AMERICA THROUGH EUROPEAN EYES

TRAVELS IN NORTH-AMERICA

TRAVELS

IN

NORTH AMERICA

IN THE

YEARS 1780-1781-1782

BY

THE MARQUIS DE CHASTELLUX

[1827]

AUGUSTUS M. KELLEY · PUBLISHERS

NEW YORK 1970

First American Edition 1827

(New York: White, Gallaher & White, 7 *Wall Street*, 1827)

Reprinted 1970 by

AUGUSTUS M. KELLEY · PUBLISHERS

REPRINTS OF ECONOMIC CLASSICS

New York New York 10001

. . . .

S B N 678 00611 3

L C N 68 55504

. . . .

PRINTED IN THE UNITED STATES OF AMERICA
by SENTRY PRESS, NEW YORK, N. Y. 10019

TRAVELS

IN

NORTH-AMERICA,

IN THE

YEARS 1780—81—82.

BY THE

MARQUIS DE CHASTELLUX,

ONE OF THE FORTY MEMBERS OF THE FRENCH ACADEMY, AND MAJOR-GENERAL IN
THE FRENCH ARMY, SERVING UNDER THE COUNT DE ROCHAMBEAU.

TRANSLATED

FROM THE FRENCH, BY AN ENGLISH GENTLEMAN,

WHO RESIDED IN AMERICA AT THAT PERIOD.

WITH NOTES BY THE TRANSLATOR.

ALSO,

A BIOGRAPHICAL SKETCH OF THE AUTHOR:

LETTERS

FROM GEN. WASHINGTON TO THE MARQUIS DE CHASTELLUX:

AND

NOTES AND CORRECTIONS,

BY THE AMERICAN EDITOR.

NEW-YORK:

WHITE, GALLAHER, & WHITE, 7 WALL-STREET.

1827.

PREFACE

TO THE AMERICAN EDITION.

———

As a memorial of the conflict which made the United States one of the nations of the earth, and a sketch of the features of the country, with some of the principal arbiters of its destiny in that momentous period, the TRAVELS OF THE MARQUIS DE CHASTELLUX will ever hold an honourable place in the interest and feelings, either of the American patriot or mere speculative reader. In following his narrative, however, it will readily be perceived, that the Author, a man of science, reflection, and literary habits, wrote more for private and individual gratification, than for critical scrutiny or the public eye. Hence the numerous little incidents and circumstances, the trivial anecdote and immaterial remark, designed only for a confidential and friendly ear ; blended with the serious observations and profound reflections on the state of society, the origin and progress of events, and the probable future condition of our embryo republic. In preparing this work for an extensive impression, to an English mind it would appear, that much of his tea-table chit-chat and travelling memoranda might as well have been omitted ; while on the graver and more weighty subjects of his inquiries, he will be perused with fixed regard and the deepest attention. A proficient in all the accomplishments of the most polished court in Europe, already distinguished by his literary attainments and productions, accustomed to modes of conduct and habits of thinking, so dissimilar to what might be expected from the retired manners, the contracted sentiments, and the entire new scenes, furnished by our home-bred rustics, it is not extraordinary that some of his remarks seem rather deficient in that frankness and courtesy, which generally prevail throughout his work. In solitary hamlets and unpeopled forests, he could not look for the balls, the theatres, and the levees of Paris. But he found a sturdy, honest, and intelligent yeomanry, rough as the soil they cultivate, resolved to defend their independence against a host of mercenaries, and successful in their object.

The uncommon merit of the French officers and soldiery, in their strict and exemplary demeanour throughout the conflict, well deserves the encomium it has received. In no instance was it known, that so much injury had been sustained by the inhabitants, from a regiment or brigade of the disciplined allies, as from a single company of the native militia.

The picture of our country, drawn by the hand of a master, in traits undoubtedly correct as far as they go, after a progress of nearly half a century, cannot but be reviewed with pleasure and gratulation by the American citizen, delighted with the present condition of the land of his nativity, and animated with its future prospects. In our improved method of travelling, the Marquis would have reached West Point from Providence, the long and tedious distance he so minutely describes, from town to town and house to house, on the same roads, very comfortably in fifty hours.

We have not admired the taste of the Translator, in some of his notes; and occasionally an observation of the Author is omitted, in a case where he would not, on the same occasion, have offered it to a Protestant neighbour. Yet when we keep in view his character as a stranger, a Frenchman, and a Roman Catholic, we must admit that he displays no common

degree of discernment, of frankness, of good sense and
liberality, in his discussion of the various topics before him;
many of which have proved the soundness of his abstract reasoning, while others, from local or incidental causes, have exhibited effects widely different from the Author's anticipations.

The letters from Gen. Washington to the Author, are extracted from the New-York Literary Journal, of 1820–1, into
which they were copied from the original manscripts of Madame Chastellux, after the death of her husband. They detract nothing from the amiable, the patriotic, and the philosophical character of their illustrious writer.

This edition of the Marquis' work, is copied from an English translation, in two volumes, published in 1787. In its
consolidated and economical form, it will doubtless be an acceptable addition to the literary and historical reading of our
country. Unwilling that the mistakes of the intelligent Author and his Translator should be extended and perpetuated
by this first American impression, the editor has added a variety of NOTES and CORRECTIONS, which it has been deemed preferable to place at the end of the volume, instead of inserting
them at the foot of the pages to which they respectively refer,
as the notes of the Translator already occupy so large a portion of the work. For the sake of method and perspicuity,
he has divided the whole into Parts and Chapters, to which
he has prepared and adapted the Table of Contents.

ADVERTISEMENT

TO THE FRENCH EDITION.

THE public have been long informed that the Marquis de Chastellux had written Journals of his Travels in North-America, and they seem to have wished to see those Journals more generally diffused. The Author, who had arranged them solely for himself and for his friends, has constantly refused to make them public until this moment. The first and most considerable, in fact, were printed in America; but only twenty-four impressions were struck off, and this with no other view than to avoid the multiplying of copies, which were become indispensably necessary, in a country and at a time when there was very little hope of any packets reaching Europe, but by the means of duplicates. Besides that, he thought proper to avail himself of the small printing press on board the squadron at Rhode-Island. Of these twenty-four impressions, not above ten or twelve reached Europe, and the Author had addressed them all to persons on whom he could rely, and whom he had requested not to suffer any copies to be taken. The curiosity, however, which every thing respecting America at that time inspired, excited much anxiety to read them. They passed successively through a great many hands, and there is reason to believe that the readers have not all been equally scrupulous; nor can it even be doubted that there exist some manuscript copies, which being hastily executed, may be presumed to be incorrect.

In the spring of 1782, the Marquis de Chastellux made a journey into Upper Virginia; and, in the autumn of the same year, another into the States of Massachusetts, and New-Hampshire, and the back part of Pennsylvania. According to custom, he wrote journals of these expeditions; but, being on his return to Europe, he reserved them to himself. These therefore are known only to a few friends, to whom he lent them; for he invariably denied the request of many

persons, and particularly our own, to empower us to lay them before
the public.   One of his friends however, who has a very extensive
correspondence in foreign countries, having pressed him much to furnish him with at least a few detached extracts from these journals, for
the purpose of inserting them in a periodical work printed at Gotha,
the object of which is to collect such works as have not been made
public, he consented ; and, during a whole year, there appeared in
each number of this Journal a few pages taken here and there from
those of the Marquis de Chastellux.   These extracts were not in a
regular series, and were indiffently taken from the first and second
parts of the Travels.   The Author had used this precaution, to prevent the foreign booksellers from collecting them, and imposing them
on the public as a complete work.   Experience has proved the insuf-
ficiency of this precaution.   A printer of Cassel, without any scruple,
has collected these detached extracts, and without announcing that
they had no coherency, has printed them under the title of *Voyages
de Monsieur le Chevalier de Chastellux*, the name the Author bore
two years ago.

   The publication of a work so mutilated and unmethodical, and
which the Marquis de Chastellux by no means expected, so far from
flattering, could not but be displeasing to him.   We deemed this a
proper opportunity for renewing our instances to him, and have, in
consequence, obtained his original manuscript.   We have lost no
time in giving it to the public, and have exerted the utmost pains to
render it, from the execution, worthy of the importance of the subject, and of the name and reputation of the Author.

BIOGRAPHICAL SKETCH

OF THE MARQUIS DE CHASTELLUX.

THE Marquis de Chastellux was of an ancient family in Bourgogne, and was born in Paris, in 1734. In his early childhood he lost his father, who was Lieutenant-General in the army of the king, and commandant in Roussillon. He entered the service at fifteen years of age, and at twenty-one, had the command of a regiment : a short time after he obtained the command of a regiment of his own name. He served during the seven years' war in Germany, with credit to himself and country. But, even among the busy and boisterous scenes of hostile movements, he pursued at every interval, his favourite literary studies. The activity of his mind was equal, in a high degree, to his thirst for knowledge. A sincere desire to be useful to mankind, and firmness to encounter every danger to gratify that desire, were characteristics of his mind.

When the subject of inoculation for the small pox was introduced, it was difficult to procure a subject who was willing to submit, to the then untried experiment in France. Chastellux. though a youth of about twenty years of age, offered to submit to the experiment. After his recovery, he called upon a friend, and made use of the following noble expression : " Here I am, safe ; and what is still more gratifying to me is, that, by my example, I shall be the means of saving many others."

In 1780 he accompanied the army commanded by Lieutenant-General Count Rochambeau to the United States ; in which army, he held the rank of Major-General. In this station he never ceased to give proofs of activity, knowledge, and firmness ; by which he received, not only the applause of his King, and the American Commander-in-Chief, but even of their enemies. In this service, he was particularly distinguished by that penetrating judge of merit, General Washington. An intimate and sincere friendship took place between them. which ended only with their lives.

He held a distinguished rank among the literary characters of France ; and some of his works are esteemed among the most valuable productions of the age. He died in 1788 ; leaving an accomplished and amiable widow, and an infant son, Alfred, who appears to possess the active disposition of his father ; and promises, like him, to pursue the road to usefulness and fame.

The Marquis of Chastellux was taken from the world, at a time when the services of such men were most needed ; but perhaps, he might, as well as the numerous friends he left behind, have been overwhelmed by the torrent of anarchy, which, soon after his death, spread terror and devastation over his beloved country. He was a sincere friend of rational liberty ; but possessed too much firmness and integrity to have been a silent spectator of that licentiousness, which, under the perverted name of liberty, was the most horrid of all tyrannies.

CONTENTS.

PART I.

Journal of a Tour from Newport to Philadelphia, Albany, &c.

PART II.

*Journal of a Tour in Upper Virginia, in the Apalachian Mountains.
and to the Natural Bridge.*

PART III.

Journal of a Tour in New-Hampshire, Massachusetts, and Upper Pennsylvania.

PART IV.

Correspondence.

TRAVELS IN NORTH-AMERICA.

PART I.

JOURNAL OF A TOUR

FROM NEWPORT TO PHILADELPHIA, ALBANY, &c.

TRAVELS IN NORTH-AMERICA.

CHAPTER I.

NEWPORT—VOLUNTOWN—WINDHAM—HARTFORD—FARMINGTON.

FROM my landing at Newport, on the 11th of July, it was hardly possible for me to be absent even for two days. On the 19th of that month the English fleet began to show itself before the port; the next day we reckoned two and twenty sail, and a few days after, we learnt that the enemy were embarking troops, nor were we informed before the middle of August of their being again disembarked at New-York, and on Long-Island. But still it appeared by no means clear that they had abandoned their undertaking: we received every day fresh advices, which bespoke new embarkations ; on our part we were adding to our fortifications, and our still recent establishment furnished me with daily employment of such a nature as not to admit of my absence. M. de Rochambeau, who had long proposed visiting his posts at Providence, was unable to carry his project into execution before the 30th of August. I accompanied him, and we returned the next day.* On the 18th of September, he set out for Hartford in Connecticut, with the Admiral Chevalier de Ternay, where General Washington had given him a rendezvous. I did not attend him in this journey, and as fortune would have it, we found ourselves in the most critical situation in which we had been since our arrival. The general belief at Rhode-Island was, that M. de Guichen, who we knew had quitted St. Domingo, was coming to join us, and we expected to go into immediate action. On the 19th, we found that instead of M. de Guichen, Admiral Rodney was arrived at New-York with ten ships of the line. Not the smallest doubt was entertained among us of an attack upon the French fleet, and even the army. The vessels

---

* Let the English reader conjecture from what this General officer has said, and from what he has probably thought proper *not* to say, whether Sir H. Clinton, and Admiral Arbuthnot, and even the *great* Rodney were *very enterprizing Officers.*—TRANSLATOR.

in consequence were laid across the harbour, with springs on their cables, and their anchorage was protected by new batteries, which were constructed with great judgment and celerity. In the beginning of October, the season being then advanced, without any thing being undertaking by Admiral Rodney, we had reason to expect that we should remain quiet for the remainder of the year, and our sole occupation was in preparing winter quarters for the troops. They took possession of them the 1st of November: and I might now without risk have absented myself from the army; but not wishing to show too much anxiety, and desirous of seeing discipline, and the arrangements relative to the cantonments well established, I deferred until the 11th setting out on a long tour upon the continent.

I left Rhode-Island that day with Mr. Lynch and M. de Montesquieu,* who had each of them a servant. I had three, one of whom had a led horse, and another drove a small cart, which I was advised to take, to convey my portmanteaus, and to avoid hurting my horses in the journey. It was then a hard frost, the earth was covered with snow, and the north-easterly wind blew very sharp. In going from Bristol to the Ferry, I went out of my way to view the fortifications of Butshill, and I reached the ferry at half past eleven†. The passage was long and difficult, because the wind was contrary. We were obliged to make three tacks, and it was necessary to make two trips, to pass over our horses, and the cart. At two o'clock I arrived at Warren, a small town in the state of Massachusetts, eighteen miles distant from Newport. I alighted at a good inn, the master of which, called Buhr, is remarkable for his enormous size as well as that of his wife, his son, and all his family. My intention was only to have baited my horses, but the cold continuing to increase, and the cart not arriving before three o'clock, I gave up all thoughts of going to sleep at Providence, and I determined to stay at Warren, where I was in very good quarters. After dinner I went to the bank of the little river Barrington, which runs near this town, to see a sloop come in which had arrived from Port au Prince. This sloop belonged to Mr. Porter, Brigadier-General of the Militia, nephew to Mr. Buhr, and still more bulky than himself. Colonel Green whom I met upon the quay, made me acquainted with Mr. Porter, and

---

* Both of these gentlemen were made Colonels en second, on their return to Europe ; the first of the regiment of Walsh, and the second, of the regiment of Bourbonnois.

† The ferries are over arms of the sea, as well as rivers, and the boats have either sails or oars.

we drank tea with him, in a simple, but comfortable house, the inside and inhabitants of which presented a specimen of American manners.

The 12th I set out at half past eight for Providence, where I arrived at noon. I alighted at the college, that is to say, at our hospital, which I examined, and dined with Mr. Blanchard, Commissary of war. At half past four I went to Colonel Bowen's where I had lodged in my first journey, I drank tea there with several ladies, one of whom, rather handsome, was called Miss Angel. I was then conducted to Mrs. Varnum's, where I again found company, and from thence to Governor Bowen's, who gave me a bed.

The 13th, I breakfasted with Colonel Peck: he is an amiable and polite young man, who passed the last summer with General Heath at Newport. He received me in a charming small house, where he lived with his wife, who is young also, and has a pleasing countenance, but without any thing striking. This little establishment, where comfort and simplicity reign, gave an idea of that sweet and serene state of happiness, which appears to have taken refuge in the New World, after compounding it with pleasure, to which it has left the Old.

The town of Providence is built on the bank of a river only six miles long, and which disembogues itself in the gulf wherein are Rhode-Island, Connecticut, Providence, &c. It has only one street, which is very long : the suburb, which is considerable, is on the other side of the river. This town is handsome, the houses are not spacious, but well built, and properly arranged within. It is pent in between two chains of mountains, one to the north, and the other to the south-west, which causes an insupportable heat in summer; but it is exposed to the north-west wind, which rakes it from one end to the other, and renders it extremely cold in winter. It may contain two thousand five hundred inhabitants. Its situation is very advantageous for commerce ; which accordingly is very considerable in times of peace. Merchant ships may load and unload their cargoes in the town itself, and ships of war cannot approach the harbour. Their commerce is the same with that of Rhode-Island and Boston ; they export staves, and salt provisions, and bring back salt, and a great quantity of molasses, sugar, and other articles from the West-Indies : they fit out vessels also for the cod and whale fishery. The latter is carried on successfully between Cape Cod and Long-Island ; but they go often as far as Baffin's Straits, and Falkland's Island. The inhabitants of Providence, like those of Newport, also carry on the Guinea trade ; they buy slaves there and carry them to the West-Indies, where they take bills of exchange on Old Eng-

land, for which they receive woollens, stuffs, and other merchandize*.

On quitting Colonel Peck, I mounted my horse for Voluntown, where I proposed sleeping. I stopped at Scituate, in a
very indifferent inn, called the Angel's Tavern; it is about
half way to Voluntown : I baited my horses there, and set out
in an hour, without seeing my cart arrive. From this place to
Voluntown the road is execrable ; one is perpetually mounting
and descending, and always on the most rugged roads. It
was six o'clock, and the night closed in, when I reached
D———'s Tavern, which is only five and twenty miles from
Providence. I dismounted with the more pleasure as the
weather was extremely bad. I was well accommodated, and
kindly received at Mr. D———'s. He is an old gentleman
of seventy-three years of age, tall, and still vigorous ; he is a
native of Ireland, first settled in Massachusetts, and afterwards
in Connecticut. His wife, who is younger than him, is active,
handy, and obliging; but her family is charming. It consists
of two young men, one twenty-eight, and the other twenty-one
years old ; a child of twelve, and two girls from eighteen to
twenty, as handsome as angels. The eldest of these young
women was sick, kept her chamber, and did not show herself.
I learnt afterwards that she was in the family way, and almost
ready to lie-in : she was deceived by a young man, who, after
promising to marry her, absented himself and did not return.†

---

* Here are several places of public worship, an university, and
other public buildings ; and a very brisk trade was carried on even at
the worst period of the war for American commerce, viz. in 1782.—
Mr. Welcome Arnold, a great plumber, and Delegate to Congress
from this state, has changed his name by act of Assembly, since the
defection of Benedict Arnold.—*Trans.*

† On the arrival of seven or eight copies of this journal, sent to
Europe by the author, the curiosity then excited by every thing relative
to the affairs of America, procured them many readers. Though the
author had addressed them only to his most intimate friends, and had
taken the precaution to apprize them that it was not his intention they
should be generally public, they passed rapidly from one hand to
another ; and as they could only be lent for a short time they were
read with as much precipitation as avidity. This anxiety could only
proceed from the general desire of forming some idea of the manners
of the Americans, of which this journal gave several details which
became interesting from the circumstances of novelty and distance.
From an inconsistency, however, more usual in France than in any
other country, some persons made no scruple to judge the author on
points of propriety, of which he alone was capable of giving them an
idea : he was taxed with wantonness and indiscretion, for having

Chagrin and the consequences of her situation had thrown her into a state of languor; she never came down to the ground-floor on which her parents lived; but great care was taken of

---

concealed neither events nor places in relating the adventure of a girl deceived by her lover. A very simple, and very natural reflection, might have convinced them, that it was by no means probable that a General Officer, a man of forty-five years of age, particularly connected with the Americans, and who has every where expressed sentiments of gratitude and attachment for those from whom he experienced kindness, should allow himself, not only to offend, but to afflict an honest family, who had shewn him every attention, and of whom he cannot speak but in terms of commendation. Besides that the simple and even serious manner in which this article is written affords not the least appearance of levity; a sufficient reason for preventing the too free observations of certain readers. Another reflection might occur naturally enough, but which demanded a little more combination. The author wishes, it might have been said, to give us an idea of American manners, which he is certainly very far from satirizing: may it not be possible that amongst a people so remote from us in every respect, a girl who should resign herself too hastily to the man she was engaged to, with the consent even of her parents, a girl without distrust, in a country where such an idea is never taught them, where morals are so far in their infancy, as that the commerce between two free persons is deemed less censurable, than the infidelity, the caprices, and even the coquetries which destroy the peace of so many European families? May it not be possible that this young woman, as interesting as she was unhappy, should be lamented rather than condemned, that she should still retain all her rights in society, and become a legitimate spouse and mother, though her story was neither unknown, nor attempted to be concealed? In fact, how could the author learn this history? Was it by the scandalous chronicles in a hamlet where he was a stranger to every person but his hosts? *I have since learnt* (says he in speaking of this girl) *that she was in the family way, and near her time of lying-in.* How did he learn this? From her own parents, who had not at first made a mystery of it, and then a matter of confidence. But had these austere judges, when they had finished their reading, happened to recollect what they saw at the beginning, they might have observed that the author being at Volun-town a second time, two months after, saw Miss D——— suckling an infant, which was continually passing from her knees to those of her mother; that she was then cherished, and taken care of by all the family. This affecting sight was described with sensibility, and not with malignity. But it is time to give over tiring the patience, not of the critics only, but of all sensible minds, those minds alone whose approbation is of any value. On another journey to Voluntown, the author had the satisfaction to see Miss D——— perfectly happy: her lover was returned, and had married her; he had expiated all his wrongs, nor had they been such as they at first appeared; he had unfortunate circumstances to plead in his excuse, if there can indeed be

her, and she had always somebody to keep her company.
Whilst a good supper was preparing for me, I went into the
room where the family was assembled, where I observed a
shelf with forty or fifty volumes on it ; on opening them I found
that they were all classical authors, Greek, Latin, or English.
They belonged to Mr. D———'s eldest son. This young
man had received a regular education, and was tutor at Providence college, until the war interrupted his studies. I conversed with him on various points of literature, and particularly
on the manner in which the dead languages should be pronounced. I found him well informed, and possessed of much
simplicity and modesty.*

We were waited on at supper by a most beautiful girl, called Miss Pearce. She was a neighbour of Mrs. D———, and
had come on a visit, and to assist her in the absence of her

---

any for a man who for a single day can leave in such agonies the
interesting and weak victim who was unable to resist him.

The translator, who has been at Voluntown, and enjoyed the society
and witnessed the happiness of this amiable family, is likewise
acquainted with the whole of this story. He is so well satisfied with
the justness of the liberal minded author's reasoning on American
manners in this particular, that in relating the circumstances of
this worthy family at length, he does not apprehend their characters
would suffer the smallest injury, where alone the imputation is of any
consequence ; nor does he fear opposing the virtue of this family, and
of these manners, to European chastity, prudery, and refinement.
The circumstances of this story were related to the translator by Mr.
and Mrs. D———, with the same sensibility, and the same innocence,
with which they appear to have told them to the Marquis de Chastellux. They are a kind, hospitable, and amiable couple, and the husband is very far from being ill informed ; he entertained the translator
with many anecdotes of the war, and with some laughable ones
respecting General Prescot, who was brought to his house, after
being carried off without his breeches from Rhode-Island ; but never
without expressing a becoming degree of sensibility for his situation,
which was peculiarly mortifying, from his gout, his naturally peevish
disposition, the humiliating mode of his capture, and the circumstance
of its being the second time of his falling into the hands of an enemy,
whom he was weak enough to despise and to insult.— *Trans.*

* The translator had a great deal of conversation with this young
man, and found him such as the Marquis represents him ; but he must
likewise add, that he met with a great number of excellent classical
scholars, in different parts of the continent, educated at Williamsburgh, Philadelphia, Yale College, New-Haven, Cambridge, and
Providence, and very few deficient, especially to the northward. The
war did infinite mischief to the rising generation of America, by
interrupting education.— *Trans.*

youngest daughter. This young person had, like all the American women, a very decent, nay even serious carriage; she had no objection to be looked at, nor to have her beauty commended, nor even to receive a few caresses, provided it was done without an air of familiarity or libertinism. Licentious manners, in fact, are so foreign in America, that the communication with young women leads to nothing bad, and that freedom itself there bears a character of modesty far beyond our affected bashfulness and false reserve. But neither my excellent supper, nor the books of Mr. D———, nor even the fine eyes of Miss Pearce, made my cart arrive, and I was obliged to go to rest without hearing any news from it. As I desired a chamber with a fire in it, Miss Pearce prepared me one, informing me at the same time, that it communicated with that of the sick lady with whom she slept, and inquired of me very politely, whether it would incommode me if she should pass through my chamber after I was in bed. I assured her, that if she disturbed my sleep, it would not be as a frightful dream. And, in fact, she came a quarter of an hour after I was in bed. I pretended to sleep, in order to examine her countenance; she passed very gently, turning her head the other way, and hiding the light for fear of awakening me. I do not know whether I shall pronounce my praise or condemnation, by saying, that I soon after fell into a profound sleep.

On my rising I found Miss Pearce, but not my cart, which it seemed more than probable was broke into a thousand pieces. I was determined to give up that mode of conveying my little baggage, which still it was necessary to have. I resolved, therefore, to wait for them, and take my breakfast, a resolution much easier adopted. At length, about eleven o'clock, my sentinels announced its appearance. It was matter of great joy to the whole crew to see it arrive, although crippled, and towed by a hired horse, which they had been obliged to put before mine. It is proper to observe, that my attendants, proud of possessing ample means of transporting my effects, had loaded it with many useless articles; that being apprised myself that wine was not always to be met with in the inns,* I had thought proper to furnish myself with cantines which held twelve bottles, and having taken the precau-

---

* The translator, when he travelled in America during the war, always carried wine with him when practicable, for at Baltimore and Philadelphia, those great sea ports, very indifferent wine, *called* claret, was sold at *two dollars*, upwards of 9 shillings a bottle, hard money. Nor was it an uncommon thing to transport wine from Boston to Philadelphia by land, when the arrivals were more fortunate in that quarter.—*Trans.*

tion to ask for two or three white loaves of bread from the commissary of provisions at Providence, he had packed up twenty, which alone weighed upwards of eighty pounds, so that my poor cart was laden till on the point of sinking. Its greatest misfortune, however, arose from striking on the rocks, which had broke one wheel and greatly damaged the other. I soon determined to leave it with Mr. D———, who undertook to get it repaired, and it was resolved that my wine should be divided into three parts, one of which should be drank the same day, the other left with the landlord, with a request to keep it till my return, and that the third should be offered him, with a request to drink it; which met with no difficulty. The remainder of the day, however, being dedicated to make new dispositions, I determined on remaining at Voluntown. I made a general inspection of my baggage; every thing unnecessary was packed up and left with Mr. D———; the rest put into portmanteaus, and by a promotion *à la Prussienne*, on the field of battle, my cart-horse was elevated to the saddle. The reading of some English poets, and the conversation with Messrs. Lynch and Montesquieu, and the good people of the house, made me pass the day very agreeably. Towards the evening, two travellers came into the room I was in, seated themselves by the fire, and began to yawn and whistle, without paying the least attention to me. The conversation, however, gradually enlivened, and became very interesting and agreeable. One of them was a colonel of militia, who had served in Canada, and had been in several engagements, wherein he was wounded. I shall observe once for all, that among the men I have met with, above twenty years of age, of whatsoever condition, I have not found two who have not borne arms, heard the whistling of balls, and even received some wounds; so that it may be asserted, that North America is entirely military, and inured to war, and that new levies may continually be made without making new soldiers. [The translator confirms this assertion, except with regard to the pacific religious sects, in the whole extent of his observations from Virginia to New-Hampshire.]

On the 15th, I set out from Voluntown at eight in the morning. I travelled five miles in the mountains, after which I saw the horizon expand itself, and my eye very soon had its full scope. On descending the hills, and before we reached the valley, is the town or hamlet of Plainfield; for what is called in America, a *town* or *township*, is only a certain number of houses, dispersed over a great space, but which belong to the same incorporation, and send deputies to the general assembly of the state. The centre or head quarters of these towns, is the meeting-house or church. This church stands sometimes single, and is sometimes surrounded by four or five houses only; whence it happens, that when a traveller asks the question : *How far is it to such a town?* He is answered, *You are there already;* but when he specifies the place he wishes to be at, whether it be the meeting, or such a tavern, he not unfrequently is told, *You are seven or eight miles from it.* Plainfield is a small town, but a large district, for there are full thirty houses within reach of the meeting.* Its situation is agreeable ; but it presents, besides, a military aspect: this was the first I had remarked. An army might encamp there on little heights, behind which the hills rise in an amphitheatre, thus presenting successive positions as far as the great woods, which would serve as the last retreat. The foot of the heights of Plainfield is fortified by morasses, only passable by one causeway, which would oblige the enemy to file off to attack you.† The right and left are supported by escarpments. On the right also is a marsh, which renders it more difficult of access. This camp is fit for six, eight, or even ten thousand men ; it might serve to cover Providence and Massachusetts state, against troops who had passed the Connecticut river. At two miles from Plainfield the road turns towards the north, and after travelling two or three miles farther, is the river of Quenebaugh, along the edge of which we travel about a mile to pass it at Canterbury, over a pretty long, and tolerably constructed, wooden bridge. This river is neither navigable, nor fordable, but flows amidst stones, which renders its bed very uneven. The inhabitants of the neighbourhood, form dams here in the shape of a projecting angle to catch the eels : the summit of the angle is in the middle of the river ; there they place nets in the shape of a purse, where the fish which follow the current of water seldom escape being caught. The bridge at Canterbury is built in rather a deep and narrow valley. The meeting-house of the town is on the right bank, as well as the greatest part of the houses, but there are some also on the eminences towards the east, which appeared to me well built and agreeably situated. These heights being of the same elevation with those to the west, Canterbury‡ offers two

---

* There is an academy or college here, with four Latin and English masters, and when the translator was there, he was present at some, not contemptible, public exhibitions of oratory in those two languages. —*Trans.*

† In summer these morasses are dry. This I have since learnt, and which it is proper to remark, that an erroneous idea may not be formed of this position.

‡ The translator reached Canterbury on a *Sunday*, a day on which travelling is forbid in the New-England states. The family at *Buck*

positions, equally advantageous for two armies, which might dispute the passage of the Quenebaugh. After passing Canterbury, we enter the woods, and a chain of hills, which must be passed by very rugged and difficult roads. Six or seven miles farther, the country begins to open, and we descend agreeably to Windham. It is a very handsome little town, or rather it is the stock from which a handsome town will spring. There are forty or fifty houses pretty near each other, and so situated as to present the appearance of a large public square, and three large streets. The Seunganick, or Windham river, runs near this town, but is of no great use to its trade, for it is no more navigable than the Quenebaugh, with which it joins its waters to form the river Thames. It may be observed in reading this journal, and still more by the inspection of the Charts, that the rivers in general, and many towns, have retained their Indian names; this nomenclature has something interesting in it, as it confirms the still recent origin of these multiplied settlements, and is perpetually presenting to the mind a very striking contrast between the former, and present state of this vast country.

Windham is fifteen miles from Voluntown. I there found Lauzun's hussars, who were stationed in it for a week, until their quarters were prepared at Lebanon. I dined with the Duke de Lauzun, and being unable to get away before half after three, the night, which soon came on, obliged me to stop at six miles from Windham, at a little solitary tavern,* kept by Mrs. Hill. As the house had an indifferent appearance, I asked if we could have beds, the only want we had; for the Duke de Lauzun's dinner had left us in no uneasiness about supper. Mrs. Hill told me, after the manner of the country, that she could only *spare* one bed, as she had a sick traveller in the house whom she would not disturb. This traveller was a poor soldier of the continental army, who was going home on a furlough for the benefit of his health. He had his furlough in his pocket in regular form, as well as the exact account of

---

house's *Tavern* were all at meeting, and it cost him innumerable entreaties, besides the most unequivocal proofs of *whiggism*, to procure a morsel of the most wretched fare, and to obtain which he was obliged to wait till the meeting was at an end. Both this town and Windham are most beautifully situated, particularly the latter, which is extremely picturesque.

* This tavern is called *Lebanon Crank*, and the translator has made similar remarks in his journal on the external appearance of, and the kindness that reigns within this little hut; where, a very uncommon circumstance at that time, he found excellent green tea, and fine loaf sugar. He also saw Mrs. Hill feed, and relieve a travelling soldier.

what was due to him, but he had not a farthing either in paper or in *hard money*. Mrs. Hill, notwithstanding, had given him a good bed, and as he was too ill to continue his journey, she had kept him, and taken care of him for four days. We arranged matters in the best way we could : the soldier kept his bed. I gave him some money to help him on his journey, and Mrs. Hill appeared to me much more affected with this charity, than with the good *hard money* I gave her to pay her bill.

The 16th, at eight in the morning, I took leave of my kind landlady, and followed the road to Hartford, beginning my journey on foot, on account of the extreme coldness of the morning. After descending by a gentle declivity for about two miles, I got into a pretty narrow, but agreeable and well cultivated valley : it is watered by a rivulet which falls into the Seunganick, and which is decorated with the name of Hope river. We follow this valley to Bolton town, or township, which has nothing remarkable. There we traverse a chain of pretty lofty mountains, which extend from north to south like all the hills in Connecticut. On quitting these mountains, we come to the first houses of East-Hartford. Though we were but five miles from Hartford Court House, we wished to rest our horses, which had travelled twenty-three miles on a stretch. The inn we stopped at was kept by Mr. Marsh : he is, according to the English phrase, a good farmer ; that is, a good cultivator. He told me that he had begun a settlement in the state of Vermont, where he had purchased two hundred acres of land for forty dollars, about two hundred livres of our money, or something more than eight pounds English. The state of Vermont is a vast country, situated to the eastward of New-Hampshire and Massachusetts,* and to the north of Connecticut, between the river of that name, and Hudson's river. As it is lately peopled, and has always been an object of contention between the states of New-York and New-Hampshire, there is properly speaking no established government. Ethan Allen, celebrated for the expedition he undertook in 1775 against Ticonderoga, of his own accord, and without any other aid than that of the volunteers who followed him, has made himself the chief of that country. He has formed there an assembly of representatives; this assembly grants lands, and the country is governed by its own laws, without having any connexion with congress. The inhabitants however are not the less enemies of the English ; but under the pretext that they form the frontier against Canada, and are obliged to guard it, they furnish no contingent to the expenses of the war. They had long no other name than that of *Green Mountain Boys*, but thinking this too ignoble an

---

* Vermont is situated west of New-Hampshire and north of Massachusetts.

appellation for their new destiny, they translated Green Mountain into French; which made *Verd Mont*, and by corruption Vermont. It remains to be seen whether it is by corruption also, that this country has assumed the title of the *state* of Vermont.*

About four in the evening, I arrived at Hartford ferry, after travelling over a very inconvenient road, a great part of which forms a narrow causeway through a marshy wood. We pass this ferry, like all the others in America,† in a flat boat with oars. I found the inns at Hartford so full that it was impossible to procure a lodging. The four eastern states, Massachusetts, New-Hampshire, Rhode-Island, and Connecticut were then holding their assemblies in that town. These four states have long maintained a particular connexion with each other, and they meet together by deputies, sometimes in one state, sometimes in another. Each legislature sends deputies. In a circumstance, so uncommon in America, as room being wanted for men collected together, Colonel Wadsworth's house offered me a most agreeable asylum; I lodged with him, as well as the Duke de Lauzun, who had passed me on the road. Mr. Dumas,‡ who belonged to the staff of the army, and was then attached to the Duke de Lauzun, Mr. Lynch and Mr. de Montesquieu were well accommodated in the neighbourhood.

Colonel Wadsworth is about two and thirty, very tall and well made, and has a noble as well as agreeable countenance. He lived formerly on Long-Island; and from his infancy was engaged in commerce and navigation: he had already made several voyages to the coast of Guinea and the West-Indies, when according to the American expression, the present *contestation* began. He then served in the army, and was in several actions; but General Washington discovering that his talents might be more usefully employed, made him Commissary of Provisions. This is a military post in America, and those

---

* In the years 1780, 1781, and 1782, the inhabitants of Vermont, who were *not* guided by Ethan Allen, annually sent deputies to congress, and were once within *one vote* of carrying their point, but had not the peace taken place, it is probable from circumstances, that in case of refusal, they would *at least* have threatened to put themselves under British protection, an event to which the Marquis seems to allude.—*Trans.*

† At the Moravian settlement of Bethlehem is a ferry passed by ropes, like that opposite the invalid hospital at Paris, and many others in France, and other parts of Europe.—*Trans.*

‡ The translator had the pleasure of meeting with this accomplished officer, at Baltimore, at Boston, and in Europe. Nature has been very favourable to his exterior, and he unites to the most perfect good manners, and a thorough knowledge of the world, and books, the most unexampled activity in his profession.—*Trans.*

who fill it, are as much respected as the first officer of the line.
The Commissary General is charged with all the purchases,
and the Quarter Master with all the conveyances; it is the latter who marks out the ground, establishes the magazines, pro-
vides carriages, and distributes the rations: it is also on his
receipts and orders that the Paymasters make their payments;
he is, in short, properly speaking, a Military Intendant, while
the Commissary General may be compared to a *Munitionnaire*
with us, who should undertake to provide forage as well as provisions. I think this arrangement as good as ours, though
these departments have not been exempt from abuses, and even
blame in the course of the present war; but it must be observed, that whenever the government wants political force, and
the treasury is without money, the administration of affairs is
always ruinous, and often culpable. This reflection alone will
afford sufficient subject for the eulogium of Colonel Wadsworth, when it is known that throughout all America, there is
not one voice against him, and that his name is never pronounced without the homage due to his talents and his probity. The particular confidence of General Washington puts
the seal upon his merit.* The Marquis de la Fayette judged
extremely well therefore in getting Mr. de Corny to employ
him, in furnishing the provisions necessary for the French
troops which were then expected. As soon as they were disembarked at Rhode-Island, he again proposed him as the most
proper man in the world to assist them in all their wants, but
those who had the direction of the army did not at that time
think proper to employ him. They even conceived some suspicions of him, from false ideas, and eagerly substituted for a
Commissary of understanding and reputation, undertakers, without fortune, and without character; who promised every thing,
performed nothing, and soon threw our affairs into confusion:
first by augmenting the price of articles by purchases hastily
made, and frequently in opposition one to another, and finally
by throwing into circulation, and offering at a great discount,
the bills of exchange they had engaged to receive for two-
thirds of all their payments. These bargains, and contracts,
succeeded eventually so ill, that we were obliged, but too late,
to have recourse to Mr. Wadsworth, who resumed the affairs
with as much nobleness as he had quitted them; always as superior to injuries by his character, as he is by his talents to the
innumerable obstacles that surrounded him.

Another interesting personage was then at Hartford, and I
went to pay him a visit: this was Governor Trumbull; Go-

---

* The translator cannot forbear adding his testimony to this brilliant
but exaggerated eulogium.—*Trans.*

vernor, *by excellence*, for he has been so these fifteen years, having been always rechosen at the end of every two years, and equally possessing the public esteem under the English government, and under that of the Congress.   He is seventy years old; his whole life is consecrated to business, which he passionately loves, whether important or not; or rather, with respect to him, there is none of the latter description.   He has all the simplicity in his dress, all the importance, and even pedantry becoming the great magistrate of a small republic. He brought to my mind the burgomasters of Holland in the time of the Heinsiuses and the Barnevelts.   I had been informed that he was employed in a history of the present revolution, and I was curious to read this work; I told him that I hoped to see him on my return at Lebanon, (his place of abode) and that I should then request permission to look over his manuscript; but he assured me that he had only written the introduction, which he had addressed to the Chevalier de la Luzerne, our ambassador.   I procured it during my stay in Philadelphia, but it is only an historical recapitulation, rather superficial, and by no means free from partiality in the manner of representing the events of the war.   The only interesting fact I found in it, was in the journal of a Governor Winthrop, in the year 1670, where he says, that the members of the council of Massachusetts, being advised by their friends in London to address themselves to the parliament, to whom the King then left a great deal of authority, as the best means of obtaining the redress of some grievances, the council, after mature deliberation, thought proper to decline the proposal, reflecting, that if they put themselves once under the protection of parliament, they should be obliged to submit to all the laws that assembly might impose, whether on the nation in general, or on the colonies in particular.   Now, nothing can more strongly prove, that these colonies, even in the very origin, never acknowledged the authority of parliament, nor imagined they could be bound by laws of their making.

The 17th, in the morning, I parted with regret from my host and the Duke de Lauzun; but it was not till after breakfast, for it is a thing unheard of in America to set off without breakfast.   By this indispensable delay I had an opportunity of making acquaintance with General Parsons.   He appeared to me a sensible man, and he is so esteemed in his country; but he has had little opportunity of displaying great military talents; he was, in fact, what one must never be, in war, or in any thing, unfortunate.   His outset was on Long-Island, where he was taken, and he has since been in all the bad affairs, so that he is better known for his capacity in business, than for the share he has had in the events of the war.

The road I had to travel becoming henceforth difficult and rather desert, it was determined that I should not exceed ten miles that day, that I might meet with good quarters; and get my horses in order for the next day's journey. The place I was to stop at was Farmington. Mr. Wadsworth, fearing I should not find a good inn there, gave me a letter of recommendation to one of his relations of the name of Lewis, where he assured me I should be well received, without incommoding any person, and without straightening myself, for that I should pay my reckoning as at an inn. In fact, when the taverns are bad, or that they are so situated as not to suit the convenience of the traveller, it is the custom in America, to ask for quarters of some individual at his ease, who can spare room in his house for you, and can give stabling for your horses : the traveller and his host then converse together on equal terms ; but he is paid merely as an inn-keeper.

The town of Hartford does not merit any attention either in travelling through, or in speaking of it. It consists of a very long street, parallel with the river ; it is pretty regular and connected, that is, the houses are not distant from each other. But it has many appendages ; every thing is Hartford six leagues round ; but East-Hartford, West-Hartford, and New-Hartford are distinct towns, though composed of houses scattered through the country. I have already mentioned what constitutes a town ; it is to have one or two meetings, particular assemblies, and the right of sending deputies to the general assembly. These *townships* may be compared to the *curiæ* of the Romans. From a very lofty plain on the road to Farmington, one discovers not only all the Hartfords, but all that part of the continent watered by the river of that name,* situated between the eastern and western chains of mountains. This place is called Rocky-hill. The houses of West-Hartford, frequently dispersed, and sometimes grouped together, and every where adorned with trees and meadows, form of the road to Farmington such a garden, in the English style, as it would be difficult for art to imitate. Their inhabitants add some industry likewise to their rich culture ; some common cloths and other woollen stuffs are fabricated here, but of a good wear, and sufficient to clothe the people who live in the country, or in any other town than Boston, New-York, and Philadelphia. I went into a house where they were preparing and dying the cloth. This cloth is made by the people of the country, and is then sent to these little manufactories, where it is dressed, pressed, and dyed, for two shillings, lawful money, per yard, which makes about thirty-five sols French,

---

* Now called Connecticut river.

or seventeen-pence English, the Connecticut pound being
equal to something more than three dollars.   I reached Farmington at three in the afternoon.   It is a pretty little town,
with a handsome meeting-house, and fifty houses collected, all
neat and well built.   It is situated on the declivity of the
mountains : the river which bears the same name runs at the
foot of them, and turns towards the north, without showing
itself; but the view of the valley is, notwithstanding, very
agreeable.   After dismounting, I took advantage of the good
weather, to take a walk in the streets, or rather in the high-
ways.   I saw through the windows of a house that they were
working at some trade ; I entered, and found them making a sort
of camblet, as well as another woollen stuff with blue and
white stripes for women's dress : these stuffs are sold at three
shillings and six-pence the yard, lawful money, or about two
and twenty-pence English.   The sons and grandsons of the
family were at work ; one workman can easily make five yards
a day.   The prime cost of the materials being only one shil-
ling currency, the day's work may amount to ten or twelve.
On my return from this walk I found an excellent dinner prepared for me, without my having said a word to the family.
After dinner, about the close of the day, Mr. Lewis, who had
been abroad on his affairs during a part of the day, came into
the parlour where I was, seated himself by the fire, lighted
his pipe, and entered into conversation with me.   I found him
an active and intelligent man, well acquainted with public affairs, and with his own : he carried on a trade of cattle, like
all the farmers of Connecticut; he was then employed in
furnishing provisions for the army, and was principally taken
up in slaughtering, and salting cattle for the state of Connecticut, to be sent to Fishkill.   For each state is obliged to furnish not only money, but other articles for the army : those to
the eastward supply it with cattle, rum, and salt ; and those to
the westward with flour and forage.   Mr. Lewis has borne
arms also for his country : he was at the affairs of Long-Island
and Saratoga, of which he gave me an exact account; in the
last he served as a volunteer.   At tea time Mrs. Lewis and
her sister-in-law gave us their company.   Mrs. Lewis had just
recovered from lying-in, and had her child in her arms : she is
near thirty, with a very agreeable face, and so amiable, and so
polite a carriage, as to present a picture of decency itself, to
every country in the world.   The conversation was interesting-
ly supported the whole evening.   The family retired at nine
o'clock ; I did not see them in the morning, and paid my bill
to the servants : it was neither dear nor cheap, but the just
price of every thing, regulated without interest, and without
compliments.

CHAPTER II.

I GOT on horseback at eight o'clock on the 18th, and at the
distance of a mile fell in with the river of Farmington, along
which I rode for some time. There was nothing interesting in
this part of my journey, except that having fired my pistol at a
jay, to my great astonishment the bird fell. This had been
for many days an object of curiosity with me, and it is really a
most beautiful creature. It is quite blue, but it unites all the
various shades of that colour so as to surpass the invention of
art, and be very difficult of imitation. I must remark by the
bye, that the Americans call it only by the name of the *blue
bird*, though it is a real jay ; but the Americans are far from
being successful in enriching their native language. On every
thing which wanted an English name, they have bestowed only
a simple descriptive one : the jay is the blue bird, the cardi-
nal, the red bird ; every water bird is a duck, from the teal to
the *canard de dois*, and to the large black duck which we have
not in Europe. They call them, red ducks, black ducks, wood
ducks. It is the same with respect to their trees ; the pine,
the cypresses, the firs, are all comprehended under the general
name of *pine-trees ;* and if the people characterize any particular tree, it is from the use to which it is applied, as the *wall-
nut*,* from its serving to the construction of wooden houses. I
could cite many other examples, but it is sufficient to observe,
that this poverty of language proves how much men's attention has been employed in objects of utility, and how much at
the same time it has been circumscribed by the only prevailing
interest, the desire of augmenting wealth, rather by dint of labour, than by industry. But to return to my jay ; I resolved to
make a trophy of it, in the manner of the savages, by scalping
it of its skin and feathers ; and content with my victory, I pursued my journey, which soon brought me amidst the steepest
and most difficult mountains I had yet seen. They are covered
with woods as old as the creation, but which do not differ
from ours. These hills heaped confusedly one upon another,

---

* Here the author is a little inaccurate respecting the English language, as the same word *wall-nut*, is applied to the same tree in English, and with no reference whatever to any such use.— *Trans.*

oblige you to be continually mounting and descending, without your being able to distinguish in this wild region, the summit, which rising above the rest, announces to you a conclusion to your labours. This disorder of nature reminded me of the lessons of him whom she has chosen for her confident and interpreter. The vision of Mr. de Buffon appeared to me in these ancient deserts. He seemed to be in his proper element, and to point out to me, under a slight crust formed by the destruction of vegetables, the inequality of a globe of glass, which has cooled after a long fusion. The waters said he, have done nothing here ; look around you, you will not find a single calcareous stone ; every thing is quartz, granite, or flint. I made experiments on the stones with aquafortis, and I could not help concluding, what has not obtained sufficient credit in Europe, not only that he speaks well, but he is always in the right.

While I was meditating on the great process of nature, which employs fifty thousand years in rendering the earth habitable, a new spectacle, well calculated as a contrast to those which I had been contemplating, fixed my attention, and excited my curiosity : this was the work of a single man, who in the space of a year had cut down several arpents of wood, and had built himself a house in the middle of a pretty extensive territory he had already cleared. I saw, for the first time, what I have since observed a hundred times ; for in fact, whatever mountains I have climbed, whatever forests I have traversed, whatever bye-paths I have followed, I have never travelled three miles without meeting with a new settlement, either beginning to take form or already in cultivation. The following is the manner of proceeding in these improvements or new settlements. Any man who is able to procure a capital of five or six hundred livres of our money, or about twenty-five pounds sterling, and who has strength and inclination to work, may go into the woods and purchase a portion of one hundred and fifty or two hundred acres of land, which seldom costs him more than a dollar or four shillings and six-pence an acre, a small part of which only he pays in ready money. There he conducts a cow, some pigs, or a full sow, and two indifferent horses which do not cost him more than four guineas each. To these precautions he adds that of having a provision of flour and cider. Provided with this first capital, he begins by felling all the smaller trees, and some strong branches of the large ones : these he makes use of as fences to the first field he wishes to clear ; he next boldly attacks those immense oaks, or pines, which one would take for the ancient lords of the territory he is usurping ; he strips them of their bark, or lays them open all round with his axe. These trees mortally wounded, are the next spring robbed of their honours; their leaves no longer spring, their branches fall, and their trunk becomes a hideous skeleton. This trunk still seems to brave the efforts of the new colonist; but where there are the small-est chinks or crevices, it is surrounded by fire, and the flames consume what the iron was unable to destroy. But it is enough for the small trees to be felled, and the great ones to lose their sap. This object completed, the ground is cleared; the air and the sun begin to operate upon that earth which is wholly formed of rotten vegetables, and teems with the latent princi-ples of production. The grass grows rapidly; there is pastu-rage for the cattle the very first year; after which they are left to increase, or fresh ones are brought, and they are employed in tilling a piece of ground which yields the enormous increase of twenty or thirty fold. The next year the same course is re-peated; when, at the end of two years, the planter has where-withal to subsist, and even to send some articles to market: at the end of four or five years, he completes the payment of his land, and finds himself a comfortable planter. Then his dwell-ing, which at first was no better than a large hut formed by a square of the trunks of trees, placed one upon another, with the intervals filled by mud, changes into a handsome wooden house, where he contrives more convenient, and certainly much cleaner apartments than those in the greatest part of our small towns. This is the work of three weeks or a month. His first habitation, that of eight and forty hours. I shall be asked, perhaps, how one man or one family can be so quickly lodged; I answer, that in America a man is never alone, never an isola-ted being. The neighbours, for they are every where to be found, make it a point of hospitality to aid the new farmer. A cask of cider drank in common, and with gaiety, or a gallon of rum, are the only recompense for these services. Such are the means by which North-America, which one hundred years ago was nothing but a vast forest, is peopled with three millions of inhabitants; and such is the immense, and certain benefit of agriculture, that notwithstanding the war, it not only maintains itself where ever it has been established, but it extends to places which seem the least favourable to its introduction. Four years ago, one might have travelled ten miles in the woods I traversed, without seeing a single habitation.

Harrington is the first township I met with on my road. This place is sixteen miles from Farmington, and eight from Litchfield. Four miles before we come to this last town, we pass a wooden bridge over the river of Waterbury; this river is pretty large, but not navigable. Litchfield, or the *Meeting-house* of Litchfield, is situated on a large plain more elevated than the surrounding heights; about fifty houses pretty near each other, with a large square, or rather area, in the middle, announces the progress of this town, which is already the county town; for America is divided into districts, called Counties, in some Provinces, as in England. It is in the capital of these counties that the court of sessions is held, where the Sheriff presides, and where the Chief Judges come every four months to decide civil and criminal affairs. Half a mile on this side of Litchfield, I remarked, on the right, a barrack surrounded by palisades, which appeared to me like a guardhouse; I approached it, and saw in this small enclosure ten pieces of brass cannon, a mortar, and a swivel. This I learnt was a part of Burgoyne's artillery, which fell to the share of the state of Connecticut, and was kept in this place as the most conveniently situated for the army, and at the same time the least exposed to the incursions of the English.

It was four o'clock, and the weather very bad, when I came near the house of a Mr. Seymour, to whom Mr. Lewis had given me a letter, assuring me that I should find better accommodation than at the taverns; but Mr. Lynch, who had gone on a little before to make inquiries, informed me, that Mr. Seymour was from home, and that from all appearance his wife would be much embarrassed to receive us. The American women, in fact, are very little accustomed to give themselves trouble, either of mind or body; the care of their children, that of making tea, and seeing the house kept clean, constitutes the whole of their domestic province. I determined therefore to go straight to the tavern, where I was still unlucky enough not to find Mr. Philips the landlord: so that I was received, at least, with indifference, which often happens in the inns in America, when they are not in much frequented situations: travellers are there considered as giving them more trouble than money. The reason of this is, that the inn-keepers are all of them cultivators, at their ease, who do not stand in need of this slight profit: the greatest number of those who follow this profession are even compelled to it by the laws of the country, which have wisely provided, that on all the great roads there shall be a public house at the end of every six miles, for the accommodation of travellers.

A still greater difficulty I had at Mrs. Philips', was, to find room for nine horses I had with me. The Quarter-Master at length made them place some of them in the stable of a private person, and every thing was arranged to my satisfaction, and that of my hostess. I cannot help remarking, that nothing can be more useful than such an officer, as well for the service of the state, as for that of any traveller of distinction. I have already spoken of the functions of the Quarter-Master-General, but I did not mention that he names a deputy Quarter-

Master-General in each state, and that the latter, in his turn, names an assistant in each district to act in his room. My horses and baggage were scarcely under cover, when a dreadful storm came on, which however was in my favour, as it brought home Mr. Philips: every thing now assumed a new face in the house, the pantry flew open, the negroes redoubled their activity, and we soon saw a supper preparing with the most favourable auspices. Mr. Philips is an Irishman, translated to America, where he has already made a fortune; he appears to be cunning and adroit; and is cautious in talking to strangers: in other respects, he is more gay than the Americans, and even given to irony; a turn of mind but little known in America, and for which they have no specific name, any more than for the different species of trees and birds. Mrs. Philips, now seconded by her husband, and more mistress of her work, soon resumed her natural serenity. She is of American birth, and a true *Yankee,** as her husband told us; her face is gentle and agreeable, and her manners correspond entirely with her features.

On the 19th I left Litchfield between nine and ten in the morning, and pursued my journey through the mountains, partly on foot and partly on horseback; for having got into the habit of travelling from morning till night without stopping, I from time to time took pity on my horses, and spared them in those deserts which seemed formed for the roebuck rather than for carriages and laden horses. The name of the first town I came to, proclaims it to be of recent origin; it is called Washington. A new county being formed in the woods of Connecticut, the state has bestowed on it this respectable name, the memory of which will indisputably exist much longer than the town intended to perpetuate it. There is another county of Washington in Virginia, belonging to the Protector of Ame-

---

* This is a name given by way of derision, and even simple pleasantry, to the inhabitants of the four eastern states. It is thought to come from a savage people who formerly occupied this country, and dwelt between the Connecticut river, and the state of Massachusetts. The name of *Buckskin* is given in the same manner to the inhabitants of Virginia, because their ancestors were hunters, and sold buck, or rather deer skins, for we shall see in another part of this work that there are no roebucks in Virginia. The English army serving in America, and England herself, will long have reason to remember the contemptuous use they made of this term in the late unhappy war, and the severe retort they met with on the occasion. The *English army*, at Bunker's Hill, marched to the insulting tune of "Yankee doodle," but from that period it became the air of triumph, the Io Pœan of *America*. It was *cuckoo* to the British ear.—*Trans.*

rica; but its great distance from this new city prevents all possible inconvenience arising from the identity of name.* This
capital of a rising county has a Meeting-house, and seven or
eight houses collected; it is in a beautiful situation, and the
cultivation appears rich and well managed : a rivulet, which
runs at the bottom of the valley, renders the meadows more
fruitful than they generally are in mountainous countries.†
From hence to Litchfield, they reckon seventeen miles: I had
ten miles to go to reach Moorhouse's tavern, where I intended
sleeping, but not taking the shortest road, I travelled at least

---

* Other states have likewise commemorated the virtues of this great
man in the same manner.— *Trans.*

† Two years after, the Author returned by this place, where he had
only seen a few houses, and a single inn. The number was almost
doubled, and there were three very good and well accommodated inns.
He has remarked the same progress through almost all the interior
parts of the country, from the bay of Chesapeake to *Piscataqua*, that
is, through a space of six hundred miles. This progress is owing, in
great measure, even to the misfortunes of the war. The English being
masters of the sea, made, or had it in their power to make, what they
called *depredatory expeditions.* Marks of these horrid expeditions
were every where to be met with in travelling within *fifty* miles of the
coasts or rivers. In one of them it was agitated by the Generals *Garth,*
Tryon, and their officers, to burn the beautiful and popular town of
New-Haven in Connecticut, with its handsome college, &c. *The latter General was for it,* but happily, more humane and wiser spirits prevailed in the council. But this term, too shameful to be adopted into
the vocabulary of war, denoted only a small part of the ravages they
actually committed; murder and conflagrations were perpetually the
incidents which occurred. Hence it happened that the citizens who
were the most easy in their circumstances, that is to say, those who,
uniting commerce with agriculture, had their plantations near the coasts,
or the mouths of rivers, abandoned them for more tranquil habitations
in the interior part of the country. The little capital they transported
with them was employed in clearing out new settlements, which soon
became prosperous. On the other hand, communications by sea becoming impracticable, it was necessary to make use of conveyances
through the country; the roads in consequence were made better,
and were more frequented; inns multiplied, as well as the establishment of all workmen useful for travellers, such as wheelwrights, black-
smiths, &c. So that, besides liberty and independence, the United
States will derive this advantage from the war, that commerce and population will be greatly increased, and that lands, which had long remained barren, have been so successfully cultivated, as to prevent them
from being again abandoned.

The Translator had the opportunity of making the same remarks,
not only in a journey from Virginia to New-Hampshire, but in many
of the interior parts of the continent.—*Trans.*

twelve, and always among the mountains. That which I took brought me to a pretty considerable hamlet, called New Milford-Bordering Skirt, or the confines of Milford. county, and from thence into so deep and wild a valley, that I thought myself completely lost, until an opening in the wood made me perceive, first a meadow surrounded by fences, then a house, and soon after another, and at length a charming valley, with several considerable farms, covered with cattle. I soon crossed this spot which belongs to the county of Kent, as well as the rivulet which flows through the middle of it, and after travelling three miles farther in the mountains, I reached the banks of the Housatonick, or the river of Stratford. It is unnecessary to remark that the first is the genuine name, that is, the name given it by the savages, the ancient inhabitants of the country. This river is not navigable, and is easily forded near Bull's iron works. We then turn to the left and pass along its banks; but if one is sensible to the beauties of nature, if on seeing the paintings of *Vernet* and *Robert*, one has learnt to admire its models, it is impossible not to be lost in admiration at the view of the charming landscape, formed by the combination of the forges, of the fall of water which seems to work them, and of the variegated prospect of trees and rocks, with which this picturesque scene is embellished. At the distance of a mile we again pass the same river on a wooden bridge; we soon meet with another called Ten-mile river, which falls into this, and which we follow for two or three miles, and then come in sight of several handsome houses, forming a part of the district called the Oblong. It is a long narrow slip of land, ceded by Connecticut to the state of New-York, in exchange for some other territory. The inn I was going to is in the Oblong, but two miles farther on. It is kept by Colonel Moorhouse; for nothing is more common in America than to see an inn-keeper a colonel: they are in general militia colonels, chosen by the militia themselves, who seldom fail to entrust the command to the most esteemed, and most creditable citizens.*

I pressed forward my horses, and hurried on to get the start of a traveller on horseback, who had joined me on the road, and who would have had the same right with myself to the lodgings, had we arrived together. I had the satisfaction, however, to see him pursue his journey; but soon learnt, with

---

* At Leesburgh in Virginia, in my way to visit General Gates, I staid three days at the house of an Englishman, a native of Bristol, a man of five foot high, who united, in his own person, the offices of *Colonel, Justice of the Peace, Parish Clerk*, and *Innkeeper*, nor was he deficient in any of these functions.—*Trans.*

concern, that the little inn where I proposed to pass that
night, was occupied by thirteen farmers, and two hundred
and fifty oxen coming from New-Hampshire. The oxen were
the least inconvenient part of the company, as they were left
to graze in a meadow hard by, without even a dog to guard
them; but the farmers, their horses, and dogs, were in possession of the inn. They were conveying to the army a part of
the contingent of provisions furnished by New-Hampshire.
This contingent is a sort of tax divided among all the inhabitants, on some of whom the imposition amounts to one hundred and fifty, on others to one hundred, or eighty pounds of
meat, according to their abilities; so that they agree among
themselves to furnish a larger, or smaller sized ox, no matter
which, as each animal is weighed. Their conveyance to the
army is then entrusted to some farmers, and drovers. The
farmers are allowed about a dollar a day, and their expenses,
as well as those of the cattle, are paid them on their return,
according to the receipts they are obliged to produce from the
inn-keepers where they have halted. The usual price is from
three-pence to five-pence English per night for each ox, and in
proportion at noon.

I informed myself of these particulars whilst my people were
endeavouring to find me lodgings; but all the rooms, and all
the beds were occupied by these farmers, and I was in the
greatest distress, when a tall, fat man, the principal person
among them, being informed who I was, came to me, and
assured me, that neither he, nor his companions would ever suffer a French General Officer to want a bed, and that they
would rather sleep on the floor; adding, that they were accustomed to it, and that it would be attended with no inconvenience. In reply, I told them I was a military man, and as
much accustomed as themselves to make the earth my bed.
We had long debates on this point of *politesse*; theirs was
rustic, but more cordial and affecting than the best turned
compliments. The result was, that I had a two-bedded room
for myself and my aids-de-camp. But our acquaintance did
not terminate there : after parting from each other, I to take
some repose, they to continue drinking their grog and cider,
they came into my room. I was then employed in tracing my
route by the map of the country; this map excited their
curiosity. They saw there with surprise and satisfaction the
places they had passed through. They asked me if they were
known in Europe, and if it was there I had bought my maps.
On my assuring them that we knew America as well as the
countries adjoining to us, they seemed much pleased; but
their joy was without bounds, when they saw New-Hampshire,
their country, on the map. They called their companions

who were in the next room; and mine was soon filled with the strongest and most robust men I had hitherto seen in America. On my appearing struck with their size and stature, they told me that the inhabitants of New-Hampshire were strong and vigorous, for which there were many reasons ; that the air was excellent, their sole occupation was agriculture, and above all that their blood was unmixed : this country being inhabited by ancient families who had emigrated from England. We parted good friends, touching, or rather shaking hands in the English fashion, and they assured me that they were very happy to have an opportunity *to shake hands with a French General.**

The horse which carried my portmanteau, not travelling so fast as me, did not come up till the next morning, so that it was ten o'clock on the 20th of December, before I could set out. Three miles from Moorhouse's is a very high hill ; we then descend, but not quite so much as we ascended ; the road here is over elevated ground, leaving large mountains on

---

* The translator, who as a disinterested, and determined friend to the rights of mankind, and to the principles of the English Constitution, could not but wish success to America in her glorious struggle ; as a native of England had many similar occasions for interesting reflections on the vicissitude of human affairs, and of the wickedness of those who too frequently direct them. But in no instance was this more striking than in Virginia, where he saw the French army encamped on the very spot, from whence *Braddock* set out on his unfortunate expedition against the French, five and twenty years before. The traces of his encampment were still evident. In this expedition he was not only well seconded by the Provincials, but had their advice been followed, his success would have been very different. It is worth observing too, that no less than *four* of the most distinguished of the American Generals, were with him on the expedition. *General Washington* was his aid-de-camp, and after dissuading him as much as possible from forming his army in the European manner, (the mistake which proved fatal to him,) received him when mortally wounded in his arms ; *General Lee,* was in a detached party from the main body of the army ; *General Gates* served in the army, and *General Stephens* was shot through the body in the engagement : Lee and Gates were Englishmen, and Stephens a Scotchman ; all the four were now become inhabitants of Virginia. On the anniversary of that unfortunate day, the translator dined in the back part of the country at General Gates', with General Stephens, from whom he had many curious particulars ; nor was the wonderful revolution in the affairs and minds of men, the subject of less anxious discussion with them, than with the translator. At the time he is speaking of, indeed, during their whole stay, nothing could be more cordial and sincere than the kind reception given to the French by the Virginians.—*Trans.*

the left. The country is well cultivated; affording the prospect of several pretty farms, with some mills; and notwithstanding the war, Hopel township is building, inhabited chiefly by Dutch people, as well as the greatest part of the state of New-York, which formerly belonged to the republic of Holland, who exchanged it for Surinam. My intention was to sleep five miles on this side of Fishkill, at Colonel Griffin's tavern. I found him cutting and preparing wood for fences: he assured me his house was full, which was easy to be believed, for it was very small. I continued my journey therefore, and reached Fishkill about four o'clock. This town, in which there are not more than fifty houses in the space of two miles, has been long the principal depot of the American army. It is there they have placed their magazines, their hospitals, their workshops, &c. but all these form a town of themselves, composed of handsome large barracks, built in the wood at the foot of the mountains; for the Americans, like the Romans in many respects, have hardly any other winter quarters, than wooden towns, or barricaded camps, which may be compared to the *hiemalia* of the Romans.

As for the position of Fishkill, that it was a post of great importance is evident from the campaign of 1777. It is clear that the plan of the English was to render themselves masters of the whole course of the North River, and thus to separate the Eastern and Western States. It was necessary therefore to secure a post on that river; West-Point was made choice of as the most important to fortify, and Fishkill as the place the best adapted to the establishment of the principal depot of provisions, ammunition, &c.: these two positions are connected together. I shall soon speak of West-Point, but I shall remark here, that Fishkill has all the qualities necessary for a place of depot, for it is situated on the high road from Connecticut, and near the North River, and is protected at the same time by a chain of inaccessible mountains, which occupy a space of more than twenty miles between the Croton river and that of Fishkill.

The approach of winter quarters, and the movement of the troops occasioned by this circumstance, made lodgings very scarce: it was with difficulty I found any, but I got at last into a middling inn, next by an old Mrs. Egremont. The house was not so clean as they usually are in America; but the most disagreeable circumstance was the want of several panes of glass. In fact, of all repairs, that of windows is the most difficult, in a country where, from the scattered situation and distance of the houses from each other, it is sometimes necessary to send twenty miles for a glazier. We made use of every thing that came to hand to patch up the windows in the best way we could, and we made an excellent fire. Soon after, the doctor of the hospital, who had seen me pass, and knew me to be a French General-Officer, came with great politeness to see if I wanted any thing, and to offer me every service in his power. I make use of the English word doctor, because the distinction of surgeon and physician is as little known in the army of Washington, as in that of Agamemnon. We read in Homer, that the physician Macaon himself dressed the wounds; but our physicians, who are no Greeks, will not follow that example. The Americans conform to the ancient custom, and it answers very well; they are well pleased with their doctors, whom they hold in the highest consideration. Doctor Craig, whom I knew at Newport, is the intimate friend of General Washington; and the Marquis de la Fayette had very lately an aid-de-camp, Colonel MacHenry, who the year before performed the functions of doctor in the same army.*

The 21st, at nine in the morning, the Quarter-Master of Fishkill, who had come the night before with the utmost politeness to offer me his services, and to place two sentinels at the door, an honour I refused in spite of every thing he could say, called upon me; and after drinking tea according to custom, he conducted me to see the barracks, the magazines, and workhouses of the different workmen employed in the service of the army. These barracks are wooden houses, well built, and well covered, having garrets, and even cellars, so that we should form a false idea, were we to judge of them by what we see in our armies, when our troops are *barraqués*. The Americans sometimes make them like like ours, but this is merely

---

* My old friend Rumney, whom I had the happiness to meet with after an absence of twenty years, during which time he has been settled at Alexandria in Virginia, (whose respectable father has been forty years master of the Latin school at Alnwick in Northumberland, and his uncle clergyman of Berwick,) had served more than one campaign as colonel, doctor, and surgeon in the army; he is held in the highest esteem, and is on terms of the greatest friendship with General Washington, at whose house I spent some days with him. But it is impossible to conceive the estimation in which all the medical men, attached to the army, were held during the war, by the people in general, as well as the military. I travelled from Philadelphia to the the American camp on the North river, with Mr. Craigie of that department, a most respectable young man, and was witness to the grateful acknowledgments his countrymen seemed every where to bestow on him, for the service he was rendering their suffering fellow-citizens, nor indeed could any thing exceed the zeal, perseverance, and attention of this department under the most discouraging circumstances.— *Trans.*

to cover the soldiers when they are more within reach of the enemy. They call these *huts*, and they are very expert in constructing one and the other. They require only three days to build the former, reckoning from the moment they begin to cut down the trees; the others are finished in four and twenty hours. They consist of little walls made of stones heaped up, the intervals of which are filled with earth kneaded with water, or simply with mud; a few planks form the roof, but what renders them very warm is that the chimney occupies the outerside, and that you can only enter by a small door, at the side of the chimney. The army has passed whole winters under such huts, without suffering, and without sickness. As for the barracks, or rather the little military town of Fishkill, such ample provision is made for every thing which the service and discipline of the army may require, that a prévôté and a prison are built there, surrounded by palisades. One gate only affords access to the enclosure of the prévôté; and before it is placed a guard-house. Through the window-bars of the prison, I distinguished some prisoners, with the English uniform; they were about thirty soldiers, or regimented tories. These wretches had accompanied the savages in the incursion they had made by Lake Ontario and the Mohawk river. They had burnt upwards of two hundred houses, killed the horses and cows, and destroyed above one hundred thousand bushels of corn. The gallows should have been the reward of these exploits, but the enemy having also made some prisoners, reprisals were dreaded, and these robbers were only confined in rigorous and close imprisonment.

After passing some time in visiting these different settlements, I got on horseback, and under the conduct of a guard which the Quarter-Master gave me, I entered the wood and followed the road to West-Point, where I wished to arrive for dinner. Four or five miles from Fishkill, I saw some felled trees, and an opening in the wood, which on coming nearer I discovered to be a camp, or rather huts inhabited by some hundred invalid soldiers. These invalids were all in very good health; but it is necessary to observe, that in the American armies, every soldier is called an invalid, who is unfit for service; now these had been sent here because their clothes were truly invalids. These honest fellows, for I will not say creatures, (they know too well how to suffer, and are suffering in too noble a cause) were not covered, even with rags; but their steady countenances, and their good arms in good order, seemed to supply the defect of clothes, and to display nothing but their courage and their patience. Near this camp I met with Major Liman, aid-de-camp to General Heath, with whom I was particularly intimate at Newport, and Mr. de Ville

Franche, a French officer, serving as an Engineer at West-Point. General Heath had been informed of my arrival by an express, sent without my knowledge, by the Quarter-Master of Fishkill, and he had despatched these two officers to meet me. I continued my journey in the woods, in a road hemmed in on both sides by very steep hills, which seemed admirably adapted for the dwelling of bears, and where in fact they often make their appearance in winter. We availed ourselves at length of a less difficult part of these mountains to turn to the westward and approach the river, but which is still invisible. Descending them slowly, at the turning of the road, my eyes were struck with the most magnificent picture I had ever beheld. It was a view of the North river, running in a deep channel formed by the mountains, through which in former ages it had forced its passage. The fort of West-Point and the formidable batteries which defend it fix the attention on the western bank, but on lifting your eyes you behold on every side lofty summits, thick set with redoubts and batteries. I leaped off my horse, and viewed them a long time with my spying glass, the only method of acquiring a knowledge of the whole of the fortifications with which this important post is surrounded. Two lofty heights, on each of which a large redoubt is constructed, protect the eastern bank. These two works have no other name than the northern, and the southern redoubts ; but from the fort of West-Point properly so called, which is on the edge of the river, to the very top of the mountain at the foot of which it stands, are six different forts, all in the form of an amphitheatre, and protecting each other. They compelled me to leave this place, where I should willingly have spent the whole day, but I had not travelled a mile before I saw the reason of their hurrying me. I perceived a corps of infantry of about two thousand five hundred men, ranged in a line of battle on the bank of the river. They had just passed it to proceed by Kingsbridge, and cover a grand foraging party which it was proposed to send towards the White-Plains, and to the gates of New-York. General Stark, who beat the English at Bennington, had the command of these troops, and General Heath was at their head ; he was desirous of letting me see them before they marched. I passed before the ranks, being saluted with the espontoon by all the officers, and the drums beating a march, an honour paid in America to Major-Generals, who are the first in rank, though it only corresponds with our *Marechal de Camp*. The troops were ill clothed, but made a good appearance ; as for the officers they were every thing that could be wished, as well for their countenance, as for their manner of marching, and giving the command. After passing the front of the line, they broke it, filed off before me, and continued their route. General Heath conducted me to the river, where his barge was waiting to carry me to the other side. A new scene now opened to my view, not less sublime than the former. We descended with our faces towards the north : on that side is an island covered with rocks, which seem to close the channel of the river, but you soon perceive, through a sort of embrasure formed by its bed in separating immense mountains, that it comes obliquely from the westward, and that it has made a sudden turn round West-Point to open itself a passage, and to endeavour to gain the sea, without making hereafter the smallest bend. The eye carrying itself towards the North Bay and Constitution-Island, (the isle I have been speaking of) again perceives the river, distinguishes New-Windsor on its left bank, and is then attracted by different amphitheatres formed by the Apalachian Mountains, the nearest summits of which, that terminate the scene, are distant upwards of thirty miles. We embarked in the barge, and passed the river, which is about a mile wide. As we approached the opposite shore, the fort of West-Point, which, seen from the eastern bank, seemed humbly situated at the foot of the mountains, elevated itself to our view, and appeared like the summit of a steep rock ; this rock however was only the bank of the river. Had I not remarked that the chinks on it, in several places, were embrasures for cannon, and formidable batteries, I should soon have been apprised of it by thirteen twenty-four pounders, which were fired successively. This was a military salute, with which General Heath was pleased to honour me in the name of the Thirteen States. Never was honour more commanding, nor more majestic ; every gun, was, after a long interval, echoed back from the opposite bank, with a noise nearly equal to that of the discharge itself. When we recollected that two years ago West Point was a desert, almost inaccessible, that this desert has been covered with fortresses and artillery, by a people, who six years before had scarcely ever seen cannon ; when we reflect that the fate of the United States depended in great measure on this important post ; and that a horse dealer,* transformed into a general, or rather become a hero, always intrepid, always victorious, but always purchasing victory at the price of his blood ; that this extraordinary man, at once the honour, and the opprobrium of his country, actually sold, and expected to deliver this *Palladium* of American liberty to the English ; when so many extraordinary circumstances are brought together in the physical and moral order of things, it may easily be imagined that I had sufficient exercise for reflection, and that I did not tire on the road.

---

* Benedict Arnold.—*Trans.*

On landing, or rather on climbing the rocks on the banks of the river, we were received by Colonel Lamb, and Major Bowman, both officers of artillery; by Major Fish, a handsome young man, witty and well formed; and Major Franks, formerly aid-de-camp to Arnold. The latter had been tried and honourably acquitted by a council of war, demanded by himself after the escape and treason of his General. He speaks good French, as well as Colonel Lamb, which they both learnt in Canada, where they were settled. The latter received a musket shot in his jaw at the attack of Quebec, fighting by the side of Arnold, and having early penetrated into the upper town. Pressed by dinner time we went immediately to General Heath's barrack. The fort, which was begun on much too extensive a plan, has been since curtailed by Mr. du Portail, so that this barrack is no longer within its precincts. Around it are some magazines, and farther to the north-west, barracks for three or four battalions; they are built of wood, and similar to those of Fishkill. Whilst dinner was preparing, General Heath took me into a little closet, which served him as a bed chamber, and showed me the instructions he had given General Stark for the grand foraging party he commanded. This expedition required a movement of troops in a space of more than fifty miles; and I can affirm, that they were as well conceived as any instructions of that kind I have ever seen, either in print, or manuscript. He showed me also a letter in which General Washington only ordered him to send this detachment, and pointed out its object, without communicating to him, however, another operation connected with it, which was to take place on the right bank of the North river. From various intelligence, by indirect ways, General Heath was persuaded, that in case the enemy collected his force to interrupt the forage, Mr. de la Fayette would attack Staten-Island, and he was not deceived; but Mr. Washington contented himself with announcing generally some movements on his side, adding, that he waited for a more safe method of communicating the nature of them to General Heath. Secrecy is strictly observed in the American army; very few persons are in the confidence of the Commander, and in general there is less said of the operations of war, of what we call news, than in the French army.

CHAPTER III.

WEST-POINT—FORT CLINTON—KING'S FERRY—STONEY POINT—
VERPLANK'S POINT—TOTOHAW FALL—WASHINGTON'S HEAD
QUARTERS.

GENERAL Heath is so well known in our little army, that I
should dispense with entering into particulars respecting him,
if this Journal, in which I endeavour to recollect what little I
have seen in this country, were not destined at the same
time to satisfy the curiosity of others who have not crossed the
sea, and to whose amusement I am desirous of contributing.
This General was one of the first who took up arms, at the
blockade of Boston, and having at first joined the army in the
quality of Colonel, he was immediately raised to the rank of
Major-General. He was at that time a substantial farmer or
rich gentleman; for we must not lose sight of the distinction,
that in America, *farmer* means cultivator, in opposition to
merchant, which every man is called who is employed in commerce. Here, as in England, by *gentleman*, is understood a
person possessing a considerable *freehold*, or land of his own.
General Heath, then, was a farmer or gentleman, and reared,
on his estate, a great number of cattle, which he sold for ships'
provisions. But his natural taste led him to the study of war;
to which he has principally applied himself since the period in
which his duty has concurred with his inclination; he has read
our best authors on tactics, and especially the Tactics of Mr.
Guibert, which he holds in particular estimation. His fortune
enabling him to continue in the service, notwithstanding the
want of pay, which has compelled the less rich to quit it, he
has served the whole war; but accident has prevented him
from being present on the most important occasions. His
countenance is noble and open; and his bald head, as well as
his corpulence, give him a striking resemblance to the late
Lord Granby. He writes well and with ease; has great sensibility of mind, and a frank and amiable character; in short,
if he has not been in the way of displaying his talents in action, it may be at least asserted, that he is well adapted to the
business of the cabinet. His estate is near Boston, and he
commanded there when Burgoyne's army were brought prisoners thither. It was he who put the English General Philips in

arrest,* for want of respect to the Congress; his conduct on this occasion was firm and noble.   On our arrival at Rhode-Island, he was sent there; and soon after, when Clinton was preparing to attack us, he assembled and commanded the militia, who came to our assistance.   During his stay at Newport, he lived honourably, and in great friendship with all the French officers.   In the month of September, General Washington, on discovering the treason of Arnold, sent for him, and gave him the command of West-Point; a mark of confidence the more honourable, as none but the most honest of men was proper to succeed, in his command, the basest of all traitors.

After giving this advantageous but just idea of General Heath, I cannot but congratulate myself on the friendship, and thorough good understanding which subsisted between us during his stay at Newport, where my knowledge of the English language rendered me the medium in all affairs we had to transact with him.   It was with real satisfaction he received me at West-Point; he gave me a plain but very good dinner.   It is true there was not a drop of wine; but I find that with excellent cider, and toddy, one may very well dispense with it.   As soon as we rose from the table, we hurried to avail ourselves of the remaining daylight to examine the fortifications.   The first fort we met with above West-Point, on the declivity of the mountain, is called Fort-Putnam, from the General of that name.   It is placed on a rock very steep on every side; the ramparts were at first constructed with trunks of trees; they are rebuilt with stone, and are not quite finished.   There is a powder magazine bomb-proof, a large cistern, and souterrains

---

* It may now be mentioned, without any invidious imputation, that the conduct of too many of the British officers, when prisoners in America, was as injurious to the honour and interest of their country, as destitute of good sense and common policy; of this the Translator saw many examples which made him blush for England.   At Lancaster in Pennsylvania, in particular, he was present at a court of inquiry, instituted into the conduct of some British officers who had broken their parole more than once, and insulted and beat the inhabitants of the country; nothing could beclearer or more decisive than the evidence, nor more polite and indulgent than the behaviour of the American officers who constituted the court, yet were they openly insulted and contemptuously treated by these magnanimous gentlemen officers.   Their names are withheld by the Translator, on account of their families; they were a part of the army taken at Yorktown, with Cornwallis.   Captain Grenville of the Guards, and others who conducted themselves really like gentlemen, can say how well they were treated.—*Trans.*

for the garrison. Above this fort, and when we reach the lofti-est summit, there are three strong redoubts lined with cannon, at three different eminences, each of which would require a formal siege. The day being nearly spent, I contented myself with judging by the eye of the very intelligent manner in which they are calculated for mutual protection. Fort Wallis, whither General Heath conducted me, was near and more ac-cessible. Though it be placed lower than fort Putnam, it still commands the river to the south. It is a large pentagonal re-doubt, built of huge trunks of trees; it is picketed, and lined with artillery. Under the fire of this redoubt, and lower down, is a battery of cannon, to range more obliquely the course of the river. This battery is not closed at the gorge, so that the enemy may take, but never keep it ; which leads me to remark that this is the best method in all field fortifications. Batte-ries placed in works, have two inconveniences : the first is, that if these works be ever so little elevated, they do not graze sufficiently ; and the second, that the enemy may at once at-tack the redoubt and the battery : whereas the latter being exterior and protected by the redoubt, must be first attacked ; in which case it is supported by troops who have nothing to fear for themselves, and whose fire is commonly better direct-ed, and does more execution. A battery yet lower, and near-er to the river, completes the security of the southern part.

In returning to West-Point, we saw a redoubt that is suffer-ed to go to ruin, as being useless, which in fact it is. It was night when we got home, but what I had to observe did not re-quire daylight. It is a vast souterrain, formed within the fort of West-Point, where not only the powder and ammunition ne-cessary for this post are kept in reserve, but the deposit of the whole army. These magazines completely filled, the nu-merous artillery one sees in these different fortresses, the pro-digious labour necessary to transport, and pile up on steep rocks, huge trunks of trees, and enormous hewn stones, impress the mind with an idea of the Americans very different from that which the English ministry have laboured to give to Parliament. A Frenchman would be surprised that a nation, just rising into notice, should have expended in two years upwards of twelve millions (half a million sterling) in this desert. He would be still more so on learning that these fortifications cost nothing to the state, being built by the soldiers, who received not the smallest gratification, and who did not even receive their stated pay ;* but he would doubtless feel some satisfaction, in hearing

---

* The zeal, perseverance, and, I may say, *honour*, which shone forth in the American army, in the most arduous and extraordinary

that these beautiful and well contrived works, were planned
and executed by two French Engineers, Mr. du Portail, and
Mr. du Gouvion, who received no more pay than their workmen.

But in this wild and warlike abode, where one seems transported to the bottom of Thrace and the dominions of the god
Mars, we found, on our return in the evening, some pretty women, and an excellent dish of tea. Mrs. Boman, wife of the
Major of that name, and a young sister who had accompanied
her to West-Point, were waiting for us. They lodged in a little
barrack neatly arranged. The room they received us in, was
hung with handsome paper, furnished with mahogany tables,
and even ornamented with several prints. After staying a
little time, it was necessary to return to General Heath's quarters, and to dispose matters for passing the night, which was
not an easy affair; for the company were much increased in

---

circumstances, almost surpass credibility. They were in general
most wretchedly clothed, seldom received any pay, were frequently in
want of every thing, from the public scarcity of money, and the con-
sequent indifference of the contractors, and had daily temptations
thrown out to them of the most alluring nature. This army was composed of all nations, yet they seemed to be pervaded but by one spirit,
and fought, and acted with as much enthusiastic ardour as the most enlightened and determined of their leaders. We all remember, when
their intolerable distresses drove part of them to revolt in 1780, when
Clinton sent emissaries among them, with the most advantageous offers,
and made a movement of his army to favour their desertion, that they
disdainfully refused his offers, appealing to their *honour*, and delivered
up with indignation, the British emissaries, who were executed at
Trenton. *Mr. Hugh Shield*, and *Mr. John Maxwell Nesbett*, two
Irish gentlemen settled at Philadelphia, who were entrusted with the
care of them, informed the Translator, that one of them was an officer
of some note in the British army. On the morning of their execution,
this gentleman desired Mr. Shield to accompany him to the necessary,
wherein he staid some time, apparently with the hopes of effecting his
escape, but this failing he addressed that gentleman as follows. " I
see, sir, that you are faithful to the trust reposed in you, and that my
die is cast ; but as you are a gentleman, I hope you will not fail to let
General Clinton know, that my fidelity is unshaken, that I die a loyal
subject to George the Third, and that I hope he will not forget my
family." He then made a hearty breakfast of cold beef, and was executed with his companion on a tree near the river Delaware, full of
courage, and making the same declarations. To account for the subordinate situation in which Messrs. Nesbett and Shield appear to have
acted on this occasion, it is necessary to observe, that on all emergencies the merchants of Philadelphia flew to arms and acted as common
soldiers.—*Trans.*

the course of the evening, by the arrival of the Vicomte de
Noailles, the Comte de Damas, and the Chevalier Duplessis.
Mauduit had reached West-Point, which post they had intended to examine minutely ; but the motions of the American
army determined them to set out with me, in order to join Mr.
de la Fayette, the next evening, or early the following morning.
Though General Heath had a great deal of company to provide for, his *Marechal de Logis*, had not much to do : there
were only three rooms in the barracks ; the General's chamber, that of his aid-de-camp, who resigned it to me ; and the
dining-room, in which some blankets were spread before a
large fire, where the other gentlemen passed as comfortable a
night as could be expected. The morning gun soon summon-
ed them from their beds ; the blankets were removed, and
the dining-room, resuming its rights, was quickly furnished
with a large table covered with beef-steaks, which we eat with
a very good appetite, swilling down from time to time a cup
of tea.   Europeans would not find this food and drink, taken
together, to their taste ; but I can assure you that it made a
very comfortable breakfast.   There now fell a very heavy rain,
which had begun in the night, and still continued, with a dreadful wind, which rendered the passage of the ferry very dangerous for our horses, and prevented us from making use of the
sail, in the barge General Heath had given us, to carry us to
King's Ferry.   In spite of all these obstacles we embarked
under the firing of thirteen guns, notwithstanding our representations to the contrary.   Another circumstance, however,
gave additional value to these honours, for the pieces they discharged had belonged to Burgoyne's army.   Thus did the artillery sent from Woolwich to Canada in 1777, now serve to
defend America, and do homage to her allies, until it was to be
employed in the siege of New-York.

General Heath, who was detained by business at West-
Point, sent Major Liman to accompany me to Verplank's-
Point, where we did not arrive till between twelve and one,
after a continued journey amidst the immense hills which
cover this country, and leave no other interval than the bed
of the river.   The highest of them is called Antony's Nose,
it projects into the river, and compels it to make a little
change in its course.   Before we arrive at this point, we see
the ruins of fort Clinton : this fort, which was named after the
governor of the state of New-York, was attacked and taken
in 1777 by the English General Clinton, as he was remounting the river to Albany to *give his hand* to Burgoyne.*   It was

* A poor fellow who was sent with a letter from Burgoyne to Clinton inclosed in a silver bullet, miscarried in his message, and lost his

then the principal fort on the river, and built on a rock, at the foot of a mountain, thought to be inaccessible, and was farther defended by a little creek which falls into the main river. Sir Henry Clinton scaled the top of the mountain, himself carrying the British colours, which he always held aloft, until his troops descended the steep rock, passed the creek, and carried the post. The garrison, consisting of 700 men, were almost all taken. Since the defeat of Burgoyne, and the alliance with France has changed the face of affairs in America, General Washington has not thought proper to repair fort Clinton; he preferred placing his communication and concentring his forces at West-Point, because the Hudson there makes a circuit which prevents vessels from remounting with the wind abaft, or with the tide; and Constitution-Isle, which is precisely at the turn of the river, in a direction north and south, is perfectly well situated to protect the chain which closes the passage for ships of war.

The English, however, had preserved a very important post at King's Ferry, where they were sufficiently well fortified; so that by the aid of their ships, they were masters of the course of the river for the space of more than fifty miles, and were thus able to repel to the northward the very important communication between the Jerseys and Connecticut. Such was the state of things, when, in the month of June, 1779, General Wayne, who commanded in the Clove a corps of 1500 men, formed the project of surprising Stoney-Point. This fort was in an entrenchment, surrounded with abattis, which crowned a steep rock, and formed a well picketed redoubt. General Wayne marched, in the night, in three columns, the principal of which was led on by Monsieur de Fleury, who, without firing a musket, forced the abattis, and entrenchments, and entered the redoubt with the fugitives.* The attack was so

---

life by the sameness of names of the American and British commanders. Falling in, in the woods, with a party of Americans clothed in British uniform, which they had taken, he inquired eagerly for *General Clinton* to whom he was instantly conducted, but on discovering that it was not *the Clinton* he was in search of, in the face of a number of spectators, he swallowed the bullet. Emetics and purgatives were instantly administered, which made him disgorge, and the unfortunate fellow was hanged on the next tree.—*Trans.*

* This officer had already distinguished himself on many occasions, particularly at the retreat of General Sullivan from Rhode-Island, and at the defence of Mud-Island. He went to America in 1777. He has since been Major of the regiment of Saint Onge, and served as Major of brigade in the army of the Count de Rochambeau. On his return to France, he was made Colonel of the regiment of Pondicherry, and is now in India.

brisk on the part of the Americans, and such the terror of the
English, that Mr. de Fleury, who was the first that entered,
found himself in an instant loaded with eleven swords which
were delivered to him by those who asked for quarter.   It
must be added to the honour of our allies, that from that moment not a drop of blood was spilt.*   The Americans, once
masters of one of the banks of the river, lost no time in getting possession of the other.   Mr. de Gouvion constructed a
redoubt at Verplank's-Point, (nearly opposite,) where we
landed, and where, by a lucky accident, we found our horses,
arrived as soon as us.   This redoubt is of a peculiar form,
hardly ever used but in America : the ditch is within the parapet, which is made steep on both sides, and picketed at the
height of the cordon ; lodgings for the soldiers are formed
below.   The middle of the work is a space constructed with
wood, and in the form of a square tower.   There are battle-
ments every where, and it commands the rampart.   An abattis formed of the tops of trees interwoven, surrounds the whole,
and is a substitute for a covered way.   We may easily perceive that such a work cannot be insulted, nor taken without
cannon.   Now as this is backed by the mountains, of which
the Americans are always masters, it is almost impossible that
the English should besiege it.   A creek which falls into Hudson river, and runs to the southward of this redoubt, renders
its position still more advantageous.   Colonel Livingston, who
commands at King's Ferry, has established himself there in
preference to Stoney-Point, to be nearer the White-Plains,

---

* I cannot here resist a pang of sorrow for the dreadful consequences of the late desperate and fatal war.   *Captain Jew* of the 17th regiment, as brave an officer, and as amiable a man as ever lived, whom
I had long known and esteemed, when serving with our common friend
Montgomery in that regiment, here lost his life, refusing to take quarter.
This gallant man was already perforated with wounds received in Canada and the West-Indies, fighting under his Colonel, *General Monck-
ton*, in the preceding war, and was such a spectacle of a wounded
body still in life, as to be particularly pointed out to the King his master's notice at a review of the regiment near London in 1770 or 1771 ;
the King asked him many questions, seemed much affected with his
situation, expressed his pity, and—he was left to pine a subaltern, and
to follow his regiment once more to scenes of war and a distant climate.
He deeply felt this ever after, and chagrin no doubt, added to his despair, had made him wish for death.   The fate of my most intimate
and lamented friend, Montgomery, who fell, as he thought in a better
cause, and on the very spot where he had attended *Wolfe* to victory
and glory, affords ample food for melancholy reflection, not easy to be
effaced from susceptible minds, and who have felt a double loss of
friends, in the horrors of this detestable war.—*Trans.*

where the English frequently made incursions. This is a very amiable and well informed young man. Previous to the war he married in Canada, where he has acquired the French language : in 1775, he was one of the first who took arms ; he fought under the orders of Montgomery, and took fort Chambly, whilst the former was besieging St. John's. He received us in his little citadel with great politeness ; but to leave it with the honours of war, the American laws required that we should breakfast : It was the second we had taken that day, and consisted of beef-steaks, and tea, accompanied with a few bowls of grog ; for the commander's cellar was no better stored than the soldiers' wardrobe. The latter had been sent into this garrison as being the worst clothed of the whole American army, so that one may form some idea of their dress.

About two o'clock we crossed the river, and stopped to examine the fortifications of Stoney-Point. The Americans finding them too extensive, had reduced them to a redoubt, nearly similar to that of Verplank's but not quite so good. There I took leave of Mr. Livingston, who gave me a guide to conduct me to the army, and I set off, preceded by Messieurs de Noailles, de Damas, and de Mauduit, who wished to join Mr. de la Fayette that night, though they had thirty miles to go, through very bad roads. This impatience was well suited to their age ; but the intelligence I collected proving to me that the army could not move before the next day, I determined to stop on the road, content to profit by the little daylight that remained to travel ten or twelve miles. On leaving the river, I frequently turned round to enjoy the magnificent spectacle it presents in this place, where its bed becomes so large, that in viewing it to the southward, it has the appearance of an immense lake, whilst the northern aspect is that of a majestic river. I was desired to observe a sort of promontory, from whence Colonel Livingston had formed the project of taking the *Vulture* sloop of war, which brought *André*, and was waiting for *Arnold*. This vessel having come too near the shore, grounded at low water ; the colonel acquainted Arnold with it, and asked him for two pieces of heavy cannon, assuring him that he would place them so as to sink her. Arnold eluded the proposal on frivolous pretences, so that the colonel could only bring one four pounder, which was at Verplank's to bear on her. This piece raked the vessel fore and aft, and did her so much damage, that if she had not got off with the flood, she must have struck. The next day Colonel Livingston being on the shore, saw Arnold pass in his barge, as he was going down the river to get on board the frigate. He declares that he had such a suspicion of him, that had his guard boats been near, he would have gone after him instantly, and asked him where he was going. This question probably would have embarrassed the traitor, and Colonel Livingston's suspicions being thence confirmed, he would have arrested him.*

My thoughts were occupied with Arnold and his treason, when my road brought me to *Smith's* famous house, where he had his interview with André, and formed his horrid plot. It was in this house they passed the night together, and where André changed his clothes. It was there that the liberty of America was bargained for and sold ; and it was there that chance, which is always the arbiter of great events, disconcerted this horrible project, and that satisfied with sacrificing the imprudent André, she prevented the crime, only by the escape of the criminal. André was repassing the river quietly, to gain New-York by the White-Plains, had not the cannon fired at the frigate, made him apprehend the falling in with the American troops. He imagined, that favoured by his disguise, he should be safer on the right bank : a few miles from thence he was stopped, and a few miles farther he found the gibbet.

Smith, who was more than suspected, but not convicted of being a party in the plot, is still in prison, where the law protects him against justice. But his house seems to have experienced the only chastisement of which it was susceptible ; it is punished by solitude ; and is in fact so deserted, that there is not a single person to take care of it, although it is the mansion of a large farm.† I pursued my route, but without being able to give so much attention as to recollect it ; I only remember

---

* There is every reason to believe that Arnold's treachery took its date from his connexion with Lieutenant *Hele,* killed afterwards on board the Formidable in the West-Indies, and who was undoubtedly a very active and industrious spy at Philadelphia in the winter of 1778, whither he was sent for that purpose in a pretended flag of truce, which being wrecked in the Delaware, he was made prisoner by Congress, a subject of much discussion between them, and the commander at New-York. That the intended plot was known in England, and great hopes built upon it, long before it was to take place, is certain. General Matthews and other officers who returned in the autumn of 1780, being often heard to declare, " that it was all over with the rebels ; that they were about to receive an irreparable blow, the news of which would soon arrive," &c. &c. Their silence from the moment in which they received an account of the failure of the plot, and the discovery of the traitor, evidently pointed out the object of their allusions.—*Trans.*

† *Smith's* is a very handsome house, and beautifully situated, but was in the same desolate state when the Translator was there in 1780.—*Trans.*

that it was as gloomy as my reflections; it brought me into a
deep vale, covered with cypresses ; a torrent rolled over the
rocks, which I passed, and soon after night came on. I had
still some miles to an inn, where I got tolerably well accommodated. It is situated in Haverstraw, and is kept by another
Smith, but who in no way resembles the former ; he assured
me he was a good whig, and as he gave me a good supper, I
readily believed him.

The 23d I set out at eight o'clock, with the intention of arriving in good time at the Marquis de la Fayette's camp ; for
I had learnt that the army was not to move that day, and I was
desirous of being presented by him to General Washington.
The shortest road was by Paramus ; but my guide insisted on
my turning to the northward, assuring me that the other road
was not safe, that it was infested by tories, and that he always
avoided it, when he had letters to carry.* I took the road to
the right therefore, and followed for some time the rivulet of
Romopog ; I then turned to the left, and soon got into the
township of Pompton, and into the Totohaw road ; but being
informed that it led me straight to the main body of the army,
without passing by the van commanded by M. de la Fayette, I
inquired for some cross road to his quarters, and one was pointed out to me, by which, passing near a sort of lake which forms
a very agreeable point of view, and then crossing some very
beautiful woods, I arrived at a stream which falls into Second
river, exactly at the spot where M. de la Fayette was encamped. His posts lined the rivulet ; they were well disposed, and
in good order. At length I arrived at the camp ; but the Marquis was not there ; apprized of my coming by the Vicomte de
Noailles, he had gone to wait for me at seven miles distance,
at head quarters, where he thought I should direct my course.
He had sent, however, Major Gimat, and one of his aids-de-
camp to meet me, but they had taken the two roads to Paramus ; so that by his precautions, and those of my guide, I was,

* The guide gave the Marquis very true information, for the Translator who took the *Paramus* road, had several well founded alarms,
in passing through that intricate country. At *Hopper's Mill,* near
Paramus, where he slept among myriads of rats in a milk house, the
family assured him, that their quarters were constantly beat up, and
horses, men, &c. carried off. At this place there was no lock to the
stable door, which they said was here a superfluous article, as these
banditti were guilty of every act of violence. He received similar
information from his friend *Doctor Brown* of Bridport in Dorsetshire,
but who has been long settled in America, and was attached to the
continental army, with whom he breakfasted, at his beautiful little
residence, next morning.— *Trans.*

as they say in English, completely disappointed, for it was
two o'clock, and I had already travelled thirty miles without
stopping.   I was in the utmost impatience to embrace M. de
la Fayette, and to see General Washington, but I could not
make my horses partake of it.   It was proposed to me to proceed directly to head quarters, because, said they, I might
perhaps arrive in time for dinner.   But seeing the impossibility of that, and being in a country where I was known, I desired some oats for my horses.   Whilst they were making this
slight repast, I went to see the camp of the *Marquis,** it is thus
they call Mr. de la Fayette; the English language being fond
of abridgments, and titles uncommon in America.   I found this
camp placed in an excellent position ; it occupied two heights
separated by a small bottom, but with an easy communication
between them.   The river Totohaw or Second river, protects
its right, and it is here that it makes a considerable elbow, and
turning towards the south, falls at length into the bay of Newark.   The principal part of the front, and all the left flank, to a
great distance, are covered by the rivulet' which comes from
Paramus, and falls into the same river.   This position is only
twenty miles from New-York island ; and was accordingly occupied by the van guard, consisting of light infantry, that is to
say, by the picked corps of the American army : the regiments,
in fact, which compose it, have no grenadiers, but only a company of light infantry, answering to our *Chasseurs,* and of whom
battalions are formed at the beginning of the campaign.   This
troop made a good appearance, were better clothed than the
rest of the army ; the uniforms both of the officers and soldiers
were smart and military, and each soldier wore a helmet
made of hard leather, with a crest of horse hair.   The
officers are armed with espontoons, or rather with half
pikes, and the subalterns with fusils : but both were provided

---

* It is impossible to paint the esteem and affection with which this
French nobleman is regarded in America.   It is to be surpassed only
by the love of their illustrious chief.   He has found the secret of win-
ning all their hearts ; nor to those who know him is it matter of any
wonder.   In the gentlest, and most courteous manner, he unites a
frankness, which is supposed to be not the general characteristic of
his countrymen ; his deportment is dignified without pride ; and his
zeal, activity, and enthusiasm in the cause of America, distinct from
all the political views of co-operation with the wishes of his court,
added to a sincere and uniform admiration of the greatest and best
character of the age, completely endeared this excellent young man
to grateful America.   *The Marquis* was never spoken of in the hearing of the Translator, without manifest tokens of attachment and
affection.—*Trans.*

with short and light sabres brought from France, and made a present of to them by M. de la Fayette. The tents agreeably to the American custom, formed only two ranks ; they were in regular lines as well as those of the officers ; and as the season was advanced, they had good chimneys, but placed differently from ours; for they are all built on the outside, and conceal the entrance of the tents, which produce the double effect of keeping off the wind, and of preserving heat night and day. I saw no piles of arms, and was informed that the Americans made no use of them. When the weather is good, each company places its fusils on a wooden horse ; but when it rains, they must be removed into the tents, which is undoubtedly a great inconvenience : this will be remedied when the means of doing it are more abundant, but I fear much, that this will not happen the next year.

As I was walking in the front of the camp, I was joined by an officer, who spoke very good French ; which was not astonishing, as he turned out to be as much a Frenchman as myself; this was Major Galvan. This officer came to America on commercial affairs, on which subject he has even had a sort of trial with the Congress ; but he was patronized by many persons, and particularly by the Chevalier de la Luzerne, our Ambassador : desiring to enter into the service, he obtained the rank of major, and the command of a battalion of light infantry. He is a man of abilities, and they are very well satisfied with him in the American army.* He led me to his

---

* Major Galvan, with whom I was well acquainted in Philadelphia, was a French West-Indian, who came, as the Marquis de Chastellux mentions, to America on commercial affairs. He was allowed to be an active good officer. During his residence at Philadelphia in 1782, he became enamoured of a beautiful and accomplished widow of the first distinction in the country. Having conceived the most flattering hopes of success to his passion, he was so shocked at finding himself deceived, that he formed the most desperate resolution. After writing a pathetic, but reproachful letter to the object of his love, and another to her female friend, sister to Mrs. Arnold, and arranging all his affairs, he spent the day cheerfully in company with some brother officers at the inn where he lodged, but with some serious intervals. As soon as the tea was over, retiring to his room, he locked the door, placed himself opposite the looking glass, and with two pistols, one in each hand, put an end to his existence. On my arrival at Bordeaux, at the end of the war, I fell in company with a gentleman, who for several days was particularly inquisitive about the Major's conduct, what the general opinion of him was, &c. Fortunately his conduct was irreproachable ; had it been otherwise, this gentleman was imprudently searching for pain to himself and me, as he, to my no small surprise and mortification, declared himself to be *his brother.—Trans.*

tent, where I found a table neatly spread : he proposed to me to dine, but I did not accept it, imagining I should lose nothing by waiting for that which General Washington would give me.   After all we had heard in Europe of the distressed state of the American army, it will appear extraordinary, perhaps, that such a thing as a dinner was to be found at the tent of a major.   Doubtless it is impossible to live without money, when every thing one eats is to be paid for ; a privilege the Americans possess no more than others.   But it must be understood, that they receive rations of provisions, rum, and flour ; that they have in each regiment a baker to bake their bread, and soldiers to serve them; so that an officer who takes the field with a tent, and a sufficiency of clothing, may do very well till winter without spending any thing.   The misfortune is, that provisions sometimes fail, or do not arrive in time ; in which case they really suffer ; but these are critical moments, which do not often occur, and may be prevented in future, if the states perform their engagements, and the Quarter-Master-General, and Commissaries do their duty.* I left Mr. Galvan sitting down to dinner, and went to prepare my horses, that I might get to head quarters before the day was spent.   Colonel MacHenry, whom I have before mentioned, took upon himself to conduct me.   We kept along the river, which was on our left.   After riding two miles we came in sight of the left of the army.   It was encamped on two heights, and in one line, in an extended but very good position, having a wood in the rear, and in the front the river, which is very difficult of passage every where except at Totohaw bridge.   But the situation would be quite in favour of an army defending the left bank, the heights on that side every where commanding those of the right.   Two miles beyond the bridge is a meeting-house of an hexagonal form, which is given to their places of worship by the Dutch Presbyterians, who are very numerous in the Jerseys.

I was pursuing my journey, conversing with Mr. MacHenry, when I was apprised by a considerable noise, that I could not be far from the great cataract, called Totohaw fall.   I was

---

* On the universal stoppage of paper money, from its enormous depreciation, the worst of specie, notwithstanding the abilities and activity of Mr. Morris, the financier, occasioned great wants in the army, and a total indifference on the part of the contractors ; insomuch, that in the end of 1782, the army was in danger of disbanding from absolute necessity.   It was on this critical occasion that *Colonel Wadsworth*, whose merit has been so well appreciated by the author, stept in, took the contract on himself, and by his *name* and *influence* restored affairs, and kept the army together.   America cannot be too grateful to this gentleman.—*Trans.*

divided between my impatience to view this curiosity, and that of approaching General Washington; but Mr. MacHenry informing me that it would not take me two hundred paces out of my way to see the cataract, I determined to avail myself of the remainder of a fine day, and I had not in fact gone a stone's throw before I had the astonishing spectacle before me a large river, which precipitates itself from a height of seventy feet, and so ingulphed in the hollow of a rock, which seems to swallow it up, but from whence it escapes by turning short to the right. It seems to me impossible to give an idea of this waterfall, but by a drawing. Let us however attempt the picture, leaving the finishing to the imagination: she is the rival of nature, and sometimes also her rival and interpreter. Let the reader figure to himself, then, a river running between mountains covered with firs, the dark green of which is in contact with the colour of its waters, and renders its course more majestic; let him represent to himself an immense rock, which would totally close up the passage, had it not by an earthquake or some other subterraneous revolution, been rent in several pieces, from its summit to its base, by this means forming long crevices perfectly vertical. One of these crevices, the depth of which is unknown, may be twenty-five or thirty feet wide. It is in this cavern that the river having cleared a part of the rock, precipitates itself with violence ; but as this rock crosses its whole bed, it can only escape by that extremity of the two, which offers it an outlet. There a fresh obstacle presents itself: another rock opposes its flight, and it is obliged to form a right angle, and turn short to the left. But it is extraordinary that after this dreadful fall, it neither froths, nor boils up, nor forms whirlpools, but goes off quietly by its channel, and gains, in silence, a profound valley, where it pursues its course to the sea. This perfect calm, after a movement so rapid, can only proceed from the enormous depth of the cavern, into which it is plunged. I did not examine the rock with aquafortis; but as there seems to be no calcareous stones in this country, I take it to be hard rock, and of the nature of quartz : but it presents a peculiarity worthy of attention, which is, that its whole surface is hollowed into little squares. Was it in a state of fusion when raised from the bowels of the earth, and it blocked up the passage of the river? These vertical crevices, these flaws on the surface, are they the effects of its cooling? These are questions I leave to the discussion of the learned: I shall only observe, that there is no volcanic appearance ; nor through this whole country are there the smallest traces of a volcano, of such at least as are posterior to the last epochas of nature.

Though Doctor MacHenry began by being a *Doctor*, before

he was an officer, and is well informed, I did not find him much versed in natural history, and I preferred questioning him on the subject of the army along the front of which I rode, meeting perpetually with posts, who took arms, the drum beating, and the officers saluting with the espontoon. All these posts were not for the safety of the army; many of them were stationed to guard houses and barns, which served as magazines. At length, after riding two miles along the right flank of the army, and after passing thick woods on the right, I found myself in a small plain, where I saw a handsome farm; a small camp which seemed to cover it, a large tent extended in the court, and several wagons round it, convinced me that this was his Excellency's quarter; for it is thus Mr. Washington is called in the army, and throughout America. M. de la Fayette was in conversation with a tall man, five foot nine inches high, (about five foot ten inches and a half English,) of a noble and mild countenance. It was the general himself. I was soon off horseback, and near him. The compliments were short; the sentiments with which I was animated, and the good wishes he testified for me were not equivocal. He conducted me to his house, where I found the company still at table, although the dinner had been long over. He presented me to the Generals Knox, Wayne, Howe, &c. and to his *family*, then composed of Colonels Hamilton and Tilgman, his secretaries and his aids-de-camp, and of Major Gibbs, commander of his guards; for in England and America, the aids-de-camp, adjutants and other officers attached to the general, form what is called his *family*. A fresh dinner was prepared for me and mine; and the present was prolonged to keep me company. A few glasses of claret and madeira accelerated the acquaintances I had to make, and I soon felt myself at my ease near the greatest and the best of men. The goodness and benevolence which characterise him, are evident from every thing about him; but the confidence he gives birth to, never occasions improper familiarity; for the sentiment he inspires has the same origin in every individual, a profound esteem for his virtues, and a high opinion of his talents.* About nine o'clock the general officers with-

---

* Rochefaucault has said, "That no man is a hero to his Valet de Chambre." Without combatting the general justice of the remark, this excellent man is most certainly an exception. Those who are the nearest to his person love him the most, but this is never separated from a marked degree of respect and admiration. This is not only the universal testimony, but I had myself the high gratification of observing it. Before the war, there was not a gentleman within the circle of his neighbourhood, who, having important concerns, or a family to leave behind him, did not close his eyes in peace, could he be so fortu-

drew to their quarters, which were all at a considerable distance; but as the general wished me to stay in his own house, I remained some time with him, after which he conducted me to the chamber prepared for my aids-de-camp and me. This chamber occupied the fourth part of his lodgings; he apologized to me for the little room he had in his disposal, but always with a noble politeness, which was neither complimentary nor troublesome.

---

nate as to get Mr. Washington for an executor : an unequivocal proof of his integrity. I have likewise the strongest testimony to refute those injurious insinuations which have been propagated by envy, ignorance, or party malevolence, with the view of depreciating his talents. I had particular business to transact with him in 1782, respecting the estates of an old friend to whom he was executor, but which from peculiar circumstances had been totally neglected by the noble heirs in England, from the year 1771, indeed I may say, from the year 1767. I found his Excellency in winter quarters at Philadelphia; on entering into conversation on the subject, which was of *a most complicated nature*, the General modestly apprized me, that from the active and turbulent situation in which he had long been placed, never having been at his own house in Virginia since the year 1775, but one night on his return from York-Town, he was ignorant of his own affairs, and was consequently afraid he could afford me but little information respecting those in question: but what was my astonishment, when, after this prelude, he entered into an accurate detail of every thing respecting them, scarcely omitting, as I afterwards found upon the spot, the most minute particular! On my arrival in Virginia, I had an opportunity of perusing, among the papers, many of his letters written whilst in the active management of the affairs, which furnished me with unquestionable proofs of the clearness of his head, the honour and disinterestedness of his heart, and the uncommon perspicuity and elegance of his style ; so as to convince me of the identity of the pen that produced those admirable epistolary performances, which did him so much honour during the war, and will ever mark the energy of his mind, and the excellence of his understanding. I have dwelt with the more satisfaction on this particular, as Envy, unable to detract from their merit, has made frequent attempts to rob his fame of the honour of having ever produced them ; and what relates to the public opinion concerning himself he always leaves to the determination of others. This heartfelt, but faithful tribute to transcendent virtue and abilities, is the effusion of a mind unaccustomed to flattery, and in an instance where flattery neither has, *nor can have any object.* I had long revered his character before I saw him, and we all know that too much prepossession is generally unfavourable on a nearer view ; but to know *him*, establishes and heightens the most favourable ideas; and I saw, and knew this truly great man, only to root in my mind the most sincere attachment, affection and veneration for his person and character.— *Trans.*

At nine the next morning they informed me that his excellency was come down into the parlour. This room served at once as audience chamber and dining-room. I immediately went to wait on him, and found breakfast prepared. Lord Stirling had come to breakfast with us. He is one of the oldest Major-Generals in the army; his birth, his titles and pretty extensive property have given him more importance in America, than his talents could ever have acquired him. The title of *Lord*, which was refused him in England, is not here contested with him: he claimed this title from inheritance, and went to Europe to support his pretensions, but without success. A part of his estate has been dissipated by the war, and by his taste for expense; he is accused of liking the table and the bottle, full as much as becomes a Lord, but more than becomes a General. He is brave, but without capacity, and has not been fortunate in the different commands with which he has been entrusted. He was made prisoner at the affair of Long-Island. In June, 1777, he got into a scrape at Elizabethtown, whilst General Washington made head against 20,000 English on the heights of Middlebrook; he there lost two or three hundred men, and three pieces of cannon: at Brandywine he commanded the right of the army, or rather the body of troops defeated by Cornwallis; but on all these occasions he displayed great personal courage and firmness. I conversed a long time with him, and found him to be a sensible man, not ill informed of the affairs of his country. He is old and rather dull; but with all this, he will continue to serve, because the employment, though not lucrative, helps to repair a little the disorder in his affairs; and not having quitted the service since the beginning of the war, he has at least zeal and seniority in his favour; thus he will retain the command of the first line, to which his rank entitles him; but care will be taken not to employ him on particular expeditions.*

---

* Lord Stirling died before the end of the war.

CHAPTER IV.

WHILST we were at breakfast, horses were brought, and General Washington gave orders for the army to get under arms at the head of the camp. The weather was very bad, and it had already began raining; we waited half an hour; but the General seeing that it was more likely to increase than to diminish, determined to get on horseback. Two horses were brought him, which were a present from the state of Virginia; he mounted one himself, and gave me the other. Mr. Lynch and Mr. de Montesquieu, had each of them, also, a very handsome blood horse, such as we could not find at Newport for any money. We repaired to the artillery camp, where General Knox received us: the artillery was numerous, and the gunners, in very fine order, were formed in parade, in the foreign manner, that is, each gunner at his battery, and ready to fire. The General was so good as to apologize to me for the cannon not firing to salute me; he said, that having put all the troops on the other side of the river in motion, and apprized them that he might himself march along the right bank, he was afraid of giving the alarm, and of deceiving the detachments that were out. We gained at length, the right of the army, where we saw the Pennsylvania line; it was composed of two brigades, each forming three battalions, without reckoning the light infantry, which were detached with the Marquis de la Fayette. General Wayne, who commanded it, was on horseback, as well as the Brigadiers and Colonels. They were all well mounted: the officers also had a very military air; they were well ranged, and saluted very gracefully.. Each brigade had a band of music; the march they were then playing was the *Huron*. I knew that this line, though in want of many things was the best clothed in the army; so that his excellency asking me whether I would proceed, and see the whole army, or go by the shortest road to the camp of the *Marquis*, I accepted the latter proposal. The troops ought to thank me for it, for the rain was falling with redoubled force; they were dismissed, therefore, and we arrived heartily wet at the Marquis de la Fayette's quarters, where I warmed myself with great pleasure, partaking, from time to time, of a large bowl of grog, which is stationary on his table, and is presented to every officer who enters. The rain appearing to cease, or inclined to cease for a moment, we availed ourselves of the opportunity to follow his excellency to the camp of the Marquis : we found all his troops in order of battle on the heights to the left, and himself at their head ; expressing by his air and countenance, that he was happier in receiving me there, than at his estate in Auvergne. The confidence and attachment of the troops, are for him invaluable possessions, well acquired riches, of which no body can deprive him; but what, in my opinion, is still more flattering for a young man of his age, is the influence and consideration he has acquired among the political, as well as the military order : I do not fear contradiction when I say, that private letters from him have frequently produced more effect on some states than the strongest exhortations of the Congress. On seeing him, one is at a loss which most to admire, that so young a man as he should have given such eminent proofs of talents, or that a man so tried, should give hopes of so long a career of glory. Fortunate his country, if she knows how to avail herself of them ; more fortunate still should she stand in no need of calling them into exertion !

I distinguished with pleasure, among the colonels, who were extremely well mounted, and who saluted with great grace, M. de Gimat, a French officer, over whom I claim the rights of a sort of military paternity, having brought him up in my regiment from his earliest youth.* This whole vanguard consisted of six battalions, forming two brigades ; but there was only one piquet of dragoons or light cavalry, the remainder having marched to the southward with Colonel Lee. These dragoons are perfectly well mounted, and do not fear meeting the English dragoons, over whom they have gained several advantages;† but they have never been numerous enough to form a solid and permanent body. The piquet that was kept with the ar-

---

* M. de Gimat made the following campaign at the head of a battalion of light infantry, always under the command of M. de la Fayette. At the siege of York, he attacked and carried jointly with Colonel Hamilton, the enemies' redoubt on their left. This attack was made at the same time with that of the Baron de Viomenil, on the right redoubt, and with the same success. Mr. Gimat was wounded in the foot : on his return to Europe, he was made Colonel of the regiment of Martinico.

† The *heroic* Tarleton has experienced that there is some difference between these dragoons and a surprised party of ill-armed infantry and peasants. This gentleman's forte was in the latter species of war ; a forced march, a surprize, and a bloody gazette, are the records of his glory.— *Trans.*

my served then as an escort to the Provost Marshal, and performed the functions of the *Marechaussée*, until the establishment of a regular one, which was intended.

The rain spared us no more at the camp of the Marquis, than at that of the main army; so that our review being finished, I saw with pleasure General Washington set off in a gallop to regain his quarters. We reached them as soon as the badness of the roads would permit us. At our return we found a good dinner ready, and about twenty guests, among whom were Generals Howe and Sinclair. The repast was in the English fashion, consisting of eight or ten large dishes of butcher's meat, and poultry, with vegetables of several sorts, followed by a second course of pastry, comprized under the two denominations of pies and puddings. After this the cloth was taken off, and apples and a great quantity of nuts were served, which General Washington usually continues eating for two hours, toasting and conversing all the time. These nuts are small and dry, and have so hard a shell, (hickory nuts) that they can only be broken by the hammer; they are served half open, and the company are never done picking and eating them. The conversation was calm and agreeable; his Excellency was pleased to enter with me into the particulars of some of the principal operations of the war, but always with a modesty and conciseness, which proved that it was from pure complaisance he mentioned it. About half past seven we rose from table, and immediately the servants came to shorten it, and convert it into a round one; for at dinner it was placed diagonally to give more room. I was surprised at this manœuvre, and asked the reason of it; I was told they were going to lay the cloth for supper. In half an hour I retired to my chamber, fearing lest the General might have business, and that he remained in company only on my account; but at the end of another half hour, I was informed that his Excellency expected me at supper. I returned to the dining-room, protesting against this supper; but the General told me he was accustomed to take something in the evening; that if I would be seated, I should only eat some fruit, and assist in the conversation. I desired nothing better, for there were then no strangers, and nobody remained but the General's family. The supper was composed of three or four light dishes, some fruit, and above all, a great abundance of nuts, which were as well received in the evening as at dinner. The cloth being soon removed, a few bottles of good claret and madeira were placed on the table.* Every sensible man will be of my opinion,

---

* On my return from the southward in 1782, I spent a day or two at the American camp at Verplank's Point on the North River, and had

that being a French officer, under the orders of General Washington, and what is more, a good whig, I could not refuse a glass of wine offered me by him; but, I confess, that I had little merit in this complaisance, and that, less accustomed to drink than any body, I accommodate myself very well to the English mode of *toasting* : you have very small glasses, you pour out yourself the quantity of wine you choose, without being pressed to take more, and the toast is only a sort of check in the conversation, to remind each individual that he forms part of the company, and that the whole form only one society. I observed that there was more solemnity in the toasts at dinner : there were several ceremonious ones; the others were suggested by the General, and given out by his aids-de-camp, who performed the honours of the table at dinner; for one of them is every day seated at the bottom of the table, near the General, to serve the company, and distribute the bottles. The toasts in the evening were given by Colonel Hamilton, without order or ceremony. After supper the guests are generally desired to give a *sentiment;* that is to say, a lady to whom they are attached by some sentiment, either of

---

the honour of dining with General Washington. I had suffered severely from an ague, which I could not get quit of, though I had taken the exercise of a hard trotting horse, and got thus far to the northward in the month of October. The general observing it, told me he was sure I had not met with a good glass of wine for some time, an article then very rare, but that my disorder must be frightened away ; he made me drink three or four of his silver camp cups of excellent madeira at noon, and recommended to me to take a generous glass of claret after dinner, a prescription by no means repugnant to my feelings, and which I most religiously followed. I mounted my horse next morning, and continued my journey to Massachusetts, without ever experiencing the slightest return of my disorder. The American camp here, presented the most beautiful and picturesque appearance : it extended along the plain, on the neck of land formed by the winding of the Hudson, and had a view of this river to the south; behind it, the lofty mountains, covered with wood, formed the most sublime back-ground that painting can express. In the front of the tents was a regular continued portico, formed by the boughs of trees in verdure, decorated with much taste and fancy; and each officer's tent was distinguished by superior ornaments. Opposite the camp, and on distinct eminences, stood the tents of some of the general officers, over which towered, predominant, that of General Washington. I had seen all the camps in England, from many of which, drawings and engravings have been taken; but this was truly a subject worthy the pencil of the first artist. The French camp during their stay at Baltimore, was decorated in the same style. At the camp at Verplank's, we distinctly heard the morning and evening gun of the British at Kingsbridge.—*Trans.*

love, or friendship, or perhaps from preference only.* This supper, or conversation, commonly lasted from nine to eleven, always free, and always agreeable.

The weather was so bad on the 25th, that it was impossible for me to stir, even to wait on the Generals, to whom M. de la Fayette was to conduct me. I easily consoled myself for this, finding it a great luxury to pass a whole day with General Washington, as if he were at his house in the country, and had nothing to do. The Generals Glover, Huntington, and some others, dined with us, and the Colonels Stewart and Butler two officers distinguished in the army. The intelligence received this day occasioned the proposed attack on Staten-Island to be laid aside. The foraging party under General Starke had met with the most complete success; the enemy not having thought proper to disturb them, so that they had not stripped the posts in the quarter where it was intended to attack them: besides, that this expedition could only have been a *coup de main*, rendered very difficult by the badness of the roads from the excessive rains. It was determined therefore that the army should march the next day to winter quarters, and that I should continue my route to Philadelphia.

The weather being fair, on the 26th, I got on horseback, after breakfasting with the general. He was so attentive as to give me the horse he rode on, the day of my arrival, which I had greatly commended: I found him as good as he is handsome; but above all, perfectly well broke, and well trained, having a good mouth, easy in hand, and stopping short in a gallop without bearing the bit. I mention these minute particulars, because it is the general himself who breaks all his own horses; and he is a very excellent and bold horseman, leaping the highest fences, and going extremely quick, without standing upon his stirrups, bearing on the bridle, or letting his horse run wild; circumstances which our young men look upon as so essential a part of English horsemanship, that they would rather break a leg or an arm than renounce them.

My first visit was to General Wayne, where Mr. de la Fayette was waiting to conduct me to the other general officers of the line. We were received by General Huntington, who appeared rather young for the rank of Brigadier-General, which he has held two years: his carriage is cold and reserved, but one is not long in perceiving him to be a man of sense and information; by General Glover, about five and forty, a little man,

---

* The English reader will see that the Author makes a small mistake here; it being the custom in America, as in England, to give a lady, *or* a sentiment, or both.—*Trans.*

but active and a good soldier; by General Howe, who is one
of the oldest Major-Generals, and who enjoys the consideration
due to his rank, though, from unfavourable circumstances, he
has not been fortunate in war, particularly in Georgia, where
he commanded with a very small force, at the time General
Provost took possession of it: he is fond of music, the arts,
and pleasure, and has a cultivated mind. I remained a considerable time with him, and saw a very curious *lusus naturæ*,
but as hideous as possible. It was a young man of a Dutch
family, whose head was become so enormous, that it took the
whole nourishment from his body; and his hands and arms
were so weak that he was unable to make use of them. He
lies constantly in bed, with his monstrous head supported by a
pillow; and as he has long been accustomed to lie on his right
side, his right arm is in a state of atrophy: he is not quite an
ideot, but he could never learn any thing, and has no more
reason than a child of five or six years old, though he is seven
and twenty. This extraordinary derangement of the animal
economy proceeds from a dropsy, with which he was attacked
in his infancy, and which displaced the bones that form the
cranium. We know that these bones are joined together by
sutures, which are soft in the first period of life, and harden and
ossify with age. Such an exuberance, so great an afflux of
humour in that, which of all the viscera seems to require the
most exact proportion, as well in what relates to the life as to
the understanding of man, afford stronger proof of the necessity
of an equilibrium between the solids and the fluids, than the
existence of the final causes.

General Knox, whom we had met, and who accompanied us,
brought us back to head-quarters, through a wood, as the
shortest way, and to fall into a road leading to his house, where
we wished to pay our compliments to Mrs. Knox. We found
her settled on a little farm, where she had passed part of the
campaign; for she never quits her husband. A child of six
months, and a little girl of three years old, formed a real *family*
for the General. As for himself, he is between thirty and
forty, very fat, but very active, and of a gay and amiable
character. Previous to the war he was a bookseller at Boston,
and used to amuse himself in reading military books in his
shop. Such was the origin and the first knowledge he acquired of the art of war, and of the taste he has had ever since
for the profession of arms. From the very first campaign, he
was entrusted with the command of the artillery, and it has
turned out that it could not have been placed in better hands.
It was he whom M. du Coudray endeavoured to supplant, and
who had no difficulty in removing him. It was fortunate for
M. du Coudray, perhaps, that he was drowned in the Schuyl-

kill, rather than to be swallowed up in the intrigues he was engaged in, and which might have been productive of much mischief.*

On our return to head quarters, we found several General Officers and Colonels, with whom he dined. I had an opportunity of conversing more particularly with General Wayne; he has served more than any officer of the American army, and his services have been more distinguished,† though he is yet but young. He is sensible, and his conversation is agreeable and animated. The affair of Stoney-Point has gained him

---

* General Knox who retained until the peace the same situation in the American army, commanded their artillery at the seige of York. One cannot too much admire the intelligence and activity with which he collected from all quarters, transported, disembarked and conveyed to the batteries the train destined for the seige, and which consisted of more than thirty pieces of cannon and mortars of a large bore: this artillery was always extremely well served, General Knox never failing to direct it, and frequently taking the trouble himself of pointing the mortars. He scarcely ever quitted the batteries; and, when the town surrendered, he stood in need of the same activity and the same resources to remove and transport the enemy's artillery, which consisted of upwards of two hundred *bouches a feu*, with all the ammunition belonging to them. The rank of Major-General was the recompense of his services.

It may be observed, that if on this occasion the English were astonished at the justness of the firing, and terrible execution of the French artillery, we were not less so at the extraordinary progress of the American artillerv, as well as the capacity and knowledge of a great number of the officers employed in it.

As for general Knox, to praise his military talents only, would be to deprive him of half of the eulogium which he merits: A man of understanding, a well formed man, gay, sincere, and honest; it is impossible to know without esteeming him, or to see without loving him. In the text, it is said that he was a bookseller at Boston before the war; this is not perfectly the truth. He carried on trade in various articles, and according to the American custom, he sold them wholesale and retail. Books, but particularly French books, made part of this commerce, but he employed himself more in reading than selling them. Before the revolution he was one of the principal citizens of Boston; at present, he belongs to the whole world by his reputation and his success. Thus have the English, contrary to their intention, added to the ornament of the human species, by awakening talents and virtues where they thought to find nothing but ignorance and weakness.

† This might in some respect be true at the time the Marquis speaks of, but let the southern campaigns be attended to, and justice will be done to the active zeal, the wonderful exertions, the unabating courage of that great officer *General Greene;* other exceptions might be made, but this stands conspicuous.—*Trans.*

much honour in the army; however, he is only a Brigadier-General! This arises from the nomination to the superior ranks being vested in the states to whom the troops belong, and that the state of Pennsylvania has not thought proper to make any promotion, apparently from principles of economy. The remainder of the day I dedicated to the enjoyment of General Washington's company, whom I was to quit the next day. He was so good as to point out to me himself my journey, to send on before to prepare me lodgings, and to give me a Colonel to conduct me as far as Trenton. The next morning all the General's baggage was packed up, which did not hinder us from breakfasting, before we parted; he for his winter quarters, and I for my journey to Philadelphia.

Here would be the proper place to give the portrait of General Washington: but what can my testimony add to the idea already formed of him? The continent of North-America, from Boston to Charleston, is a great volume, every page of which presents his eulogium. I know, that having had the opportunity of a near inspection, and of closely observing him, some more particular details may be expected from me; but the strongest characteristic of this respectable man is the perfect union which reigns between the physical and moral qualities which compose the individual; one alone will enable you to judge of all the rest. If you are presented with medals of Cæsar, of Trajan, or Alexander, on examining their features, you will still be led to ask what was their stature, and the form of their persons; but if you discover, in a heap of ruins, the head or the limb of an antique *Apollo*, be not curious about the other parts, but rest assured that they all were conformable to those of a god. Let not this comparison be attributed to enthusiasm! It is not my intention to exaggerate, I wish only to express the impression General Washington has left on my mind; the idea of a perfect whole, that cannot be the produce of enthusiasm, which rather would reject it, since the effect of proportion is to diminish the idea of greatness. Brave without temerity, laborious without ambition, generous without prodigality, noble without pride, virtuous without severity; he seems always to have confined himself within those limits, where the virtues, by clothing themselves in more lively, but more changeable and doubtful colours, may be mistaken for faults. This is the seventh year that he has commanded the army, and that he has obeyed the Congress; more need not be said, especially in America, where they know how to appreciate all the merit contained in this simple fact. Let it be repeated that Condé was intrepid, Turenne prudent, Eugene adroit, Catinat disinterested. It is not thus that Washington will be characterized. It will be said of him, AT THE END OF

A LONG CIVIL WAR, HE HAD NOTHING WITH WHICH HE COULD RE-PROACH HIMSELF. If any thing can be more marvellous than such a character, it is the unanimity of the public suffrages in his favour. Soldier, magistrate, people, all love and admire him; all speak of him in terms of tenderness and veneration. Does there then exist a virtue capable of restraining the injustice of mankind; or are glory and happiness too recently established in America, for envy to have deigned to pass the seas?

In speaking of this perfect whole of which General Washington furnishes the idea, I have not excluded exterior form. His stature is noble and lofty, he is well made, and exactly proportioned; his physiognomy mild and agreeable, but such as to render it impossible to speak particularly of any of his features, so that in quitting him, you have only the recollection of a fine face. He has neither a grave nor a familiar air, his brow is sometimes marked with thought, but never with inquietude; in inspiring respect, he inspires confidence, and his smile is always the smile of benevolence.*

But above all, it is in the midst of his general officers, that it is interesting to behold him. General in a republic, he has not the imposing stateliness of a Marechal de France who gives *the order;* a hero in a republic, he excites another sort of respect, which seems to spring from the sole idea, that the safety of each individual is attached to his person. As for the rest, I must observe on this occasion, that the general officers of the American army have a very military and a very becoming carriage; that even all the officers, whose characters were brought into public view, unite much politeness to a great deal of capacity; that the head-quarters of this army, in short, neither present the image of want, nor inexperience. When one sees the battalion of the general's guards encamped within the precincts of his house; nine wagons, destined to carry his baggage, ranged in his court; a great number of grooms taking care of very fine horses belonging to the general officers and their aids-de-camp; when one observes the perfect order that reigns. within these precincts, where the guards are exactly

---

* It is impossible for any man who has had the happiness to approach the General, not to admire the accuracy of this description, and the justness and happiness with which it is developed, or to read it without the strongest emotion. It is here above all, the Translator must apologize for his author; it is not possible to do justice to the original, to feel all its elegance it must be read in the language in which it was written. Posterity, future historians, will be grateful to the Marquis de Chastellux for this exquisite portrait; every feature, and every tint of which will stand the test of the severest scrutiny, and be handed down to distant ages in never fading colours.—*Trans.*

stationed, and where the drums beat an alarm, and a particular retreat, one is tempted to apply to the Americans what Pyrrhus said of the Romans : *Truly these people have nothing barbarous in their discipline!*

The reader will perceive that it is difficult for me to quit General Washington : let us take our resolution briskly then, and suppose ourselves on the road. Behold me travelling with Colonel Moyland, whom his excellency had given me, in spite of myself, as a companion, and whom I should have been glad to have seen at a distance, for one cannot be too much at one's ease in travelling. In such situations, however, we must do the best we can. I began to question him, he to answer me, and the conversation gradually becoming more interesting, I found I had to do with a very gallant and intelligent man, who had lived long in Europe, and who has travelled through the greatest part of America. I found him perfectly polite ; for his politeness was not troublesome, and I soon conceived a great friendship for him. Mr. Moyland is an Irish catholic ; one of his brothers is catholic bishop of Cork, he has four others, two of whom are merchants, one at Cadiz, the other at L'Orient ; the third is in Ireland with his family ; and the fourth is intended for the priesthood.* As for himself, he came to settle in America some years ago, where he was at first engaged in commerce ; he then served in the army as aid-de-camp to the general, and has merited the command of the light cavalry. During the war he married the daughter of a rich merchant in

---

* I was acquainted with four brothers of this family ; they were all amiable, sensible and lively men, and remarkably active and useful in the revolution. The colonel, in the military line ; another brother whom I *suppose* to have been the merchant at Cadiz, was afterwards in America, and clothier general to the army ; another is a lawyer at Philadelphia ; and Mr. Moyland, who is lately dead at L'Orient, was singularly useful in the year 1777, by managing a treaty between the American Commissioners and the Farmers General of France, for an annual supply of tobacco from America, which he concluded *during Lord Stormont's residence at the Court of France*, and many months previous to the open rupture with that Court. I speak of this with personal knowledge of the fact, nor was it so secret as to have escaped the English Ambassador, or the *vigilant Mr. Forth*. There could not be a more direct attack on England and English claims, than this transaction, which *must* have had the sanction of the French Government, yet England was lulled to sleep by her Ministers, or rather was so infatuated as to shut her ears against the most interesting truths. I could say much more on this subject, but why enter into discussions which have long ceased to be either seasonable or useful ? England was, literally, in the case of the *Quos Deus vult perdere.—Trans.*

the Jerseys, who lived formerly at New-York, and who now
resides on an estate at a little distance from the road we were
to pass the next day. He proposed to me to go and sleep
there, or at least to take a dinner; I begged to be excused,
from the fear of being obliged to pay compliments, of straightening others, or of being myself straightened; he did not insist, so that I pursued my journey, sometimes through fine
woods, at others through well cultivated lands, and villages inhabited by Dutch families. One of these villages, which forms
a little township, bears the beautiful name of Troy. Here the
country is more open and continues so to Morristown. This
town, celebrated by the winter-quarters of 1779, is about three
and twenty miles from Prakeness, the name of the head-quarters from whence I came. It is situated on a height, at the
foot of which runs the rivulet called Vipenny river; the houses
are handsome and well built, there are about sixty or eighty
round the Meeting-house. I intended stopping at Morristown
only to bait my horses, for it was but half past two, but on
entering the inn of Mr. Arnold, I saw a dining-room adorned
with looking-glasses and handsome mahogany furniture, and a
table spread for twelve persons. I learnt that all this preparation was for me; and what affected me more nearly, was to
see a dinner, corresponding with these appearances, ready to
serve up. I was indebted for this to the goodness of General
Washington, and the precautions of Colonel Moyland, who had
sent before to acquaint them with my arrival. It would have
been very ungracious to have accepted this dinner at the expense of Mr. Arnold, who is an honest man and a good whig,
and who has not a particle in common with *Benedict Arnold;*
it would have been still more awkward to have paid for the
banquet without eating it. I therefore instantly determined
to dine and sleep in this comfortable inn. The Vicomte de
Noailles, the Comte de Damas, &c. were expected to make up
the dozen; but these young travellers, who had reckoned
during their stay with the army, on being witnesses to some
encounters, were desirous of indemnifying themselves by riding
along the bank of the river, to take a look at York island, and
try if they could not tempt the enemy to favour them with a
few shot. M. de la Fayette himself conducted them, with an
escort of twenty dragoons. They deferred for a day therefore
their journey to Philadelphia, and I had no other guests but a
secretary and aid-de-camp of M. de la Fayette, who arrived
as I was at table, well disposed to supply the deficiency of the
absent.

After dinner I had a visit from General St. Clair, whom I
had already seen at the army, which he had left the preceding

evening to sleep at Morristown. It was he who commanded
on Lake Champlain, at the evacuation of Ticonderoga; a terrible clamour was raised against him on that occasion, and he
was tried by a council of war, but *honourably acquitted,** not
only because his retreat was attended with the best consequences; Burgoyne having been forced to capitulate; but because it was proved that he had been left in want of every
thing necessary for the defence of the post entrusted to him.
He was born in Scotland, where he has a family and property;
he is esteemed a good officer, and, if the war continues, will
certainly act a principal part in the army.†

I set out from Morristown the 28th, at eight in the morning,
with very lowering weather, which did not hinder me, however, from observing, to the right of the road, the huts occupied by the troops in the winter of 1779—80. Some miles
from thence, we met a man on horseback, who came to meet
Colonel Moyland with a letter from his wife. After reading it,
he said to me, with a truly European politeness, that we must
always obey the women; that his wife would accept of no excuse, and expected me to dinner; but he assured me that he
would take me by a road which should not be a mile out of my
way, whilst my people pursued their journey, and went to wait
for me at Somerset court-house. I was now too well acquainted with my colonel, and too much pleased with him, to refuse
this invitation; I followed him, therefore, and after crossing a
wood, found myself on a height, the position of which struck
me at first sight. I remarked to Colonel Moyland, that I was
much mistaken if this ground was not well calculated for an
advantageous camp: he replied, that it was precisely that of
Middlebrook, where General Washington had stopped the
English in June, 1777, when Sir William Howe was endeavouring to traverse the Jerseys to pass the Delaware, and take
Philadelphia. Continuing my journey, and looking about me
as far as my view would reach, the shape alone of the ground
made me imagine, that the right could not be very good; I
then learnt with pleasure that General Washington had built
two strong redoubts there. The reader will permit me the following short reflection, that the best method for military men,
in following on the ground, the campaigns of great generals,
is not to have the different positions pointed out and explained

---

* The terms of his acquittal are—*with the highest honour.*—*Trans.*

† General St. Clair's defence on this trial, which was lent me by Mr.
Arthur Middleton, one of the Delegates in Congress for South-Carolina, is an admirable piece of reasoning and eloquence.—*Trans.*

to them : it is much better, before they are made acquainted
with these details, to visit the places, to look well about on
every side, and to propose to themselves some problems on the
nature of the ground, and on the advantages to be derived
from it; then to compare ideas with facts, by which means they
will be enabled to rectify one, and to appreciate the other.

On descending from the heights, we turned a·little to the
left, and found ourselves on the side of a rivulet, which brought
us into a deep vale. The various cascades formed by this
stream, in precipitating itself over the rocks ; the ancient fir-
trees with which it is surrounded, a part of which have fallen
from age, and lie across its course ; the furnaces belonging to
some copper mines, half destroyed by the English ; these ruins
of nature, and these ravages of war, composed the most poetic,
or according to the English expression, the most romantic
picture ; for it is precisely what is called in England a romantic
prospect. It is here that Colonel Moyland's father-in-law has
fitted a little rural asylum, where his family go to avoid the
heats of the summer, and where they sometimes pass whole
nights in listening to the song of the *mocking bird,* for the
nightingale does not sing in America. We know that great
musicians are oftener to be met with in the courts of despots,
than in republics. Here the songster of the night is neither
the graceful *Melico,* nor the pathetic *Tenducci ;* he is the *Bouffon Caribaldi:* he has no song, and consequently no sentiment
peculiar to himself: he counterfeits in the evening what he
has heard in the day. Has he heard the lark or the thrush, it
is the lark or the thrush you hear. Have some workmen been
employed in the woods, or has he been near their house, he will
sing precisely as they do. If they are Scotchmen, he will
repeat you the air of some gentle and plaintive tale ; if they are
Germans, you will discover the clumsy gaiety of a Swabian, or
Alsatian. Sometimes he cries like a child, at others he laughs
like a young girl : nothing, in short, is more entertaining than
this comic bird ; but he performs only in summer, and so it
happened that I never had the good fortune to hear him.*

After travelling two miles in this sort of gorge, the woods
begin to open, and we soon found ourselves beyond the mountains. On the brow of these mountains, to the south, were
the huts occupied by a part of the army in 1779, after the battle of Monmouth. We soon arrived at Colonel Moyland's or
rather at Colonel Vanhorn's, his father-in-law. This manor is
in a beautiful situation ; it is surrounded by some trees, the

---

* The translator, as well as most travellers in America, particularly
in the middle states, can testify the accuracy of this account.—*Trans.*

approach is decorated with a grass plot, and if it was better taken care of, one would think ones-self in the neighbourhood of London, rather than in that of New-York. Mr. Vanhorn came to meet me : he is a tall, lusty man, near sixty years of age, but vigorous, hearty, and good humoured; he is called Colonel from the station he held in the militia, under the English government. He resigned some time before the war : he was then a merchant and cultivator, passing the winter at New-York, and the summer in the country ; but since the war he has quitted that town, and retired to his manor, always faithful to his country, without rendering himself odious to the English, with whom he has left two of his sons in the Jamaica trade, but who, if the war continues, are to sell their property and come and live with their father. Nothing can prove more strongly the integrity of his conduct, than the esteem in which he is held by both parties. Situated at ten miles from Staten-Island, near to Rariton, Amboy, and Brunswick, he has frequently found himself in the midst of the theatre of war ; so that he has sometimes had the Americans with him, sometimes the English. It even happened to him once in the same day, to give a breakfast to Lord Cornwallis and a dinner to General Lincoln. Lord Cornwallis, informed that the latter had slept at Mr. Vanhorn's, came to take him by surprise ; but Lincoln, getting intelligence of his design, retired into the woods. Lord Cornwallis, astonished not to find him, asked if the American General was not concealed in his house: "No," replied Mr. Vanhorn, bluntly. "On your honour?" says Cornwallis. "On my honour, and if you doubt it, here are the keys, you may search every where." "I shall take your word for it," said Lord Cornwallis, and asked for some breakfast; an hour afterwards he returned to the army. Lincoln, who was concealed at no great distance, immediately returned, and dined quietly with his hosts.

The acquaintance I made with Mr. Vanhorn being very prompt and cordial, he conducted me to the parlour, where I found his wife, his three daughters, a young lady of the neighbourhood, and two young officers. Mrs. Vanhorn is an old lady, who, from her countenance, her dress, and her deportment, perfectly resembled a picture of Vandyke. She does the honours of the table with exactness, helps every body without saying a word, and the rest of the time is like a family portrait. Her three daughters are not amiss : Mrs. Moyland, the eldest, is six months advanced in her pregnancy ; the youngest only twelve years old, but the second is marriageable. She appeared to be on terms of great familiarity with one of the young officers, who was in a very elegant undress, forming a good representation of an agreeable country squire ; at table he picked her nuts for her, and often took her hands. I imagined that he was an intended husband; but the other officer, with whom I had the opportunity of conversing as he accompanied us in the evening, told me that he did not believe there was any idea of marriage between them. I mention these trifles only to show the extreme liberty that prevails between the two sexes, as long as they are unmarried. It is no crime for a girl to embrace a young man; it would be a very heinous one for a married woman even to show a desire of pleasing.* Mrs. Carter,† a handsome young woman, whose husband is concerned in furnishing our army with provisions, and lives at present at Newport, told me, that going down one morning into her husband's office, not much decked out, but in a rather elegant French undress, a farmer of the Massachusetts state, who was there on business, seemed surprised at seeing her, and asked who that young lady was. On being told, Mrs.

---

* Though this freedom prevails among all ranks, it is particularly striking among the middling classes and common people. Not to speak of the New-England *bundling*, a practice which has been so often mentioned, the Translator has seen a grave Quaker and his wife sitting on their bench at their door, as is the custom at Philadelphia in the summer evenings and along side of them the apprentice boy of sixteen, and the servant girl, or perhaps one of the daughters of the family, not only kissing and embracing each other, but proceeding to such familiarities as would shock modesty, and draw down the vengeance of the virtuous citizen of London; and all this, not only without reprehension, but even with marks of complacency on the part of the good old folks. Even the *last slip*, is no essential blemish in the character of the frail fair one. Both sexes arrive early at puberty, their constitutions are warm, there are few restraints, and they lose no time in completing the great object, the population of the country.— *Trans.*

† Mrs. Carter is the daughter of General *Schuyler*, and is now called *Church*; her husband, *Mr. John Barker Church*, having re-assumed his real name on his return to England since the peace. He is an English gentleman of a very respectable family and connexions; but having been unfortunate in business in London in the outset of life, retired to America, where, from his known principles he was received as a good whig. He took the name of *Carter*, that his friends might hear nothing of him, until by his industry he had retrieved his affairs. His activity in the revolution, brought him acquainted with General Schuyler, whose daughter he soon after married; and on the arrival of the French troops, got a principal share of the contract for supplying them, in conjunction with Col. Wadsworth. Since the war he has returned to Europe, with a very considerable fortune, settled all his affairs, and is happily and honourably restored to his friends and family.— *Trans.*

Carter—"*Aye!*" said he, loud enough for her to hear him, "*A wife and a mother, truly, has no business to be so well dressed.*"

At 3 o'clock I got on horseback, with Colonel Moyland, and Captain Herne, one of the young officers I had dined with. He is in the light cavalry, and consequently in Colonel Moyland's regiment. His size and figure, which I had already remarked, appeared to still more advantage on horseback. I observed that he was seated in a very noble and easy manner, and in perfect conformity to our principles of horsemanship. I asked where he had studied horsemanship. He told me at his own regiment; that his desire to teach the soldiers induced him to learn it; and that he made it his business to render them as expert in the exercise as himself. Though but one and twenty, he had already acquired great experience, and distinguished himself the preceding year, in an affair where a small body of American light horse beat a much more considerable one of English dragoons. I had a long conversation with him, and he always spoke to me with a modesty, and a grace which would be favourably received by all the military in Europe, and which to all appearance, would be as successful at Paris as in camps.

We had scarcely proceeded three miles, before we found ourselves in the Princeton road, and on the banks of the Rariton, which may be easily passed by fording, or over a wooden bridge. Two miles farther we crossed the Millstone, the left bank of which we followed to Somerset Court-house. Of all the parts of America I had hitherto passed through, this is the most open; we meet with handsome little plains here, where from fifteen to twenty thousand men might be encamped. General Howe had not less when he passed the Rariton in 1777. His right was supported by a wood, beyond which runs the Millstone; his left also extended towards other woods. General Washington at that time occupied the camp at Middlebrook, and General Sullivan, at the head of only 1500 men, was six miles from the army, and three miles from the left of the enemy. In this position he was near enough to harass them, without committing himself as he had in his rear the mountains of Saourland. They who in the last war, have passed through Saourland, will easily conceive that the country to which the German emigrants have given this name, is not very easy of access. I found my suite at Somerset court-house, where they were waiting for me in a pretty good inn, but as there was still some daylight, and I had calculated my next day's journey, which required that I should gain something in the present, I determined to proceed farther. The night, which soon came on, prevented me from making any more observations on the country. After once more passing the Millstone, and getting well out of a horrible slough, we halted at Greggtown, where we slept at Skilman's tavern, an indifferent inn, but kept by very obliging people. Captain Herne continued his route. Our next day's ride presented us with very interesting objects: we were to see two places which will be for ever dear to the Americans, since it was there the first rays of hope brightened upon them, or, to express it more properly, that the safety of the country was effected. These celebrated places are Princeton, and Trenton. I shall not say I went to see them, for they lay precisely in the road. Let the reader judge then how much I was out of humour, on seeing so thick a fog rising, as to prevent me from distinguishing objects at fifty paces from me : but I was in a country where one must despair of nothing. The fortune of the day was like that of America ; the fog suddenly dispersed, and I found myself travelling on the right bank of the Millstone, in a narrow valley. Two miles from Greggtown we quit this valley, and mount the highest of Rocky-hill, where are a few houses. Kingstown is a mile farther, but still on the Millstone ; the Maidenhead road ends here, and its communication is facilitated by a bridge built over the rivulet. It is here that General Washington halted after the affair of Princeton. After marching from midnight until two o'clock in the afternoon, almost continually fighting : he wished to collect the troops, and give them some rest ; he knew, however, that Lord Cornwallis was following him on the Maidenhead road ; but he contented himself with taking up some planks of the bridge, and as soon as he saw the vanguard of the English appear, he continued his march quietly towards Middlebrook. Beyond Kingstown, the country begins to open, and continues so to Princeton. This town is situated on a sort of platform not much elevated, but which commands on all sides : it has only one street formed by the high road ; there are about sixty or eighty houses, all tolerably well built, but little attention is paid them, for that is immediately attracted by an immense building, which is visible at a considerable distance. It is a college built by the state of Jersey some years before the war ; as this building is only remarkable from its size, it is unnecessary to describe it ; the reader will only recollect, when I come to speak of the engagement, that it is on the left of the road in going to Philadelphia, that it is situated towards the middle of the town, on a distinct spot of ground, and that the entrance to it is by a large square court surrounded with lofty palisades. The object which excited my curiosity, though very foreign from letters at that moment, brought me to the very gate of the college. I dismounted for a moment to visit this vast edifice, and was soon joined by Dr. Witherspoon, President of the university. He is a man of at least sixty, is a member of Congress, and much respected in this country. In accosting me he spoke French, but I easily perceived that he had acquired his knowledge of that language, from reading, rather than conversation ; which did not prevent me, however, from answering him, and continuing to converse with him in French, for I saw that he was well pleased to display what he knew of it. This is an attention which costs little, and is too much neglected in a foreign country. To reply in English to a person who speaks French to you, is to tell him, you do not know my language so well as I do yours : in this, too, one is not unfrequently mistaken. As for me, I always like better to have the advantage on my side, and to fight on my own ground. I conversed in French, therefore, with the President, and from him I learnt that this college is a complete university ; that it can contain two hundred students, and more, including the out boarders : that the distribution of the studies is formed so as to make only one class for the *humanities ;* which corresponds with our first four classes ; that two others are destined to the perfecting the youth in the study of Latin and Greek ; a fourth to Natural Philosophy, Mathematics, Astronomy, &c. and a fifth to Moral Philosophy. Parents may support their children at this college at the annual expense of forty guineas. Half of this sum is appropriated to lodgings and masters ; the rest is sufficient for living, either in the college, or at board in private houses in the town. This useful establishment has fallen into decay since the war ; there were only forty students when I saw it. A handsome collection of books had been made ; the greatest part of which has been embezzled. The English even carried off from the chapel the portrait of the king of England, a loss for which the Americans easily consoled themselves, declaring they would have no king among them, not even a painted one. There still remains a very beautiful astronomical machine ; but as it was then out of order, and differs in no respect from that I saw afterwards in Philadelphia, I shall take no notice of it.* I confess also that I was rather anxious to exa-

---

* This is the celebrated *Orrery of Rittenhouse*, the supposed destruction of which made so much noise at the beginning of the civil war, and sullied the English name in the eyes of all enlightened Europe. Justice, however, requires from the Translator to declare, that from his inquiries, and examination on the spot, the report had no other foundation than, that they intended to remove, and send it as a present to the King. It may possibly be said, and would to God that such a conjecture were not too well warranted by the whole conduct of the war, that to this motive only may be attributed its preservation ; however that may be, their sudden dislodgement from Princeton. preserved the Orrery, and, as far as that goes, the national character.— *Trans.*

mine the traces of General Washington, in a country where every object reminded me of his successes. I passed rapidly therefore from Parnassus to the field of Mars, and from the hands of President Witherspoon * into those of Colonel Moyland. They were both equally upon their own ground ; so that while one was pulling me by the right arm, telling me, here is the philosophy class ; the other was plucking me by the left, to show me where one hundred and eighty English laid down their arms.

Every person who, since the commencement of the war, has only given himself the trouble of reading the Gazettes, may recollect that General Washington surprised the town of Trenton the 25th of December, 1776 ; that, immediately after this expedition, he retired to the other side of the Delaware, but that having received a small addition to his force, he repassed the river a second time, and encamped at Trenton. Lord Cornwallis had now collected his troops, before dispersed, in winter-quarters. He marched against Washington, who was obliged to place the Assampik, or river of Trenton, between the enemy and him. By this means the town was divided between the two armies ; the Americans occupying the left bank of the creek, and the English the right. Lord Cornwallis' army was receiving hourly reinforcements ; two brigades from Brunswick were expected to join him, and he only waited their arrival to make the attack.† General Washington on the other hand, was destitute of provisions, and cut off from all communication with the fertile country of the Jerseys, and the four eastern states. Such was his position, when, on the second of January, at one o'clock in the morning, he ordered the fires to be well kept up, and some soldiers to be left to take care of them, whilst the remainder of the army should march by the

---

* This gentleman is so well known in Europe as to render it unnecessary to enter into any particulars respecting him. He certainly played a much more important part on the theatre of this grand revolution, than by heading the low church party, as it is called in Scotland, and displaying his eloquence, as I have seen him, at presbyteries and synods.—*Trans.*

† Lord Cornwallis made one or two attempts to force the small stone bridge over the creek at Trenton, but was so galled by a small battery which commanded it, and a body of chosen men, placed by General Washington in the Mill-house, that he gave up the attempt, from a contempt of his enemy ; looking upon them as his certain prey, their retreat over the Delaware, then full of ice, being impracticable ; for the same reason, probably he made no attempt to cross the creek in any other part.—*Trans.*

right, to fall back afterwards on the left, pass the rear of the English army, and enter the Jerseys. It was necessary to throw themselves considerably to the right, in order to reach Allenstown, and the sources of the Assampik, and then to fall on Princeton. About a mile from this town, General Washington's vanguard, on entering the main road, fell in with Colonel Mawhood, who was marching quietly at the head of his regiment in his way to Maidenhead and thence to Trenton. General Mercer immediately attacked him, but was repulsed by the enemies fire ; he then attempted to charge with the bayonet, but unfortunately, in leaping a ditch, was surrounded and put to the sword by the English. The troops, who were in general militia, discouraged by the loss of their commander, retreated into the woods, to wait for the remainder of the army, which arrived soon after : but Colonel Mawhood had continued his route to Maidenhead, so that General Washington had only to do with the forty-eighth regiment, part of which had appeared upon the main road on the first alarm of the attack. He pushed these troops vigorously, dispersed them, and made fifty or sixty prisoners. General Sullivan, however, was advancing rapidly, leaving on his left the Princeton road, with the design of turning that town, and of cutting off the retreat of the troops, who occupied it, to Brunswick. Two hundred English had thrown themselves into a wood by which he was to pass, but they did not long hold it, and returned in disorder to Nassau-hall, the name of the college I have been speaking of. This they ought to have taken possession of, and have there made a vigorous defence. To all appearance their officers were bewildered, for instead of entering the house, or even the court, they remained in a sort of wide street, where they were surrounded and obliged to lay down their arms, to the number of one hundred and eighty, not including fourteen officers. As for General Washington, after taking or dispersing every thing before him, he collected his troops, marched on to Kingstown, where he halted, as I have already mentioned, and continued his route towards Middlebrook ; having thus marched near thirty miles in one day, but still regretting that his troops were too much fatigued to proceed to Brunswick, which he could have taken without any difficulty. Lord Cornwallis had now nothing left but to hasten thither as fast as possible with his whole army. From this moment Pennsylvania was in safety, the Jerseys were evacuated, and the English reduced to the towns of Brunswick and Amboy, where they were obliged to act always on the defensive, not being able to stir, nor even to forage, without being driven back, and roughly handled by the militia of the country. Thus we see that the great events of war are not always great battles, and humanity may receive some consolation from this sole reflection, that the art of war is not necessarily a sanguinary art, that the talents of the commanders spare the lives of the soldiers, and that ignorance alone is prodigal of blood.

The affair of Trenton, whence this originated, cost no dearer, and was perhaps more glorious, without being more useful. Addison said, in visiting the different monuments of Italy, that he imagined himself treading on classic ground ; all my steps were on martial ground, and I was in the same morning to see two fields of battle.

CHAPTER V.

I ARRIVED early at Trenton, having remarked nothing interesting on the road, unless it be the beauty of the country,
which every where corresponds with the reputation of the
Jerseys, called the garden of America. On approaching Trenton, the road descends a little, and permits one to see at the
east end of the town the orchard where the Hessians hastily
collected, and surrendered prisoners. This is almost all that
can be said of this affair, which has been amplified by the Gazettes on one side and the other. We know that General
Washington, at the head only of three thousand men, passed
the Delaware in dreadful weather, on the night of the 24th
and 25th of December; that he divided his troops into two
columns, one of which made a circuit to gain a road upon the
left leading to the Maidenhead-road, whilst the other marched
along the river, straight to Trenton; that the main guard of
the Hessians was surprised, and that the brigade had scarcely
time to get under arms. The park of artillery was near a
church, they were attempting to harness the horses, when the
American vanguard, which had forced the piquet, fired on and
killed almost all of them. General Washington arrived with the
right column; the Hessians were surrounded, and fired a few
random shot, without order. General Washington suffered
them to do so, but he availed himself of the first moment of
the slackening of their fire, to send an officer who spoke French
to them, for our language supplies the want of all others. The
Hessians hearkened very willingly to his proposal. The general promised that the effects they had left in their houses should
not be pillaged, and they soon laid down their arms, which
they had scarcely had time to take up. Their position was certainly not a good one; nor can I conceive it possible that this
could be a field of battle fixed upon in case of an alarm. They
would have had a sure retreat by passing the bridge over the
creek at the south end of the town, but the vanguard of the
right column had got possession of it. Such, in a few words,
was this event, which is neither honourable nor dishonourable
for the Hessians; but which proves that no troops existing can
be reckoned on, when they suffer themselves to be surprised.
After viewing so many battles, it was but right to think of

dinner. I found my head-quarters well established in a good inn kept by Mr. Williams. The sign of this inn is a philosophical, or, if you will, a political emblem. It represents a beaver at work, with his little teeth, to bring down a large tree, and underneath is written, *perseverando.* I had scarce alighted from my horse, before I received a visit from Mr. Livingston,* governor of the Jerseys. He is an old man much respected, and who passes for a very sensible man. He was pleased to accompany me in a little walk I took before dinner, to examine the environs of the town, and see the camp occupied by the Americans before the affair of Princeton. I returned to dinner with Colonel Moyland, Mr. de Gimat, and two aids-de-camp of M. de la Fayette, who arrived some time before me. We were all acquainted, very happy to meet together and to dine at our ease, when a justice of the peace, who was at Trenton on business, and a captain of the American artillery, came and sat down to table with us, without any ceremony ; it being the custom of the country for travellers, when they meet at the hour of dinner, to dine together. The dinner, of which I did the honours, was excellent ; but they did not seem to know that it was I who had ordered it. There was wine at table, a very rare and dear article in America ; they drank moderately of it, and rose from table before us. I had given orders that the dinner should be charged to me ; they learnt this on going out, but set off without saying a word to me on the subject. I have often had occasion to observe, that there is more of ceremony than compliment in America. All their politeness is mere form, such as drinking healths to the company, observing ranks, giving up the right hand, &c. But they do nothing of this but what has been taught them, not a particle of it is the result of sentiment ; in a word, politeness here is like religion in Italy, every thing in practice, but without any principle.

At four o'clock I set out, after separating, but not without regret, from the good Colonel Moyland. I took the road to Bristol, crossing the river three miles below Trenton. Six miles from thence you pass a wood ; and then approach the Delaware, which you do not quit till you arrive at Bristol. It was night when I got to this town. The inn I alighted at is kept by a Mr. Benezet, of French extraction, and of a very re-

---

* This gentleman was so active and useful in the revolution, that he was long the marked object of tory vengeance, he was obliged, for many months, to shift his quarters every day, and under the necessity of sleeping every night in a different place ; but nothing could abate his zeal, he never quitted his government, and was indefatigable in his exertions to animate the people.—*Trans.*

spectable quaker family; but he is a deserter from their com-
munion. He is of the church of England, and has retained
none of the acknowledged principles of his brethren, except
that of making you pay dearer than other people: in other
respects his inn is handsome, the windows look upon the Delaware, and the view from them is superb; for this river is nearly
a mile broad, and flows through a very delightful country.*

I left Bristol the 30th of November, between nine and ten
in the morning, and arrived at Philadelphia at two. The road
leading to this city is very wide and handsome; one passes
through several small towns or villages, nor can one go five
hundred paces without seeing beautiful country houses. As
you advance you find a richer and better cultivated country,
with a great number of orchards and pastures; every thing, in
short, answers the neighbourhood of a large town, and this
road is not unlike those round London.   Four miles from Bristol you pass the creek of Neshaminy over a ferry.   It is pretty
large, and runs in such a direction as to form a sort of peninsula of the country between it and the Delaware. It had
struck me from the view of the country, and from inspecting
the chart, that on the retreat of Clinton, General Washington
might have passed the sources of this river, and marched along
it towards the Delaware. It would have covered his right flank,
and, by this precaution, he would have been at liberty to have
approached the Delaware, and to have crossed it as soon as
Clinton.   Mr. de Gimat, to whom I made this observation,
answered me, that General Washington never being sure of
the moment when the English would evacuate Philadelphia,
was afraid of quitting Lancaster, where he had all his magazines.   The town of Frankfort, which is about fifteen miles
from Bristol, and five from Philadelphia, is pretty considerable.
A creek runs in the front of this town, over which are two
stone bridges; for it divides itself into two branches, one of
which appeared to me to be artificial, and destined to turn a
great number of mills, that furnish Philadelphia with flour.
These mills, so necessary for the subsistence of the two armies,
made the town of Frankfort for a long time an object of contention, which brought on several skirmishes; but the position
is such as to be advantageous to neither party, for the river

---

* This landlord, like his brethren at Richmond and Shooter's-hill,
makes his guests pay for the prospect, and he has the same temptations; the ride from Philadelphia here on parties of pleasure being
very common in summer, and the situation of his house on the great
road to the Jerseys, and the northward, always ensuring him a number
of travellers.— *Trans.*

runs in a bottom, and the ground is of an equal elevation on both sides.

The nearer you approach to Philadelphia, the more you discover the traces of the war. The ruins of houses destroyed, or burnt, are the monuments the English have left behind them; but these ruins present only the image of a transient misfortune, and not that of long adversity. By the side of these ruined edifices, those which still exist proclaim prosperity and abundance. You imagine you see the country after a storm, some trees are overthrown, but the others are still clothed with flowers and verdure. Before you enter Philadelphia, you traverse the lines thrown up by the English in the winter of 1777—8; they are still discoverable in many places. The part of the lines I now saw, is that of the right, the flank of which is supported by a large redoubt, or square battery, which commands also the river. Some parts of the parapet have been constructed with an elegance which increases labour, more than it fortifies the work : they are made in the form of a *saw*, that is to say, composed of a series of small *redans*, each of which is capable only of containing three men. As soon as I had passed these lines, my eye, was struck with several large buildings; the two principal were a range of barracks constructed by the English, and a large hospital lately built at the expense of the quakers. Insensibly I found myself in the town, and after following three or four very wide streets, perfectly straight, I arrived at the gate of M. le Chevalier de la Luzerne.

It was just twenty days since I left Newport, during which time I had only stayed one at Voluntown, and three at the American army. I was not sorry therefore to get into quarters of refreshment, and could not desire any more agreeable than the house of the Chevalier de la Luzerne. I had a great deal of time to converse with him before dinner ; for at Philadelphia, as in London, it is the custom to dine at five, and frequently at six. I should have liked it as well had the company been not so numerous, as to oblige me to make acquaintance with a part of the town ; but our minister maintains a considerable state, and gives frequently great dinners, so that it is difficult not to fall into this sort of ambuscade. The guests, whose names I recollect, were Mr. Governeur Morris,*

---

* This gentleman lost his leg by a fall from a phaeton. He is a man of exquisite wit, and an excellent understanding. An admirable companion at the table, and the toilet, he was in universal request ; he was in all the secrets of his namesake the financier, and refined in the dark history of political intrigue. Notwithstanding his misfortune. nature did not form him for inactivity.—*Trans.*

a young man full of wit and vivacity, but unfortunately maimed, having lost a leg by accident. His friends congratulated
him on this event, saying, that now he would wholly dedicate
himself to public business. Mr. Powel, a man of considerable
fortune, without taking any part in the government, his attachment to the common cause, having appeared hitherto rather
equivocal. Mr. Pendleton, Chief Justice of South-Carolina, a
remarkably tall man, with a very distinguished countenance ;
he had the courage to hang three tories at Charleston, a few
days before the surrender of the town, and was accordingly in
great danger of losing his life, had he not escaped out of the
hands of the English, though comprised in the capitulation.
Colonel Laurens, son of Mr. Laurens, late President of Congress, and now a prisoner in the tower of London ; he speaks
very good French, which is not surprising as he was educated
at Geneva ; but it is to his honour, that being married in London, he should quit England to serve America ; he has distinguished himself on several occasions, particularly at Germantown where he was wounded.* Mr. White, Chaplain to

---

* Among the numerous traits that might be cited to do honour to
this illustrious young man, so prematurely, and unfortunately lost to his
family and his country, the translator has selected the following ; extracted from the journals of Congress.

Thursday, November 5, 1778.
Resolved, " That John Laurens, Esq. aid-de-camp to General
Washington, be presented with a continental commission of Lieutenant-
Colonel, in testimony of the sense which Congress entertain of his
patriotic and spirited services as a volunteer in the American army,
and of his brave conduct in several actions, particularly in that of
Rhode-Island on the 29th of August last ; and that General Washington be directed, whenever an opportunity shall offer, to give Lieutenant-Colonel Laurens command agreeable to his rank."

Friday, November 6, 1778.
" A letter of this day from Lieutenant-Colonel John Laurens was
read," expressing " his gratitude for the unexpected honour which
Congress were pleased to confer on him by the resolutions passed
yesterday, and the high satisfaction it would have afforded him, could
he have accepted it without injuring the rights of the officers in the
line of the army, and doing an evident injustice to his colleagues in
the family of the commander-in-chief : that having been a spectator
of the convulsions occasioned in the army by disputes of rank, he
holds the tranquillity of it too dear to be instrumental in disturbing
it ; and therefore entreating Congress to suppress the resolve of yesterday, ordering him a commission of Lieutenant-Colonel ; and to
accept his sincere thanks for the intended honour." Whereupon,
Resolved, That Congress highly approve the disinterested and
patriotic principles upon which Lieutenant-Colonel Laurens has

Congress, a handsome man, and of a mild and tolerant character.* General Mifflin,† whose talents have shone alike in war and politics; he has been Quarter-Master-General of the army; but quitted that place on account of some preference shown to to General Greene. Don Francesco, Chargé des Affaires of Spain: and I believe that is all that can be said of him: M. de Ternan, a French officer in the service of America; he had been employed in some commissions in America, and after executing them, he took to the profession of arms; he is a young man of great wit and talents; he draws well, and speaks English like his own language; he was made prisoner at Charleston :‡ the last whose name I recollect is Colonel Armand, that is, M. de la Rouerie, nephew of M. de la Belinage. He was as celebrated in France for his passion for Mademoiselle B——, as he is in America for his courage and capacity. His family having compelled him to abandon an attachment the consequences of which they dreaded, he buried himself in a celebrated and profound retirement, (the monas-

---

declined to accept the promotion conferred on him by Congress.— *Trans.*

* Mr. White is the Clergyman of St. Peter's church, and brother to Mrs. Morris, the financier's lady.— *Trans.*

† I had the happiness of enjoying the particular acquaintance of the General. He is a smart, sensible, active, and agreeable little man. I never saw him without thinking of *Garrick;* he is about the same size and figure, and his countenance sparkles with significance and expression. To him and his brother I am indebted for the most hospitable reception, and continued civilities and attention; and the General, besides showing me on the spot, the whole manœuvres of Germantown, and the proceedings on the Marquis de la Fayette's expedition over the Schuylkill, furnished me with many interesting particulars respecting the conduct of the war. I knew there was a disgust, and the cause of it, but all his narratives seemed to be those of a man of honour, unmixed with personal considerations. On signifying my intention of making a tour into the interior parts of Pennsylvania, he was so good as to give me the following letter of introduction, to his friend Colonel Patton, in case I passed by his neighbourhood. I have preserved it as characteristic at once of his own frankness, and American hospitality.

Dear Patton—Mr. ——, my particular friend, will favour you with a visit at the Spring. I have assured him that he will meet a hearty welcome.   Yours,

        THO. MIFFLIN.

Philadelphia, 3d May, 1782.

‡ He is at present a Colonel in the service of Holland, in the legion of Maillebois.

tery of La Trappe. T.) but he soon quitted it for America,*
when he devoted himself to a more glorious abstinence, and to
more meritorious mortifications. His character is gay, his
wit agreeable, and nobody would wish to see him make the
vow of silence.

Such were the guests with whom I got acquainted ; for I do
not speak of M. de Dannemours, Consul of France, at Baltimore, M. de Marbois, Secretary of the embassy, nor of the family of M. de la Luzerne, which is pretty considerable. The
dinner was served in the American, or if you will in the English
fashion ; consisting of two courses, one comprehending the
entrées, the roast meat, and the warm side dishes ; the other,
the sweet pastry, and confectionary. When this is removed,
the cloth is taken off, and apples, nuts, and chestnuts are
served : it is then that healths are drank ; the coffee which
comes afterwards serves as a signal to rise from table. These
healths or toasts as I have already observed, have no inconvenience, and only serve to prolong the conversation, which
is always more animated at the end of the repast ; they oblige
you to commit no excess, wherein they greatly differ from the
German healths, and from those we still give in our garrisons
and provinces. But I find it an absurd, and truly barbarous
practice, the first time you drink, and at the beginning of dinner, to call out successively to each individual, to let him know
you drink his health. The actor in this ridiculous comedy is
sometimes ready to die with thirst, whilst he is obliged to inquire the names, or catch the eyes of five and twenty or thirty
persons, and the unhappy persons to whom he addresses himself, with impatience, for it is certainly not possible for them
to bestow a very great attention to what they are eating, and

---

* *M. le Marquis de la Rouerie* was then very young : his subsequent conduct has proved, that nature, in giving a susceptible and
impassioned mind, has not made him a present likely to be always fatal
to him, glory and honour have employed all its activity ; and it is an
observation which merits to be consigned in history, as well as in this
journal, that carrying with him, as he did to America, all the heroic
courage, and romantic notions of chivalry of the ancient French
noblesse, he could so well conform to republican manners, that far
from availing himself of his birth, he would only make himself known
by his Christian name : hence he was always called Colonel *Armand*.
He commanded a legion which was destroyed in Carolina, at the battle of Camden, and in the remainder of that unfortunate campaign.
In 1781, he went to France, purchased there every thing necessary
for arming and equipping a new legion, and, on his return to America,
he advanced the cost of them to Congress. Before the peace he was
advanced to the rank of Brigadier-General.

what is said to them, being incessantly called to on the right
and left, or pulled by the sleeve by charitable neighbours, who
are so kind as to acquaint them with the politeness they are
receiving. The most civil of the Americans are not content
with this general call ; every time they drink they make partial ones, for example, four or five persons at a time. Another
custom completes the despair of poor foreigners, if they be
ever so little absent, or have good appetites : these general
and partial attacks terminate in downright duels. They call
to you from one end of the table to the other ; *Sir, will you permit me to drink a glass of wine with you ?* This proposal always
is accepted, and does not admit the excuse of the Great-Cousin,
one does not drink without being acquainted. The bottle is then
passed to you, and you must look your enemy in the face, for
I can give no other name to the man who exercises such an
empire over my will : you wait till he likewise has poured out
his wine, and taken his glass ; you then drink mournfully with
him, as a recruit imitates the corporal in his exercise. But to
do justice to the Americans, they themselves feel the ridicule
of these customs borrowed from old England, and since laid
aside by her. They purposed to the Chevalier de la Luzerne
to dispense with them, knowing that his example would have
great weight ; but he thought proper to conform, and he did
right. The more the French are known to be in possession of
giving their customs to other nations, the more should they
avoid the appearance of changing those of the Americans.
Happy our nation if her ambassadors, and her travellers, had
always so correct an understanding, and if they never lost sight
of this observation, that of all men, the dancing master should
have the most negligent air !

After this dinner, which I may possibly have spun out too
long, according to the custom of the country, the Chevalier de
la Luzerne took me to make visits with him.* The first was

---

* The conduct of the Chevalier de la Luzerne in America justified
every idea that has been formed of the superior skill and address of the
French nation on embassies, and in the cabinet. He not only con-
formed to the manners, and customs of the country, but he studied
the character of every individual of the least importance. He rose
early in the morning, and watched the hour that best suited their convenience, to wait on the members of Congress, and the leading men of
state ; at dinner he received company of all political complexions, except *offensive* tories ; his afternoons were chiefly employed in visiting
the ladies, and in passing from one house to another ; in these visits
he made no political exceptions, but on the contrary, paid his court
particularly to the ladies in the suspected families, an evidently wise
policy ; in this class, he was supposed to have a very agreeable, as

to Mr. Reed, President of the State. This post corresponds with that of Governor in the other provinces, but without the same authority ; for the government of Pennsylvania is purely democratic, consisting only of a General Assembly, or House of Commons, who name an executive council, composed of twelve members possessing very limited powers, of the exercise of which they are obliged to give an account to the Assembly, in which they have no voice. Mr. Reed has been a general officer in the American army, and has given proofs of courage, having had a horse killed under him in a skirmish near White-

---

well as useful acquaintance, in the two Miss C———'s, who put no restraint upon their tongues, but were well informed of all the transactions of their party. Wherever he could not himself be present, Mr. Marbois, and Mr. Ottaw, the Secretaries were distributed, so that you could not make an afternoon's visit to a *whig* or *tory* family in the city, without being sure to meet with this political General or one of his aids-de camp. When he made a public entertainment, and the presence of the tory ladies gave offence to those of the patriotic party, he always pleaded ignorance, contrived to shift the blame from himself, and throw it on the Secretaries, who were left to fight the battle in the best way they could over the tea table ; but all this was carried on with undescribable address, and so managed as to keep all parties in good humour with him. He indulged every man's peculiarities, and bestowed the *petites attentions* on all. It is thus the French maintain their ascendency in the cabinet, which is worth a thousand victories, and their superiority in the Courts of Europe, under every varied form of government, from Holland to Constantinople. I cannot help contrasting with this policy, an instance of English diplomatic conduct.—— A very respectable senator of Sweden, previous to the revolution in that country, told me, that in a very hard struggle, between the English and French parties in the senate, on some leading question, the English minister applied to him in his turn, for his suffrage ; on his starting some objection, the minister turned angry, assumed a haughty tone, and observed that the Swedes did not know their true interest, that they might do as they thought proper, that England was the *only country* that could support them, and left him much out of humour ; the same language he held to all the senators. The French ambassador, on the contrary, was paying his court to each senator, in his family, distributing favours and making entertainments, and carried his point with barely *insinuating*, what would be agreeable to his Court. Compare this anecdote with the well known conduct in Holland, of a minister mightily extolled for his wisdom and experience, *Sir Joseph Yorke*, and his memorials, before the late fatal breach with that country, and the success of the Duke de la Vauguyon, which nothing but such haughty, ill-timed language could have so rapidly produced, and judge whether *Sir William Temple* would have done the same.—*Trans.*

marsh. It is he, whom Governor Johnstone attempted to corrupt in 1778, when England sent Commissioners to treat with Congress; but this attempt was confined to some insinuations, entrusted to Mrs. Ferguson. Mr. Reed, who is a sensible man, rather of an intriguing character, and above all eager of popular favour, made a great clamour, and published, and exaggerated the offers that were made him. The complaints of Mrs. Ferguson, who found herself committed in this affair, a public declaration of Governor Johnstone, whose object was to deny the facts, but which served only to confirm them; various charges, and refutations, printed and made public, produced no other effect than to second the views of Mr. Reed, and to make him attain his end, of playing a leading part in the country. Unfortunately his pretensions, or his interest led him to declare himself the enemy of Dr. Franklin.* When I was at Philadelphia, it was no less than matter of question to *recall* that respectable man; but the French party, or that of General Washington, or to express it still better the really patriotic party prevailed, and the matter finished by sending an officer to France to represent the wretched state of the army, and to ask for an aid of clothes, tents, and money, of which it stood in much need. The choice fell on Colonel Laurens.†

---

* I make no doubt that the M. de Chastellux is correct in this assertion, but thus much I can say from personal knowledge, that Mr. Reed is one of the warmest and most strenuous supporters of the present democratic constitution of Pennsylvania, the work of Dr. Franklin, and to subvert which almost all the personal enemies of Mr. Reed have been labouring for some years past. In Philadelphia, in 1782, the parties of constitutionalists, and anti-constitutionalists ran so high, as to occasion frequent personal quarrels. Another fact is well known to many persons in Europe, and to every body in America, that the attack on Dr. Franklin came from a much more powerful and intriguing quarter than that of Mr. Reed, who never was of any weight *in Congress*. Mr. Reed too was much attached to General Washington, whom the opposers of Dr. Franklin's constitution of Pennsylvania, *affected* to hold in no very high respect. I never exchanged a word with Mr. Reed, my only wish is to ascertain the truth.—*Trans.*

† Colonel Laurens obtained six millions of livres from the French court, the greatest part of which was expended in clothing and necessaries for the American army, on his arrival in Europe in the spring of 1781. Mr. Gillon, who had the commission of commodore from the state of Carolina, and had been sent over to purchase three frigates for that state, came immediately from Holland to Paris, and prevailed on Colonel Laurens, who was of the same state, to purchase a large quantity of the clothing at Amsterdam, a measure highly offensive to the French court, to be shipped on board his frigate the *South-Carolina*, which was to sail *immediately*, and besides her great force, carrying

Mr. Reed has a handsome house arranged, and furnished in the English style. I found there Mrs. Washington, who had just arrived from Virginia, and was going to stay with her husband, as she does at the end of every campaign. She is about forty, or five and forty, rather plump, but fresh, and with an agreeable face.* After passing a quarter of an hour at Mr. Reed's, we waited on Mr. Huntington, president of Congress:

---

twenty-eight forty-two pounders, and twelve eighteens, had the legion of Luxembourg on board. The purchase was made accordingly at Amsterdam, the goods shipped on board the frigate, by which many private purposes were answered to Mr. Gillon, who, on some pretext however, after many month's delay, and the Colonel's return, removed the goods from the frigate, and shipped them on board two Dutch vessels *to be taken under his convoy;* but to these he soon gave the slip, leaving them in September in the Texel, without saying a word of his intention; finding he did not return, they were conveyed back in October to Amsterdam, and relanded at an enormous expense to America, and to the great loss of the army, for whom they were intended as a supply that winter; yet, on his return, he had address enough to elude every inquiry into this very extraordinary transaction, to which escape, the universal esteem in which Mrs. Gillon, his wife, was held by every person in Carolina, contributed not a little. It may here be proper to correct an error which has slipped into all the English public prints of the day, and particularly into *Dodsley's Annual Register*, on the subject of the frigate, the South-Carolina. This frigate is mentioned in the list of Admiral Zoutman's fleet in the engagement off the Dogger's Bank in August, 1781. The translator was then at the Texel, saw the Dutch fleet sail, and return after the engagement; during that interval had the frigate lying at anchor before his eyes, and was close to her, on board another vessel off the end of the *Haaks*, a great shoal at the mouth of the Texel, when the Dutch fleet entered in the most shattered condition. Mr. Gillon is himself a native of Rotterdam, but was on very bad terms with all the officers of the Dutch fleet, and indeed with almost all his countrymen.—*Trans.*

* I had the pleasure of passing a day or two with Mrs. Washington, at the general's house in Virginia, where she appeared to me to be one of the best women in the world, and beloved by all about her. She has no family by the general, but was surrounded by her grand-children, and Mrs. Custis, her son's widow. The family were then in mourning for Mr. Custis, her son by a former marriage, whose premature death was subject of public and private regret. He was brought up by the general as his own son, and formed himself successfully on his model. He succeeded him as representative for Fairfax county, and promised to be a very distinguished member of society, but having gone down to Yorktown, after the capture of Cornwallis, to view the works, he caught a malignant fever at one of the hospitals, and was rapidly carried off. The general was uncommonly affected at his death, insomuch that many of his friends imagined they percei-

We found him in his cabinet, lighted by a single candle. This simplicity reminded me of that of the Fabricius and the Philopemens. Mr. Huntington is an upright man, who espouses no party, and may be relied on. He is a native of Connecticut, and was delegate for that state, when chosen president.

My day having been sufficiently taken up, the Chevalier de la Luzerne, conducted me to the house where he had ordered lodgings to be prepared for me. It was at the Spanish minister's, where there were several vacant apartments; for M. Miralé, who had occupied it, died a year before at Morristown. His secretary has remained charge des affaires, master of the house, and well contented to enjoy the *incarico*, which includes in it, besides the correspondence, a table maintained at the expense of the king of Spain. The Chevalier de la Luzerne, though very well, and agreeably lodged, had no apartments to spare;* he made them, however, contrive me one the next day, which contributed greatly to my happiness during my stay at Philadelphia, for I was situated exactly between M. de Marbois and him, and able to converse with them every moment of the day.

That of the 22d commenced like every other day in America, by a great breakfast. As the dinners are very late at the minister's, a few loins of veal, some legs of mutton, and other *trifles* of that kind are always introduced among the tea-cups,

---

ved some change in his equanimity of temper, subsequent to that event. It is certain that they were upon terms of the most affectionate and manly friendship.—*Trans.*

* The French Ambassador's was a very handsome house, hired of Mr. John Dickinson, and very near the seat of Congress. In one of those dreadful storms of thunder with which America is so frequently visited in the summer months, this house, though lower than the State-house, and that of his neighbour, Mrs. Allen, was struck by lightning, and a French officer, sitting alone in one of the rooms, burnt to death ; the lightning had set fire to his clothes, and thrown him into a fainting fit, during which, part of his body was miserably scorched, and his private parts reduced to ashes, so that he survived but a few hours ; but the principal ravage was in a chamber containing an *iron bedstead*, in which the Ambassador himself slept, by way of security from the bugs ; in that room, large blocks of marble were rent in pieces, and torn from the chimney-piece ; its effects, in short, were so singular in many respects, and in some so contrary to received opinions, that Mr. Arthur Lee, and Dr. Rush, thought proper to publish a very long and curious account of it ; and indeed, as far as I am able to judge, this stroke presented many new phenomena of electricity. It may be proper to add, that this was the only house in the neighbourhood *unprovided with an electrical apparatus.—Trans.*

and are sure of meeting a hearty welcome. After this slight
repast, which only lasted an hour and a half, we went to visit
the ladies, agreeable to the Philadelphia custom, where the
morning is the most proper hour for paying visits. We began
by Mrs. Bache; she merited all the anxiety we had to see her,
for she is the daughter of Mr. Franklin. Simple in her manners, like her respectable father, she possesses his benevolence.
She conducted us into a room filled with work, lately finished
by the ladies of Philadelphia. This work consisted neither of
embroidered tambour waistcoats, nor net work edging, nor of
gold and silver brocade—it was a quantity of shirts for the
soldiers of Pennsylvania. The ladies bought the linen from
their own private purses, and took a pleasure in cutting them
out, and sewing them themselves. On each shirt was the name
of the married, or unmarried lady who made it, and they
amounted to 2200. Here is the place, no doubt, to make a
very *moral*, but very *trivial* reflection on the difference between
our manners and those of America; but as for myself, I am of
opinion that, on a similar occasion, our French women would
do as much, and I even venture to believe that such works
would inspire as agreeable verses as those which accompany
the annual presents of cradles, coaches, houses, castles, &c.
laboriously and awkwardly brocaded. · It must be allowed that
this custom is an abundant source of most ingenious ideas;
but their harvest is past, and they begin to be exhausted. But
should any rigid French philosopher be disposed to censure
French manners, I would not advise him to address himself to
Mrs. P———, whom I waited upon on quitting Mrs. Bache.
This is the agreeable woman of Philadelphia; her taste is as
delicate as her health: an enthusiast to excess for all the French
fashions, she only waits for the termination of this little revolution, to effect a still greater one in the manners of her
country.

After paying due homage to this admirable female patriot, I hurried to make acquaintance with Mr. Morris.
He is a very rich merchant, and consequently a man of
every country, for commerce bears every where the same character. Under monarchies it is free; it is an egotist in republics; a stranger, or if you will, a citizen of the universe, it
excludes alike the virtues and the prejudices that stand in the
way of its interest. It is scarcely to be credited, that amidst
the disasters of America, Mr. Morris, the inhabitant of a town
just emancipated from the hands of the English, should possess a fortune of eight millions, (between 3 and 400,000*l.* sterling.) It is, however, in the most critical times that great fortunes are acquired. The fortunate return of several ships, the
still more successful cruises of his privateers, have increased

his riches beyond his expectations, if not beyond his wishes. He is, in fact, so accustomed to the success of his privateers, that when he is observed on a Sunday to be more serious than usual, the conclusion is, that no prize has arrived in the preceding week.* This flourishing state of commerce, at Philadelphia, as well as in Massachusetts bay, is entirely owing to the arrival of the French squadron.† The English have

---

* Mr. Morris has certainly enriched himself greatly by the war, but the house of *Willing & Morris* did a great deal of business, and was well known in all the considerable trading towns of Europe, previous to that period. Mr. Morris had various other means of acquiring wealth besides privateering; among others, by his own interest, and his connexions with Mr. *Holker*, then Consul-General of France, at Philadelphia, he frequently obtained exclusive permissions to ship cargoes of flour, &c. in the time of general embargoes, by which he gained immense profits. His situation gave him many similar opportunities, of which his capital, his credit, and abilities always enabled him to take advantage.—On the strength of his office, as Financier-General, he circulated *his own notes of Robert Morris*, as cash, throughout the continent, and even had the address to get some assemblies, that of Virginia in particular, to pass acts to make them current in payment of taxes. What purchases of tobacco, what profits of every kind might not a man of Mr. Morris' abilities make with such powerful advantages? The house the Marquis speaks of, in which Mr. Morris lives, belonged formerly to Mr. *Richard Penn;* the Financier has made great additions to it, and is the first who has introduced the luxury of hot-houses, and ice-houses on the continent. He has likewise purchased the elegant country house formerly occupied by the traitor, Arnold, nor is his luxury to be outdone by any commercial voluptuary of London. This gentleman is a native of Manchester in England, is at the head of the aristocratical party in Pennsylvania, and has eventually been instrumental in the revolution; in private life he is much esteemed, by a very numerous acquaintance.—*Trans.*

† Very large fortunes were made from nothing during this period, but this state of prosperity was not of long duration ; in 1781 and 1782, so numerous were the King's cruisers, and privateers, that frequently not one vessel out of seven that left the Delaware escaped their vigilance. The profits on successful voyages were enormous, but it was no uncommon thing to see a man one day worth forty or fifty thousand pounds, and the next reduced to nothing; indeed these rapid transitions were so frequent, that they almost ceased to affect either the comfort or the credit of the individual.—Flour shipped at Philadelphia, cost *five* dollars, and produced from twenty-eight to thirty-four dollars a barrel in *specie* at the Havana, which is generally but a short run, and the arrival of one European cargo, out of three, amply repaid the merchant, so that notwithstanding the numerous captures, the stocks were continually full of new vessels to supply such as were lost or taken. In short, without having been upon the spot at that period, it

abandoned all their cruises, to block it up at Newport, and in that they have succeeded ill, for they have not taken a single sloop coming to Rhode-Island or Providence.   Mr. Morris is a large man, very simple in his manners : but his mind is sub-tle and acute, his head perfectly well organized, and he is as well versed in public affairs as in his own.   He was a member of Congress in 1776, and ought to be reckoned among those personages who have had the greatest influence in the revolution of America.   He is the friend of Dr. Franklin, and the decided enemy of Mr. Reed.   His house is handsome, resem-bling perfectly the houses in London ; he lives there without ostentation, but not without expense, for he spares nothing which can contribute to his happiness, and that of Mrs. Mor-ris, to whom he is much attached.   A zealous republican, and an epicurean philosopher, he has always played a distinguish-ed part at table and in business.*   I have already mentioned Mr. Powel, at present I must speak of his wife ; and indeed it would be difficult to separate from each other, two persons, who for twenty years have lived together in the strictest union : I shall not say as man and wife, which would not convey the idea of perfect equality in America, but as two friends, hap-pily matched in point of understanding, taste, and informa-tion.   Mr. Powel, as I have before said, has travelled in Eu-rope, and returned with a taste for the fine arts ; his house is adorned with the most valuable prints, and good copies of se-veral of the Italian masters.   Mrs. Powel has not travelled, but she has read a great deal, and profitably : it would be un-just, perhaps, to say, that in this she differs from the greatest part of the American ladies; but what distinguishes her the most is, her taste for conversation, and the truly European use she knows how to make of her understanding and informa-tion.

I fear my readers (if ever I have any) may make this natu-ral reflection, that visits are very tiresome pieces of business

---

is impossible to conceive the activity and perseverance of the Ameri-cans.   There was scarcely a captain, or even common sailor, who had not been taken six or seven times during the war, nor a merchant who had not been, more than once, rich and ruined.—*Trans.*

* **Mr. Morris** has since filled for three years the post of Financier, or Comptroller-General, which was created for him.   He had for his colleague Mr. *Governeur Morris*, whom I have already mentioned, and who has amply justified the opinion entertained of his talents.   It may safely be asserted, that Europe affords few examples of a perspicuity, and a facility of understanding equal to his, which adapts itself with the same success to business, to letters, and to sciences.

every where, and as it is impossible to escape the epigrammatic turn of the French, without making great haste, I am determined to get the start. I apprise them, however, that I acquit them of a long dinner, which the Chevalier de la Luzerne gave that day to the southern delegates. I shall have occasion to speak elsewhere of some of these delegates, and as for those who will not give me that opportunity, they deserve to be passed over in silence.

CHAPTER VI.

FEARFUL lest the pleasures of *Capua* should make me forget the campaigns of *Hannibal*, and of *Fabius*, I determined to get on horseback, on the second of December, to visit the field of battle of Germantown. Many recollect, that after the defeat of Brandywine, in 1777, the American army, not thinking proper to defend Philadelphia, retired to the upper Schuylkill, whilst the English took possession, without resistance, of the capital of Pennsylvania. Elated with their success, and full of that confidence which has invariably deceived them, they had divided and dispersed their forces: the greatest part of their troops encamped upon the Schuylkill, four miles from Philadelphia; another division occupied Germantown, eight miles to the northward of that place, and they sent a considerable detachment to Billingsport, to favour the passage of their fleet, which was making fruitless endeavours to get up the Delaware. Thus circumstanced, General Washington thought it was time to remind the English that there still existed an American army. One is at a loss whether most to extol the sage intrepidity of the chief, or the resolution displayed by his army in making an attack on the same troops, whose shock they were unable to sustain a month before. Germantown is a long town, or village, consisting of a single street, not unlike La Villitre, or Vauginard, near Paris. From the first house, at the south, to the last, at the north end of the town, it is near two miles and a half. The English corps which occupied, or rather covered it, was encamped near the last houses to the northward, and so situated as that the street, or main road intersected the camp at right angles. This body might amount to three or four thousand men. General Washington, who occupied a position of ten miles distance,* on Skippack Creek, left his

---

* There are many striking differences between this account, and that given by General Howe in his public despatches, in his own narrative to the house of commons, and in the examination of his witnesses. The English General reports, that Washington's camp near Skippack Creek, from whence he moved, was *sixteen* miles from Germantown—the Marquis says, only *ten*. The English General

camp towards midnight, marching in two columns, one of which was to turn Germantown on the eastward, the other on the left; two brigades of the right column were ordered to form the corps de reserve, to separate themselves, from that column, at the instant of the attack, and follow the main street of Germantown. A very thick fog came on, favourable to the march of the enemy, but which rendered the attack more difficult, as it became impossible to concert the movements, and extend the troops. The militia marched on the right and left, without the two columns, not being committed in the affair, and always skirting the woods, on the Frankfort side, as well as on that of the Schuylkill. General Washington halted a moment before daylight, at a cross road, distant only half a mile from the picket, or advanced post of the enemy. There he learnt from an English dragoon, who was intoxicated, and had lost his way, that the Billingsport detachment was returned. This unexpected intelligence did not change the General's project; he continued his march at the head of the right column, and fell upon the English picket who were surprised, put to rout, and driven to the camp, where they brought the first news of the arrival of the Americans. The troops flew to arms, and precipitately fell back, leaving their tents standing, and abandoning all their baggage. This was a moment not to be lost, and French troops would certainly have availed themselves of it, nay it would have been difficult to prevent them either from pursuing the enemy too far, or from dispersing to plunder the camp. It is here we may form a judgment of the American character. Perhaps this army, notwithstanding the slowness of its manœuvres, and its inexperience in war, may merit the praises of Europeans. General Sullivan who commanded the column on the right, calmly and slowly formed the three brigades

---

strongly asserts, that this affair was no surprise, (see his *narrative*, and his examination of *Sir George Osborne;*) the Marquis seems to be well authorised to call it a *complete surprise.* The General affirms he was prepared for it. The Marquis *proves*, nay, the English General's letters and narrative demonstrate how narrowly, and by what means his army, and the British affairs escaped total ruin. The General says, " The enemy retired near twenty miles to Perkyoming Creek, and are now encamped near Skippack Creek, about *eighteen* miles distance from hence." The Marquis asserts, that " The retreat was executed in good order, that General Washington took an excellent position within *four* miles of Germantown, so that on the evening of the battle, he was six miles nearer the enemy than before." How shall we reconcile these essential contradictions, which ought unquestionably to be discussed, for the interest of truth, and the benefit of history?— *Trans.*

ahead; and after ranging them in order of battle, he traversed the English camp, without a single soldier stopping for plunder: he advanced in this manner, leaving the houses on the left, and driving before him all resistance from the gardens and inclosures: he penetrated into the town itself, and was some time engaged with the troops who defended a small square near the market.

Whilst every thing thus succeeded on the right, General Washington, at the head of the reserve was expecting to see his left column arrive, and pursued his march by the main street. But a fire of musketry, which proceeded from a large house within pistol shot of the street, suddenly checked the van of his troops. It was resolved to attack this house; but cannon were necessary, for it was known to be of stone, and could not therefore be set fire to. Unfortunately they had only six pounders: the Chevalier Duplessiis-Mauduit, brought two pieces near another house, two hundred paces from the former. This cannonade produced no effect, it penetrated the walls, but did not beat them down. The Chevalier de Mauduit, full of that ardour, which, at the age of sixteen, made him undertake a journey into Greece, to view the fields of *Platea* and *Thermopylæ*, and at twenty go in search of laurels in America, resolved to attack by main force this house, which he was unable to reduce by cannon.* He proposed to Colonel Laurens to take with him some determined men, and get some straw and hay from a barn, to set fire to the princi-

---

* In 1782 I visited and passed a very agreeable day at this celebrated stone-house, so bravely, and judiciously defended by *Colonel Musgrove*, and saw many marks of cannon and musket shot in the walls, doors, and window shutters, besides two or three mutilated statues which stood in front of it. It is a plain gentleman's country-house, with four windows in front, and two stories high, calculated for a small family, and stands single, and detached from every other building, so that defended as it was by six companies, commanded by so gallant an officer, it was calculated to make a long resistance against every thing but heavy cannon. I here saw, what to me was perfectly new, but in this perhaps I betray my ignorance; a cock, though surrounded by hens, in frequent copulation with a duck. Being in company with ladies, I had no opportunity of inquiring whether there was any, and what sort of produce. From the different size of their bodies, the difference of their organization, and the mode of union, I could not help considering it as not much less extraordinary than the Brussels fable of the Hen and Rabbit; but in this, perhaps, every peasant can set me right. This house formerly belonged to Mr. Chew, a loyalist, and was purchased by Mr. *Blair MacClenaghan;* who, from a very small beginning, has, by his industry, fairly and honourably acquired a a very considerable fortune.—*Trans.*

pal door. One may conceive such an idea presenting itself to two spirited young men ; but it is scarcely credible, that of these two noble adventurous youths, one should be at present on his way to France, and the other in good health at Newport.* M. de Mauduit making no doubt that they were following him with all the straw in the barn, went straight to a window on the ground floor, which he forced, and on which he mounted. He was received, in truth, like the lover who mounting a ladder to see his mistress found the husband waiting for him on the balcony: I do not know whether, like him too, on being asked what he was doing there, he answered, *I am only taking a walk ;* but this I know, that whilst a gallant man, pistol in hand, desired him to surrender, another less polite entering briskly into the chamber, fired a musket shot, which killed, not M. de Mauduit, but the officer who wished to take him. After these slight mistakes, and this little quarrel, the difficulty was for him to retire. On one hand he must be exposed to a smart fire from the first and second floor ; on the other, a part of the American army were spectators, and it would have been ridiculous to return running. M. de Mauduit, like a true Frenchman, chose rather to expose himself to death than ridicule ; but the balls respected our prejudices ; he returned safe and sound, and Mr. Laurens, who was in no greater haste than he, escaped with a slight wound in his shoulder. I must not here omit a circumstance which proves the precarious tenure of a military existence. General Washington thought that on summoning the commander of this post. he would readily surrender : it was proposed to M. de Mauduit to take a drum with him, and make this proposal ; but on his observing that he spoke bad English, and might not, perhaps, be understood, an American officer was sent, who being preceded by a drum, and displaying a white handkerchief, it was imagined, would not incur the smallest risk ; but the English answered this officer only by musket shot, and killed him on the spot.

By this time the enemy began to rally : the English army had marched from their camp near Schuylkill to succour Germantown, and Cornwallis was coming with all expedition from Philadelphia, with the grenadiers and chasseurs, whilst the corps de reserve of the American army were losing their time at the stone-house, and the left column was scarcely ready for the attack. The contest was now become too unequal, and it

---

* Mr. Laurens has since fallen a victim to his too inconsiderate valour : he was killed in Carolina, in a skirmish of little importance. a short time before the signing of the peace.

became necessary to think of a retreat, which was executed in good order, and General Washington took an excellent position four miles from Germantown ; so that on the evening of the battle, he was six miles nearer the enemy than before. The capacity he had just displayed on this occasion, the confidence he had inspired into an army they thought disheartened, and which, like the Hydra of the fable, re-appeared with a more threatening head, astonished the English, and kept them in awe, till the defeat of Burgoyne changed the aspect of affairs. This is the most favourable light in which we can view this day, unfortunately too bloody for any advantages derived from it. Military men who shall view the ground, or·have before them an accurate plan, will, I imagine, be of opinion, that the extensiveness of the object occasioned the failure of this enter-prize. The project of first beating the advanced corps, then the army, and afterwards of becoming masters of Philadelphia, was absolutely chimerical : for the village of Germantown being upwards of two miles in length, presented too many obstacles for the assailants, and too many points of rallying for the English ; besides that it is not in intersected countries, and without cavalry, that great battles are gained, which destroy or disperse armies. Had General Washington contented himself with proceeding to Whitemarsh, and covering his march with a large body of troops, which might have advanced to Germantown, he would have surprised the English van-guard, and forced them to retire with loss; and if satisfied with this sort of lesson given to a victorious army, he had fallen back on the new position he wished to occupy, he would have completely fulfilled his object, and the whole honour of the day been his. But, supposing the project of attack to be, such as was adopted, it appears to me that two faults, rather excusable, it is true, were committed ; one, the losing time in ranging in line of battle General Sullivan's column, instead of marching directly to the camp of the enemy ; the other, the amusing themselves in attacking the stone-house. The first fault will appear very pardonable to those who have seen the American troops such as they then were ; they had no instruction, and were so ill-disciplined, that they could neither preserve good order in marching in a column, nor spread themselves when it became necessary ; for experience, which is always differing with M. de Menil Durand, teaches us, that profound order is the most subject to disorder and confusion, and which consequently demands the most phlegm and discipline. The second error may be justified by the hope they always had of getting possession of the stone-house, the importance of which was measured by the obstinacy of the enemy in defending it. It is certain, that two better measures might have been adopted :

the first to pursue their march without regarding the fire of musketry, which could always have been sufficiently slackened by detaching a few men to fire at the windows; and the second, that of leaving the village on the left, to enter it again three hundred paces further on, where it would then have been sufficient to take possession of another house opposite to those occupied by the enemy; though this house be not quite so high as the former, the fire from it would have checked the English, and secured a retreat in case of necessity.*

In allowing myself this sort of censure, I feel how much I ought to mistrust my own judgment, especially as I was not present at the action; but I made the same observations to M. Laurens, M. de Mauduit, and M. de Gimat, who seemed to be unable to refute them. We have seen the share the two former had in the engagement; the third has several times viewed the field of battle with General Washington, who explained to him the motions of the two armies, and nobody is better calculated to hear well, and to give a good account of what he has heard.

After sufficiently examining the position of Germantown, I returned to Philadelphia by the shortest road, and quicker than I came, for the cold was very piercing, and I had only time to dress myself to accompany the Chevalier de la Luzerne to dine with the northern delegates. It must be understood, that the Delegates, or if you will, the Members of Congress, have a tavern to themselves, where they give frequent entertainments; but that the company may not be too numerous at a time, they divide themselves into two sets, and as we see, very geographically; the line of demarkation being from east to west.† The dinner was plain and good, and our reception

---

* Possibly the Marquis does not know that there were *six companies* of the 40th regiment in this house; no despicable enemy to leave in the rear of such an army as General Washington's was composed of. — *Trans.*

† There is a great probability of seeing this line of demarkation more distinctly marked, by a separation of the federal union into *two parts*, at no very distant day; but not on hostile, or unfriendly terms. This was matter of frequent discussion during my stay at Philadelphia, and seemed to be an opinion which was daily gaining ground. Indeed it seems to be a measure which sooner or later must take place, from the obvious difficulties attending the management, and operations of a confederacy extending from Florida to Nova-Scotia, a country, every day increasing in population, and branching out into *new states*. Such a division must, in my opinion, give new force and energy to each part of it, and produce more union and activity in their councils: nor do I see any bad consequences arising from such an ami-

polite and cordial, but not ceremonious. Two Delegates, placed at each end, did the honours of the table. Mr. Duane, Deputy from the state of New-York, occupied the side I was on. He is of a gay and open character, has no objection to talk, and drinks without repugnance. I conversed some time, but less than I could have wished with Mr. Charles Thompson, Secretary of Congress. He passes, with reason, for one of the best informed men in the country, and though he be a man of the cabinet, and mixing little with society, his manners are polite and amiable. Mr. Samuel Adams, Deputy for Massachusetts Bay, was not at this dinner, but on rising from table I went to see him. When I entered his room, I found him *tête-à-tête* with a young girl of fifteen who was preparing his tea, but we shall not be scandalized at this, on considering that he is at least sixty. Every body in Europe knows that he was one of the prime movers of the present revolution. I experienced in his company the satisfaction one rarely has in the world, nay even on the theatre, of finding the person of the actor corresponding with the character he performs. In him, I saw a man wrapt up in his object, who never spoke but to give a good opinion of his cause, and a high idea of his country. His simple and frugal exterior, seemed intended as a contrast with the energy and extent of his ideas, which were wholly turned towards the republic, and lost nothing of their warmth by being expressed with method and precision; as an army, marching towards the enemy, has not a less determined air for observing the laws of tactics. Among many facts he cited in honour of his country, I shall relate one which merits to be transmitted to posterity. Two young soldiers had deserted from the army, and returned to their father's house. Their father, incensed at this action, loaded them with irons, and conducted them himself to their general, Lord Sterling. He did what every other officer would have done, in his place, he pardoned them. The father, as patriotic, but less austere than a Roman, was happy to preserve his children; nevertheless he seemed astonished, and approaching the general, my lord, says he, with tears in his eyes, "'Tis more than I hoped for." I quitted Mr. Adams with regret, but with a full intention of seeing him again, and my evening terminated by a visit to Colonel

---

cable separation, except in the case of a war exactly similar to the last, a case which I believe every man will agree is scarcely within the line of possibility. *Local* obstacles to a long continuance of the present state of things, must alone infallibly produce it. They who are acquainted with America will add many reasons, which it is unnecessary for me to enumerate.—*Trans.*

Bland, one of the Delegates for Carolina. He is a tall hand-some man, who has been in the West-Indies, where he ac-quired French. He is said to be a good soldier, but at present serves his country, and serves it well in Congress. The Southern Delegates, in fact, have great credit, they are inces-santly labouring to draw the attention of the government towards them, and to avert every idea of purchasing peace on their account.

The weather was so bad on the third that it was impossible to stir out. I had no reason to complain, however, of the em-ployment of this day, which I passed either in conversation with M. de la Luzerne, and M. de Marbois, or in reading such interesting papers as they were pleased to communicate. Mr. Huntington having informed me, that the next day he would show me the hall in which the Congress assembles, I went there at ten o'clock, and found him waiting for me, accompanied by several delegates. This hall is spacious, without magnifi-cence; its handsomest ornament is the portrait of General Washington, larger than life : He is represented on foot, in that noble and easy attitude which is natural to him; cannon, colours, and all the attributes of war form the accessories of the picture. I was then conducted into the secretary's hall, which has nothing remarkable but the manner in which it is furnished; the colours taken from the enemy serve by way of tapestry. From thence you pass to the library, which is pretty large, but far from being filled; the few books it is composed of, appear to be well chosen. It is in the town-house that Congress hold their meetings : this building is rather hand-some ; the staircase in particular is wide and noble : as to ex-ternal ornaments, they consist only in the decoration of the gate, and in several tablets of marble placed above the win-dows. I remarked a peculiarity in the roof, which appeared new to me ; the chimneys are bound to the two extremities of the building, which is a long square, and are so con-structed, as to be fastened together in the form of an arch, thus forming a sort of portico.

After taking leave of the President and Delegates, I re-turned to the Chevalier de la Luzerne's, and as the streets were covered with ice, I staid at home, where I received a visit from Mr. Wilson,* a celebrated lawyer and author of se-veral pamphlets on the present affairs. He has in his library all our best authors on public law and jurisprudence ; the works

---

* Mr. Wilson is a Scotchman, and is making a fortune rapidly in the profession of the law at Philadelphia. He is about four and forty, a man of real abilities, and Mr. Morris's intimate friend and coadjutor in his aristocratic plans.— *Trans.*

of President Montesquieu, and of the Chancellor d'Aquessau, hold the first rank among them, and he makes them his daily study. After dinner, which was private and *a la Francoise*, I went to see Mrs. Bingham, a young and handsome woman, only seventeen : her husband, who was there, according to the American custom, is only five and twenty :* he was Agent of Congress at Martinico, from whence he is returned with a tolerable knowledge of French, and with much attachment to the Marquis de Bouillé. I passed the remainder of the evening with Mrs. Powell, where I expected to have an agreeable conversation ; in which I was not deceived, and forgot myself there till pretty late.

I went again to the town-house, on the 5th, but it was to be

---

* Mr. Bingham, even at this age, returned from Martinico with a very handsome fortune. In the year 1782, he gained a very considerable sum by opening policies on the capture of the Count de Grasse in the Ville de Paris ; an event, of which there is little doubt he had secret and sure intelligence from his connection with the islands. They first opened at 10, and afterwards were done at 25 and 30 per cent. Very large sums were underwritten, chiefly by the *whigs*, who were unwilling, and could not be brought to credit this piece of news. Circumstances were peculiarly favourable to this speculation, for, notwithstanding the great intercourse between the West-Indies and the Continent, only *two* accounts of this affair arrived for six weeks after the engagement ; the event of which was sooner known, with certainty, in England. The one was in Rivington's New-York paper, copied from the Antigua Gazette, and lamely given ; besides, that his paper was deservedly in universal discredit : the other was brought to Philadelphia by the *Holker* privateer, Captain Keane, who saw part of the engagement, but whose account contradicted the principal facts in Rivington's. The two fleets having gone to leeward after the battle, no fresh intelligence was received from the *leeward*, or more properly speaking here, in the *windward* islands, so that this gambling was carried to so high a pitch, as to induce the French Ambassador to go in person to the coffee-house to communicate a letter he had received from Martinique, subsequent to the battle ; from which fair conclusions might be drawn *against* the capture ; but this, instead of putting a stop to the gambling, by encouraging the whigs, increased it :—Mr. Bingham and his friends in the secret, indulged them to the utmost extent of their enthusiasm ; and if the policies were all paid, a matter which began to be a subject of discussion when I left Philadelphia, must have gained *prodigious sums*, for no less than from £80,000 to £100,000 sterling were calculated to have been written. It is a singular circumstance, that the first *authentic* account of this great battle, which appeared in America, was copied from the *London Gazette*. Whereas we had at Boston the account of the loss of the *Royal George*, at Spithead, the 16*th day* after the accident, by way of Newfoundland.— *Trans.*

present at the Assembly of the State of Pennsylvania; for the hall, where this sort of parliament meets, is under the same roof with the Congress. I was with M. de la Fayette, the Vicomte de Noailles, the Comte de Damas, M. de Gimat, and all the French, or *Gallo-Americans*, at Philadelphia. We seated ourselves on a bench opposite the Speaker's chair: on his right was the President of the State: the Clerks were placed at a long table before the Speaker. The debates turned on some misconduct, imputed to the Commissioners of the Treasury. The executive council were sent for, and heard. General Mifflin was almost the only speaker; he delivered himself with grace and spirit, but with a marked intention of opposing the President of the State, who is not one of his friends. His manner of expressing himself, his gestures, his deportment, the air and ease of superiority he invariably assumed, perfectly reminded me of those members of the House of Commons who are accustomed to give the tone to others, and to make every thing bend to their opinion. The affair not being terminated in the morning, the Speaker left the chair; the house went into a committee, and adjourned.

The morning was not far spent, and I had enough to employ it; I was expected in three places; by a lover of natural history, by an anatomist, and at the college, or rather university of Philadelphia. I began by the cabinet of natural history. This small and scanty collection, is greatly celebrated in America, where it is unrivalled; it was formed by a painter of Geneva, called *Cimetiere*, a name better suited to a physician, than a painter. This worthy man came to Philadelphia twenty years ago, to take portraits, and has continued there ever since; he lives there still as a bachelor, and a foreigner, a very uncommon instance in America, where men do not long remain without acquiring the titles of husband and citizen. What I saw most curious, in this cabinet, was a large quantity of the vice, or screw, a sort of shell pretty common, within which a very hard stone, like *jade*,* is exactly moulded. It appears clear to me, that these petrefactions are formed by the successive accumulation of lapidific molecules conveyed by the waters, and assimilated by the assistance of fixed air. After fatiguing my legs, and satisfying my eyes, which is always the case in cabinets of natural history, I thought proper to quit the earth for heaven; or, in the vulgar style, I went to the library of the university, to see a very ingenious machine (an Orrery) representing all the celestial motions. I lose no time in de-

---

* See Chamber's *Encyclopedia*—a green sort of precious stone, called in France *la pierre divine,* from its supposed mystic qualities.

claring that I shall not give a description of it : for nothing is
so tiresome as the description of any machine; it is enough
for me to say, that one part of it gives a perfect view, on the
vertical point, of all the motions of the planets in their orbits ;
and that the other, which is designed only to represent that of
the moon, displays, in the clearest manner, her phases, her
nodes, and her different altitudes.   The President of the college,* and Mr. Rittenhouse, the inventor and maker of this
machine, took the pains of explaining to me every particular :
they seemed very happy that I knew English, and astronomy
enough to understand them ; on which I must observe, that the
latter article is more to the shame of the Americans than to
my praise ; the almanack being almost the only book of Astronomy studied at Philadelphia.   Mr. Rittenhouse is of a
German family, as his name announces ; but he is a native of
Philadelphia, and a watch maker by profession.   He is a man
of great simplicity and modesty, and though not a mathematician of the class of the Eulers, and the D'Alemberts, knows
enough of that science to be perfectly acquainted with the motions of the heavenly bodies.   As for his mechanical talents,

---

* The President is Dr. Ewing.   I had the gratification of being present at a public exhibition at the college, at which the Congress, the
President and executive council of the state, General Washington, the
French Minister, and all the strangers of distinction, &c. assisted.   Some
excellent declamations were made in Latin, and in English, by the young
men who were about to leave college, and obtain degrees ; by no
means inferior to those I have heard at Oxford and Cambridge.   Their
compositions in general were elegant, and their elocution easy, dignified, and manly ; but, whatever was the subject, the great cause of liberty and their country never was lost sight of, nor their abhorrence of
the tyranny of Britain.   This language in the mouths of some of these
young men, who were the sons of *tories*, illustrated the remark of the
shrewd and sensible *author of Common Sense*, that whilst the war was
pending, the old prejudiced friends of Britain were dropping off, and
the rising generation, in the course of seven years knew nothing of
that country but as an enemy, nor saw or heard of any thing but her
cruelties and devastation.   To them the independence of America appeared as much the natural and established government of the country,
as that of England does to an Englishman.   " Time and Death, says
he, hard enemies to contend with, fight constantly against the interests
of Britain ; and the bills of mortality, in every part of America are
the thermometers of her decline.   The children in the streets are from
their cradle bred to consider her as their only foe.   They hear of her
cruelties : of their fathers, uncles, and kindred killed ; they see the remains of burnt and destroyed houses, and the common tradition of the
school they go to, tells them *those things were done by the British.*"

it is unnecessary to assign a reason for them; we know that of all others, they are less the result of study, and most generally the gift of nature ; and it is a fact worthy of observation, that, notwithstanding the little connection to be perceived between that particular disposition and the delicacy of our senses, or the perfection of our organs, men are more frequently born mechanics, than painters and musicians. Education, nay, even the rigour of education, frequently makes great artists in the two latter ; but there is no example of its making a mechanical genius.

This morning seemed devoted to the sciences, and my walks were a sort of encyclopedia, for, on quitting the university library, I went to call upon a celebrated anatomist, called Dr. Showell. The following, in a few words, is his history : he was born in England upwards of seventy years ago. After studying medicine and surgery there, he went to France to improve himself under M. Winslow. In 1734, he went to the West-Indies, where he since practised medicine, sometimes at Barbadoes, sometimes at Jamaica ; but is invariably a man of application, and laborious. In the war of 1744, a prize being brought into Barbadoes, with a great deal of wax on board, Mr. Showell took this opportunity to make different anatomical experiments in wax, and he succeeded so well as to carry this art to the highest degree of perfection. On seeing him, one can with difficulty conceive how so much patience and perseverance could consist with his natural vivacity ; for it seems as if the sun of the tropic had preserved in him all the heat of youth; he speaks with fire, and expresses himself as well in French as if he were still in our schools of surgery. In other respects, he is a perfect original : his reigning taste is disputation ; when the English were at Philadelphia he was a whig, and has become a tory since they left it ; he is always sighing after Europe, without resolving to return, and declaiming constantly against the Americans, he still remains among them. His design in coming to the continent, was to recover his health, so as to enable him to cross the seas : this was about the commencement of the war ; and, since that time, he imagines he is not at liberty to go, though no body prevents him. He was to me a greater curiosity than his anatomical preparations, which, however, appeared superior to those of Bologna, but inferior to the preparations of Mademoiselle Bieron ; the wax having always a certain lustre which makes them less like nature.

At the end of this morning's walk I was like a bee, so laden with honey that he can hardly regain his hive. I returned to the Chevalier de la Luzerne's, with my memory well stored, and after taking food for the body as well as mind, I dedicated my evening to society. I was invited to drink tea at Colonel Bland's, that is to say, to attend a sort of assembly pretty much like the *conversazzioni* of Italy; for tea here, is the substitute for the *rinfresco*. Mr. Howley, governor of Georgia, Mr. Izard, Mr. Arthur Lee, (the two last lately arrived from Europe,) M. de la Fayette, M. de Noailles, M. de Damas, &c. were of the party. The scene was decorated by several married and unmarried ladies, among whom, Miss Shippen, daughter of Dr. Shippen, and cousin of Mrs. Arnold, claimed particular distinction. Thus we see that in America the crimes of individuals are not reflected on their family; not only had Dr. Shippen's brother given his daughter to the traitor Arnold, a short time before his desertion, but it is generally believed, that being himself a tory, he had inspired his daughter with the same sentiments, and that the charms of this handsome woman contributed not a little to hasten to criminality a mind corrupted by avarice, before it felt the power of love.*

On our return to the Chevalier de la Luzerne's, we assembled all the French and Gallo-American military, and laid our plan for a very agreeable jaunt, we took next day. The 6th, in the morning, M. de la Fayette, the Vicomte de Noailles, the Comte de Damas, the Chevalier du Plessis Mauduit, Messieurs de Gimat and De Neville, aids-de-camp of M. de la Fayette, M. de Montesquieu, Mr. Lynch, and myself, set out to visit the field of battle of Brandywine, thirty miles from Philadelphia. M. de la Fayette had not seen it, since, at the age of twenty, separating from his wife, his friends, the pleasures of the world, and those of youth, at the distance of three thousand miles, he there shed the first drop of blood he offered to glory, or rather to that noble cause he has invariably supported with the same zeal, but with better fortune. We passed the Schuylkill at the same ferry where Mr. Du Coudray was drowned in 1777. We there discovered the traces of some entrenchments thrown up by the English, after they became masters of Philadelphia; then turning to the left, we rode on fourteen miles to the little town of Chester. It is built at the junction of the creek of that name, with the Delaware, and is a sort of port

---

* Mrs. Arnold is said to be very handsome; but this I know, that her two sisters are charming women, and must have been very dangerous companions for a wavering mind, in the least susceptible of the most powerful of all passions. But an apology for Arnold, on this supposition, is too generous for a mind so thoroughly base and unprincipled as his. With what delicacy could be beloved a woman by that miscreant, who made the mysteries of the nuptial bed the subject of his coarse ribaldry to his companions, the day after his marriage!—*Trans.*

where vessels coming up the river sometimes anchor. The houses, to the number of forty or fifty, are handsome and built of stone or brick.* On leaving Chester, and on the road to Brandywine, we pass the stone bridge where M. de la Fayette, wounded as he was, stopped the fugitives, and made the first dispositions for rallying them behind the creek. The country beyond it has nothing particular, but resembles the west of Pennsylvania, that is to say, is interspersed with woods and cultivated lands. It was too late when we came within reach of the field of battle, and as we could see nothing till next morning, and were too numerous to remain together, it was necessary to separate into two divisions. Messieurs de Gimat, De Mauduit, and my two aids-de-camp, staid with me at an inn, three miles on this side Brandywine; and M. de la Fayette, attended by the other travellers, went farther on to ask quarters at a quaker's called Benjamin Ring, at whose house he lodged with General Washington the night before the battle. I joined him early the next morning, and found him in great friendship with his host, who, quaker as he was, seemed delighted to entertain the marquis. We got on horseback at nine, provided with a plan, executed under the direction of General Howe, and engraved in England; but we got more information from an American major, with whom M. de la Fayette had appointed a place of meeting. This officer was present at the engagement, and his house being on the field of battle, he knew it better than any body.

We must recollect, that in 1777, the English having in vain attempted to cross the Jerseys to get to Philadelphia by land, were obliged to embark, and doubled the capes to reach the bay of Chesapeake, and the mouth of the river Elk. They arrived there the 25th of August, after a passage dreadful by sea, but fortunate in the bay, which they remounted with much less difficulty than they expected. Whilst the sea, the winds, and three hundred vessels were assisting the manœuvres of the enemy's army, Mr. Washington remained some days at Middlebrook, in one of the most embarrassing positions in which the general of an army can be placed. To the north, the troops of Burgoyne, after taking Ticonderoga, were advancing towards Albany; to the south, an English army of fifteen thousand men were embarked, and might either proceed to Chesapeake bay, as they did, penetrate by the Delaware, or go up Hudson's river as far as Crest Point, to form a junction with Burgoyne, and cut off the American army, which from that

---

* Not far from this town, is found an astonishing quantity of *ashestos.—Trans.*

moment would have been for ever separated from the eastern
and northern states. Of all the chances, this was certainly
the most to be dreaded ; accordingly General Washington did
not abandon his position at Middlebrook, till he received certain intelligence that the enemy had doubled Cape May. Let
us figure to ourselves the situation in which a general must find
himself, when obliged to comprehend in his plan of defence,
an immense country, and a vast extent of coast, he is at a loss
to know, within one hundred and fifty miles, where the enemy
is likely to appear; and having no longer any intelligence of
them, either by patroles, or detachments, or even by couriers,
is reduced to the necessity of observing the compass, and of
consulting the winds, before he can form any resolution. As
soon as the movement of the enemy was decided, General
Washington lost no time in marching his army ; I should rather
say his soldiers, for a number of soldiers, however considerable, does not always form an army. His was composed of at
most 12,000 men. It was at the head of these troops, the
greatest part of them new levies, that he traversed in silence
the city of Philadelphia, whilst the Congress were giving him
orders to fight, yet removing their archives and public papers
into the interior parts of the country ; a sinister presage of the
success which must follow their council.

The army passed the Schuylkill, and occupied a first camp
near Wilmington, on the banks of the Delaware. This position had a double object ; for the ships of war, after convoy-
ing General Howe to the river Elk, had fallen down the bay of
the Chesapeake, remounted the Delaware, and seconded by
some troops landed from the fleet, appeared inclined to force
the passages of that river. General Washington, however,
soon perceived that the position he had taken became every
day more dangerous. The English, having finished their de-
barkation, were ready to advance into the country; his flank
was exposed, and he left uncovered, at once, Philadelphia and
the whole county of Lancaster. It was determined, therefore, that the army should repass the creek of Brandywine,
and encamp on the left bank of that river. The position
made choice of, was certainly the best that could be taken to
dispute the passage. The left was very good, and supported
by thick woods extending as far as the junction of the creek
with the Delaware. As it approaches its conflux, this creek
becomes more and more embanked, and difficult to ford : the
heights are equal on the two banks ; but for this reason the
advantage was in favour of him who defended the passage.
A battery of cannon with a good parapet, was pointed towards Chaddsford, and every thing appeared in safety on that
side ; but to the right the ground was so covered, that it was

impossible to judge of the motions of the enemy, and to keep in a line with them, in case they should attempt, as they did, to detach a corps by their left, to pass the river higher up. The only precaution that could be taken was to place *five* or *six brigades** in steps from each other, to watch that manœuvre. General Sullivan had the command of them; he received orders to keep in a line with the enemy, should they march by their left; and on the supposition that they would unite their forces on the side of Chaddsford, he was himself to pass the river, and make a powerful diversion on their flank.

When a general has foreseen every thing, when he has made the best possible dispositions, and his activity, his judgment, and his courage in the action correspond with the wisdom of his measures, has he not already triumphed in the eyes of every impartial judge? and if by any unforeseen accidents, the laurels he has merited drop from his hands, is it not the historian's duty carefully to collect, and replace them on his brow? Let us hope that history will acquit herself of this duty better than us, and let us see how such wise dispositions were disconcerted by the mistakes of some officers, and the inexperience of the troops.

The 11th of September, General Howe occupied the heights on the right of the creek; he there formed part of his troops in line of battle, and prepared some batteries opposite Chaddsford, whilst his light troops were attacking and driving before them a corps of riflemen, who had passed over to the right bank more closely to observe his motions. General Washington seeing the cannonade continue, without any disposition of the enemy to pass the river, concluded they had another object. He was informed that a great part of their army had marched higher up the creek, and were threatening his right; he felt the importance of keeping an attentive eye on all the movements of this corps; but the country was so covered with thickets, that the patroles could discover nothing. It must be observed that General Washington had a very small number of horse, and those he had sent to the right, towards *Dilworth*, to make discoveries on that side. He ordered an officer of whom he had a good opinion, to pass the river, and inform himself accurately of the route Lord Cornwallis was taking; for it was he who commanded this separate corps. The officer returned, and assured him that Cornwallis was marching by his right to join Knyphausen, on the side of Chaddsford. According to this report, the attack seemed to be determined on the left. Another officer was then sent, who reported that Cornwallis had changed his direction, and

---

* General Howe calls them 10.000 men—*Trans.*

that he was rapidly advancing by the road leading to Jefferies Ford, two miles higher than Birmingham church. General Sullivan was immediately ordered to march thither with all the troops of the right. Unfortunately the roads were badly reconnoitred, and not at all open: with great difficulty General Sullivan got through the woods, and when he came out of them to gain a small eminence near Birmingham church, *he found the English columns mounting it on the opposite side*. It was no easy matter to range into order of battle such troops as his; he had neither the time to choose his position, nor to form his line. The English gained the eminence, drove the Americans back on the woods, to the edge of which they pursued them, and they were totally dispersed.*

During the short time this action lasted, Lord Stirling and General Conway, had time to form their brigade on pretty advantageous ground: it was a gentle rising, partly covered by the woods which bounded it, their left was protected by the same woods, and on the right of this rising ground, but a little in the rear, was the Virginia line, who were ranged in line of battle, on a high spot of ground, and on the edge of an open wood. The left column of the enemy, who had not been engaged with Sullivan, formed rapidly, and marched against these troops with as much order as vivacity and courage. The Americans made a very smart fire, which did not check the English, and it was not till the latter were within twenty yards of them, that they gave way, and threw themselves into the woods. Lord Stirling, M. de la Fayette, and General Sullivan himself, after the defeat of his division fought with this body of troops, whose post was the most important, and made the longest resistance. It was here that M. de la Fayette was wounded in his left leg, in rallying the troops who were beginning to stagger. On the right, the Virginia line made some resistance; but the English had gained a height, from whence their artillery took them *en écharpe:* this fire must have been very severe, for most of the trees, bear the mark of bullets or cannon shot. The Virginians in their turn gave way, and the right was then entirely uncovered.

Though this was three miles from Chaddsford, General Knyphausen heard the firing of the artillery, and musketry, and judging that the affair was serious, the confidence he had in

---

* General Howe's account says, "General Washington detached General Sullivan to his right with 10,000 men, who *took a strong position* on the commanding ground above Birmingham church," and then relates the manœuvres to *dislodge* them. There is a material difference in these accounts.—*Trans.*

the English and Hessian troops, made him conclude they were
victorious.   Towards five in the evening, he descended from
the heights in two columns,* one at John's Ford, which turned
the battery of the Americans, and the other lower down at
Chaddsford.   The latter marched straight to the battery and
took it.   General Wayne, whose brigade was in line of battle,
the left on an eminence, and the right drawing towards the
battery, then made that right fall back, and strengthened the
heights, thus forming a sort of change of front.   In a country
where there are neither open columns, nor successive positions
to take, in case of accident, it is difficult to make any disposition for retreat.   The different corps who had been beaten, all
precipitated themselves into Chester road, where they formed
but one column ; artillery, baggage and troops being confusedly mixed together.   At the beginning of the night General
Washington also took this road, and the English, content with
their victory, did not disturb their retreat.

Such is the idea I have formed of the battle of Brandywine,
from what I have from General Washington himself, from M.
de la Fayette, Messieurs de Gimat and De Manduit and from
the Generals Wayne and Sullivan.   I must observe, however,
that there is a disagreement in some particulars ; several persons, for example, pretend that Knyphausen, after passing the
river, continued his march in one column to the battery, and
it is thus marked in the English plan, which gives a false direction to that column ; besides that General Washington, and
General Wayne assured me there were two, and that the left
column turned the battery, which otherwise would not have
been carried.†   It is equally difficult to trace out on the plan,
all the ground on which Cornwallis fought.   The relations on
both sides throw hardly any light upon it ; I was obliged therefore to draw my conclusions from the different narratives, and
to follow none of them implicitly.

---

* Several persons, amongst others some English officers who were
prisoners, whom I have questioned, assured me that Knyphausen's
corps passed the river only in one column at Chaddsford ; and then
separated into two, one of which turned the battery, and the other attacked it in front.

† Howe's account says, there were two divisions, one under Grant,
the other under Knyphausen ; the fourth and fifth regiments turned the
battery.—*Trans.*

CHAPTER VII.

Whilst we were examining the field of battle with the greatest minuteness, our servants went on to Chester to pre-pare dinner and apartments, but we soon followed them, and got there at four o'clock. The road did not appear long to me; for chance having separated M. de la Fayette, M. de Noailles, and myself from the rest of the company, we entered into a very agrèeable conversation, which continued till we got to Chester. I could not help observing to them that after talking of nothing but war for three hours, we had suddenly changed the subject, and got on that of Paris, and all sorts of discussions relative to our private societies. This transition was truly French, but it does not prove that we are less fond of war, than other nations, only that we like our friends better. We were scarcely arrived at Chester, before we saw some state barges or boats coming down the river, which the president had sent to conduct us back to Philadelphia, it being our plan to remount the Delaware next day, in order to examine the fort of Redbank, and fort Mifflin, as well as the other posts which had served for the defence of the river. An officer of the American navy who was come with these barges, to con-duct us, informed us that two vessels were arrived at Philadel-phia in thirty-five days from L'Orient. The hopes of receiving letters, or news from Europe, almost tempted us to relinquish our projects, and set out immediately for Philadelphia; but as the weather was fine, and we should have the tide in our favour next day, which rendered our voyage more easy, we determined to remain at Chester, and M. de la Fayette sent off a man and a horse to Philadelphia, to bring back news, and letters, if there were any. This courier returned before nine; and only brought us a line from the Chevalier de la Luzerne, by which we learnt that these ships had no letters; but that the captains assured him, that Monsieur de Castries was made minister of the marine.

Whilst the courier was going and coming, we had got to the

inn, where dinner and lodgings were prepared.* The exterior
of this house is not very tempting, and several of the company
were preparing to look out elsewhere, but after a minute examination, we found room enough for a dozen masters, as many
servants, and nineteen horses. In addition to our company
we had the major, who met us on the field of battle of Brandywine, and the officer who had brought us the barges. We
had an excellent dinner, and very good wine. The tea which
followed pretty close on dinner succeeded as well; so that all
my fellow-travellers, were in the best humour, and so gay as
never to cease laughing, singing, and dancing during the
whole-evening. The people of the house, who saw nothing in
this company but two General officers, one French, the other
American, accompanied by their families, and not a society of
friends joyous to meet together in another hemisphere, could
not conceive how it was possible to be so gay without being
drunk, and looked upon us as people descended from the
moon. This evening, which was lengthened to eleven o'clock,
terminated well, for we had excellent beds, such as one might
expect to find in a well furnished country house. We rose at
six in the morning, and assembled in the dining-room, where a
good breakfast was prepared for us by candle light. At seven
we embarked, and crossing the Delaware, obliquely a little
higher up, we landed at Billingsport. This is a fort constructed in 1776, to support the left of the first barrier of the chevaux de frise, destined to block the passage of the river. This
post was of no use, for the fortifications having been commenced on too extensive a plan for the number of troops which
could be spared, it was thought proper to abandon it. They
have since been reduced, which is the better, as they are now
removed from some points which commanded the fort. The
present situation of affairs, not drawing the attention of Government to this quarter, the fortifications are rather neglected. All the battery there was, consisted of one pretty good
brass mortar, and five eighteen pounders, (English twenty-
fours) which Major Armstrong, who commands on the river,
and came to receive me, fired on my arrival. When America
has more money, and leisure, she will do well not to neglect
this post, as well as all those for the defence of the river. For
this war once terminated, she will see no more European armies
on the Continent, and all she can have to fear from England,
in case of a rupture with her, will be a few maritime expedi-

---

* Mrs. Witby's inn at Chester, is one of the best on the continent,
and a favourite house for parties of pleasure from Philadelphia.—
Trans.

tions, the sole object of which can be to destroy shipping, to ravage the country, and even to burn the towns within reach of the sea. Unfortunately Billingsport belongs to the state of Jersey, which can reap no advantage from it; and that of Pennsylvania, whose safety it would constitute, has no other means to employ towards fortifying it than its own request, and the recommendations of Congress, which are not always attended to. However this may be, Philadelphia took other precautions for her defence, which depended only on the state of Pennsylvania, and to this advantage is united that of an excellent position, which will soon be made impregnable; I mean Fort Mifflin, whither we went on leaving Billingsport, still ascending the river. The isle on which it is built, and that called Mud-Island, support the right of a second barrier of chevaux de frise, the left of which is defended by the fort of Red Bank ;* but it must be observed that the barrier only blocked the main channel of the river, the only passage by which it was thought that vessels could pass.† Near the right bank is Hog-Island, about two miles long, the surface of which, like that of most of the islands in the Delaware is so low, that at high water, nothing is to be seen but the tops of the reeds with which it is covered. Between this island, and the main land, a small passage remained open, but the Americans were persuaded that there was not water enough for any ship with guns to pass it. At the extremity of this channel, and in remounting it, we leave on the left a marshy ground, so surrounded by creeks, and inlets, as to form a real island, called Province-Island.‡ This post was in the possession of the enemy; who established batteries there, which incommoded those of Fort Mifflin, but not sufficiently to make the Americans abandon it.

The English army were at that time in a singular situation : they had purchased and maintained possession of Philadelphia at the price of two bloody battles ; but they were still shut up between the Schuylkill and the Delaware, having in their

---

* This fort too, is liable to the same difficulties with Billingsport, being on the Jersey side.—*Trans.*

† The person principally employed in sinking the chevaux de frise, and in securing the passage of the river, was one White, who is supposed to have left this channel open designedly, as he afterwards turned out a decided traitor, went over to the enemy, and distinguished himself by every act of hostile virulence against his country.—*Trans.*

‡ This is one of the richest spots of land in America, and being part of the proprietary estate, was parcelled out, and sold in lots by the Assembly of the State.

front Washington's army, which kept them in awe, and behind them several forts occupied by the Americans, which shut the passage of the Delaware. A large city, however, and a whole army must have subsistence; it became necessary therefore to open the communication by sea, and to secure the navigation of the river. When one recollects the innumerable obstacles the English had to surmount in the present war, it is difficult to assign the cause of their successes; but if we turn our eyes on all the unforeseen events which have deceived the expectation of the Americans, and frustrated their best concerted measures, one cannot but be persuaded that they were devoted to destruction, and that the alliance with France alone proved the means of their preservation. In this voyage, in particular, I saw fresh proofs of it every instant. When the place was pointed out to me where the *Augusta*, of sixty-four guns, took fire, and blew up in attempting to force the chevaux de frise, and farther, on the remains of the *Merlin*, of two and twenty, which ran ashore in the same action, and was burnt by the English themselves, whilst the Hessians were vainly sacrificing five or six hundred men before the fort of Redbank, I figured to myself the English army starved in Philadelphia, retreating with disgrace and difficulty through the Jerseys, and my imagination already enjoyed the triumph of America. But of a sudden the scene changed, and I saw nothing but the fatality which collected towards the channel of Hog-Island the waters long confined by the chevaux de frise, and recollected with pain, that on the 15th of November, three weeks after the fruitless attempts I have mentioned, the English succeeded in passing over the bar of this channel, the Vigilant, and another small ship of war; that they thus got up the river, and turned Fort Mifflin, the batteries of which they took from behind, and left the Americans no other resource but to abandon the defence of the chevaux de frise in all parts, and make a precipitate retreat by the left shore of the Delaware.

Taught by sad experience, the Americans have provided in future against the misfortunes which cost them so dear. I saw them with pleasure extending the fortifications of Mifflin's-Island, so as to enclose the fort on every side, which will be surrounded also by the Delaware in place of a ditch; and as the garrison will have a safe asylum in souterrains, bomb-proof, this fort may henceforth be deemed impregnable. The plan of these works was given by M. du Portail; Major Armstrong showed me them upon the spot, and I found them correspond perfectly with the just reputation of their author.

We now had to visit Redbank; for which purpose we had again to cross the Delaware, which in this place is a mile wide.

The gentleman who was to do the honour there, was impatient
to arrive. We had amused ourselves by telling him that the
morning being far spent, and the tide about to turn, we should
be obliged to omit Redbank, and return directly to Philadelphia. This conductor, whom we diverted ourselves in torment-
ing, was M. du Plessis Mauduit, who in the double capacity of
engineer, and officer of artillery, had the charge of arranging
and defending this post, under the orders of Colonel Green.
On landing from our boat, he proposed conducting us to a
Quaker's, whose house is half a musket shot from the fort, or
rather the ruins of the fort ; for it is now destroyed, and there
are scarcely any *reliefs* of it remaining. " This man, said M.
de Mauduit, is a little of a tory ; I was obliged to knock down
his barn, and fell his fruit trees ; but he will be glad to see M.
de la Fayette, and will receive us well." We took him at his
word, but never was expectation more completely deceived.
We found our Quaker seated in the chimney corner, busied in
cleaning herbs : he recollected M. de Mauduit, who named M.
de la Fayette, and me, to him ; but he did not deign to lift his
eyes, nor to answer any of our introducer's discourse, which at
first was complimentary, and at length jocose.   Except *Dido's*
silence, I know nothing more severe, but we had no difficulty in
accommodating ourselves to this bad reception, and made our
way to the fort. We had not gone a hundred yards before we
came to a small elevation, on which a stone was vertically placed, with this short epitaph : *here lies buried Colonel Donop.*
M. de Mauduit could not refrain from expressing his regret
for this brave man, who died in his arms two days after the action ; he assured us that we could not make a step without
treading on the remains of some Hessians ; for near three hundred were buried in the front of the ditch.
    The fort of Redbank was designed, as I have said above, to
support the left of the chevaux de frise. The bank of the Delaware at this place is steep; but even this steepness allowed
the enemy to approach the fort, under cover, and without being exposed to the fire of the batteries. To remedy this inconvenience, several gallies armed with cannon, and destined to
defend the chevaux de frise, were posted the whole length of
the escarpement, and took it in reverse. The Americans, little
practised in the art of fortifications, and always disposed to
take works beyond their strength, had made those of Redbank
too extensive. When M. de Mauduit obtained permission to
be sent thither with Colonel Green, he immediately set about
reducing the fortifications, by intersecting them from east to
west, which transformed them into a sort of large redoubt nearly of a pentagonal form. A good earthen rampart, raised to
the height of the cordon, a fossé, and an abattis in front of the

fossé, constituted the whole strength of this post, in which were placed *three hundred men,*[*] and fourteen pieces of cannon. The 22d of October, in the morning, they received intelligence that a detachment of two thousand five hundred Hessians were advancing; who were soon after perceived on the edge of a wood to the north of Redbank, nearly within cannon shot. Preparations were making for the defence, when a Hessian officer advanced, preceded by a drum ; he was suffered to approach, but his harangue was so insolent that it only served to irritate the garrison, and inspire them with more resolution. " *The King of England,* said he, *orders his rebellious subjects to lay down their arms, and they are warned, that if they stand the battle, no quarters whatever will be given.*" The answer was, that they accepted the challenge, and that there should be no quarter on either side. At four o'clock in the afternoon, the Hessians made a very brisk fire from a battery of cannon, and soon after they opened, and marched to the first entrenchment, from which, finding it abandoned, but not destroyed, they *imagined* they had driven the Americans. They then shouted *victoria,* waved their hats in the air, and advanced towards the redoubt. The same drummer, who a few hours before had come to summon the garrison, and had appeared as insolent as his officer, was at their head beating the march ; both he, and that officer were knocked on the head by the first fire. The Hessians, however, still kept advancing within the first entrenchment, leaving the river on their right : they had already reached the abattis, and were endeavouring to tear up, or cut away the branches, when they were overwhelmed with a shower of musket shot, which took them in front, and in flank ; for as chance would have it, a part of the courtine of the old entrenchment, which had not been destroyed, formed a projection at this very part of the intersection. M. de Mauduit had contrived to form it into a sort of *caponiere,* (or trench with loop-holes) into which he threw some men, who flanked the enemy's left, and fired on them at close shot. Officers were seen every moment rallying their men, marching back to the abattis, and falling amidst the branches they were endeavouring to cut. Colonel Donop was particularly distinguished by the marks of the order he wore, by his handsome figure, and by his courage ; he was also seen to fall like the rest. The Hessians, repulsed by the fire of the redoubt, attempted to secure themselves from it by attacking on the side of the escarpement, but the fire from the gallies sent them back with a great loss of

---

[*] General Howe calls them *about* 800 men.—*Trans.*

men.   At length they relinquished the attack, and regained the
wood in disorder.

    While this was passing on the north side, another column
made an attack on the south, and, more fortunate than the
other, passed the abattis, traversed the fosse, and mounted the
berm; but they were stopped by the fraises, and M. de Mauduit
running to this post as soon as he saw the first assailants give
way, the others were obliged to follow their example.   They
still did not dare however to stir out of the fort, fearing a surprise; but M. de Mauduit wishing to replace some palisades
which had been torn up; he sallied out with a few men, and
was surprised to find about twenty Hessians standing on the
berm, and stuck up against the shelving of the parapet.   These
soldiers who had been bold enough to advance thus far, sensible that there was more risk in returning, and not thinking
proper to expose themselves, were taken and brought into the
fort.   M. de Mauduit, after fixing the palisades, employed himself in repairing the abattis; he again sallied out with a detachment, and it was then he beheld the deplorable spectacle
of the dead and dying, heaped one upon another.   A voice
arose from amidst these carcases, and said in English,
"whoever you are, draw me hence."   It was the voice of Colonel Donop: M. de Mauduit made the soldiers lift him up, and
carry him into the fort, where he was soon known.   He had
his hip broken; but whether they did not consider his wound
as mortal, or that they were heated by the battle, and still irritated at the menaces thrown out against them a few hours before, the Americans could not help saying, aloud: "Well! is it
determined to give no quarter?"   "I am in your hands," replied the colonel, "you may revenge yourselves."   M. de
Mauduit had no difficulty in imposing silence, and employed
himself only in taking care of the wounded officer.   The latter,
perceiving he spoke bad English, said to him: "you appear to
me a foreigner, Sir, who are you?"   "A French officer," replied
the other.   "*Je suis content*," said Donop, making use of our
language, "*je meurs entre les mains de l'honneur meme.*" I am content; I die in the hands of honour itself.   The next day he
was removed to the quaker's house, where he lived three days,
during which he conversed frequently with M. de Mauduit.   He
told him that he had been long in friendship with M. de Saint
Germain, that he wished in dying to recommend to him his
vanquisher, and benefactor.   He asked for paper, and wrote
a letter, which he delivered to M. de Mauduit, requiring of him,
as the last favour, to acquaint him when he was about to die:
the latter was soon under the necessity of acquitting himself
of this sad duty: "it is finishing a noble career early," said the
colonel: "but I die the victim of my ambition, and of the ava-

rice of my sovereign." Fifteen wounded officers were found, like him, upon the field of battle ; M. de Mauduit had the satisfaction to conduct them himself to Philadelphia, where he was very well received by General Howe. By singular accident, it happened that the English that very day received indirect intelligence of the capitulation of Burgoyne, of which he knew more than they. They pretended to give no credit to it: " you who are a Frenchman," said they, " speak freely, do you think it possible ?" " I know," replied he, " that the fact is so ; explain it as you think proper."

Perhaps I have dwelt too long on this event; but I shall not have to apologize to those who will partake of the pleasing satisfaction I experience, in fixing my eyes upon the triumphs of America, and in discovering my countrymen among those who have reaped her laurels. At present I hasten my return to Philadelphia, where, on my arrival, I had only time to dress myself to attend the Chevalier de la Luzerne, and the companions of my journey, to dinner at Mr. Huntington's, the president of Congress. Mrs. Huntington, a good looking, lusty woman, but not young, did the honours of the table, that is to say, helped every body without saying a word. I did not remain long after dinner, having a little snug rendezvous, which I was not inclined to miss. The reader will think it time for me to throw some variety into this journal ; but I am obliged to confess that this rendezvous was with Mr. Samuel Adams. We had promised ourselves at our last interview to set an evening apart for a tranquil tete-à-tete, and this was the day appointed. Our conversation commenced with a topic of which he might have spared himself the discussion ; the justice of the cause he was engaged in. I am clearly of opinion that the parliament of England had no right to tax America without her consent, but I am more clearly convinced that when a whole people say *we will be free*, it is difficult to demonstrate they are in the wrong. Be that as it may, Mr. Adams very satisfactorily proved to me, that New-England, comprehending the states of Massachusetts, New-Hampshire, Connecticut, and Rhode-Island, were not peopled with any view to commerce and aggrandizement, but wholly by individuals who fled from persecution, and sought an asylum at the extremity of the world, where they might be free to live, and follow their opinions; that it was of their own accord, that those new colonists put themselves under the protection of England; that the mutual relationship, springing from this connexion, was expressed in their charters, and that the right of imposing, or exacting a revenue of any kind was not comprised in them.

From this subject we passed to a more interesting one ; the form of government which should be given to each state ; for it is only on account of the future, that it is necessary to take a retrospect of the past. The revolution has taken place, and the republic is beginning ; it is an infant newly born, the question is how to nourish, and rear it to maturity. I expressed to Mr. Adams some anxiety for the foundations on which the new constitutions are formed, and particularly that of Massachusetts. Every citizen, said I, every man who pays taxes, has a right to vote in the election of representatives, who form the legislative body, and who may be called the sovereign power. All this is very well for the present moment, because every citizen is pretty equally at his ease, or may be so in a short time, but the success of commerce, and even of agriculture, will introduce riches among you, and riches will produce inequality of fortunes, and of property. Now, wherever this inequality exists, the real force will invariably be on the side of property ; so that if the influence in government be not proportioned to that property, there will always be a contrariety, a combat between the form of government, and its natural tendency, the right will be on one side; and the power on the other ; the balance then only can exist between the two equally dangerous extremes, of aristocracy and anarchy. Besides, the ideal worth of men must ever be comparative : an individual without property is a discontented citizen, when the state is poor ; place a rich man near him, he dwindles into a clown. What will result then, one day, from vesting the right of election in this class of citizens ? The source of civil broils, or corruption, perhaps both at the same time. The following was pretty nearly the answer of Mr. Adams. I am very sensible of the force of your objections ; we are not what we should be, we should labour rather for the future, than for the present moment. I build a country house, and have infant children ; I ought doubtless to construct their apartments with an eye to the time in which they shall be grown up and married : but we have not neglected this precaution. In the first place, I must inform you, that this new constitution was proposed and agreed to in the most legitimate manner of which there is any example since the days of Lycurgus. A committee chosen from the members of the legislative body, then existing, and which might be considered as a provisional government, was named to prepare a new code of laws. As soon as it was prepared, each county or district was required to name a committee to examine this plan : it was recommended to them to send it back at the expiration of a certain time, with their observations. These observations having been discussed by the committee, and the necessary alterations made, the plan was sent back to each particular committee. When they had all approved it, they received orders to communicate it to the people at large, and to demand their suffrages. If two-thirds of the voters approved it, it was to have the force of law, and be regarded as the work of the people themselves; of two and twenty thousand suffrages, a much greater proportion than two-thirds was in favour of the new constitution. Now these were the principles on which it was established: a state is never free but when each citizen is bound by no law whatever that he has not approved of, either by himself, or by his representatives; but to represent another man, it is necessary to have been elected by him; every citizen therefore should have a part in elections. On the other hand, it would be in vain for the people to possess the right of electing representatives, were they restrained in the choice of them to a particular class; it is necessary therefore not to require too much property as a qualification for the *representative of the people*. Accordingly the house of representatives which form the legislative body, and the true *sovereign*, are the people themselves represented by their delegates. Thus far the government is purely democratical; but it is the permanent and enlightened will of the people which should constitute law, and not the passions and sallies to which they are too subject. It is necessary to moderate their first emotions, and bring them to the test of inquiry and reflection. This is the important business entrusted with the Governor and Senate, who represent with us the negative power, vested in England in the upper-house, and even in the crown, with this difference only, that in our new constitution the senate has a right to reject a law, and the governor to suspend the promulgation, and return it for a reconsideration; but these forms complied with, if, after this fresh examination, the people persist in their resolution, and there is then, not as before, a mere majority, but two thirds of the suffrages in favour of the law, the governor and senate are compelled to give it their sanction. Thus this power moderates, without destroying the authority of the people, and such is the organization of our republic, as to prevent the springs from breaking by too rapid a movement, without ever stopping them entirely. Now, it is here we have given all its weight to property. A man must have a pretty considerable property to vote for a member of the senate; he must have a more considerable one to be himself eligible. Thus the democracy is pure and entire in the assembly, which represents the *sovereign*; and the aristocracy, or, if you will, the *optimacy*, is to be found only in the moderating power, where it is the more necessary, as men never watch more carefully over the state than when they have a great interest in its destiny. As to the power of commanding armies, it ought neither to be vested in a great, nor even in a small number of men: the governor alone can employ the forces by sea and land according to the necessity; but the land forces will consist only in the militia, which, as it is composed of the people themselves, can never act against the people.*

Such was the idea Mr. Adams gave me of his own work,† for it is he who had the greatest part in the formation of the new laws. It is said, however, that before his credit was employed to get them accepted, it was necessary to combat his private opinion, and to make him abandon systems in which he loved to stray, for less sublime, but more practicable projects. This citizen, otherwise so respectable, has been frequently reproached with consulting his library, rather than the present circumstances, and of always beginning by the Greeks and Romans, to get at the whigs and tories; if this be true, I shall only say that study has also its inconveniences, but not such as are important, since Mr. Samuel Adams, heretofore the enemy of regular troops, and the most extravagant partisan of the democracy, at present employs all his influence to maintain an army, and to establish a mixed government. Be that as it may, I departed well content with this conversation, which was only interrupted by a glass of Madeira, a dish of tea, and an old American General, now a member of Congress, who lodges with Mr. Adams.

I knew that there was a ball at the Chevalier de la Luzerne's, which made me less in a hurry to return thither : it was, however, a very agreeable assembly ; for it was given to a private society, on the occasion of a marriage. There were near twenty women, twelve or fourteen of whom were dancers ; each of them having her partner, as is the custom in America. Dancing is said to be at once the emblem of gaiety and of love ; here it seems to be the emblem of legislation, and of marriage ; of legislation, inasmuch as places are marked out, the country dances named, and every proceeding provided for, calculated and submitted to regulation ; of marriage, as it furnishes each

---

* As there appears to be some little inaccuracy in this account of the conversation, the reader is referred to the *Constitution of the Massachusetts*, as republished in England with those of the other states, where he will see the respective privileges and powers of the *Senate* and *Governor* and *Council* clearly discriminated, which are here confounded. The Translator has endeavoured to free the original from its obscurity, *the Senate* being there wholly overlooked, and its duties blended with those of the Governor and Council ; and materially to preserve the drift of Mr. Adams' argument.—*Trans.*

† I have some reason to think that the admirable form of government for Massachusetts Bay, is *not* the work of Mr. Samuel Adams, but of Mr. *John Adams*, the present Minister Plenipotentiary from the United States, in England.—*Trans.*

lady with a partner, with whom she dances the whole evening, without being allowed to take another.   It is true that every severe law requires mitigation, and that it often happens, that a young lady after dancing the two or three first dances with her partner, may make a fresh choice, or accept of the invitation she has received; but still the comparison holds good, for it is a marriage in the *European fashion.*   Strangers have generally the privilege of being complimented with the handsomest women.   The Comte de Darnes, had Mrs. Bingham for his partner, and the Vicomte de Noailles, Miss Shippen.   Both of them, like true philosophers, testified a great respect for the manners of the country, by not quitting their handsome partners the whole evening; in other respects they were the admiration of all the assembly, from the grace and nobleness with which they danced; I may even assert, to the honour of my country, that they surpassed a Chief-Justice of Carolina (Mr. Pendleton) and two members of Congress, one of whom (Mr. Duane) passed however for being by 10 per cent. more lively than all the other dancers.   The ball was suspended, towards midnight, by a supper, served in the manner of coffee, on several different tables.   On passing into the dining-room, the Chevalier de la Luzerne presented his hand to Mrs. Morris, and gave her the precedence, an honour pretty generally bestowed on her, as she is the richest woman in the city, and all ranks here being equal, men follow their natural bent, by giving the preference to riches.   The ball continued till two in the morning, as I learnt the next morning on rising, for I had seen too many attacks and battles the day before not to have learnt to make a timely retreat.

Our young folks standing in need of repose after their journey and exercise of the evening, did not appear at breakfast.   In their stead, we had an old quaker of the name of Benezet, whose diminutive figure, and humble and scanty physiognomy, formed a perfect contrast to Mr. Pendleton.   This Mr. Benezet may rather be regarded as the model, than as a specimen of the sect of quakers: wholly occupied with the welfare of mankind, his charity and generosity made him be held in great consideration in happier times, when the virtues alone sufficed to render the citizen illustrious.   At present the noise of arms deafens the ears against the sighs of charity, and the amor patriæ has prevailed over the love of humanity.   Benezet, however, still exercises his benevolence: he came to get some information respecting the new methods invented in France of restoring drowned persons to life.   I promised not only to send them to him from Newport, but to transmit to him such a box, with the necessaries, as our government has distributed in the sea-port towns.   Confidence being established between us, we fell on the topic of the miseries of war. " Friend, says he to me, I know thou art a man of letters, and a member of the French Academy : the men of letters have written a great many good things of late ; they have attacked errors and prejudices, and, above all, intolerance; will they not endeavour too, to disgust men with the horrors of war, and to make them live together like friends and brethren ?" " Thou art not deceived, friend, replied I, when thou buildest some hope on the progress of enlightened philosophy. Many active hands are labouring at the grand edifice of public happiness ; but vainly will they employ themselves in finishing some parts of it, as long as there is a deficiency at the base, and that base, thou hast said it, is universal peace. As for intolerance and persecution, it is true that these two enemies of the human race, are not bound by strong enough chains ; but I will whisper a word in thy ear, of which thou wilt not perhaps feel all the force, though thou art well acquainted with the French ; *they are out of fashion;* I should even believe them to be on the point of annihilation, but for some little circumstances thou art not informed of; which are, *that they who attack them are now and then imprisoned, and Abbies of a hundred thousand livres a year bestowed on such as favour them."* " A hundred thousand livres a year ! cried Benezet, there is wherewithal to build hospitals and establish manufactures ; this doubtless is the use they make of their riches." " No, friend, replied I, persecution must be kept in pay ; though it must be confessed that it is but indifferently paid, for the most splendid of these persecutors content themselves with giving a pension of ten or twelve hundred livres to a few satirical poets, or journalists, enemies of letters, whose works are greatly read, but little sold."—" Friend, says the quaker, this persecution is a strange thing : I can hardly believe what has happened to myself. My father was a Frenchman, and I am a native of thy country. It is now sixty years, since he was obliged to seek an asylum in England, taking with him his children, the only treasure he could save in his misfortunes. Justice, or what is so called in thy country, ordered him to be hung in effigy, for explaining the gospel differently from thy priests. My father was not much better pleased with those of England; wishing to get out of the way of all hierarchy, he came and settled in this country, where I led a happy life until this war broke out. I have long forgot all the persecutions my family underwent. I love thy nation, because it is mild and sensible, and as for thee, friend, I know that thou servest humanity as much as in thy power. When thou shalt get to Europe, engage thy brethren to second thee, and, in the mean time, permit me to place under thy protection our brethren of Rhode-Island." He then recommended to me specifically the quakers living in that state, and who are pretty numerous ; after which he took leave, desiring my permission to send me some pamphlets, *in his way*, which were principally apologies for his sect. I assured him I would read them with great pleasure, and he did not fail to send them the next morning.

Of whatever sect a man may be who is inflamed with an ardent love of humanity, he is undoubtedly a respectable being ; but I must confess that it is difficult to bestow upon this sect in general, that esteem which cannot be refused to some individuals. The law observed by many of them, of saying neither *you*, nor *sir*, is far from giving them a tone of simplicity and candour. I know not whether it be to compensate for that sort of rusticity, that they in general assume a smooth and wheedling tone, which is altogether jesuitical. Nor does their conduct belie this resemblance : concealing their indifference for the public welfare under the cloak of religion, they are sparing of blood, it is true, especially of their own people ;* but they trick both parties out of their money, and that

---

* In confirmation of this remark, I cannot avoid referring to a circumstance which made a considerable noise at the time, and has been grossly perverted to the discredit of American humanity. Every reader attentive to the events of the war in that country, must recollect the execution of Carlisle and Roberts, two considerable quakers, after the evacuation of Philadelphia by General Clinton ; the barbarity of putting to death two members of a sect so peaceable and inoffensive, who *had not borne arms*, and whose principles forbid an active opposition to *any* form of government, was much enlarged upon. In justice to America, and for the benefit of future historians, I shall give the fact, the truth of which will bear inquiry, as I had it from men of every party and description in that city, and leave the decision to every impartial man. The quakers in America, I speak generally, had long belied their principles, and covertly and openly done every thing in their power to thwart the measures adopted by a vast majority of their countrymen, then in possession of the government ; their secret intrigues and open defiance were long overlooked and borne with, until danger became so critical as to demand some precautions for the common safety. A few of the most *active* spirits amongst these pacific and *passive* sectaries were arrested, and sent from the immediate scene of action into Virginia, where they suffered only a temporary restraint from mischief. Carlisle and Roberts, though well known for a malignant hatred to the cause of America, unfortunately for them, escaping this temporary exile, continued their clandestine practices until General Howe got possession of the city, when they no longer set any bounds to their inveteracy. They were both employed by the general, or his honest and grateful agent Mr. Galloway, in the administration of the police, or in other words, they undertook. Carlisle in

without either shame or decency. It is a received maxim in trade to beware of them, and this opinion, which is well founded, will become still more necessary. In fact, nothing can be worse than enthusiasm in its downfall ; for what can be its substitute, but hypocrisy ? That monster so well known in Europe, finds but too easy an access to all religions ; he found none, however, in a company of young ladies, who were invited, as well as myself, to drink tea with Mrs. Cunningham. They were well dressed, seemed desirous of pleasing, and it is fair to conclude, that their private sentiments were in unison with their appearance. The mistress of the house is amiable, and her conversation graceful and interesting. This assembly recalled to my mind in every respect, those of Holland, and Geneva, where one meets with gaiety without indecency, and the wish to please without coquetry.

---

particular, to discriminate between the loyalists and the friends to America. Carlisle granted permissions to pass the lines, watched at the gates, to point out obnoxious persons coming in from the country, who were frequently committed to prison on his bare suggestion, and exercised, in short, the office of sub-inquisitor to Mr. Joseph Galloway. Nor was this the only method by which they manifested the peaceable principles of their sect. General Howe having received information of a party of militia lying in the woods, in the county of Bucks, at sixteen miles distance, under General Lacy, despatched Lieutenant-Colonel Abercrombie with a considerable detachment by the Frankfort road to attack them ; and one or both of these harmless quakers who would not *bear arms* for the wealth of Britain, conscientiously undertook to conduct this man of blood to a successful surprise and massacre of their own countrymen. These, and a variety of other facts being proved against them, after the evacuation of the town, where they had the *presumption* to remain, and there being an evident necessity for making an example of these most dangerous of all enemies, lenity would have been as ill-timed as unjust to the suffering citizens. Such, I am sorry to say it, was the undoubted conduct of too many of this once respectable body, during the war, a conduct, which must not only be condemned by every honourable and feeling mind, but I may venture to say, is wholly repugnant to the principles of a Lettsom, a Fothergill, a Barclay, or a William Penn ; for, it may be pronounced with no intolerant spirit, that in cases of critical emergency, no society can endure such members. In opposition, however, to newspaper reports, and their cries of persecution, I can myself bear testimony to the unpunished license these quietests gave their tongues in the very seat of Congress, and in defiance of the assembly of the state, and to their ostentatious display of the portraits of the king and queen of England, which, however, there is every reason to believe, was more the result of obstinacy, and the spirit of contradiction, than of loyalty or reason, in this selfish set of people.— *Trans.*

On Sunday the 10th I had resolved to make a circuit through the churches, and different places of worship. Unluckily the different sects, who agree in neither point, take the same hour to assemble the faithful, so that in the morning I was only able to visit the quaker's meeting, and in the afternoon the church of England. The hall the quakers meet in is square; there are, on every side, and parallel with the walls, benches and desks, by which means they are placed opposite to each other, without either altar or pulpit to attract the attention. As soon as they are assembled, one of the more elderly makes an extempore prayer, of whatever comes uppermost in his mind; silence is then observed until some man or woman feels inspired, and rises to speak. Travellers must be taken at their word, however extraordinary their motives. Like Ariosto, I shall recount prodigies, *diro maraviglia;* but it is a fact that I arrived at the moment a woman was done holding forth; she was followed by a man who talked a great deal of nonsense about internal grace, the illumination of the spirit, and the other dogmas of his sect, which he bandied about, but took special care not to explain them; and at length finished his discourse to the great content of the brethren, and the sisterhood, who had all of them a very inattentive and listless air. After seven or eight minutes silence, an old man went on his knees, dealt us out a very unmeaning prayer, and dismissed the audience.*

---

* Mention has been frequently made in the public prints of the new sect of *shakers* in Massachusetts Bay, who carry their frantic orgies to still more ridiculous and licentious excesses than the pristine quakers, with George Fox at their head; but I have seen no notice taken of another, which sprung up at Rhode-Island about the year 1780. A very comely *young woman* is, or pretends to be, impressed with the belief that she is in her person *the saviour of the world* revived, and travels from place to place, attended by twelve young men, whom she calls *her apostles;* who, if the general assertion be credited, have literally followed the precept of "making eunuchs of themselves for Christ's sake." General Gates told me he heard her preach at Rhode-Island, and I made an attempt to hear her at Philadelphia in October 1782, but the crowd was so great, and, what is very uncommon in America, so turbulent, that it was impossible to get near the place of worship. Two of her apostles came to the house I boarded in, to obtain lodgings for her, and some of the brethren; by which means I had an opportunity of seeing a specimen of them, but they would enter into no conversation; they were tall, handsome young men, the youngest not above nineteen, with large round flapped hats, and long flowing strait locks, with a sort of melancholy wildness in their countenances, and an effeminate, dejected air, which seemed to justify the truth of what I believe literally to be their unfortunate situation.—*Trans.*

On quitting this melancholy, homespun assembly, the service of the English church appeared to me a sort of *opera*, as well for the music as the decorations : a handsome pulpit placed before a handsome organ ; a handsome minister in that pulpit, reading, speaking, and singing with a grace entirely theatrical, a number of young women answering melodiously from the pit and boxes, (for the two side galleries form a sort of boxes) a soft and agreeable vocal music, with excellent sonatas, played alternately on the organ; all this, compared to the quakers, the anabaptists, the presbyterians, &c. appeared to me rather like a little paradise itself, than as the road to it. If however we consider the different sects, whether rigid, or frivolous, but all imperious, all exclusive, we think we see men reading in the great book of nature, like Montauciel at his lesson, when, instead of *vous etes un blanc bec*, he persists in repeating *trompette blessé*. It is a million to one that a man should hit upon a line of writing without knowing how to spell his letters ; but should he come to ask your assistance, beware how you meddle with him ; it is better to leave him in his error than to cut throats with him.*

I shall only mention my dinner this day at Mrs. Powell's, to say that it was excellent and agreeable in every respect. The conversation carried us so far into the evening, that it was near eleven when I returned home.

---

* For this allusion the reader is referred to the humorous prison scene, between *Montauciel* and the *Deserter*, in the *comic opera* of that name. Montauciel is the *Skirmish* of the English theatre, in their copy from the French.—*Trans.*

CHAPTER VIII.

M. DE LA FAYETTE had made a party with the Vicomte de Noailles and the Comte de Damas, to go the next morning, first to Germantown (which the two latter had not yet seen) and from thence to the old camp at Whitemarsh. Though I had already viewed the former, I had no objection to going over it a second time, besides that I was curious to see the complete Whitemarsh. It is that which was occupied by General Washington after the unsuccessful attempt of the 7th of October. As this was a bold position which the English never dared to attack, it is very celebrated in the American army, where they assert that they had *no other entrenchment than two redoubts.* The fact is, that the position is excellent, and does great honour to General Washington, who could discover it, as if by instinct, through those woods with which the country was then covered; but it is no less true, that General Howe had every reason for not attacking it, and, among others, for the following : descending from the heights of Germantown, there are very thick woods; on coming out of them, to the west, is a pretty high hill, the foot of which is watered by a rivulet, with steep banks, which turns towards the north and protects the right of the camp. Six pieces of cannon were placed on this eminence, with four hundred men, who formed an advanced *pion.* It is called Chestnut-Hill, from a little church of that name, situated on its summit; behind this eminence, and behind the woods which stretch from east to west, the ground rises considerably, and forms two hills with a gentle declivity, which commands Chestnut church; here the army was encamped. These hills are only separated by a small bottom; each summit was fortified with a redoubt, and the slope of it defended by an abattis. The hill on the left was still farther protected by a rivulet, which might be increased at pleasure, as it ran behind the camp, and it was easy to make the dams necessary for raising the waters. The front of this position, it is true, is covered with wood; but these woods terminate at three hundred yards from the line formed abreast; an enemy therefore must have come out of them uncovered, and how get through a wood where there is no road, and which was filled with militia and *riflemen*? I.

pointed out the more minutely all the advantages of this position, that I might amuse myself in exaggerating them to M.
de la Fayette, to convince him that he was a Gascon as well
as the rest of them. He owned to me that the camp was a
good one, and that if the English had given them room for
pleasantry, it was only by inserting in their relations that the
rebels were so well *entrenched* that it was impossible to attack
them. But we were unanimous in our conclusion, that the
more respectable this position was, the more honour it did to
General Washington, who had divined, rather than discovered
it. This was really, an eagle's-eye view, for it seems as if he
must have hovered above the trees to examine the ground concealed by them.*

Having taken our view, we returned briskly to the Chevalier
de la Luzerne's, where dinner came very apropos, after being
eight hours on horseback, and riding six and thirty miles. In
the afternoon we drank tea with Miss Shippen. This was the
first time, since my arrival in America, that I had seen music
introduced into society, and mix with its amusements. Miss
Rutledge† played on the harpsichord, and played very well.
Miss Shippen sung with timidity, but with a pretty voice.
Mr. Ottaw, Secretary to M. de la Luzerne, sent for his harp,‡
he accompanied Miss Shippen, and played several pieces.
Music naturally leads to dancing : the Vicomte de Noailles,
took down a violin, which was mounted with harp strings, and
he made the young ladies dance, while their mothers and
other grave personages chatted in another room. When music, and the fine arts come to prosper at Philadelphia ; when
society once becomes easy and gay there, and they learn to
accept of pleasure when it presents itself, without a formal
invitation, then may foreigners enjoy all the advantages peculiar to their manners and government, without envying any
thing in Europe.§

---

* See General Howe's account of his attempt upon this camp.—
Trans.

† Miss Rutledge is since married to M. de Marbois, who is at present Secretary to M. de la Luzerne, in his government of St. Domingo.—*Trans.*

‡ He is now Consul General, and Chargé des Affaires at Philadelphia in the absence of the Chevalier de la Luzerne.—The Chevalier
does not return to America, being appointed to the government of St.
Domingo, and no other minister is yet named.—*Trans.*

§ It is very certain that any person educated in Europe, and accustomed to the luxury of music and the fine arts, and to their enjoyment
in the two capitals of France and England, must find a great void in

The 12th, in the morning, a new cavalcade, and a new reconnoitring party. M. de la Fayette was to do the honours of this. The just interest he inspires, has given still more celebrity to an event, of itself singular enough. The alliance with France being already public in June 1778, it seemed probable that the English would not delay the evacuation of Philadelphia. In this state of things, though it was General Washington's business to risk nothing, it was important nevertheless to watch the motions of the enemy. M. de la Fayette received orders to march from Valley Forge, with two thousand infantry, fifty dragoons, and as many savages, to pass the Schuylkill, and take post on a height called Barrenhill, about twelve miles distant from Philadelphia. The position was critical, he might be attacked, or turned, by three different roads; but M. de la Fayette guarded the most direct of the three; a Brigadier-General of militia, named Potter, had orders to watch the second, and patroles kept an eye upon the third, which was the most circuitous. Though these precautions seemed sufficient at first sight, they must not have been deemed so by General Howe; for he thought he had now fairly caught *the Marquis*, and even carried his gasconade so far as to invite ladies to meet him at supper the next day, and while the principal part of the officers were at the play,* he put in movement the main body of his forces, which he marched in three columns. The first, commanded by General Howe in person, took the direct road to Barrenhill, passing by Schuylkill Falls, and keeping along the river; the second, led by General Gray, kept the high road of Germantown, and was to

---

these particulars in America. This the translator experienced during his residence in that country, and felt the contrast with greater force on his return to Europe. After a long absence, in which he heard scarcely any other music than church hymns, the cannon, and the drum; or viewing any paintings but the little sketches of *Cimetiere*, or the portraits of *Peele*, of Philadelphia: on his arrival at Bordeaux after the peace, the common orchestra at the theatre afforded him more exquisite delight than he had ever felt from one of *Hayden's* best symphonies at Bach's, or than he should now feel perhaps at the Westminster commemoration of Handel; and the very moderate exhibition at the Louvre, was, to him, a groupe of Raphaels, Titians, and Vandykes.—*Trans.*

* The English had brought with them from New-York, a company of players, and the officers themselves frequently performed the principal characters. [An excellent trait this for the future historians of the civil war, as well as the *meschianza*, that illustrious act of folly and infatuation; facts truly characteristic of the dissipation, and decline of a great people.—*Trans.*]

fall on M. de la Fayette's left flank ; the third, under the orders of General Grant, made a long circuit, marching first by Frankfort, then turning upon Oxford, to reach the only ford by which the Americans could retreat.

This complicated march, was executed the more easily, as the English had positive intelligence that the militia did not occupy the post assigned them. Fortunately for M. de la Fayette, two officers had set out early from the camp to go into the Jerseys, where they had business ; these officers having successively fallen in with two columns of the enemy, resolved to return to the camp through the woods, as quick as possible. General Howe's column was not long in reaching the advanced posts of M. de la Fayette; which gave rise to a laughable enough adventure. The fifty savages he had with him, were placed in an ambuscade, in the woods, after their manner, that is to say, lying as close as rabbits. Fifty English dragoons, who had never seen any Indians, marching at the head of the column, entered the wood where they were hid, who on their part had never seen dragoons. Up they start, raising a horrible cry, throw down their arms, and escape by swimming across the Schuylkill. The dragoons, on the other hand, as much terrified as they were, turned about their horses, and did not recover their panic until they got back to Philadelphia. M. de la Fayette, now finding that he was turned, concluded very justly like a warrior, that the column marched against him would not be the first to make the attack, and that it would wait until the other was in readiness. He immediately changed his front, therefore, and took a good position opposite the second column, having before him Barrenhill church, and behind him the opening which served as a retreat. But he had scarcely occupied this position, before he learnt that General Grant was on his march to the Schuylkill Ford, and was already nearer to it than himself. Nothing remained but to retreat : but the only road he had, made him approach the column of General Grant, and exposed him to be attacked by it in front, whilst Grey and Howe fell upon his rear. The road, it is true, soon turning to the left, became separated by a small valley from that General Grant was on, but this valley itself was crossed by several roads, and it must, in short, be traversed to reach the Ford. In this situation, his own greatness of mind alone suggested to the young soldier the proper conduct, as well as consummate experience could possibly have done. He knew that more honour is lost, than time gained, in converting a *retreat* into a *flight*. He continued his march, therefore, in so tranquil and regular an order, that he imposed on General Grant, and made him believe, that he was sustained by Washington's whole army, which was waiting for him at the end of the defile. On the other hand, Howe himself, on arriving on the heights of Barrenhill, was deceived by the first manœuvre of M. de la Fayette ; for seeing the Americans in line of battle, on the very spot where the second column was to appear, he imagined it was General Grey who had got possession of this position, and thus lost some minutes in looking through his glass, and in sending to reconnoitre. General Grey also lost time in waiting for the right and left columns. From all these mistakes it followed, that M. de la Fayette had the opportunity of effecting his retreat, as if by enchantment, and he passed the river with all his artillery without losing a man. Six alarm guns, which were fired at the army, on the first news of this attack, served, I believe, to keep the enemy in awe, who imagined the whole American army were in march. The English, after finding the bird flown, returned to Philadelphia, spent with fatigue, and ashamed of having done nothing. The ladies did not see M. de la Fayette, and General Howe himself arrived too late for supper.

In reciting this affair, I give at the same time an account of my ride, for I followed the exact road of the left column, which leads to Schuylkill Falls, where there is a sort of scattered village, composed of several beautiful country houses ; among others, that of the Chevalier de la Luzerne.* A small creek which falls into the Schuylkill, the height of ten or twelve feet, the mills turned by this creek, the trees which cover its banks, and those of the Schuylkill, form a most pleasing landscape, which would not escape the pencil of *Robert* and *Le Prince.*

---

* The beautiful banks of the Schuylkill are every where covered with elegant country houses ; among others, those of Mr. Penn, the late proprietor, Mr. Hamilton, and Mr. Peters, late Secretary to the Board of War, are on the most delightful situations. The tasty little box of the last gentleman is on the most enchanting spot that nature can embellish, and besides the variegated beauties of the rural banks of the Schuylkill, commands the Delaware, and the shipping mounting and descending it, where it is joined at right angles by the former. From hence is the most romantic ride up the river to the Falls, in which the opposite bank is likewise seen beautifully interspersed with the country houses of the opulent citizens of the capital. On your arrival at the Falls, every little knowl or eminence is occupied by one of these charming retreats ; among which General Mifflin's stands conspicuous, nor is the exterior belied by the neatness, the abundance, and hospitality which reign within ; the easy politeness, the attention, good sense, gaiety, and information of the owner ; the order, arrangement, and elegance of Mrs. Mifflin, who still adhering to her sect, which her husband renounced for " the ear-piercing fife and spirit-

This expedition not being so long as that of the other day,
left me two hours at my disposal; and I employed them in visiting the left of the English lines, which I had not yet seen.   M.
de Gimat was so good as to separate from the rest of the company, and instead of returning to Philadelphia, we kept to the
right, to follow the lines, as far as the Schuylkill.   I found that
from the centre, to the left, their position was nothing less than
advantageous, particularly near a burnt house, towards which
I should have directed my attack had I been in the way of
making one.   From a ridge of ground, where indeed the English had formed a semicircular battery towards the Schuylkill;
the glacis is against the lines ; so that the assailant might first
march under cover, and then command the batteries which defend them.   To the left, and close to the Schuylkill, the ground
has suddenly a very considerable rise, of which the English
did not fail to avail themselves, by constructing a large redoubt,
and a battery ; but this summit itself is commanded, and taken
in reverse by the heights on the other side of the river.   Be
this as it may, these works were sufficient to secure an army
of fifteen thousand men, against one of seven or at most eight
thousand.   At every step one takes in America, one is astonished at the striking contrast between the contempt in which the
English affected to hold their enemies, and the extreme precautions they took on every occasion.

Nothing can equal the beauties of the coup d'œil which the
banks of the Schuylkill present, in descending towards the
south to return to Philadelphia.

I found a pretty numerous company assembled at dinner at
the Chevalier de la Luzerne's, which was augmented by the
arrival of the Comte de Custine and the M. de Laval.   In the
evening we took them to see the President of the Congress,
who was not at home, and then to Mr. Peters, the Secretary
to the Board of War, to whom it was my first visit.   His house
is not large, nor his office of great importance ; for every thing

---

stirring drum," possesses all its excellencies, and is what a most
amiable female Quaker ought to be, render this (and I speak from
knowledge and gratitude) a most delicious abode.   Below this house,
and close to the Falls, is a building erected by Mr. John Dickinson,
the celebrated author of the Farmer's Letters, for a select society of
friends, who held a weekly meeting there, before the war, during the
season for eating shad.   Good humour, harmony, and good sense, are
said to have characterised these meetings, presided by this eminent
and amiable man, whose figure, countenance, and manners always reminded me of the urbanity and virtues so characteristically portrayed
in the person of the lamented, great, good man, Lord *Rockingham.*—
Trans.

which is not in the power of the General of the army, depends on each particular state, much more than on Congress ; but he possesses what is preferable to all the departments in the world, an amiable wife, [the Marquis might have added, *very beautiful*] excellent health, a good voice, and great gaiety and humour. We conversed some time together, and he spoke of the American army with as much freedom as good sense. He confessed that formerly their army knew no discipline, and he insisted strongly on the obligations they owed to the *Baron de Steuben*, who performed the duties of Inspector-General. Passing then to the eulogium of Messieurs de Fleury, du Portal, and all the French officers who had served in the late campaigns, he observed, that those who offered their service in the beginning, had not given a very advantageous idea of their country. They were almost all furnished, however, with letters of recommendation from the Governors or Commandants of our colonies ; in which they seem to me very reprehensible. The weakness which prevents men from refusing a letter of recommendation, or the desire of getting rid of a good for nothing fellow, continually gets the better of justice and good faith ; we deceive, we expose the reputation of our allies, but we still more essentially betray the interests of our country, whose honour and character are thus shamefully prostituted.

I shall only speak of Mr. Price, with whom we drank tea and spent the evening, to bear witness to the generosity of this gallant man, who, born in Canada and always attached to the French, lent two hundred thousand livres, *hard money*, to M. de Corny, whom the court had sent with fifty thousand livres only, to make provision for our army.

The 13th, I went with the Chevalier de la Luzerne, and the French travellers, to dine with the Southern Delegates.*

---

* The Marquis de Chastellux seems unfortunately to have known but little of the Southern Delegates, particularly those of *South Carolina*, whom, without any invidious comparison, he would have found men of the greatest liberality and understanding : as firm in their principles, and as ready to hazard their lives in the defence of their liberty, as the most zealous inhabitant of New-England ; they possessed, in general, all the taste, urbanity, and enlightened knowledge of polished Europe. In Mr. *Ramsey*, he would have found a cultivated understanding, a persevering mind, and an active enthusiasm, founded on a thorough knowledge of the cause he was engaged in, and the most perfect conviction of its rectitude. In Mr. *Izard*, the fire and zeal of a gentleman republican, filled with indignation at the violence and excesses he had *witnessed* in the English government. In Mr. *Rutledge*, a manly, principled determination to risk and suffer every thing, rather than again submit to the yoke of Britain, with elegant

Messieurs Sharp, Flowy,† and Maddison, were the nearest
to me ; I conversed a great deal with them, and was much
satisfied with their conversation. But I was still more so with
that I had in the afternoon at Mrs. Meredith's, General Cadwallader's daughter : this was the first time I had seen this
amiable family, although the Chévalier de la Luzerne was very
intimate with them; but they had only just arrived from the
country, where General Cadwallader was still detained by
business. It is this gentleman who had a duel with Mr. Chace,
formerly a Delegate for Maryland, and severely wounded him
in the jaw with a pistol shot. Mrs. Meredith has three or four
sisters, or sisters-in-law. I was astonished at the freedom and
gaiety which reigned in this family, and regretted not having
known them sooner. I chattered more, particularly with Mrs.
Meredith, who appeared to me very amiable and well informed. In the course of an hour we talked of literature, poetry,
romances, and above all, history ; I found she knew that of
France very well ; the comparison between Francis I. and
Henry IV. between Turenne and Condé, Richelieu and Maza-
rine, seemed familiar to her, and she made them with much
grace, wit and understanding. While I was talking with
Mrs. Meredith, Mr. Lynch had got possession of Miss Polly
Cadwallader, who had likewise made a conquest of him, insomuch that the Chevalier de la Luzerne was much entertained
at the enthusiasm with which this company had inspired us,
and the regret we expressed at not having become sooner ac-

---

ideas of the enjoyments of life, and all the domestic virtues. In Mr.
Arthur Middleton, the plainest manners, with the most refined taste ;
great reading, and knowledge of the world, concealed under the reserve of the mildest, and most modest nature ; a complete philanthro-
pist, but the firmest patriot ; cool, steady, and unmoved at the general
wreck of property and fortune, as far as he was personally concerned,
but with a heart melting for the suffering and woes of others. He
would have found him, in short, a model of private worth, and public
virtue, a good citizen, a good father, and an exemplary husband,
accomplished in the letters, in the sciences, and fine arts, well
acquainted with the manners and the courts of Europe, from whence
he has transplanted to his country nothing but their embellishments
and virtues. I speak of him with enthusiasm, for he really excited my
admiration. He had made a handsome collection of paintings when in
Italy, and on his travels, which were mutilated and destroyed by the
ruffian hands of the European savages, who took possession of his
house in Carolina.—*Trans.*

† There must be an error in this name, but as the translator can
find no similitude between it and that of any of the Southern Delegates, he has inserted it literally.—*Trans.*

quainted with them. It must be acknowledged, with regard
to the ladies who compose it, that none of them are what may
be called handsome ; this mode of expression is, perhaps, a
little too circuitous for the American women, but if they have
wit enough to comprehend, and good sense enough to be flattered with it, their eulogium will be complete.

I know not how it happened, that since my arrival in Philadelphia, I had not yet seen Mr. Payne, that author so celebrated in America, and throughout Europe, by his excellent work,
entitled *Common Sense,* and several other political pamphlets.
M. de la Fayette and I asked the permission of an interview
for the 14th in the morning, and we waited on him accordingly with Colonel Laurens.   I discovered, at his apartments, all
the attributes of a man of letters ; a room pretty much in disorder, dusty furniture, and a large table covered with books
lying open, and manuscripts begun.   His person was in a cor-
respondent dress, nor did his physiognomy belie the spirit that
reigns throughout his works.   Our conversation was agreeable and animated, and such as to form a connexion between
us, for he has written to me since my departure, and seems desirous of maintaining a constant correspondence.   His existence at Philadelphia is similar to that of those political writers
in England, who have obtained nothing, and have neither
credit enough in the state, nor sufficient political weight to
obtain a part in the affairs of government.   Their works are
read with more curiosity than confidence, their projects being
regarded rather as the play of imagination, than as well concerted plans, and sufficient in credit ever to produce any real
effect : theirs is always considered as the work of an individual,
and not that of a party ; information may be drawn from them,
but not consequences; accordingly we observe, that the influence of these authors is more felt in the satirical, than in the
dogmatical style, as it is easier for them to decry other men's
opinions than to establish their own.   This is more the case
with Mr. Payne than any body; for having formerly held a
post in government, he has now no connexion with it ; and as
his patriotism and his talents are unquestionable, it is natural
to conclude that the vivacity of his imagination, and the independence of his character, render him more calculated for
reasoning on affairs, than for conducting them.*   Another

---

* Mr. Payne has since written a very interesting pamphlet on the
finances of America, entitled *the Crisis ;* an answer to the history of
the American Revolution by the Abbé Raynal; and several other
works, which confirm the reputation he so justly acquired by his first
production.   [The author is inaccurate in this particular, *the Crisis*

literary man, as much respected, though less celebrated, expected us at dinner ; this was Mr. Wilson, whom I have already
mentioned : his house and library are in the best order ; he
gave us an excellent dinner, and received us with a plain and
easy politeness.   Mrs. Wilson did the honours of the table
with all possible attention ; but we were particularly sensible
to the mark of it she gave us, by retiring after the desert, for
then the dinner assumed an air of gaiety.   Mr. Peters, the
minister at war, gave the signal of joy and liberty by favour-
ing us with a song of his composition, so jolly, and so free, that
I shall dispense with giving either a translation, or an extract.
This was really a very excellent song.   He then sung another
more chaste, and more musical ; a very fine Italian *contabile*.*
Mr. Peters is, unquestionably, the minister of the two worlds,
who has the best voice, and who sings the best, the pathetic
and the *bouffon*.   I was told that the preceding year there were
some private concerts at Philadelphia, where he sung among
other pieces of comic operas, a burlesque part in a very pleasant

---

was a sort of periodical publication, many numbers of which had appeared previous even to the arrival of the French army in America,
and was adapted by Mr. Payne to every great house, or crisis of the
government, whether favourable, or unfavourable ; either to urge to
energy, and as a spur against supineness, or to give a countenance to
misfortune, and stimulate to fresh exertions ; the subject of finance
was only the occasional topic of *one number* of the Crisis, and so great
was the weight of this writer, whose situation was very different indeed
from that of an English pamphleteer, however ingenious the comparison, that on great emergencies, where almost despondency might be
looked for, the whole continent waited with suspense for consolation
and council from *Common Sense*, his general appellation.   His productions were instantly published in every town, of every state, (for
every town has a newspaper,) on grey, brown, yellow, and black, but
seldom on white paper, a very rare commodity ; the people took fresh
courage, and, " have you read *the Crisis*," was the specific against
every political apprehension.   In short, never was a writer better calculated for the meridian under which he wrote, or who knew how to
adapt himself more happily to every circumstance.   Considering the
wonderful effect of his pamphlet of Common Sense, known to every
man in America, and the universal ascendency he had justly acquired
over the minds of the people, it is impossible, in a general distribution
of cases, to appreciate the share Mr. Payne had in producing this momentous revolution.   It were the height of injustice, and ingratitude,
to rob him of that share of glory, which if not his only, is at least his
noblest recompense.—*Trans.*

   * So varied and universal are the talents of Mr. Peters, and he is
so excellent a companion, that it is not saying too much, to add, that
he would form the delight of any society in Europe.—*Trans.*

trio, by himself, which he seasoned with all the humourous strokes usual on such occasions, and afforded the highest amusement to the company, so that this was not the time for saying, *one cannot lose a kingdom more gaily*, but, *it is impossible to be more gay in forming a republic.*   After this, conclude from particulars to generals, judge of whole nations by one specimen, and establish principles without exceptions!

The assembly, or subscription ball, of which I must give an account, may here be properly introduced.   At Philadelphia, as at London, Bath, Spa, &c. there are places appropriated for the young people to dance in, and where those whom that amusement does not suit, play at different games of cards; but at Philadelphia, games of commerce are alone allowed. A manager, or master of ceremonies presides at these methodical amusements: he presents to the gentlemen and ladies, dancers, billets folded up containing each a number; thus fate decides the male or female partner for the whole evening. All the dances are previously arranged, and the dancers are called in their turns.   These dances, like the *toasts* we drink at table, have some relation to politics: one is called *the success of the campaign*, another, *the defeat of Burgoyne*, and a third, *Clinton's retreat*.   The managers are generally chosen from among the most distinguished officers of the army; this important place is at present held by Colonel Wilkinson, who is also clothier general of the army.   Colonel Mitchell, a little fat, squat man, fifty years old, a great judge of horses, and who was lately contractor for carriages, both for the American and French armies, was formerly the manager; but when I saw him, he had descended from the magistracy, and danced like a private citizen.   He is said to have exercised his office with great severity, and it is told of him, that a young lady who was figuring in a country dance, having forgot her turn by conversing with a friend, he came up to her, and called out aloud, " give over, Miss, take care what you are about; do you think you come here for your pleasure ?"

The assembly I went to on leaving Mr. Wilson, was the second of the winter.   I was apprised that it would be neither numerous nor brilliant, for at Philadelphia, as at Paris, the best company seldom go to the balls before Christmas.   On entering the room, however, I found twenty or five and twenty ladies ready for dancing.   It was whispered me, that having heard a great deal of the Vicomte de Noailles, and the Comte de Damas, they were come with the hopes of having them for partners; but they were completely disappointed, those gentlemen having set out that very morning.   I should have been disappointed also, had I expected to see pretty women.   There were only two passable, one of whom, called Miss Footman, was rather contraband, that is to say, suspected of not being a very good whig, for the tory ladies are publicly excluded from this assembly. I was here presented to a ridiculous enough personage, but who plays her part in the town ; a Miss Viny, celebrated for her coquetry, her wit, and her sarcastic disposition : she is thirty, and does not seem on the point of marriage. In the mean time she applies red, white, blue, and all possible colours, affects an extraordinary mode of dressing her hair and person, and a staunch whig in every point, she sets no bounds to her liberty.

I intended leaving Philadelphia the 15th, but the President of the State, who is also President of the Academy, was so good as to invite me to a meeting of that body to be held that day. It was the more difficult for me to refuse his invitation, as it was proposed to elect me a foreign member. The meetings are held only once a fortnight, and the elections take place but once a year : every candidate must be presented and recommended by a member of the academy; after which recommendation his name is placed up during three succeeding sittings, in the hall of the academy, and the election is at length proceeded to by ballot. I had only heard of mine three days before. It was unanimous, which very rarely happens. M. de la Fayette himself, who was elected at the same time, had one black ball against him, but it was thought to have been an accident. Out of one and twenty candidates, only seven were chosen, although the others had been strongly recommended, and there were several vacancies.

As the sittings of the academy did not begin till seven in the evening, I employed my morning in paying visits, after which I dined at Mr. Holker's,* with the Chevalier de la Luzerne,

---

* Mr. Holker, the son of the Chevalier Holker, died a few months ago at Rouen, who being condemned to die for acting as an officer in the Manchester regiment, in the rebellion of 1745, made his escape from prison, and fled to France, where he was tempted by the government to establish the Manchester manufactory ; this he repeatedly refused, until, from the wretched policy of Mr. Pelham and other Ministers to whom he represented the offers held out to him, with a request of his pardon, he was driven to accept of the proposals of the French court. England knows too well, at this hour, the success with which his endeavours have been crowned. On the arrival of the American commissioners in France, Mr. Holker was among the first, and most zealous in his offers of every assistance in his power, and entered into the most intimate connexion with them. In 1777 his son was sent to Paris to be near Dr. Franklin, and had many opportunities of rendering essential services. In 1778 he went out to America with Monsieur Gerard, the first French Ambassador, in D'Estaign's squadron, as Consul General of France. He had not been long in the

M. de la Fayette, and all the French officers : from thence I went to the academy accompanied by M. Marbois, a member of that body, as well as M. de la Luzerne, who having other business, excused himself from attending me, but left me in very good hands. Mr. Marbois, unites to all political and social qualities, a great deal of literature, and a perfect knowledge of the English language. The assembly consisted of only fourteen or fifteen persons ; the President of the college performed the office of Secretary. A memoir was read on a singular plant, a native of the country ; the Secretary then gave an account of correspondence and read a letter, the object of which was, for the academy of Philadelphia to associate with, or rather adopt several learned societies which are forming in each State. This project tended to make of this academy

---

country before he entered into very advantageous commercial speculations, jointly with his father's countryman, Mr. Robert Morris, and by means of his situation as Consul, had many opportunities of shipping flour, &c. under permissions for the French fleet, in the time of a general and strict embargo ; he speculated largely too in paper money, with which he purchased, for almost nothing, a very handsome house at Philadelphia, and an elegant country house, and estate a few miles from that city. Mr. Holker displayed, during the whole war, a taste and luxury hitherto strangers in America ; his house was the resort of all the first people on the Continent, and after the arrival of the French army, of all their officers of distinction. The French court, however, on some representations of the Chevalier de la Luzerne, thought fit to prohibit their Consuls from all private commerce, a wise regulation universally established by them ; and Mr. Holker preferring the advantages of trade, to those of his office, resigned the latter, about the beginning of 1781, which for some time occasioned a coolness between the Minister and him ; he had likewise a difference with Mr. Morris on settling their accounts to a very large amount, which has detained him in America, since the peace ; but, if I am rightly informed, it is at length terminated. In 1777, I supped with Mr. Deane, *then* a strenuous friend to his country, on his return from Havre de Grace ; where he told me, that on giving the usual toasts of " the Congress," &c. after dinner, the old gentleman could not forbear reflecting on the mutability of human affairs, and that he who was an exile, and had nearly suffered death for his zealous attachment to the cause of arbitrary monarchy, should now be as ardent in his wishes for the success of the most pure democracy that had ever been proposed to human understanding. And in fact this is more striking, as the most strenuous supporters of the American war were found in Scotland, and his native town of Manchester ; in the very seat, and sources of rebellion against liberty ; in the persons of the very actors, in the attempt to overthrow the English constitution, and dethrone the Brunswick family.—*Trans.*

a sort of literary congress, with which the particular legislatures should keep a correspondence, but it was not thought proper to adopt this idea ; the members seeming to be afraid of the trouble inseparable from all these adoptions, and the academy not wishing to make the following lines of Racine's *Athalie* applicable to them :

> D'Ou lui viennent de tous côtés
> Ces enfans qu' en son sein elle n' a pas portés !

I returned as soon as possible to the Chevalier de la Luzerne's, to have a still farther enjoyment of that society which had constituted my happiness for the last fortnight : for it is unquestionably a very great one, to live with a man whose amiable and mild character never varies on any occasion ; whose conversation is agreeable and instructive, and whose easy and unaffected politeness is the genuine expression of the best disposition. But however allowable it may be to declare one's own sentiments, when dictated by justice and gratitude, there is always a sort of personality in regarding public men only as they respect their connexions with ourselves : it is to the King's Minister, in America ; it is to a man who most ably fills a most important post, that I owe my testimony and my praises. I shall say, without fear of contradiction, that the Chevalier de la Luzerne is so formed for the station he occupies, that one would be led to imagine no other could fill it but himself ; noble in his expenses, like the minister of a great monarchy, but as plain in his manners as a republican, he is equally proper to represent the King with Congress, or the Congress with the King. He loves the Americans, and his own inclination attaches him to the duties of his administration ; he has accordingly obtained their confidence, both as a private and a public man ; but in both these respects he is equally inaccessible to the spirit of party, which reigns but too much around him : whence it results, that he is anxiously courted by all parties, and that, by espousing none, he manages them all.

It was the 16th of December that I quitted the excellent winter quarters I had with him, and turned my face towards the north, to seek after the traces of General Gates and General Burgoyne, amidst heaps of snow. I had sent forward my horses to Bristol, where I was conveyed in a carriage which the Chevalier de la Luzerne was so kind as to lend me. By this means I arrived there time enough to reach Princeton that night, but not before it was dark, leaving behind me some of my servants and horses.

CHAPTER IX.

PHILADELPHIA—PRINCETON—BASKENRIDGE—POMPTON—NEW WIND-
SOR—POUGHKEEPSIE—RHINEBECK—CLAVERACK—KINDERHOOK.

THE detail of my daily occupations having prevented me
from giving a general idea of Philadelphia, I must, on quitting
it, take a retrospective view, and consider at once its present
state and the destiny which seems to await it. In observing
its geographical situation, we may readily admit that *Penn*
proceeded upon no erroneous idea, when he conceived his
plan of making it one day the capital of America. Two large
rivers,* which take their rise in the neighbourhood of Lake
Ontario, convey to it the riches of all the interior parts of the
country, and at length, by their junction considerably higher
up, form a magnificent port at this city. This port is at once
far enough from the sea to shelter it from every insult ; and so
near, as to render it as easy of access as if situated on the
shore of the ocean. The Schuylkill, which runs to the west of
Philadelphia, and nearly parallel with the Delaware, is rather
ornamental than useful to this city and its commerce. This
river, though wide and beautiful near its conflux, is not navigable for boats, on account of its shallow and rocky bed.
Philadelphia, placed between these two rivers, on a neck of
land only three miles broad, ought to fill up this space, but
commerce has given it another turn. The regular plan of
William Penn has been followed, but the buildings are along
the Delaware, for the convenience of being near the warehouses and shipping. Front-street, which is parallel with the
river, is near three miles long, out of which open upwards of
two hundred quays, forming so many views terminated by vessels of different sizes.† I could easily form an idea of the

---

* The two branches of the Delaware form two considerable rivers,
the sources of which are distant several miles from each other, but
they are only distinguished by the names of the *Eastern* and *Western*
Branches.

† The author has by no means given an adequate idea of Philadelphia,
which, however, has so often been described as to render it less necessary ; but as he names only one street extending along the river, it may

commerce of Philadelphia, from seeing above three hundred
vessels in the harbour, though the English had not left a single
bark in it in 1778. Two years tranquillity, and, above all, the
diversion made by our squadron at Rhode-Island, have sufficed
to collect this great number of vessels, the success of which in
privateering, as well as in trade, have filled the warehouses
with goods, insomuch that purchasers alone are wanting. The
wisdom of the legislative council, however, has not corresponded with the advantages lavished by nature. Pennsylvania is
very far from being the best governed of the United States.
Exposed, more than others, to the convulsions of credit, and
to the manœuvres of speculation, the instability of the public
wealth has operated on the legislation itself. An attempt was
made to fix the value of the paper currency, but commodities
augmented in price, in proportion as money lost its value; a
resolution was then taken to fix the price also of commodities,
which almost produced a famine. A more recent error of the
government, was the law prohibiting the exportation of corn.
The object they had in view, was on one hand to supply the
American army at a cheaper rate, and on the other, to put a
stop to the contraband trade between Philadelphia and New-
York; the ruin of the farmers and the state was the result,
as the latter could not obtain payment of the taxes. This law
is just repealed, so that I hope agriculture will resume its vigour, and commerce receive an increase. Corn sent to the
army will be something dearer, but there will be more money

---

be proper to observe, that parallel with Front-street, are *second*, *third*,
fourth, *fifth*, and *sixth* streets ; these are intersected at right angles by
Arch-street, *State*-street, and *Market*-street, &c. &c. the latter, which
is of a great breadth, and length, and cuts the centre of the city, would
be one of the finest streets in the world, were it not for the market
situated in the middle of it ; but the upper part is occupied by the
houses of opulent citizens, and will in time become truly noble. It
may be added, that so far from the buildings following the river, they
are extended rapidly towards the common, where many new streets
were marked out and begun in 1782 ; and it may safely be predicted
that if the trade of Philadelphia continue to flourish, the plan of *William Penn* will be accomplished, judging from the very rapid progress
of the past, at no very distant period, and the ground be covered with
perhaps, the noblest of modern cities, extending from the Delaware to
the Schuylkill. This will be accelerated too, by the sale of the common, which was taken by the Assembly from the proprietor, Mr. John
Penn, at the beginning of the revolution, with the rest of the proprietary estate, in consideration of a certain sum, and disposed of in lots
to the best bidders.—*Trans.*

to pay for it; and should there be some smuggling with New-York, English money will circulate among their enemies.*

It were greatly to be wished that paper might at length obtain an established credit, no matter what value; for it signifies little whether the price of a sheep be represented by one hundred and fifty paper dollars, or two dollars in specie. This depreciation of the paper is not felt in those places where it remains the same; but Philadelphia is, so to speak, the great sink, wherein all the speculations of America terminate, and are confounded together. Since the capture of Charleston, many of the inhabitants of Carolina hastily sold their estates and crops, and having been only paid in paper, they brought this article with them to Philadelphia already overstocked with it.† The quakers and tories, on the other hand, with which

---

* The votes of the House of Commons, and the account of Messieurs Drummond and Harley, will show the immense sums, in Portugal and Spanish gold alone, sent to America; these, as well as English guineas, found their way, towards the middle period of the war, in great abundance into the American part of the continent, where they circulated in a variety of mutilated forms, the moidores, and six-and-thirties, had all of them holes punched in them, or were otherwise diminished at New-York, before they were suffered to pass the lines; from whence they obtained the name of *Robertson's*, in the *rebel* country; but the profits, if any, of that commander, on this new edition of the coin, remain a secret. In the country, almost all the specie of every denomination was cut by individuals, and appeared under the forms of half, quarter, and eighth parts, the latter of which received the name of *sharp shins*; by this arbitrary division of the money, which was never weighed, great frauds were inevitable.—*Trans.*

† The wonderful resources derived in the commencement from this paper money, its extraordinary depreciation, and total disappearance without producing any great shock, or convulsion in an infant country, struggling with a complication of difficulties, will certainly form an epocha in the general history of finances, as well as in that of this great revolution. I saw *hundreds of millions* of paper dollars piled up, effaced, in the office of Congress at Philadelphia, which, never possessing any real value, had served all the purposes of a difficult, and uncommonly expensive war, and were now quietly laid aside, with scarce a murmur on the part of the public; the variety of the depreciation, at different periods, and in different parts of the Continent, whilst it gave rise to great temporary abuses, had been so divided, and balanced, by alternate profit and loss among all classes of citizens, that on casting up the account, some very unfortunate cases excepted, it seems to have operated only as a general tax on the public; and the universal joy on its annihilation, with the satisfactory reflection on the necessity under which it was issued in the critical moment of danger, seemed to

this province abounds, two classes of men equally dangerous, one from their timidity, and the other from their bad intentions, are incessantly labouring to secure their fortune ; they lavish the paper for a little gold or silver, to enable them to remove wherever they may think themselves in safety ; from these reasons, the paper money is more and more decried, not only because it is too common, but because gold and silver are extremely scarce, and difficult to be obtained.

In the midst of these convulsions the government is without force, nor can it be otherwise. A popular government can never have any, whilst the people are unsteady and fluctuating in their opinions ; for then the leaders rather seek to please, than serve them ; obliged to gain their confidence before they merit it, they are more inclined to flatter, than instruct them, and fearing to lose the favour they have acquired, they finish by becoming the slaves of the multitude whom they pretended to govern. Mr. Franklin has been blamed for giving too democratical a government to his country, but they who censure him do not reflect that the first step was to make her renounce monarchical government, and that it was necessary to employ a sort of seduction in order to conduct a timid and avaricious people to independence, who were besides so divided in their opinions, that the republican party was scarcely stronger than the other. Under these circumstances he acted like *Solon ;* he has not given the best possible laws to Pennsylvania, but the best of which the country was susceptible. Time will produce perfection ; in pleading to recover an estate, the first object is to obtain possession, the rest follows of course.*

---

conciliate all minds, to a total oblivion of its partial mischief. Here and there great fortunes are to be seen, reared upon its now visionary basis, and families reduced from opulence to mediocrity by means of this destructive medium, but these instances are by no means so frequent as they have been represented in Europe, and were often the result of ill judged, but avaricious speculations ; but I repeat it, that the continued use, the general circulation, the astonishing depreciation, and total destruction of such an immense imaginary property, will always exhibit a phœnomenon infinitely more striking, than that a few, or even a great number of individuals should have suffered, as must always be the case in every civil commotion. The fact is unparalleled, and will probably stand single in the annals of the world.— *Trans.*

* The author might have added in corroboration of his argument, that the constitution of Pennsylvania is, for this reason, only a constitution of experiment, from seven years to seven years, in which it is expressly reserved to a *Council of Censors*, to revise the past operations of government, to judge of the effects produced from it as then consti-

Philadelphia contains about forty thousand inhabitants. The streets are large and regular, and intersect each other at right angles. There are footways here, as in London for the passengers. This city has every useful establishment, such as hospitals, workhouses, houses of correction, &c. but it is so deficient in an essential article of comfort and enjoyment, that there is not a single public walk.* The reason of this is, that hitherto every thing concerning the police, and particular government of the city has been in the hands of the quakers, and these sectaries consider every species of private or public amusement as a transgression of their law, and as a *pomp of Satan.* Fortunately, the little zeal, (to say no more) they have displayed on the present crisis, has made them lose their credit. This revolution comes very opportunely, at a time when the public has derived every benefit from them they could expect; the walls of the house are finished, it is time to call in the carpenters and upholsterers.

It is time also for me to return to Princeton, to continue my journey to Albany, by New-Windsor, General Washington's head-quarters. I intended setting out early on the 17th; it was necessary, in fact, to be alert, that I might reach Morristown, but my baggage horse not being able to pass the Delaware, at the same time with myself, I left one of my people to wait for, and conduct him. It so happened that neither the servant I was waiting for, nor the other arrived. One of the servants was an Irishman, the other a German, both newly entered into my service. As soon as I saw the morning of the 17th approach, without their making their appearance, the neighbourhood of New-York began to give me some uneasi-

---

tuted, and to call a *general convention of the people,* for the purpose of amending the deficient parts and of correcting its exuberancies and vices. It is a glorious experiment, worthy the philanthropic heart, and the enlightened understanding of Doctor Franklin,—*Quod felix, faustumque sit!*—*Trans.*

* The city of Philadelphia is not only at present destitute of public walks, but, in summer, the heat renders walking in the streets intolerably inconvenient; the houses and footpaths being generally of brick, are not even cooled until some hours after sunset. This extreme heat, and the abundance of excellent water, with which Philadelphia is supplied, occasion many accidents among the lower class of people, for it is no uncommon thing to see a labourer after quenching his thirst at a pump, drop down dead upon the spot, nor can the numerous examples of this kind every summer, prevent them from frequently occurring; but it is to be observed, that if the heat be intense, the water is uncommonly cold.—*Trans.*

ness. I was apprehensive they might have taken that road
with my little baggage, and I was already making dispositions
to pursue them, when, to my great satisfaction, I saw the head
of my baggage column appear, that is, one of the three horses
which were left behind, the remainder following soon after.*

---

* After Sir Guy Carleton's arrival at New-York with the vote of
Parliament to discontinue offensive war, the translator, who was travelling to the northward, and meant to call on General Washington,
then in camp at Verplank's-Point, on the North River, thought he
might with safety take the lower road by Brunswick and Elizabethtown, but he had not been an hour in bed, before he and his companion, a surgeon in the American army, were alarmed by a scattering
fire of musketry. Before they had time to dress themselves, and take
their pistols, the landlord entered their apartment, and informed them,
that a party from Staten-Island was marching towards the town, and
advised them to make their escape ; with much difficulty they got
their horses out of the stable, hid their baggage in the church-yard,
and hearing the English officer order his men to *form* at the end of
the town, they took different roads, leaving their servants, who were,
one a Scotch prisoner to the Americans, the other an English deserter,
and whose conduct appeared very suspicious, to take care of themselves, and the horses they rode on. The translator, who followed
the great road to Newark, was mounted on a white horse, which
made him a good object, and had several shot fired at him, but the
ground rising, and his horse going at full gallop, the balls luckily fell
short. After endeavouring to rouse the country, but without being
able to collect a sufficient force, he took shelter at an honest carpenter's, about a mile from the town, where he remained till a little before daybreak, when concluding from the general silence, that the
party had retired, he returned, and went to search for his baggage in
the church-yard, for which, however, he sought in vain, and his anxiety was not a little increased on not finding his other horse in the
stable, nor seeing either of the servants. But from which he was
soon relieved by his friend, who had watched the first moment of the
enemy's departure, ordered the baggage up into his room, and assured
him that the servants had conducted themselves with the greatest
fidelity. His alarm was, it seems, much greater than that of the
translator, as General Washington had declared publicly in orders,
that any officer of his army, taken near the lines, unless on duty,
should be the last exchanged. The translator imagines the party to
have been Refugees from Staten-Island, who, from their separate institution, under the direction of *a Board*, not unfrequently set at defiance the orders of the Commander-in-Chief ; a remarkable instance
of which occurred in the case of Captain Huddy, whom they obtained, under false pretences, from the guard-house, where he was a prisoner, and murdered without either scruple or apprehension. All
Europe knows the consequence, in the imminent danger of *Captain
Asgill;* and all America saw with shame and indignation the English

To pass the time, however, I entered into conversation with my landlord, Colonel Howard, who is a very good man, and with his son the Captain, a great talker, and genuine *Capitan*. He recounted to me with many gestures, oaths and imprecations, all his feats of prowess in the war ; especially at the affair of Princeton, where he served as a lieutenant of militia in his father's regiment ; and indeed the action he boasted of would have merited an eulogium, had he related it with simplicity.   We may recollect that after beating the English, General Washington continued his route towards Middlebrook. An American officer, who had his leg broke by a musket ball, was dragged into a house, where the English sooner or later must have found him : young Howard, and some soldiers as well disposed as himself, set out at night from Middlebrook, took a circuitous road, arrived at the house, found the officer, took him on their shoulders and carried him to their quarters. During the remainder of the winter, the Jersey militia were constantly under arms to restrain the English, who occupied Elizabethtown and Brunswick. It was a sort of continual chace, to which Lieutenant Howard one day led his little brother, a boy of fifteen, and who was lucky enough to begin his career by killing a Hessian grenadier ; as these stories were very tedious, I shall drop them here for fear of not improving on the narration : I must mention however, the manner in which my *Capitan* entered into the service, as it will serve to discover the spirit which reigned in America at the beginning of the present revolution.   He was an apprentice to a hatter at the time of the affair of Lexington, and the blockade of Boston ; three of his companions and himself set out one morning from Philadelphia with four dollars among them in their pockets : they travelled four hundred miles on foot to join the army, in which they served as volunteers the remainder of the campaign ; from thence they set out with Arnold on his expedition to Canada, and did not return home until the theatre of war was removed into their own country.

Eleven o'clock had struck before I could rally the horses in my train, and begin my march ; I abandoned therefore the plan of sleeping at Morristown, and determined to stop at Baskenridge, eight miles nearer Princeton.   I first left the Millstone on the right, then crossed it twice before I reached the Rariton, which I passed at the same place ; as in my journey to Philadelphia.   Three miles from thence I was told to

general unable to enforce discipline in his own army, and shrinking under the apprehensions of irritating Governor Franklin, and his envenomed board of Loyalists.—*Trans.*

take a road to the right, which leads into the woods, and over the summit of the hills; this route was opened for the army, during the winter quarters of 1778—9; it appears to have been made with care, and is still passable; but after some time, daylight failing me, I lost myself, and went a mile or two out of my way. Luckily for me, I found a hut inhabited by some new settlers; there I got a guide who conducted me to Baskenridge, where I arrived at seven o'clock, and alighted at Bullion's Tavern, got tolerable lodgings, with the best people in the world. Our supper was very good : bread only was wanting ; but, inquiring of us what sort we liked, in an hour's time we had such as we desired. This will appear less extra- ordinary, on being told that in America, little cakes, which are easily kneaded and baked in half an hour, are often substituted for bread. Possibly one would soon tire of them, but they suited my taste extremely well. Mr. Bullion had two white servants, one a man about fifty, the other a woman, younger, with a tolerable good face : I had the curiosity to inquire what wages he gave them, and was told that the man earned half a crown a day and the woman six shillings a week, or ten pence a day. If we pay attention to the circumstance, that these servants are lodged and fed, and have no expenses, we may see that it is easy for them very shortly to acquire a piece of ground, and to form such a settlement as I have described.

The 18th I set out at eight in the morning, and made only one stage to Pompton; which is six and thirty miles, without baiting my horses or stopping, except for a quarter of an hour to pay a visit to General Wayne, whose quarters were on the main road. He was posted to cover the Jerseys, and had under his orders the same Pennsylvania line which revolted a fort- night after. I again saw with pleasure the environs of Morris- town, which are agreeable and well cultivated; but after passing the Rockaway, and approaching Pompton, I was as- tonished at the degree of perfection to which agriculture is carried, and particularly admired the farms of Messieurs Man- deville. They are the sons of a Dutchman, who first cleared the ground from which they now reap such rich harvests. Their domains join each other. In each of them the manor is very simple and small the barns alone are lofty and spacious. Always faithful to their national economy, they cultivate, reap, and sell, without augmenting either their houses or their enjoy- ments ; content with living in a corner of their farm, and with being only the spectators of their own wealth. By the side of these old farms we see new settlements forming, and have more and more reason to be convinced, that if the war has retarded the progress of agriculture and population, it has not entirely suspended them. The night, which surprised me on my journey, deprived me of the beautiful prospect this country would have continued to afford. Being very dark, it was not without difficulty I passed two or three rivulets, on very small bridges, and got to Courtheath's Tavern. This inn is lately established, and kept by young people without fortune, consequently the best parts of the furniture are the owner and his family. Mr. Courtheath is a young man of four and twenty, who was formerly a travelling dealer in stuffs, toys, &c. The depreciation of paper money, or perhaps his own imprudence so far ruined him as to oblige him to leave his house at Morristown, and set up a tavern in this out of the way place, where nothing but the neighbourhood of the army can procure him a few customers. He has two handsome sisters, well dressed girls, who wait on travellers with grace and coquetry. Their brother says, he will marry them to some fat clumsy Dutchmen, and that as for himself, as soon as he has got a little money, he shall resume his commerce, and travel about as formerly. On entering the parlour, where these young women sit, when there are no strangers, I found on a great table, *Milton, Addison, Richardson,* and several other works of that kind. The cellar was not so well stored as the library, for there was neither wine, cider, nor rum; nothing in short but some vile cider-brandy, with which I must make grog. The bill they presented me the next morning amounted nevertheless to sixteen dollars.* I ob-

---

* Travelling in America was wonderfully expensive during the war, even after the abolition of paper money, and when all payments were made in specie ; you could not remain at an inn, even the most indifferent, one night, with a servant and two horses, living in the most moderate way, under from five to eight dollars. At Grant's Tavern at Baltimore, where the translator staid some days, with only one horse and no servant, though he either dined or supped out every day, he never escaped for less than five dollars. I cannot here avoid relating the pleasant manner in which one Bell, a shrewd Scotch bookseller and auctioneer of Philadelphia, paid his bills in travelling through the country. I had given him at Irish copy of Sheridan's School for Scandal, with the prologue and epilogue taken from Dodsley's Annual Register, which he reprinted and sold for a dollar. In travelling through Virginia some months after, I was surprised to see in many of the inns, even in the most remote parts of the country, this celebrated comedy ; and, upon inquiry, found that Mr. Bell, who travelled with his family in a covered cart, had passed in his way to the Springs, (the Harrowgate, or Matlock of America) and successfully circulated in payment this new species of paper currency ; for, as he observed, " Who would not prefer Sheridan's Sterling, to the counterfeit creations of Congress, or even of Robert Morris ?" Nor was any depreciation attempted, where the intrinsic value was so unequivocally stamped with the character of wit and freedom.—*Trans.*

served to Mr. Courtheath, that if he made one pay for being
waited on by his pretty sisters, it was by much too little ; but
if only for lodgings and supper, it was a great deal.   He seemed a little ashamed at having charged too high, and offered to
make a pretty considerable abatement, which I refused, content with having shewn him, that though a foreigner, I was no
stranger to the price of articles, and satisfied with the excuse
he made me, that being himself a stranger and without property in the country, he was obliged to purchase every thing.   I
learnt, on this occasion, that he hired the inn he kept, as well
as a large barn which served for his stable, and a garden of two
or three acres, for eighty-four bushels of corn a year : in fact,
the depreciation of paper has compelled people to this manner
of making bargains, which is perhaps the best of all, but is
unquestionably an effectual remedy to the present disorder.

At eight o'clock I took leave of my landlord and young
landladies, to penetrate through the woods by a road with
which nobody was very well acquainted.   The country I was
to pass through, called *the Clove*, is extremely wild, and was
scarcely known before the war : it is a sort of valley, or gorge,
situated to the westward of the high mountains between New-
Windsor and King's ferry, and at the foot of which are West-
Point and Stony-Point, and the principal forts which defend
the river.   In times when the river is not navigable, on account of
ice, or contrary winds, it is necessary to have communication by
land between the states of New-York and the Jerseys, between
New-Windsor and Morristown.   This communication traversing
the Clove when General Green was Quarter-Master-General, he
opened a road for the convoys of provisions and the artillery.
This was the road I took, leaving on my right the Romopog road,
and ascending by that which comes from Ringwood.   Ringwood is only a hamlet of seven or eight houses, formed by
Mrs. Erskine's manor and the forges, which are profitable
to her.   I had been told that I should find there all sorts of
conveniences, whether in point of lodgings, if I chose to stop,
or in procuring every information I might stand in need of.
As it was early in the day, and I had travelled but twelve
miles, I alighted at Mrs. Erskine's, only to desire her to point
out to me some inn where I might sleep, or to recommend me
to some hospitable quarters.   I entered a very handsome house
where every body was in mourning, Mr. Erskine being dead
two months before. Mrs. Erskine, his widow, is about forty, and
did not appear the less fresh or tranquil for her misfortune. She
had with her one of her nephews, and Mr. John Fell, a member of Congress.   They gave me all the necessary information,
and after drinking a glass of Madeira, according to the custom
of the country, which will not allow you to leave a house with-

out tasting something, I got on horseback, and penetrated afresh into the woods, mounting and descending very high mountains, until I found myself on the borders of a lake, so solitary and concealed, that it is only visible through the trees with which it is surrounded. The declivities which form its banks are so steep, that if a deer made a false step on the top of the mountain, he would infallibly roll into the lake, without being able to rise up. This lake which is not marked upon the charts, and is called *Duck Sider*, is about three miles long and two wide. I was now in the wildest and most desert country I had yet passed through ; my imagination was already enjoying this solitude, and my eyes were searching through the woods for some extraordinary animals, such as elks or caribous (supposed to be the same as the reindeer) when I perceived, in an open spot, a quadruped which seemed very large. I started with joy, and was advancing slowly, but on a nearer observation of the monster of the desert, to my great regret I discovered it to be a horse peaceably browsing the grass ; and the opening, no other than a field belonging to a new settlement. On advancing a few steps farther, I met two children of eight or ten years old, returning quietly from school carrying under their arms a little basket, and a large book. Thus was I obliged to lay aside all the ideas of a poet or a sportsman, to admire this new country, where one cannot travel four miles without finding a dwelling, nor find one which is not within reach of every possible succour, as well in the natural as in the moral order. These reflections, and the fine weather we had all the afternoon, made the end of my day's journey very agreeable. At the beginning of the night, I arrived at the house of Mr. Smith, who formerly kept an inn, though at present he lodges only his friends ; but as I had not the honour to be of that number, I was obliged to go a little farther, to Hern's tavern, a very indifferent house, where I supped and slept. I left it the 19th, as early as possible ; having still twelve miles to New-Windsor, and intending to stay only one night, I was anxious to pass at least the greatest part of the day with General Washington. I met him two miles from New-Windsor ; he was in his carriage with Mrs. Washington, going on a visit to Mrs. Knox, whose quarters were a mile farther on, near the artillery barracks. They wished to return with me, but I begged them to continue their way. The general gave me one of his aid-de-camps, (Colonel Humphreys*) to conduct me to his house, assured me that

---

* He is at present secretary of the embassy to the court of France. This brave and excellent soldier is at the same time a poet of great

he should not be long in joining me, and he returned accordingly in half an hour. I saw him again with the same pleasure, but with a different sentiment from what he had inspired me with at our first interview. I felt that internal satisfaction, in which self-love has some share, but which we always experience in finding ourselves in an intimacy already formed, in real society with a man we have long admired without being able to approach him. It then seems as if this great man more peculiarly belongs to us than to the rest of mankind; heretofore we desired to see him; henceforth, so to speak, we exhibit him; we knew him, we are better acquainted with him than others, have the same advantage over them, that a man having read a book through, has in conversation over him who is only at the beginning.

The General insisted on my lodging with him, though his house was much less than that he had at Prakness. Several officers, whom I had not seen at the army, came to dine with us. The principal of whom were Colonel Malcomb, a native of Scotland, but settled in America, where he has served with distinction in the continental army; he has since retired to his estate, and is now only a militia Colonel; Colonel Smith,*

---

talents: he is the author of a poem addressed to the American army, a work recently known in England, where, in spite of the national jealousy, and the affectation of depreciating every thing American, it has had such success, as to have been several times publicly read in the manner of the ancients. [The Marquis de Chastellux may be assured that it is not by that part of the English nation who are "jealous of America, and who affect to depreciate every thing American," that the poem of Colonel Humphreys is admired, it is by that numerous and enlightened class of free spirits, who have always supported, and wished prosperity to the glorious struggle of America, who rejoiced at her success, and who look forward with hope and pleasure to her rising greatness.—*Trans.*]

* The author having since been very intimate with Colonel Smith, can take it upon himself to assert, that this young man is not only a very good soldier, but an excellent scholar. The manner of his entering into the service merits relation: he was designed for the profession of the law, and was finishing his studies at New-York, when the American army assembled there after the unfortunate affair of Long-Island. He immediately resolved to take arms in defence of his country, but his parents disapproving of this step, he enlisted as a common soldier, without making himself known, or pretending to any superior rank. Being one day on duty at the door of a General officer, he was discovered by a friend of his family, who spoke of him to that General officer. He was immediately invited to dinner; but he answered that he could not quit his duty; his corporal was sent for to relieve him.

an officer highly spoken of, and who commanded a battalion of light infantry under M. de la Fayette ; Colonel Humphreys, the General's aid-de-camp, and several others, whose names I have forgot, but who had all the best *ton*, and the easiest deportment. The dinner was excellent ; tea succeeded dinner, and conversation succeeded tea, and lasted till supper. The war was frequently the subject : on asking the General which of our professional books he read with the most pleasure ; he told me, the King of Prussia's Instructions to his Generals, and the Tactics of M. de Guibert ; from whence I concluded that he knew as well how to select his authors as to profit by them.

I should have been very happy to accept of his pressing invitation to pass a few days with him, had I not made a solemn promise, at Philadelphia, to the Vicomte de Noailles, and his travelling companions, to arrive four and twenty hours after them if they stopped there, or at Albany, if they went straight on. We were desirous of seeing Stillwater and Saratoga, and it would have been no easy matter for us to have acquired a just knowledge of that country had we not been together, because we reckoned upon General Schuyler, who could not be expected to make two journies to gratify our curiosity. I was thus far faithful to my engagement, for I arrived at New-Windsor the same day that they left Cress Point ; I hoped to overtake them at Albany, and General Washington finding that he could not retain me, was pleased himself to conduct me in his barge to the other side of the river. We got on shore at Fishkill Landing Place, to gain the eastern road, preferred by travellers to the western. I now quitted the General, but he insisted that Colonel Smith should accompany me as far as Poughkeepsie. The road to this town passes pretty near Fishkill, which we leave on the right, from thence we travel on the heights, where there is a beautiful and extensive prospect, and traversing a township, called Middlebrook, arrive at the creek, and at Wapping Fall. There I, halted a few minutes to consider, under different points of view, the charming landscape formed by this river, as well from its cascade, which is roaring and picturesque, as from the groups of trees and rocks, which

---

and he returned to his post after dinner. A few days only elapsed before that General officer, charmed with his zeal, made him his aid-de-camp. In 1780, he commanded a battalion of light infantry, and the year following was made aid-de-camp to General Washington, with whom he remained until the peace.—[He is now Secretary to the Embassy to the court of Great Britain, and has lately married the daughter of his Excellency John Adams, Minister Plenipotentiary to that court.—*Trans.*]

combined with a number of saw mills and furnaces, compose the most capricious and romantic prospect.

It was only half past three when I got to Poughkeepsie, where I intended sleeping ; but finding that the *sessions* were then holding and that all the taverns were full, I took advantage of the little remaining day to reach a tavern I was told of at three miles distance. Colonel Smith who had business at Poughkeepsie remained there, and I was very happy to find myself in the evening with nobody but my two aids-de-camp. It was, in fact, a new enjoyment for us to be left to ourselves, at perfect liberty to give mutual accounts of the impression left on our minds by so many different objects. I only regretted not having seen Governor Clinton, for whom I had letters of recommendation. He is a man who governs with the utmost vigour and firmness, and is inexorable to the tories, whom he makes tremble, though they are very numerous : he has had the address to maintain in its duty this province, one extremity of which borders on Canada, the other on the city of New-York. He was then at Poughkeepsie, but taken up with the business of the sessions : besides, Saratoga, and Burgoyne's different fields of battle, being henceforth the sole object of my journey, I was wishing to get forward for fear of being hindered by the snow, and of the roads becoming impassable. On my arrival at Pride's tavern, I asked a number of questions of my landlord respecting the appearance he thought there was of a continuance or a change of weather, and perceiving that he was a good farmer, I interrogated him on the subject of agriculture, and drew the following details from him. The land is very fertile in Duchess County, of which Poughkeepsie is the capital, as well as in the state of New-York, but it is commonly left fallow one year out of two or three, less from necessity than from their being more land than they can cultivate. A bushel of wheat at most is sown upon an acre, which renders twenty, and five and twenty for one. Some farmers sow oats on the land that has borne wheat the preceding year, but this grain in general is reserved for lands newly turned up :* flax is also a considerable object of cultivation : the land is ploughed with horses, two or three to a plough ; sometimes

* Flax has become a very great and profitable article of cultivation in the Middle and Eastern states, the principal cultivators are settlers from the north of Ireland, who know the value of it in their own country. In Massachusetts, there is a very considerable and flourishing settlement, called Londonderry, peopled entirely by emigrants from that city, where they apply themselves particularly to the growth of flax.—*Trans.*

even a greater number when on new land, or that which has long lain fallow. Mr. Pride, while he was giving me these details, always flattered me with the hopes of fine weather the next day. I went to rest, highly satisfied with him and his prognostics ; in the morning, however, when I awakened, I saw the ground already entirely white, and snow, which continued to fall in abundance, mixed with hail and ice. There was nothing to be done under such circumstances, but to continue my journey, as if it was fine weather, only taking a little better breakfast than I should otherwise have done. But I regretted most that the snow, or rather small hail that drove against my eyes, prevented me from seeing the country ; which, as far as I could judge, is beautiful and well cultivated. After travelling about ten miles, I traversed the township of Strasbourg, called by the inhabitants of the country, Strattsborough. This township is five or six miles long, yet the houses are not far from each other. As I was remarking one which was rather handsome, the owner came to the door, doubtless from curiosity, and asked me, in French, if I would alight, and step in and dine with him. Nothing can be more seducing in bad weather, than such a proposal ; but on the other hand, nothing is more cruel, when one has once got under shelter, than to quit the fire-side, a second time to expose oneself to frost and snow.

I refused therefore the dinner offered me by this gallant man, but not the questions he put to me. I asked him, in my turn, whether he had not seen some French officers pass, meaning the Vicomte de Noailles, the Comte de Damos, and the Chevalier de Mauduit, who, as they had three or four servants, and six or seven horses, might have been remarked on the road. My Dutchman, for I have since learnt that his name is Le Roy,* a Dutch merchant, born in Europe, and acquainted with France, where he lived some time ; my Dutchman, replied like a man who knew France, and who speaks French ; " Sir, it is very true that the Prince de Conti passed by here yesterday evening, with two officers, in their way to Albany." I could not discover whether it was to the Vicomte de Noailles, or to the Comte de Damos, that I ought to do homage for his principality ; but

---

* The translator had the pleasure of being well acquainted with one of the sons of Mr. Le Roy, a most amiable young man, whom he knew at Amsterdam, when residing with his aunt Madame Chabanel, the widow of a rich merchant, who did a great deal of business with America previous to the war. He saw him afterwards at Philadelphia and Boston, and has only to regret, that his affairs rendered it impossible to accept of a kind invitation to pay him a visit at Strattsborough. Mrs. Chabanel's house, at Amsterdam, was open to all the Americans in Holland during the war.—*Trans.*

as they are both my relations, I answered with strict truth, that
my cousin having gone on before, I was very glad to know at
what hour they passed, and when I should be able to join them;
so that if Mr. Le Roy, as no doubt he did, consulted his almanack, he will have set me down for the Duke of Orleans, or the
Duke of Chartres; which was the more probable as I had nine
horses with me, whilst the Prince de Conti, being farther removed from the crown, had only seven.

You scarcely get out of Strasbourgh, before you enter the
township of Rhynbeck. It is unnecessary to observe, that all
these names discover a German origin. At Rhynbeck, nobody
came out to ask me to dinner. But this snow mixed with hail
was so cold, and I was so fatigued with keeping my horse
from slipping, that I should have stopped here even without
being invited by the handsome appearance of the inn called
Thomas' Inn. It was no more, however, than half past two;
but as I had already come three and twenty miles, the house
was good, the fire well lighted, my host a tall good looking
man, a sportsman, a horse dealer, and disposed to chat, I determined, according to the English phrase, to spend the rest of
my day there. The following is all I got interesting from Mr.
Thomas. In time of peace, he carried on a great trade of
horses, which he purchased in Canada, and sent to New-York,
there to be shipped for the West-Indies. It is incredible with
what facility this trade is carried on in winter; he assured me
that he once went to Montreal, and brought back with him,
in a fortnight seventy-five horses which he bought there. This
is effected by travelling in a right line, traversing Lake George
upon ice and the snow, the desert between that Lake and
Montreal. The Canadian horses easily travel eighteen or
twenty hours a day, and three or four men, mounted, are sufficient to drive one hundred before them. " It was I," added
Mr. Thomas, " who made, or rather who repaired the fortune
of that rogue, *Arnold*. He had conducted his affairs ill, in the
little trade he carried on at New-Haven;*· I persuaded him to

---

* Arnold was brought up to the business of an apothecary, being
taken from his mother, out of charity, by Doctor Lothrop of Norwich
in Connecticut, who was at once a physician, surgeon, apothecary,
merchant, and shopkeeper, as is usual in America; after his appren-
ticeship expired, his master gave him 500*l.* and letters of recommendation to his correspondents in London, by which means he obtained
credit for some thousands, and returning to Connecticut, settled at
New-Haven, set up an equipage, with ten horses, a carriage, and a
number of servants, failed in two years, and was thrown into jail, where
he remained till released by a bankrupt act passed the Assembly. He
then seduced, and afterwards married the daughter of Mr. Mansfield.

purchase horses in Canada, and to go himself and sell them at Jamaica. This speculation alone was sufficient to pay his debts, and set him once more afloat." After talking of trade, we got

---

High Sheriff of New-Haven, much against the will of the latter; who at length, became reconciled to him, and employed him as a supercargo to the West-Indies, where he usually went in the spring, and returned in the autumn with molasses, rum, and sugar. In winter, he went among the Dutch towards the head of Hudson's River, and into Canada, with various sorts of woollen goods, such as stockings, caps, mittens, &c. &c. and also cheese, which sold to great profit in Canada. These articles he either exchanged for horses, or purchased them with the money arising from his sales. With these horses, which generally made a part of a Connecticut cargo, together with poultry, corn, and fish, he went to the islands, whilst his father-in-law was selling the rum, molasses and sugars of the last voyage, and collecting woollens for Arnold's next winter trip to Canada. It was in these voyages that Arnold became an expert seaman, which qualified him for the command of the fleet on the lakes, where he behaved with his usual gallantry against a much superior enemy. The translator had an opportunity, during his residence at Porto Rico during the war, of seeing several of these Connecticut sloops make very advantageous sales of their little cargoes. After disembarking their horses, they ran their vessels up to the quay, and converted them into retail shops, where they dealt out their onions, potatoes, salt fish, and *apples*, (an article which brought a very high price,) in the smallest quantities, for which they received hard dollars, although *it is a fact*, that specie was uncommonly scarce in this *Spanish* island, almost all the intercourse being carried on in *paper dollars*, whilst the *French* part of the neighbouring island of Hispaniola was full of Spanish money, and the French fleet and army were paid in dollars from the Havana. The translator hopes that he shall here be pardoned a digression on the subject of this *charming island*, which in the hands of any other nation would certainly become one of the most valuable possessions in the American Archipelago. Its central situation between the windward and leeward islands, its capacious harbour, the number of springs and rivers with which it is watered, (the latter abounding with fish,) the excellence of its soil, the greatest part of which is nearly in a virgin state, the strong position of the peninsula of St. John, are advantages, which if in the possession of a great *active* maritime power, such as France or England, can scarcely be appreciated. In the possession of Spain, it is at most but a negative advantage ; for I am well assured that the king only receives the inconsiderable revenue of 100,000 piasters, from this island, whilst he expended, in the course of the late war, no less than *eight millions* on the fortifications, which I had the *very singular favour* to visit, accompanied by the first engineer, and the strength of which is now deemed not less formidable than those of fort Moro, and the Havana. Nor could England, with her then force in the West-Indies, have attacked this island with any prospect of suc-

to agriculture : he told me, that in the neighbourhood of Rhynbeck, the land was uncommonly fruitful, and that for a bushel
of sown wheat, he reaped from thirty to forty. The corn is so
abundant that they do not take the trouble of cutting it with a
sickle, but mow it like hay. Some dogs of a beautiful kind
moving about the house, awakened my passion for the chase ;
on asking Mr. Thomas what use he made of them, he told me,
that they were only for hunting the fox ; that deer, stags, and
bears, were, pretty common in the country, but they seldom
killed them except in winter, either by tracing on the snow, or
by tracking them in the woods. All American conversation
must finish with politics. Those of Mr. Thomas appeared to
me rather equivocal ; he was too rich, and complained too much
of the flour he furnished for the army to let me think him a
good whig. He gave himself out for such notwithstanding, but
I observed that he was greatly attached to an opinion *which I
found generally diffused throughout the state of New-York ; that
there is no expedition more useful, nor more easy than the conquest
of Canada. It is impossible to conceive the ardour the inhabitants
of the north still have to recommence that enterprise.* The reason
is, that their country is so fertile, and so happily situated for
commerce, that they are sure to become very wealthy as soon
as they have nothing to fear from the savages ; now the savages

---

cess, though many persons in Jamaica were sanguine for such an expedition. Besides an immense train of very fine artillery, three of the
best regiments in the Spanish service were there in garrison, in full
health, viz.: the regiments *de Bruxelles, de la Couronne,* and *de la
Victoire,* and a most numerous militia. Indeed, so secure did they
think themselves, that they embarked, when I was there, the regiment
de la Couronne, consisting of 1200 men for Carthagena. The interior of the country, which I was likewise allowed to visit, is delightful ;
land may be had for nothing, but every settler must not only be a Catholic, but a rigid one, *the Inquisition* having an officer here ; he must
likewise marry, and wretched is his choice, within a year, nor is he
ever allowed to remove any property from the island, should he wish
to quit it, except what he can carry off clandestinely. Several Irish
are settled here, but all under the predicament of sacrificing to the
most gloomy superstition, the most arbitrary jealousy of despotic power, and to the most horrid state of nuptial slavery, with the ugliest and
filthiest of women. The officers of the *Dragon* man-of-war of 60
guns, and of the frigates which were lying there, and the military in
garrison were anxious to peruse the European and American Gazettes
I had with me, but even this communication was obliged to be confined to very few, and under the strictest injunctions of secrecy, for
our mutual safety. In other respects it is impossible to have met with
a more hospitable reception.—*Trans.*

are only formidable when they are supported and animated by the English.

I left Thomas' inn the 23d, at 8 in the morning, and travelled three hours always in Livington's Manor. The road was good, and the country rich and well cultivated. We pass several considerable villages, the houses of which are handsome and neat, and every object here announces prosperity. On leaving this district, we enter that of Claverack, then descend from the hills, and approach Hudson's River. We soon after come to a creek, which is also called by the name of Claverack, and which falls not far from this into the Hudson. As soon as you have passed this creek, an immense rock, which runs, across in the direction of the road, obliges you to turn to the right to reach Claverack meeting-house, and to pursue the road to Albany. This rock, or rather chain of rocks, merits all the attention of naturalists. It is about three miles in length. As I did not traverse it, I am ignorant of its width, but it is so steep to the south, that it can be ascribed to nothing but a shrinking of the earth, occasioned by a violent shock. Yet one does not find, either in the space between this rock and the little river, or on the opposite bank, any correspondence with the accidental separation it announces. Its flank, which is almost exposed, presents parallel beds, but rarely horizontal, which made me conjecture that it was of a calcareous nature ;* I tried it with aquafortis, and found my conjecture just. But I was the most struck with the strength and beauty of the trees which grow in the midst of it, the trunks of which rise out of the chinks formed by the separation of the rock. Unless you closely examine these trees, it is impossible to believe that they can grow, and get to such a height without an inch of earth to nourish their roots. Several of them grow horizontally, to a certain distance, and then assume a vertical direction. Others have their roots quite naked, which proves that their origin is prior to the catastrophe, whatever it was, which one cannot refuse admitting. These roots are in the most whimsical directions imaginable, resem-

---

* The Marquis having, in his account of *Totahaw Falls*, observed that there is little or no calcareous stone in *this country*, by which I am at a loss to know whether he means the state of New-Jersey, where he then was, or the United States in general ; I take this opportunity of mentioning, that limestone abounds in a great part of the Continent ; the interior parts of Pennsylvania, Maryland, and Virginia in particular are intersected by immense strata of this invaluable stone, which lie every where exposed to the day, or very near the surface.

bling serpents crawling amidst the ruins of an immense edifice. The principal part of the trees I speak of, are of that sort of fir called hemlock by the English, but they are mixed with others, which I took to be walnut-trees, and other white wood; but I must observe that this conjecture cannot be relied on, as I did not see the leaves, and am not well enough acquainted with trees to distinguish by their branches and their structure.*

Claverack is a pretty considerable township, and extends very far. On quitting it you traverse several woods to arise at the first houses of Kinderhook. I found in these woods new improvements, and several log-huts. But on approaching one of them, I perceived, with regret, that the family who inhabited it had been long settled there, without thinking of building a better house, an uncommon circumstance in America, and which is almost unexampled, except in the Dutch settlements; for that people are more economical than industrious, and are more desirous of amassing wealth than of adding to their comfort. When you arrive at the first hamlet of Kinderhook, you must make a long circuit to reach the meeting-house, which is in the centre of what may be properly called the town of Kinderhook. There you pass a pretty considerable stream, and have the choice of three or four inns; but the best is that of Mr. Van Burragh. The preference given to this, however, does no honour to the others; it is a very small house, kept by two young people of a Dutch family; they are civil and attentive, and you are not badly off with them, provided you are not difficult to please. It would have ill become me now to have been so, for I had nothing but snow, hail, and frost during the whole day, and any fireside was an agreeable asylum for me.

---

* With great submission to the author, he appears to have laid a greater stress on this phenomenon than it has any claim to from its singularity; every mountainous country in Europe abounds with such appearances, which, though curious, may possibly be accounted for on principles more simple, and less *systematical*, than those great convulsions so enthusiastically imagined by the disciples of the *buffonic* school. The translator too owns himself ignorant of the species of *fir*, called *hemlock* by the English.— *Trans.*

CHAPTER X.

It was a difficult question to know where I should the next day pass the North river, for I was told that it was neither sufficiently broken to cross it on the ice, nor free enough from flakes to venture it in a boat. Apprized of these obstacles, I set out early on the 24th, that I might have time to discover the easiest passage. I was only twenty miles from Albany; so that after a continued journey through a forest of fir trees, I arrived at one o'clock on the banks of the Hudson. The vale in which this river runs, and the town of Albany, which is built in the form of an amphitheatre on its western bank, must have afforded a very agreeable coup d'oeil, had it not been disfigured by the snow. A handsome house half way up the bank opposite the ferry, seems to attract attention, and to invite strangers to stop at General Schuyler's, who is the proprietor as well as architect. I had recommendations to him from all quarters, but particularly from General Washington and Mrs. Carter. I had besides given the rendezvous to Colonel Hamilton, who had just married another of his daughters,* and was preceded by the Vicomte de Noailles, and the

---

* Colonel Hamilton is so well known by all those who have had any connexion with America, that it would be unnecessary to point him out more particularly, were not this journal, at length destined for publication, likely to fall into the hands of several readers who were ignorant of, or have forgotten, many details relative to this revolution, to which their attention may still be awakened. Colonel Hamilton, a native of Sainte Croix, and some time settled in America, was destined to the profession of the law, and had scarcely completed his studies, when General Washington, versed as* all great men are in the discovery of talents, and in the employment of them, made him at once his aid-de-camp and secretary, a post as eminent as important in the American army. From that time his correspondence with the French, which language he speaks and writes perfectly well, the details of every kind, political and military, entrusted to him, developed those talents, the general had known how to discover, and put in activity; whilst the young soldier, by a prudence and secrecy still more beyond his age than his information, justified the confidence with which he

Comte de Damas, who I knew were arrived the night before. The sole difficulty therefore consisted in passing the river. Whilst the boat was making its way with difficulty through the flakes of ice, which we were obliged to break as we advanced. Mr. Lynch, who is not indifferent about a good dinner, contemplating General Schuyler's house, mournfully says to me, " I am sure the Vicomte and Damas are now at table, where they have good cheer, and good company, whilst we are here kicking our heels, in hopes of getting this evening to some wretched alehouse." I partook a little of his anxiety, but diverted myself by assuring him that they saw us from the windows, that I even distinguished the Vicomte de Noailles who was looking at us through a telescope, and that he was going to send somebody to conduct us on our landing to that excellent house, where we should find dinner ready to come on table; I even pretended that a sledge I had seen descending towards the river was designed for us. As chance would have it, never was conjecture more just. The first person we saw on shore, was the Chevalier de Mauduit, who was waiting for us with the general's sledge, into which we quickly stepped and were conveyed in an instant into a handsome saloon, near a good fire, with Mr. Schuyler, his wife and daughters. Whilst we were warming ourselves, dinner was served, to which every one did honour, as well as to the Madeira which was excellent,

---

was honoured. He continued to serve in this capacity till the year 1781, when desirous of distinguishing himself in the command of troops, as he had done in all his other functions, he took that of a battalion of light infantry. It was at the head of this battalion, that jointly with M. de Gimat, he carried by assault one of the enemy's redoubts at the siege of Yorktown. The reader will perhaps be surprised to hear, that the next year, before the peace was made, Mr. Hamilton turned advocate, and became a member of Congress. The explanation of this enigma is, that the war being considered as at an end, it was necessary for him to think of his fortune, which was very inconsiderable. Now the profession of a *lawyer*, which comprehends those of attorney and notary, is not only the most respectable in America, but likewise the most lucrative; and there is no doubt that, with such talents and such knowledge, Mr. Hamilton must be in peace, as well as in war, one of the most considerable citizens in his new country. At present he is settled at New-York. [To this just eulogium, the translator takes the liberty of adding, that Colonel Hamilton is a most elegant writer, and a perfectly accomplished gentleman, and as such could not fail of distinguishing himself in the first European circles. His account of the behaviour and death of the unfortunate *Andre*, to which he was a witness, published at the time in the American and English prints, does equal honour to his understanding and his heart.—*Trans.*]

and made us completely forget the rigour of the season, and the fatigue of the journey.

General Schuyler's family was composed of Mrs. Hamilton, his second daughter, who has a mild agreeable countenance; of Miss Peggy Schuyler, whose features are animated and striking; of another charming girl, only eight years old, and of three boys, the eldest of whom is fifteen, and are the handsomest children you can see. He is himself about fifty, but already gouty and infirm. His fortune is very considerable, and it will become still more so, for he possesses an immense extent of territory, but derives more credit from his talents and information, than from his wealth. He served with General Amherst in the Canadian war, as deputy Quarter-Master-General. From that period he made himself known, and became distinguished; he was very useful to the English, and was sent for to London after the peace, to settle the accounts of every thing furnished by the Americans. His marriage with Miss Rensselaer, the rich heiress of a family which has given its name to a district, or rather a whole province, still added to his credit and his influence; so that it was not surprising he should be raised to the rank of Major-General at the beginning of the war, and have the command of the troops on the frontiers of Canada. It was in this capacity, that he was commissioned in 1777 to oppose the progress of General Burgoyne; but having received orders from Congress, directly contrary to his opinion, without being provided with any means necessary for carrying them into execution, he found himself obliged to evacuate Ticonderoga, and fall back on the Hudson. These measures, undoubtedly prudent in themselves, being unfavourably construed in a moment of ill humour and anxiety, he was tried by a court martial, as well as General St. Clair, his second in command, and both of them were soon after *honourably acquitted.* St. Clair resumed his station in the army, but General Schuyler, justly offended, demanded more satisfactory reparation, and reclaimed his rank which, since this event, was contested with him by two or three generals of the same standing. This affair not being settled, he did not rejoin the army, but continued his services to his country. Elected a member of Congress the year following, he was nearly chosen president in opposition to Mr. Laurens; since that time he has always enjoyed the confidence of the government, and of General Washington, who are at present paying their court to him, and pressing him to accept the office of secretary at war.

Whilst we were in this excellent asylum, the weather continued doubtful, between frost and thaw; there was a little snow upon the ground, and it was probable there soon would be a fall. The council of travellers assembled, and it ap-

peared to them proper not to delay their departure for Saratoga.   General Schuyler offered us a house which he has upon
his own estate; but he could not serve us as guide, on account
of an indisposition, and his apprehension of a fit of the gout.
He proposed giving us an intelligent officer to conduct us to
the different fields of battle, whilst his son should go before to
prepare us lodgings.   We could still travel on horseback, and
were supplied with horses of the country to replace ours which
were fatigued, and a part of which still remained on the other
side of the river.   All these arrangements being accepted, we
were conveyed to Albany in a sledge.   On our arrival, we
waited on Brigadier-General Clinton, to whom I delivered my
letters of recommendation.   He is an honest man, but of no
distinguished talents, and is only employed out of respect to
his brother the governor.   He immediately ordered the horses
for our journey, and Major Popham, his aid-de-camp, an amiable and intelligent officer, was desired to conduct us.   He was
to take with him Major Græme, who knows properly the
ground, and served in the army under General Gates.

All our measures being well concerted, we each of us retired
to our quarters ; the Vicomte de Noailles and his two companions to an inn, kept by a Frenchman, called Louis, and I to
that of an American of the name of Blennissens.   At daybreak, tea was ready, and the whole caravan assembled at my
quarters ; but melted snow was falling, which did not promise
an agreeable ride.   We were in hopes that it was a real thaw,
and set out upon our journey.   The snow however fell thicker
and thicker, and was six inches deep when we arrived at the
junction of the Mohawk with the Hudson river.   Here is a
choice of two roads to Saratoga : one obliges you to pass the
Hudson, to keep some time along the left bank, and pass it a
second time near the Half-Moon ; the other goes on the Mohawk river till you get above the cataract, when you pass that
river, and traverse the woods to Stillwater.   Even had there
been no difficulty in passing the North river on account of the
ice, I should have preferred the other road, to see the cascade
of Cokes, which is one of the wonders of America.   Before
we left the Hudson, I remarked an island in the middle of its
bed, which offers a very advantageous position for erecting
batteries, to defend the navigation.   The two majors, to whom
I communicated this observation, told me that this point of defence was neglected, because there was a better one, a little
higher up, at the extremity of one of the three branches into
which the Mohawk river divides itself, in falling into the Hudson.   They added that this position was very slightly reconnoitred ; that which was begun to be fortified higher up, being
sufficient to stop the progress of the enemy.   Thus the more

you examine the country, the more you are convinced that the expedition of Burgoyne was extravagant, and must sooner or later have miscarried, independent of the engagements which decided the event.

The junction of the two rivers is six miles north of Albany, and after travelling two more in the woods, we began to hear a murmuring noise, which increased till we came in sight of Cohoes Fall. This cataract is the whole breadth of the river, that is to say, near two hundred toises, about 1200 English feet wide. It is a vast sheet of water, which falls 76 English feet.* The river in this place is contracted between two steep banks formed by the declivity of the mountains; these precipices are covered by an earth as black as iron ore, and on which nothing grows but firs and cypresses. The course of the river is straight, both before and after its fall, and the rocks forming this cascade are nearly on a level, but their irregular figure breaks the water whilst it is falling, and forms a variety of whimsical and picturesque appearances. This picture was rendered still more terrible by the snow which covered the firs, the brilliancy of which gave a black colour to the water, gliding gently along, and a yellow tinge to that which was dashing over the cataract.

After feasting our eyes with this awful spectacle, we travelled a mile higher up to the ferry where we hoped to pass the river; but on our arrival, found the boat so entangled in the ice and snow, that it was impossible to make use of it. We were assured, that people had passed a ferry two miles higher, that morning, whither we immediately went, determined to pursue our route, though the snow was greatly increased, and we were benumbed with wet and cold. The boatmen of this ferry made many objections on account of the bad weather and the smallness of their boat, which could only transport three horses at a time; but this difficulty did not stop us, and we agreed to make several trips. The first attempt was made to pass over my valet de chambre, with three horses: I was waiting by the fireside for my turn, when they came to inform me that the boat was coming back to shore, with some difficulty, and that the current had almost driven it towards the cataract. We were obliged therefore to submit to our destiny,

---

* Madame *la Comtesse de Genlis* in speaking of this cataract in one of the notes to her *Veilles du Chateau*, says it is only 50 feet, but from other accounts confirming this of M. de Chastellux, I am inclined to think, that is between 70 and 80 feet. This invaluable and correct writer, the pride of her son, and of humanity, has in this instance been unavoidably misled by the American travellers she consulted.—*Trans.*

which was not yet disposed to let us fulfil the object of our
voyage.   On this occasion I displayed a magnanimity which
placed me high in the esteem of the whole company: whilst
others were storming, and growing impatient, uncertain of the
measures to be taken, I serenely gave the signal for a retreat,
and thought no more of any thing but supper, for which I
made the most prudent dispositions on the spot.   The inn-
keeper of M. de Noailles being a Frenchman, and consequently
a better cook, or at least more active than mine, it was decided
that he should provide our supper: the best mounted cavalier
of the troop was despatched to give the necessary orders,
whom we followed in half an hour; we arrived as night was
coming on, and presently sat down to table.   Thus passed the
day's work of the 25th, which was not very agreeable till the
hour of supper, but terminated very happily; for what consolation does not one derive under disappointment, from a good
fire, a good supper, and good company?

The 26th, the rivers not being yet frozen, nor the roads
hard enough to make a long journey in a sledge, I determined
to remain at Albany.   My morning was employed in adjusting
my notes, which occupation was only interrupted by a visit
from Colonel Hamilton.   He told us that Mrs. Schuyler was a
little indisposed, but that the General would be equally glad
to receive us.   Accordingly he sent us his sledges the beginning of the evening.   We found him in his saloon with Mr.
and Mrs. Hamilton.   A conversation soon took place between
the General, the Vicomte de Noailles and me.   We had
already talked, when we were last with him, of some important
faults relative to the northern campaigns, of which we had asked some explanations.   Mr. Schuyler appeared no less desirous
of giving them.   He is pretty communicative, and is well
entitled to be so; his conversation is easy and agreeable; he
knows well what he says, and expresses himself well on every
thing he knows.   To give the best answer to our questions, he
proposed to us to read his political and military correspondence with General Washington, which we accepted with great
pleasure, and leaving the rest of the company with Mr. and
Mrs. Hamilton, we retired into another room.   The General
opening his pocket-book, the Vicomte and I divided the different manuscripts, containing upwards of sixty pages of close
writing on paper à la Telliere.   The first despatch I read was
a letter written by him to General Washington, in November
1777: it contained a plan of attack on Canada, which originated in the following circumstance: Two English officers after
being made prisoners with Burgoyne's army, obtained permission to return to Canada on their parole, and on the road stopped at General Schuyler's at Saratoga.   The conversation, as

we may easily suppose, soon turned on the great event, the impression of which was so recent. One of these officers being attached to General Burgoyne, criminated Governor Sir Guy Carleton, whom he accused of having retained too many troops in Canada; the states maintained that he had not even reserved sufficient for the defence of the country. From assertions they came to proofs, which proofs could only be an exact detail of all the forces then remaining in Canada, and their distribution. General Schuyler was attentive, and took advantage of the dispute. He learns by this means, that Canada was in real danger; and proposed, in consequence, to General Washington to retake Ticonderoga, in case that post was not abandoned, as it actually has been, and to proceed from thence to Montreal. This plan is extremely well conceived, and exhibits a great knowledge of the country; and what struck me as the most worthy of attention, is the immensity of the resources to be found in this country for a winter expedition, and the extreme facility with which an army may rapidly advance, by means of sledges to transport the provisions and stores, and even sick and lame soldiers. It is possible, in a months time, to collect, between the Connecticut and Hudson river, fifteen hundred sledges, two thousand horses and as many oxen; the latter may be shod for the ice, like horses, and serve to draw the sledges with provisions; and as these are consumed, or the oxen fatigued, they may be slain for the food of the army. Nor must it be imagined that these expeditions are so dreadful for the soldiers as we are accustomed to suppose them. With the feet and legs well fortified, and proper clothing, which it was easy to procure before the finances and resources of the country were exhausted, they support extremely well the fatigue of long marches; and as they pass all the night in the woods, they easily find shelter, and light great fires, by which they sleep better than under tents; for it is to be observed, that if the cold be severe in this country, it is always a dry cold, against which it is much more easy to provide than against rain and moisture.

General Schuyler never received any answer to this letter, nor does he know with whom the fault lies. M. de la Fayette however came to Albany in January to prepare and command an expedition similar to that he had projected: he showed his instructions to General Schuyler, who discovered it to be his own plan, of which he supposes some other person wished to claim the honour, but as no orders had come to him, he had made no preparations, nor were there any made on the side of Connecticut; so that M. de la Fayette, how agreeable soever this expedition might be to him, had so much good sense and attachment to the interest of America as to admit the difficulties, and divert Congress from pursuing it.

The winter following, after the evacuation of Philadelphia, and the affair of Monmouth, General Washington, always more occupied in putting an end to the misfortunes of his country, than in prolonging the duration of the brilliant part he was acting in America, wrote to Mr. Schuyler, to consult him on an expedition to Canada, and on the means of executing it with success. In answer to this letter, he sent a memoir perfectly well conceived, and no less well written, in which he proposed three different plans. The first was to collect his forces near the sources of the Connecticut, at a place called Coos; from thence there is only a trifling carrying place to the rivers which fall into the St. Lawrence, below Lake Saint Pierre, near to Quebec. But this plan would be difficult of execution, from the scarcity of resources on the Connecticut river, and from the great difficulties to be encountered in approaching those to be provided on the Hudson and Mohawk rivers, besides that the attack would thus be carried into the heart of the English forces, and too near the sea, from whence they derive their principal aid. The second project was to remount the Mohawk river, then to embark on Lake Oneida, and crossing Lake Ontario, proceed westward to besiege Niagara; then returning by the same route, to descend the river, and attack Montreal by the north. In this plan, General Schuyler foresaw two great inconveniences; one, from the long circuit it would be necessary to make, thus giving the English time to collect their troops at the point of attack; the other from the impossibility there was of deceiving the enemy by threatening them on the side of Lake Champlain, and Sorel, since the preparations on the Mohawk and Hudson River could not fail of disclosing the whole system of the campaign. It was by Lake Champlain therefore, and in the winter, that General Schuyler proposed marching directly to Montreal; leaving St. John's on the right, and postponing the attack of that post until spring, which was not to be secured, before the Isle of Montreal, and *all the upper country* should be got possession of: on this plan there would be no difficulty in concealing its real object; as the necessary preparations might be collected on the rivers Hudson and Connecticut; the shifting from one to the other being an easy measure. Thus the enemy would be alarmed at once for Quebec, St. Johns, and Montreal. On this supposition, it is probable they would prefer sacrificing Montreal. There an advantageous establishment might be formed, and measures taken to attack Quebec; but in case of their being obliged to abandon it, an easy retreat would always be secured by the *Beaver hunting place*,* and Lake Champlain. Such was the object of this long despatch which I read with great attention and much pleasure, and of which I have attempted to give some idea, convinced as I am that this article of my journal will not be uninteresting to military men ; others may render it amusing, by surveying the chart, and running over the immense country embraced by these different projects.

The next memoir which fell into my hands was the answer of General Washington. After testifying the greatest confidence in General Schuyler, he enters into discussion with him, and offers his reflections with a modesty as amiable, as worthy of estimation. He is of opinion that the expedition by Lake Ontario is perhaps too highly rejected without sufficient reason ; that it would be easy for him to favour the attack of Niagara, by a diversion he could make on Lake Erie, by marching the Virginia troops on the side of the Ohio and Fort Pitt : he inquires whether it be possible to build boats on Hudson's river, and transport them on carriages to the Mohawk ; his object in this was evidently to obviate one of the principal objections I have mentioned ; that the preparations for this expedition revealed too much the real object. All the other points are treated with wisdom and precision ; which renders the reply of General Schuyler still more curious and interesting. It is worthy both of the importance of the subject, and of the great man to whom it is addressed. Mr. Schuyler persists in his opinion ; and invariably attached to his project of attack by Lake Champlain, he proves that it may be executed in summer as well as in winter. Every thing depends, according to him, on possessing a naval superiority,† which he is of opinion may

---

* This is the name given in the English charts to the deserts between Lake Ontario, the River St. Lawrence, and the Lakes George and Champlain, and the River of Sorel.

† From these accounts it appears very evident that General Carleton acted with great prudence in retaining the force he did in Canada, for which he has been blamed by some, when Burgoyne went on his expedition ; in the catastrophe of which, 1500 or 2000 men more would probably have made little difference, but the want of which would have totally enfeebled the defence of Canada, and thrown that province into the hands of the United States. The American ideas too, on the subject of an expedition into Canada, and which may possibly be carried into execution at some future period, merit the attention of the English government, more particularly as America, since she is put in possession of the Kennebec and the boundary line, cuts the Sorel river below Lake Champlain, can now carry on her operations at her ease, and unmolested on the lakes, and by Arnold's route ; but, in fact, Canada must, on a rupture, follow the fortune of the United States :

be easily obtained by constructing larger vessels than those of
the English, and he is persuaded that two fifty gun ships would
be sufficient to secure it. People are wrong, added he, in

---

that province can only be prevented from falling rapidly before such a
force as the Eastern States can put in motion, by *very strong* forts
built at the head of the *Kennebec*, *St. Croix*, and *Connecticut* rivers,
by forts on *both* sides of the Sorel, where cut by the boundary line, on
both sides the St. Lawrence where it joins that river, at *the head* of the
carrying place above Niagara, on the English side, where a new carrying place, must if possible be formed, and *opposite* the fort of Detroit and Michilimazance, (now Michilimackinac.) All must be
strong, *regular* works, capable of containing garrisons with stores sufficient to stop the progress of an enemy's army, till relief can arrive
from the interior of the country, where 6 or 8000 regular forces must
be kept, besides strong garrisons at Quebec, and Montreal, the fortifications of which must be repaired and strengthened. Unless England
be determined to adopt, and rigorously to maintain all these necessary defences, perhaps after all inadequate, it is impossible that Canada
should long resist an American expedition. On such a tenure, and at
such an enormous expense, will that province be worth holding ? *Mr.
Payne*, in his admirable letter to the Abbé Raynal, makes the following judicious observations on this subject :—" Respecting *Canada*,
one or other of these two events will take place, viz.; if Canada should
become populous, it will revolt ; and if it do not become so, it will
not be worth the expense of holding. But Canada *never will* become
populous ; Britain may put herself to great expenses in sending settlers to Canada, but the descendants of those settlers will be Americans, as other descendants have been before them. They will look
round and see the neighbouring States sovereign and free, respected
abroad, and trading at large with the world ; and the natural love of
liberty, the advantages of commerce, the blessings of independence,
and of a *happier climate and a richer soil* will draw them *southward*,
and the effects will be, that Britain will sustain the expense, and America reap the advantage, and the same may be said of *Halifax* and the
country round it. One would think that the experience Britain has
had of America, would entirely sicken her of all thoughts of *continental* colonization ; and any part she may retain, will only become to her
a field of jealousy and thorns, of debate and contention, for ever struggling for privileges, and meditating revolt. She may form *new settlements*, but they will be for us ; *they will become part of the United
States of America;* and that against all her contrivances to prevent it,
or without any endeavour of ours to promote it. In the first place she
cannot draw from them a revenue until they are able to pay one, and
when they are so, they will be above subjection. Men soon become
attached to the soil they live upon, and incorporated with the prosperity of the place ; and it signifies but little what opinions they come
over with, for time, interest and new connections will render them ob-
solete, and the next generation know nothing of them.—To speak ex-

dreading the navigation of the Lakes, and in not daring to trust large ships on them. On all these subjects, he speaks as an enterprising well informed man; and capable of. executing what he proposes. I shall conclude this detail, by giving the project of a campaign against the savages, different from that adopted by Congress in 1779, the execution of which was entrusted to General Sullivan. According to this, five hundred men only should have marched by *Wioming* and *Tioga*, whilst the remainder of the army made its appearance by the head of the Mohawk river, and Lake *Oneida* to take the savages in the rear, and cut off their retreat to Lake Ontario; which appeared to me reasonable, because by this means, the double object was fulfilled of destroying the savages, and of avoiding a long and difficult march for the main body of the army, across the *Great Swamp* of Wioming.

To comprehend this, it must be recollected that in 1779, the Congress, seeing their enemies confined to New-York and Rhode-Island, thought they might spare a body of troops of

---

plicitly on the matter, I would not, were I an European, have Canada, under the conditions that Britain must retain it, could it be given to me. It is one of those kinds of dominion that is, and ever will be, a constant charge upon any foreign holder.—There are, I doubt not, thousands of people in England, who suppose that Canada and Nova-Scotia are a profit to the nation, whereas they are directly the contrary, and instead of producing any revenue, a considerable part of the revenue of England is annually drawn off to support the expense of holding them."—What it costs England to maintain Canada alone, may be known from the following accurate *abstract*, verified by the treasury accounts, of the *expenses of that Province, from the 1st of June*, 1776, *to the 24th of October*, 1782, *being six years and four months.*

	£	s.	d.
Military—Ordinaries,	688,385	18	$2\frac{1}{2}$
Extraordinaries,	4,510,790	12	7
Civil Establishment and Contingencies,	100,343	8	9
Total,	£5,299,519	19	$6\frac{1}{2}$
Which for 6 years and 4 months, is	£836,766	6	3 per ann.

It is true that the war extraordinaries must not be taken into the estimate of a peace establishment, but will not the independence of the United States render a larger force necessary than during the former peace, besides the garrisons above mentioned, &c.; and is war so very improbable in that quarter? Perhaps the most fortunate event for Britain will be, to receive the news, some spring or other, after the opening of the St. Lawrence, that Canada has been taken in the winter, with little or no bloodshed.—*Trans.*

three or four thousand men against the five nations, of whose cruelties they had many proofs. The plan was to carry off or destroy them, and thus relieve the country lying between the *Susquehannah* and the *Delaware*. General Sullivan, after taking every sort of precaution to secure the subsistence and health of the soldiers, made a very long and well conducted march, drove the savages before him, and burnt their villages and harvests. But this was the whole fruit of his expedition, for he never had it in his power to cut them off; the corps under General Clinton, which had penetrated by the Mohawk river, being found too weak to act of itself, was obliged to join the main body of the army.

I did not finish my reading before ten o'clock; and I continued in conversation with General Schuyler, whilst the company was at supper. It cannot be supposed that I was able to reason upon all the subjects he had laid before me. I contented myself therefore with remarking that every partial expedition against Canada, and which did not tend to the total conquest, or rather the deliverance of that country, would be dangerous and ineffectual; as it would not be strengthened by the concurrence of the inhabitants, they having been already deceived in their expectations in Montgomery's expedition, and dreading the resentment of the English, should they a second time show themselves favourable to the Americans. It gave me pleasure to find him of the same opinion. We then separated well pleased with each other, and I returned home to await the decision of the weather, respecting the next day's journey.

The 27th in the morning, understanding that the rivers were not yet frozen, and the weather being fine but very cold, I wished to take advantage of it to go to Schenectady. This is a town situated 14 miles from Albany, on the Mohawk river. It excites some curiosity, from being built in the very country of the savages ; from its being picketed, that is to say, surrounded with lofty palisades, like their villages, and from their still retaining some habitations there, which form a sort of suburb, to the east of the town. It was rather late when I thought of this ride, and it was noon before I got a sledge; but General Schuyler had assured me that I should be there in two hours, on the supposition, doubtless, that my sledge would be better provided with horses. I found the roads very bad, and the horses still worse ; for they would not draw, and if M. de Montesquieu had not himself taken the reins, and pressed them forward with more vivacity than their merciful conductor, I believe I should have remained in the snow, with which this country is covered six months in the year. The country which lies between Albany and Schenectady, is nothing but an immense forest of pine-trees, untouched by the hatchet. They are lofty and robust, but thin sown; and as nothing grows under their shade, a line of cavalry might traverse this woods without breaking their ranks, or defiling. It was three o'clock, and myself half dead with cold when I reached Schenectady. This town stands at the foot of a small declivity, on your coming out of the woods; it is regularly built, and contains five hundred houses within the palisades, without reckoning some dwellings which form a suburb, and the Indian village adjoining to the suburb. Two families, and eight inhabitants are reckoned to a house. Beyond the town, to the westward, the country is more open, and the land very fertile; it produces a great deal of corn, of which they carry on a great trade. I alighted at Colonel Glen's, the Quarter-Master-General of this district, a lively, active man. He received me in the politest manner; an excellent fire, and two or three glasses of toddy, warmed me, so as to enable me to ask him some questions, and to return immediately, for night was coming on, and the Vicomte de Noailles expected me at dinner at five o'clock. Colonel Glen lent me horses to return to Albany, and was so good as to conduct me himself into the Indian village. As we were preparing to set out, one of these savages entered his house : he was a messenger despatched by their hunters, who came to inform him of a party of one hundred and fifty *Senecas*, and several tories, making their appearance a few miles from Saratoga, and having even carried off one of their young men. This messenger spoke very good French, and very bad English; born of a Canadian, or European father, he had mixed with the savages, among whom he had lived twenty years, rather from libertinism than any other motive. The news he brought was not very encouraging for the journey I was about to take, but I gave little credit to it, and I was in the right.

The Indian village Mr. Glen conducted me to, is nothing but an assemblage of miserable huts in the wood, along the road to Albany. He took me into that of a savage *du Saut Saint Louis*, who had long lived at Montreal, and spoke good French. These huts are like our barracks in time of war, or those run up in vineyards, or orchards, to watch the fruit when it is ripe. All the timber consists in two up-rights and one cross pole; it is covered with a matted roof, but this is well lined within by a quantity of bark. The inner space is rather below the level of the ground, and the entrance by a little side-door; in the middle of the hut is the fire-place, from which the smoke ascends by an opening in the roof. On each side of the fire, are raised two branches, which run the length of the hut, and serve to sleep on; these are covered with skins and bark. Besides the savage who spoke French, in this hut.

there was a squaw, the name given to the Indian women, who had taken him as her second, and was bringing up a child by her first husband ; two old men composed the remainder of the family, which had a melancholy and poor appearance. The squaw was hideous, as they all are, and her husband almost stupid, so that the charms of this society did not make me forget that the day was advancing, and that it was time to set out. All that I could learn from the Colonel, or from the savages was, that the State gives them rations of meat, and sometimes of flour ; that they possess also some land, where they sow Indian corn, and go a hunting for skins, which they exchange for rum. They are sometimes employed in war, and are commended for their bravery and fidelity. Though in subjection to the Americans, they have their chiefs, to whom application is made for justice, when an Indian has committed any crime. Mr. Glen told me, that they submitted to the punishments inflicted on them ; but had no idea that it was right to punish them with death, even for homicide. Their number at present is three hundred and fifty ; which is constantly diminishing, as well as that of *the five nations.* I do not believe that these five nations can produce four thousand men in arms. The savages of themselves therefore, would not be much to be dreaded, were they not supported by the English, and the American tories. As an advanced guard, they are formidable, as an army they are nothing. But their cruelty seems to augment in proportion as their numbers diminish ; it is such as to render it impossible for the Americans to consent to have them long for neighbours ; and a necessary consequence of a peace, if favourable to the Congress, must be their total destruction, or their exclusion at least from all the country within the lakes.* Those who are attached to the Americans, and live in some manner under their laws, such as the Mohawks of the environs of Schenectady, and part of the Oneidas, will ultimately become civilized and be confounded with them. This is what every feeling and reasonable man should wish, who, preferring the interests of humanity to those of his own celebrity, disdains

---

* Dr. Franklin, whose amiable and philosophic mind sincerely laments all the evils attendant on humanity, used frequently to regret the painful necessity under which we foresaw America would shortly find herself of using violence against the savages, from the bloody scenes into which they were led by the policy of the English Government. The translator has often heard him express himself with the utmost sensibility on the subject, and suggest many expedients to prevent the probability of matters being urged to that horrid extremity, but reason, philosophy and eloquence were in vain opposed by good and wise men to the headlong career of that mad war.—*Trans.*

the little artifice so often and so successfully employed, of extolling ignorance and poverty, to extort praises in senates and academies.

I had time enough to make these and a great many other reflections, whilst, by the sole light of the snow, I was passing through these majestic woods, where the silence which reigns in the night is seldom disturbed even in the day. I did not arrive at the apartments of the Vicomte de Noailles till near eight o'clock, where supper, tea, and conversation detained me till midnight. Still nothing was decided respecting our journey, and the news we had received was by no means satisfactory. The next morning I received a letter from General Schuyler, to inform me, that having sent the evening before, he was told that I was gone to Schenectady, and from thence to Saratoga ; but that he was glad to know I was detained at Albany, for that finding himself much better of his gout, he intended accompanying me the next day. He requested me to come and pass the evening with him, to settle our route, and our departure. I answered his letter, by accepting of all his propositions, and employed part of the morning in walking about Albany, not without taking many precautions, for the streets were covered with ice. My first visit was to the artillery park, or rather the trophies of the Americans ; for there is no other artillery in this place than eight handsome mortars, and twenty ammunition wagons, which made part of Burgoyne's artillery.* I entered a large workshop where they were employed in making muskets for the army. The barrels of these muskets, and the bayonets, are forged a few miles from Albany, and polished and finished here. I inquired the price of them, and found that the weapon complete costs about five dollars. The armourers are enlisted, and receive besides their rations, very considerable salaries, if they were well paid. From thence I went to another barrack situated towards the west of the town, which serves as a military hospital. The sick are served by women. Each of them has a separate bed, and they appear in general to be well taken care of, and kept very clean. At dinner all the company who were to be of the Saratoga party collected at my lodgings, and we went afterwards to General Schuyler's to settle matters for our journey, and, in consequence, set out the next day at sun rise, in five different sledges. General Schuyler took me in his own. We passed the Mohawk river on the ice, a mile above the cataract. It

---

* The principal part of Burgoyne's artillery was conveyed to Philadelphia, where I saw a very fine park, formed of them and the pieces taken from the Hessians, in various engagements.—*Trans.*

was almost the first attempt, and succeeded with all but Major Popham, whose two horses broke through the ice, and sunk into the river. This event will appear fatal to Europeans ; but let them not be alarmed at the consequences. It is a very common accident, and is remedied in two ways : one by dragging the horses on the ice by force, and, if possible, by the help of a lever or plank to raise them up ; the other by strangling them with their halter, or the reins : as soon as they have lost their respiration, and motion, they float on the water, and are lifted by their fore-feet on the ice ; the stricture is loosened, they are bled, and in a quarter of an hour are reinstated in the harness. As there were a great many of us, the first method which is the surest, was employed. All this may be easily conceived, but it will be asked what becomes of the sledge, and how one does to approach the gulf opened by the horses ? The answer is, that these animals being much heavier than the sledge, and supported by four slender bases, break the ice under their feet, without causing the sledge to sink, which is light of itself, and its weight supported by long pieces of wood which serve by way of shafts. The travellers are not less safe, the ice being always thicker than is necessary to bear them. As for the horses, they easily keep themselves up on the surface of the water, by means of their fore-legs, and by resting their heads upon the ice.

The accident which happened to Major Popham's sledge, did not detain us above seven or eight minutes ; but we went a little astray in the woods we had to pass to reach the high road. We came into it between Half Moon and Stillwater. A mile from thence, I saw on the left, an opening in the wood, and a pretty extensive plain, below which runs a creek, and observed to General Schuyler, that there must be a good position there : he told me I was not deceived, and that it had been reconnoitred for that purpose in case of need. The creek is called Anthony's Rill ; the word *rill*, among the Dutch, having the same signification as *creek* with the Americans. Three miles farther on, we traversed a hamlet called Stillwater Landing-place, for it is here that boats coming down from Saratoga are obliged to stop to avoid the rapids. From hence there is a portage of eight or ten miles to the place where the river is navigable. I imagine the name of *Stillwater* is derived from its tranquillity here previous to the commencement of the rapids. General Schuyler showed me some redoubts he had constructed to defend the park, where his boats and provisions were collected, after the evacuation of Fort Anne and Fort Edward. We stopped there to refresh our horses. The General had given the rendezvous to a militia officer, called Swang, who lives in this neighbourhood, and served in the army of General Gates :

he put me into his hands, and continued his route to Saratoga, to prepare our reception. I presently got into a sledge with my guide, and, at the end of three miles, we saw two houses on the bank of the river; it was here that General Gates had his right, and his bridge of boats defended by a redoubt on each bank. We alighted to examine this interesting position, which dissipated all the hopes of Burgoyne, and prepared his ruin. I shall attempt to give some idea of it, which though incomplete indeed, may throw some light on the relations of General Burgoyne, and even serve to rectify his errors.

The eminences, called *Bream's Heights*, from whence this famous camp is named, are only a part of those high grounds which extend along the right bank of the Hudson, from the river Mohawk to that of Saratoga. At the spot chosen by General Gates for his position, they form, on the side of the river, two different slopes, or terraces. In mounting the first slope, are three redoubts placed in parallel directions. In front of the last, on the north side, is a little hollow, beyond which the ground rises again, on which are three more redoubts, placed nearly in the same direction as the former. In front of them is a deep ravine which runs from the west, in which is a small creek. This ravine takes its rise in the woods, and all the ground on the right of it is extremely thick set with wood. If you will now return upon your steps, place yourself near the first redoubts you spoke of, and mount to the second slope proceeding to the westward, you will find, on the most elevated platform, a large entrenchment which was parallel with the river, and then turns towards the north-west, where it terminates in some pretty steep summits, which were likewise fortified by small redoubts. To the left of these heights, and at a place where the declivity becomes more gentle, begins another entrenchment which turns towards the west, and makes two or three angles, always carried over the tops of the heights to the south-west. Towards the north-west, you come out of the lines to descend another platform, which presents a position the more favourable, as it commands the surrounding woods, and resists every thing which might turn the left flank of the army. It is here that Arnold was encamped with the advanced guard.

If you descend again from this height, proceeding towards the north, you are presently in the midst of the woods near Freeman's farm, and on the ground where the actions of the 19th of September, and the 7th of October happened. I avoid the word *field of battle*; for these two engagements were in the woods, and on ground so intersected and covered, that it is impossible either *to conceive or discover the smallest resemblance between it and the plan given to the public by General Burgoyne.* But what appears to me very clear is, that this general who was encamped about four miles from the camp of Bream's Heights, wishing to approach, and reconnoitre the avenues to it, marched through the woods in four columns, and that having several ravines to pass, he made General Frazer, with the advanced guard, turn them at their origin ; that two other columns traversed the ravines, and the woods, as well as they could, without either communicating or materially waiting for each other ; that the left column, chiefly composed of artillery, followed the course of the river, where the ground is more level, and built bridges over the ravines and rivulets, which are deeper on that side, as they all terminate in the river ; that the engagement first began with the *riflemen* and American militia, who were supported as necessity required, without any prior disposition; that the advanced guard, and the right column were the first engaged, and that the combat lasted until the columns on the left arrived, that is to say, till sunset; that the Americans then retired to their camp, where they had taken care to convey their wounded ; that the English advanced guard, and the right column greatly suffered ; both one and the other having been very long engaged in the woods without any support.

General Burgoyne purchased dearly the frivolous honour of sleeping on the field of battle : he now encamped at Freeman's farm, so near the American camp, that it was impossible for him to manœuvre, so that he found himself in the situation of a chess-player, who suffers himself to be stalemated. In this position he remained until the 7th of October, when seeing his provisions expended, hearing nothing of Clinton, and being too near the enemy to retreat without danger, he tried a second attack, and again made an attempt for his advanced guard to turn their left. The enemy, with whom the woods were filled, penetrated his design, themselves turned the left flank of the corps which threatened theirs, put them to route, and pursued them so far as to find themselves, without knowing it, opposite the camp of the Germans. This camp was situated *en potence*, and a little in the rear of the line. Arnold and Lincoln, animated with success, attacked and carried the entrenchments : both of them bought the victory at the price of their blood ; each of them had a leg broke* with musket shot. I saw the spot where Arnold, uniting the hardiness of a *jockey*† with that of a soldier, leaped his horse over the entrenchment of the enemy. It was like all those of this country, a sort of parapet, formed by the trunks of trees piled one

---

* Lincoln was not wounded till the next day.

† The name given in America to horse-dealers, as well as those who take care of horses.

upon another. This action was very brisk, to which the fir trees, which are torn by musket and cannon shot, will long bear testimony; for the term of their existence seems as remote, as is the period of their origin.

I continued reconnoitring here till night; sometimes walking in the snow, where I sunk to the knees, and sometimes travelling still less successfully in a sledge, my conductor having taken care to overset me, very gently indeed, in a great heap of snow.   After surveying Burgoyne's lines, I at length got down to the high road, passing through a field where he had established his hospital.   We then travelled more easily, and I got to Saratoga at seven in the evening, after a seven and thirty miles journey, we found good rooms well warmed, an excellent supper, and had a gay and agreeable conversation; for General Schuyler, like many European husbands, is still more amiable when he is absent from his wife.   He gave us instructions for our next day's expedition, as well to Fort Edward, as to the great cataract of Hudson's river, eight miles above that fort, and ten from lake George.

CHAPTER XI.

In consequence of these arrangements, we set out the next
morning at eight o'clock, with the Majors Græme and Popham,
whom he had requested to accompany us. We remounted the
right bank of the Hudson for near three miles, before we found
a safe place to pass the river in our sledges. That we made
choice of exposed us to no danger, the ice being as thick as
we could wish it; but, on approaching the opposite side, the
banks appeared to me so high and steep that I could not conceive how we should get up them. As it is my principle to
form no judgment of any thing I do not understand, and always
to conform myself in travelling as in navigation, to the persons who are habituated to the roads, I was sitting quietly in
my sledge, waiting the event, when my conductor, a farmer of
the country, *called* his horses with a ferocious cry, something
like that of the savages; and in an instant, without a stroke
of the whip, they set off with the sledge, and, in three bounds,
were at the top of a precipice, of twenty feet high, nearly per-
pendicular.

The road to Fort Edward is almost always on the side of
the river, but you frequently lose sight of it in the fir woods
you pass through. From time to time you discover tolerable
handsome houses on the two banks. That of the unfortunate
Miss MacRea, who was killed by the savages, was pointed out
to me. If the whigs were superstitious, they would attribute
this event to the Divine vengeance. The parents of Miss
MacRea were whigs, nor did she belie the sentiments with
which they had inspired her, until she became acquainted with
an English officer at New-York, who triumphed at once over
her virtue, and her patriotism. From that moment she espoused the interests of England, and waited till she had an
opportunity of marrying her lover. The war, which soon extended to New-York, as well as Boston, obliged her father to
retire to his country-house, which he abandoned immediately
on the approach of Burgoyne's army. But Miss MacRea's
lover was in this army; she wished to see him again as a con-

queror, to marry him, and then partake of his toils and his successes. Unfortunately the Indians composed the vanguard of
this army; these savages are not much accustomed to distinguish friends from foes; they pillaged the house of Miss Mac-
Rea, and carried her off. When they had conducted her to
their camp, it was a matter of dispute to whom she should belong; they could not agree, and to terminate the quarrel,
some of them killed her with a tomahawk.* The recital of
this sad catastrophe, whilst it made me deplore the miseries of
war, concentrated all my interest in the person of the English
officer, to whom it was allowable to listen at once to his passion and his duty. I know that a death so cruel and unforeseen,
would furnish a very pathetic subject for a drama, or an elegy;
but nothing short of the charms of eloquence and poetry is
capable of moving the heart, for such a destiny, by exhibiting
only the effect, and throwing the cause into the shade; for
such is the true character of love, that all the noble and generous affections seem to be its natural attendants, and if it be
that it can sometimes ally itself with blameable circumstances,
every thing at least which tends to humiliate or degrade it,
either annihilates or disguises its genuine features.

As you approach Fort Edward the houses become more rare.
This fort is built sixteen miles from Saratoga, in a little valley
near the river, on the only spot which is not covered with
wood, and where you can have a prospect to the distance of a
musket-shot around you. Formerly it consisted of a square,
fortified by two bastions on the east side, and by two demi-bas-
tions on the side of the river; but this old fortification is
abandoned, because it was too much commanded, and a large
redoubt, with a simple parapet and a wretched palisade, is
built on a more elevated spot: within are small barracks for
about two hundred soldiers. Such is Fort Edward, so much
spoken of in Europe, although it could in no time have been
able to resist five hundred men, with four pieces of cannon.
I stopped here an hour to refresh my horses, and about noon
set off to proceed as far as the cataract, which is eight miles
beyond it. On leaving the valley, and pursuing the road to
Lake George, is a tolerable military position, which was occupied in the war before the last: it is a sort of entrenched
camp, adapted to abattis, guarding the passage from the
woods, and commanding the valley.

I had scarcely lost sight of Fort Edward, before the spectacle

* A particular account of this melancholy occurrence is to be found
in the "Northern Traveller," published by Mr. Goodrich, New-
York.

of devastation presented itself to my eyes, and continued to distress them as far as the place I stopped at.   Peace and industry had conducted cultivators amidst these ancient forests, men content and happy, before the period of this war.   Those who were in Burgoyne's way alone experienced the horrors of his expedition ; but on the last invasion of the savages, the desolation has spread from Fort Schuyler, (or Fort Stanwise,) even to Fort Edward ; I beheld nothing around me but the remains of conflagrations ; a few bricks, proof against the fire, were the only indications of ruined houses ; whilst the fences still entire, and cleared out lands, announced that these deplorable habitations had once been the abode of riches, and of happiness.   Arrived at the height of the cataract it was necessary to quit our sledges, and walk half a mile to the bank of the river.   The snow was fifteen inches deep, which rendered this walk rather difficult, and obliged us to proceed in Indian files, in order to make a path.   Each of us put ourselves alternately at the head of this little column, as the wild geese relieve each other to occupy the summit of the angle they form in their flight.   But had our march been still more difficult, the sight of the cataract was an ample recompense.   It is not a sheet of water as at Cohoes, and at Totohaw : the river confined, and interrupted in its course by different rocks, glides through the midst of them, and precipitating itself obliquely forms several cascades.   That of Cohoes is more majestic, this, more terrible : the Mohawk river seems to fall from its own dead weight ; that of Hudson frets, and becomes enraged, it foams and forms whirlpools, and flies like a serpent making its escape, still continuing its menaces by horrible hissings.

It was near two when we regained our sledges, having two and twenty miles to return to Saratoga, so that we trod back our steps as fast as possible ; but we still had to halt at Fort Edward to refresh our horses.   We employed this time, as we had done in the morning, in warming ourselves by the fire of the officers who command the garrison.   They are five in number, and have about one hundred and fifty soldiers.   They are stationed in this desert for the whole winter, and I leave the reader to imagine whether this garrison be much more gay than those of Gravelines, or Briancon.*   We set off again in an hour, and night soon overtook us ; but before it was dark, I had the satisfaction to see the first game I had met with in my journey : it was a bevy of quails ; by some called partridges, though they have a much greater resemblance of quails.   They were perched to the number of seven, upon a

---

* Two of the most melancholy garrisons in France.—*Trans.*

fence. I got out of my sledge to have a nearer view of them; they suffered me to approach within four paces, and to make them rise I was obliged to throw my cane at them; they all went off together, in a flight similar to that of partridges, and like them they are sedentary.*

Our return was quick and fortunate : we had no accident to fear but at the second passage of the river, and the descent of the precipice we had mounted. I waited for this fresh trial with as much confidence as the former; but a sledge, which was before mine, stopping at that place, and the darkness of the night preventing me from distinguishing any thing, I imagined that the company were going to alight, the first sledge was that of the Vicomte de Noailles, and the Comte de Damas; but I was scarcely alighted, before I saw this sledge set out with all its lading, and slide down the precipice with such rapidity that it could not be stopped at thirty yards from the bottom. They make no more ceremony in descending these precipices, than in mounting them : the horses accustomed to this manœuvre, precipitate themselves, as rapidly as they launch off the carriage, so that the sledge sliding like the Ramasse of mount Cenis, cannot touch their hind legs and make them fall.

At half past six, we reached General Schuyler's, where we spent our evening as agreeably as the former.

The 31st we got on horseback at eight o'clock, and Mr. Schuyler conducted us himself to the camp occupied by the English when General Burgoyne capitulated. We could not have a better guide, but he was absolutely necessary for us in every respect; for besides that this event happened before his eyes, and that he was better able than any body to give us an

---

* This bird can neither be classed in the species of quails, nor in that of partridges; it is larger than the former, and smaller than the latter; the feathers of the wings and body are nearly of the same colour with the grey partridge, those of the belly are mixed with grey and black, like the *bartavelle*. The neck of the cock is white, that of the hen yellow, both of them have a handsome black collar. It whistles like a quail, but with more force; and has four notes, whereas the quail has only three. In other respects its manners resemble more those of the red partridge than the quail, for it perches, and is always in a flock; it haunts the woods and morasses. This bird is very common in America, more so to the southward, than in the northern parts. It is no exaggeration to assert that in one winter only, and in a circle of five or six leagues, the officers in winter quarters at Williamsburgh and York, killed upwards of six thousand, and that they bought as many of the negroes, which they had taken in little snares, yet it was difficult to perceive any diminution of their numbers the following spring.

account of it, no person but the proprietor of the ground himself was able to conduct us safely through the woods; the fences and entrenchments being covered a foot deep with snow.

In throwing your eyes upon the chart, you will see that Saratoga is situated on the bank of a small river which comes from
a lake of that name, and falls into the Hudson. On the right
bank of the Fishkill, the name of that little river, stood formerly a handsome country-house belonging to General Schuyler;
a large farm depending on it, two or three saw-mills, a meeting-house, and three or four middling houses, composed all the
habitations of this celebrated place, the name of which will be
handed down to the latest posterity. After the affair of the
7th of October, General Burgoyne began his retreat; he
marched in the night between the 8th and 9th, but did not pass
the creek till the 13th, so much difficulty he had in dragging
his artillery, which he *persisted in preserving*, although the greatest part of his horses were killed, or dead with hunger. He
took four days therefore to retire eight miles, which *gave the
Americans time* to follow him on the right bank of the Hudson,
and to get before him on the left bank, where they occupied
in force all the passages. General Burgoyne had scarcely
reached the other side of the creek, before he set fire to General Schuyler's house, *rather from malice,* than for the safety of
his army;* since this house, situated in a bottom, *could afford*

---

* This is a matter in which General Burgoyne's honour and humanity, seem to be directly called in question. The General in his
examination of witnesses on the inquiry into the failure of his expedition before the House of Commons, was particularly anxious to excul-
pate himself on the subject, and to prove not only that it always was
necessary in a military point of view to destroy this house, but that
General Schuyler himself afterwards admitted that *necessity*—in opposition to which we have here the assertion of a man of rank distinguished in the military and literary world, as well as the General, who on the
testimony of General Schuyler, asserts, " *Que le General Burgoyne fut
à peine de l'autre côté de la creek, qu'il fit mettre lefeu à la maison
du General Schuyler, plutôt par humblur, que pour la sûreté de son ar-
mée ;* &c. &c." The Translator knows General Burgoyne to be a
soldier of honour, who in that capacity never wishes to forget the par-
amount duties of the citizen, and the man ; the Marquis de Chastellux too, deservedly stands high in the public estimation ; it is with infinite concern therefore, that the Translator finds himself unable to refute the injurious assertion, or reconcile the contradiction. That the
matter may be fairly brought to issue, he subjoins an extract from
General Burgoyne's speech in the House of Commons, in answer to
" a call upon him by Mr. Wilkes, for explanation respecting the burning of the country during the progress of the army under his command."

no advantage to the Americans, and he left the farm standing, which is at present the only asylum for the owner. It is here that Mr. Schuyler lodged us in some temporary apartments he fitted up, until happier times allow him to build another house. The creek runs between two steep ascents, the summits of which are about the same height ; it then descends by several rapids which turn the mills : there the ground is more open, and continues so to the north river ; that is to say, for half a mile. As to General Burgoyne's position, it is difficult to describe it, because the ground is so very irregular, and the Ge-

---

" I am ignorant, said the General, of any such circumstance : I do not recollect more than one accident by fire ; I positively assert there was no fire by order, or countenance of myself, or any other officer, except at Saratoga. That district is the property of Major-General Schuyler of the American troops ; there were large barracks built by him, which took fire the day after the army arrived on the ground in their retreat ; and I believe, I need not state any other proof of that matter being merely accident, than that the barracks were then made use of as my hospital, and full of sick and wounded soldiers. General Schuyler had likewise a very good dwelling-house, exceeding large store-houses, great saw-mills, and other out-buildings, to the value altogether perhaps of *ten thousand pounds* : a few days before the negotiation with General Gates, the enemy had formed a plan to attack me : a large column of troops was approaching to pass the small river, preparatory to a general action, and was *entirely covered from the fire of my artillery by those buildings.* Sir, I avow that I gave the order to set them on fire ; and in a very short time the whole property I have described was consumed. But, to show that the person most deeply concerned in that calamity did not put the construction upon it which it has pleased the honourable gentleman to do, I must inform the House, that one of the first persons I saw, after the convention was signed, was *General Schuyler.* I expressed to him my regret at the event which had happened, and the reasons which occasioned it. He desired me to think no more of it ; said *that the occasion justified it* according to the principles and rules of war, and *he should have done the same upon the same occasion,* or words to that effect. He did more—he sent an aid-de-camp to conduct me to Albany, in order as he expressed, to procure me better quarters than a stranger might be able to find. This gentleman conducted me to a very elegant house, and to my great surprise, presented me to Mrs. Schuyler and her family : and in this General's house I remained during my whole stay at Albany, with a *table of more than twenty covers* for me and my friends, and every other possible demonstration of hospitality ; a situation painful as it is true in point of sensibility at the time, but which I now contemplate with some satisfaction, as carrying undeniable testimony how little I deserved the charges of the honourable gentleman."—*Trans.*

neral finding himself surrounded, was obliged to divide his troops into three camps, forming three different fronts ; one facing the creek, another Hudson river, and the third the mountains to the westward.   General Burgoyne's plan, gives a tolerable just idea of this position, which was not ill taken, and is only defective on the side of the Germans, where the ground forms a rising, the declivity of which was against them.   All that it is necessary to observe is, that the woods continually rise towards the west ; so that the General might very well occupy some advantageous eminences, but never the summits.   Accordingly, General Gates who arrived at Saratoga, almost as soon as the English passed two thousand men over the creek, with orders to begin to fire on the 14th and considerably incommode the English.   General Schuyler criticises this position ; he pretends that this corps so advanced as to be in danger, without being strong enough to oppose the retreat of the enemy.   But when we consider that these two thousand men were posted in very thick woods ; that they were protected by abattis ; had a secure retreat in the immense forest in their rear, and that they had only to harass a flying enemy, whose courage was broken, every military man will think with me that this was rather the criticism of a severe rival, than of a well informed and methodical tactician.   Be this as it may, it is very certain that Burgoyne had no other alternative than to let his troops be slaughtered, or capitulate. His army had only five days provision, and it was impossible for him to retain his position.   It was proposed to him to restore an old bridge of boats, which had been constructed in the very front of his camp ; but a corps of two thousand men were already posted on the heights on the opposite side of the river, where they had raised a battery of two pieces of cannon. Had he undertaken to remount by the right bank, to attain the fords which are near Fort Edward, he had ravines to pass and bridges to repair ; besides that these defiles were already occupied by the militia, and the vanguard alone must have been engaged with them, whilst he had a whole army on his rear, and on his flanks.   He had scarce time to deliberate, the cannon shot began to shower into the camp ; one of which fell in the house where the council of war was holding, and obliged them to quit it to take refuge in the woods.

Let us now compare the situation of General Burgoyne, collecting his trophies, and publishing his insolent manifesto at Ticonderoga, with that in which he now stood, when vanquished, and surrounded as he was by a troop of peasants, not a place was left him even to discuss the terms of supplication. I confess when I was conducted to the spot where the English laid down their arms, and to that where they filed off before

Gates' army, I could not but partake of the triumph of the Americans, and at the same time admire their magnanimity; for the soldiers and officers beheld their presumptuous and sanguinary enemies pass, without offering the smallest insult, without suffering an insulting smile or gesture to escape them. This majestic silence conveyed a very striking refutation of the vain declarations of the English general, and seemed to attest all the rights of our allies to the victory. Chance alone gave rise to an allusion with which General Burgoyne was very sensibly affected. It is the custom in England, and in America, on approaching any person for the first time, to say, *I am very happy to see you;* General Gates chanced to make use of this expression in accosting General Burgoyne: *I believe you are;* replied the general, *the fortune of the day is entirely yours.* General Gates pretended to give no attention to this answer, and conducted Burgoyne to his quarters, where he gave him a good dinner, as well as to the principal part of the English officers. Every body ate and drank heartily, and seemed mutually to forget their misfortunes, or their successes.

Before dinner, and at the moment when the Americans were striving who should entertain the English officers, somebody came to ask where Madame Riedesel, the wife of the Brunswick general, was to be conducted. Mr. Schuyler, who had followed the army as a volunteer, since he had quitted the command, ordered her to be shown to his tent, where he went soon after, and found her trembling and speechless, expecting to find in every American a savage, like those who had followed the English army. She had with her two charming little girls, about six or seven years old. General Schuyler caressed them greatly; the sight of this touched Madame de Riedesel and removed her apprehension in an instant; *you are tender and sensible*, said she, *you must then be generous, and I am happy to have fallen into your hands.*

In consequence of the capitulation, the English army was conducted to Boston. During their march the troops encamped, but lodgings were to be procured for the generals, and there being some difficulty in procuring near Albany a proper quarter for General Burgoyne and his suite, Mr. Schuyler offered him his handsome house. He was himself detained by business at Saratoga, where he remained to visit the ruins of his other house, which General Burgoyne had just destroyed; but he wrote to his wife to prepare every thing for giving him the best reception, and his intentions were perfectly fulfilled. Burgoyne was extremely well received by Mrs. Schuyler, and her little family; he was lodged in the best apartment in the house. An excellent supper was served him in the evening, the honours

of which were done with so much grace, that he was affected
even to tears; and could not help saying, with a deep sigh,
*Indeed this is doing too much for the man who has ravaged their
lands and burnt their asylum.* The next morning, however, he
was again reminded of his disgraces by an adventure which
would have appeared gay to any one but him. It was always
innocently that he was afflicted. His bed was prepared in a
large room; but as he had a numerous suite, or *family*, several
mattresses were spread upon the floor for some officers to sleep
near him. Mr. Schuyler's second son, a little spoilt child of
about seven years old, very forward and arch, as all the American children are, but very amiable, was running all the morning about the house, according to custom, and opening the
door of the saloon, he burst out a laughing on seeing all the
English collected, and shutting it after him, crying, *Ye are all
my prisoners:* this stroke of nature was cruel, and rendered
them more melancholy than the preceding evening.

I hope I shall be pardoned these little anecdotes, which only
appeared interesting to myself, perhaps solely from their proceeding from the source, and being acquired upon the spot.
Besides, a plain journal merits some indulgence, and when one
does not write history, it is allowable to write little stories.
Henceforth I have only to take leave of General Schuyler, detained by business at Saratoga, and to tread back my steps as
fast as possible to Newport.

In repassing near Bream's Height, and Stillwater, I had
again an opportunity of examining the right flank of General
Burgoyne's camp, of which it seemed to me that his plan gives
a pretty accurate idea. I was assured that I might return to
Albany by the eastern road, but on arriving at Half-Moon,
I learnt that the ice was broken in several places, so that after
reposing some time in a handsome inn, kept by Madam People, a Dutchman's widow, I took the road by the Mohawk
river, which I passed without accident, and arrived at Albany
about six in the evening. We immediately assembled (I speak
only of the six French travellers) to concert measures for our
return. Not a moment was to be lost, for the wind having got
to the southward, the thaw was beginning; and it might very
well happen that we should be detained a considerable time
at Albany: for, when you cannot pass the river on the ice, you
are sometimes obliged to wait eight or ten days before it is
navigable, and you can pass the ferry. It was necessary therefore to set out immediately; but as we were too many to travel
together, it was determined that the Vicomte de Noailles and
his two companions should set off the next morning at daybreak, and sleep thirty miles from Albany; and that I should
set out at noon, and stay all night at Kinderhook. The Vi-

comte de Noailles had left his horses on the other side of the river, and had already sent over his sledge, nothing therefore stood in the way of his departure, the ice being certainly thick enough for him to pass on foot. My situation was very different; I had, at Albany, two sledges, which belonged to the state, and were furnished me by the aid-Quarter-Master-General, an excellent man, called Quakerbush. My intention was to pay for them; but he would not allow it, assuring me that I had only to deliver them to the Quarter-Master of Rhode-Island, who would return them by the first opportunity. This is a very convenient arrangement for the military on the continent, and for all such as are employed in commissions for the public service : each state maintains horses for travelling, nothing more being requisite than to deliver them to the Quarter-Master of the place at which you leave them. In the northern states, there are sledges also for the same purpose.

As we were deliberating on our journey, Colonel Hughes, Quarter-Master of the State of New-York, came to call upon us : he had just arrived from an expedition towards Fishkill, and testified great regret at not having been at Albany during our stay. I must repeat here what I have already said, that it is impossible to imagine a more frank, and more noble politeness, a more courteous behaviour, than I experienced from the greatest part of the American officers with whom I had any concern. Mr. Hughes was so good as undertake to conduct me to the other side of the river, and promised to call upon me the next day at eleven o'clock.

I had travelled far enough in the day to hope for a quiet sleep, but, at four in the morning, I was awakened by a musket fired close to my windows : I listened, but heard not the smallest noise or motion in the street, which made me imagine it was some musket discharged of itself without causing any accident. I again attempted to go to sleep, but a quarter of an hour after a fresh musket or pistol shot interrupted my repose; this was followed by several others; so that I had no longer any doubt that it was some rejoicing, or feast, like our village christenings. The hour indeed struck me as unusual, but at length a number of voices mingled with musketry, crying out, *new year*, reminded me that we were at the first of January, and I concluded that it was thus the Americans celebrate that event. Though this manner of proclaiming it was not, I must own, very pleasing to me, there was nothing for it but patience; but at the end of half an hour, I heard a confused noise of upwards of a hundred persons, chiefly children, or young people, assembled under my windows, and I very soon had farther indication of their proximity, for they fired several musket shot, knocked rudely at the door, and threw

stones against my windows. Cold and indolence still kept me
in bed, but Mr. Lynch got up, and came into my chamber to
tell me that these people certainly meant to do me honour,
and get some money from me. I desired him to step down,
and give them two Louis: he found them already masters of
the house, and drinking my landlord's rum. In a quarter of
an hour, they went off to visit other streets, and continued
their noise till daylight. On rising, I learnt from my landlord, that it was the custom of the country for the young
folks, the servants, and even the negroes, to go from tavern to
tavern, and to other houses, to wish a good new year, and ask
for drink ; so that there was no particular compliment to me
in this affair, and I found, that after the example of the Roman emperors, I had made a largess to the people. In the
morning, when I went out to take leave of General Clinton, I
met nothing but drunken people in the streets ; but what astonished me the most was too see them not only walk, but run
upon the ice without falling, or making a false step, whilst it
was with the utmost difficulty I kept upon my legs.

As soon as my sledges were ready, I took one of them to go
and bid adieu to Mrs. Schuyler and her family, whence I returned to Colonel Hughes, who was waiting for me at the entrance of the town. He had learnt, since he left us, that the
Baron de Montesquieu was grandson of the author of *The Spirit of Laws*. Rejoiced at this discovery, he desired me to introduce him a second time to the gentleman whe bore so respectable a name ; and a few minutes after, as I was expressing my sensibility for the services he had done us, and my
regret at the same time at not having it in my power to repay
them, he said to me with a sentiment truly amiable, " Well
then ! since you wish to do something for me, try to procure
a French copy of the Spirit of Laws. I do not speak your
language, but I understand your books, and shall be happy to
read that in the original." I proposed to send him a copy,
and have been so lucky as to be able to fulfil my promise on
my return to Newport. After this conversation he took me to
the river-side, at the place he thought the safest; but, as I
was about to venture myself, the first object I beheld was a
sledge, the horses of which were sinking under the ice, at
twenty paces from me. Judge of my consternation ; I must
tread back my steps, and remain perhaps a week at Albany till
the thaw was complete, and the river free from floating ice.
Colonel Hughes bid me to return to my inn, and remain there
quietly, until he sent a man and horse along the river to inquire for a place to pass over. Three sledges, however, with
rum for the state storehouses appeared on the other side, and
seemed determined to risk the passage, but he sent a man on

foot to stop them, after which I left him sorrowfully enough. About one o'clock, as I was reading by my fireside, Mr. Hughes' secretary entered, and told me that the sledges he had sent to stop, had persisted in passing, and succeeded by avoiding the hole made by the horses I had seen sinking, and which were extricated with great difficulty.   As the thaw continued, I had not a moment to lose, the horses were instantly put to, and I set out, under the auspices of Colonel Hughes, who was waiting for me at the river-side.   As soon as I got over I parted from him; but had still half a mile to go upon the ice, before I could get to a landing place which led me to the high road; all danger was now over, and I reached Kinderhook with ease towards six o'clock.

I set out the next morning at nine, and after passing the bridge of Kinderhook, left the Clavarack road on the right, to follow that of Nobletown.   I stopped in this township, and alighted at Makingston's Tavern, a small neat inn, in which two travellers may be conveniently lodged.   Having an opportunity of conversing with the cousin and neighbour of Mr. Makingston, of the same name with himself; he told me he had been a Major in the American army, and received a ball through his thigh in Canada.   He said that his nerves, irritated with the wound, became contracted, and he halted for upwards of a year; but that at the affair of Princeton, after travelling eighteen miles on foot, he happening to leap over a fence, by this effort the contracted nerves broke or rather lengthened themselves, so that he has never since been lame.

As soon as my horses had rested a little, I continued my journey, and travelling among woods and mountains, it was night before I got to Sheffield.   I traversed this whole town, which is about two miles long, before I got to Mr. Dewy's inn. Sheffield is a very pretty place, there are a good many well built houses, and the high road that separates them is upwards of a hundred paces wide.   My inn gave me pleasure the moment I entered it; the master and mistress of the house appeared polite and well educated; but I admired above all a girl of twelve years old, who had all the beauty of her age, and whom *Greuze* would have been happy to have taken for a model, when he painted his charming picture of the young girl crying for the loss of her canary bird.   When I was shown into my chamber, I amused myself in looking at some books scattered on the tables.   The first I opened was the Abridgment of Newton's Philosophy: this discovery induced me to put some questions to my landlord on physics, and geometry, with which I found him well acquainted, and that he was besides very modest, and very good company.   He is a surveyor.

a very active employment in a country where there is perpetually land to measure, and boundaries to fix.

The 3d in the morning, I was sorry to find that the weather, which had been hitherto uncertain, was ended in a thaw. I had to traverse the *Greenwoods*, a rugged, difficult, and desert country. The snow remaining on the ground, and giving me still hopes of being able to continue my route in a sledge, I kept mine, and proceeded tolerably well as far as Canaan, a small town situated on the left bank of the Housatonick, seven miles from Sheffield meeting-house; there I turned to the left, and began to climb the mountains; unfortunately the snow failed me where it was the most necessary, and I was obliged to walk almost always on foot to relieve my horses, which were sometimes labouring to drag the sledge out of the mud, and at others to pull it over stones two or three feet high. This road is, in fact, so rough, that it is hardly possible to make use of sledges, unless there be a foot and a half of snow upon the ground. It was with the utmost difficulty therefore I travelled fifteen miles to a wretched inn dependant on Norfolk. On leaving this inn, I got into the Greenwoods. This forest is part of the same chain of mountains I had passed in going to Fishkill by the Litchfield road; but here the trees are superb; they are firs, but so strong, so straight and lofty, that I doubt whether there are any like them in all North-America. I regret that Salvator Rosa, or Gaspard Poussin, never saw the majestic and truly *grandioso* picture a deep valley here affords, through which runs the small river called the Naragontad. This valley appears still more narrow from the immense firs that shade it; some of which, rising in an oblique direction, seem to unite their tops purposely to intercept the rays of the sun. When you have passed this river, you mount for four or five miles, and then descend as much; continually bounding from one large stone to another which cross the road, and give it the resemblance of stairs. Here one of my sledges broke, and night approaching, I was at a loss how to repair it, imagining myself in an uninhabitable desert; I tried to get it forward broken as it was, but despaired of succeeding, when two hundred steps farther on, I found a small house, and opposite to it a forge, where the fire was lighted, and the blacksmith at work. A pilot who discovers land in unknown seas, is not more happy than I was at this sight. I politely requested the honest man to leave his work and repair my sledge, which he agreed to, and I continued to follow that in good condition, on foot, despairing of ever seeing the other, which arrived however an hour after me. Such are the resources travellers meet with in America, and such the excellent police* of this country, that no road is destitute of what is necessary for their wants.

This day was destined to be full of contrarieties. It was seven in the evening when I arrived at New-Hartford, where I expected to find a good inn, called Gilbert's House. Three American officers who, having rode on horseback, had very easily passed me, were so polite as to go farther on, in order to leave me the whole house ; but I was told, and it was evident on entering, that it was impossible I could be accommodated. The masons were repairing it, and at work every where : so that I had now no other hope but at the inn of a Mr. Case, two miles farther, beyond Farmington river; but learning that the American officers were there, I inquired whether I could not be lodged elsewhere, and was recommended to an old woman, called Mrs. Wallen, who formerly kept an inn, and I was flattered with hopes of her receiving me. I continued therefore to follow my sledge on foot, and having, with difficulty, reached this house, I implored Mrs. Wallen's hospitality, who consented, but merely to oblige me. I remained here some time, but finding it a very poor house, and the apartments wretched, I sent one of my people to Case's, to try if he could find me some corner to lodge in. They contrived to let me have one, and I went thither on foot, leaving my horses at the other house. I was lucky enough to find a good bed, and a supper, such as it was, but which appeared to me excellent, less because I had a good appetite, than from being waited on by a tall woman of five and twenty, handsome, and of a noble appearance. I inquired of my landlady if she was her daughter, but she, a good,

---

* The word *police* is certainly inapplicable in this case, although the fact be, as the Marquis states it. The respective governments of America, never dreamt of compelling persons to keep public houses, or blacksmith's and wheelwright's shops, nor could such a regulation be enforced without infinite difficulty, even in established and arbitrary governments. A moment's reflection, but above all, a knowledge of the constitutions, and the nature of the country, may convince any person that this assertion, which is repeated in this work, can only be the result of misinformation, or misapprehension. I have said that the existence of these resources is a fact, having experienced their utility and frequency in all parts of the country, but this arises from the necessity of such occupations, in the innumerable new settlements which are spread over great part of the continent, wherein every settler is obliged more or less to be a handicraftsman, and where they are all compelled mutually to administer to each other's wants. In them too, the publican, who is so far from being precluded from other pursuits, that he frequently becomes the first farmer, the first magistrate, the first military officer of the district, is a necessary appendage.—*Trans.*

fat woman, very industrious and talkative, and who had taken me into favour for giving ready answers to the questions she had put, told me she had never had any children, although she then had one in her arms, which she was dandling and caressing. To whom does that belong then, said I? To the tall woman you see, replied she—and who is her husband?—She has none—She is a widow then?—No, she was never married. It is an unlucky affair, too long to tell you : the poor girl was in want, I took her to live with me and provide for the mother and child.—Is it advancing a paradox to say, that such conduct proves, more than any thing, the pure and respectable manners of the Americans? With them vice is so strange, and so rare, that the danger of example has almost no effect ; so that a fault of this nature is regarded only as an accidental error, of which the individual, attacked with it, must be cured, without taking any measures to escape the contagion. I must add too, that the acquisition of a citizen in this country is so precious, that a girl, by bringing up her child, seems to expiate the weakness which brought it into existence. Thus morality, which can never differ from the real interest of society, appears sometimes to be local and modified by times and circumstances. When an infant without an asylum, and without property, shall become a burthen to the state, a being devoted to misfortune, owing its preservation to pity alone, and not to the public utility, we shall then see the mother humbled, nay perhaps punished, and this severity will then be vindicated here, as well as elsewhere, by all those austere dogmas which at present are neglected or forgotten.*

I proposed making a short journey the next day to Hartford, fifteen miles only from the place I slept at, but it seeming to me impossible to perform it except on horseback, I left the

---

* It is to be hoped that it will be long, very long ere the *barbarous* prejudices and punishments of polished Europe shall be introduced into this happy country. At present, the natural commerce between the sexes universally takes place, to the exclusion of exotic vices, and without involving the weak and unprotected female in all the horrors of shame, misery and child-murder. Here libertinism is by no means the consequence of an accidental frailty, nor is the mother, who in following the strong impulse of Nature, has given a member to society, thrown an outcast upon the world, lost to herself, and compelled to become vicious. The error of passion, though condemned, is venial, and she is neither driven to despair by cruelty, nor excluded from the sweet prospect of giving birth to future offspring, under the sanction of every legitimate and sacred title. Nothing is more common in this country, than such slips in the first violence of an early puberty, nor less frequent than a repetition of the same weakness.—*Trans.*

two State sledges with Mr. Case, taking a receipt from him, which I afterwards delivered to Mr. Wadsworth. At first I was not satisfied with the exchange, as I travelled some time on heights covered with snow, well calculated for the sledge, but on descending towards Farmington river, I found the thaw complete, and mud instead of snow. The woods I had just passed through, were very different from the Greenwoods; they were full of small firs, whose verdant hue pleased the eye, and the road was by accident so prettily laid out, that it is impossible to imagine a better model for walks in the English style.

When I had passed Farmington river, I mounted a pretty long and steep hill, on which I observed, from time to time, objects interesting to the lovers of natural history. You see, among other things, large masses of rocks, or rather vast blocks of stone, which have no sort of correspondence with the rest of the mountain, and appear as if they had been launched there by some volcano. I remarked one more singular than the rest, and stopped to measure it : it is a sort of socle, or long square, thirty feet long by twenty high, and as many wide, not unlike the pedestal of the statue of Peter the Great one sees at Petersburgh. On the east side, it is split from top to bottom, the crack is about a foot and a half wide at the top, but much less at bottom. Some shrubs vegetate in the little earth there is, and on the very summit of the rock grows a small tree, but I could not tell of what species. The stone is hard, of the nature of quartz, and is no wise volcanized.

I got to Hartford about three, and being informed that Mr. Wadsworth was absent, I was afraid of incommoding his wife and sister by going to lodge there, and went to a very good inn kept by Mr. Bull, who is accused of being rather *on the other side of the question;* a polite method of designating a tory. I only made a transient visit therefore to Mrs. Wadsworth, to invite myself to breakfast the next morning. The 5th I did not set out till eleven, although I had thirty miles journey to Lebanon. At the passage of the Ferry, I met with a detachment of the Rhode-Island regiment, the same corps we had with us all the last summer, but they have since been recruited and clothed. The greatest part of them are negroes or mulattoes ; but they are strong, robust men, and those I have seen had a very good appearance. We had fine weather all day, and got to Lebanon at sunset. Not that I got to Lebanon meeting-house, where the Duke de Lauzun was quartered with his Hussars, that was six miles farther, still travelling in Lebanon. Who would not think, after this, that I am speaking of an immense city? and in fact, this is one of the most considerable towns in the country, for it consists of at least one hundred houses; but it is unnecessary to add, that they are much scattered, and distant from each other frequently more than four or five hundred paces.

It will be easily imagined that I was not sorry to find myself in the French army, of which these Hussars formed the advanced guard, although their quarters be seventy-five miles from Newport; but there are no circumstances in which I should not be happy with M. de Lauzun. For two months I had been talking, and listening, with him I conversed : for it must be allowed that conversation is still the peculiar forte of the amiable French; a precious appendage for our nation, which it neglects possibly too much, and may one day chance to forfeit. It is told of an Englishman accustomed to be silent, that he said, *talking spoils conversation*. This whimsical expression contains great sense : every body can talk, but nobody knows how to listen; insomuch that the society of Paris, such as I left it, resembles the chorus of an opera, which a few *coryphées* alone have a right to interrupt; each theatre has its particular coryphæus; each theatre has its chorus too, which chime in, and its pit which applaud without knowing why. Transplant the actors, or change the theatre, the effect of the piece is lost. Fortunate for the spectators, when the stock is abundant, and they are not satiated with a repetition of the same production.

But I am got very far from America, where I must return however, if it be only to hunt a few squirrels. The Duke de Lauzun entertained me with this diversion, which is much in fashion in this country. These animals are large, and have a more beautiful fur than those in Europe; like ours, they are very adroit in slipping from tree to tree, and in clinging so closely to the branches as to become almost invisible. You frequently wound them, without their falling; but that is a slight inconvenience, for you have only to call or send for somebody, who applies the hatchet to the tree, and presently knocks it down. As squirrels are not rare, you will conclude then, and very justly, that trees are very common. On returning from the chase, I dined at the Duke de Lauzun's, with Governor Turnbull and General Huntington. The former lives at Lebanon, and the other had come from Norwich. I have already painted Governor Turnbull, at present you have only to represent to yourself this little old man, in the antique dress of the first settlers in this colony, approaching a table surrounded by twenty Hussar officers, and without either disconcerting himself, or losing any thing of his formal stiffness, pronouncing, in a loud voice, a long prayer in the form of a *benedicite*. Let it not be imagined that he excites the laughter of his auditors; they are too well trained : you must, on the contrary, figure to yourself twenty Amens issuing at once from the midst of forty mustaches,* and you will have some idea of this little scene. But M. de Lauzun is the man to relate, how this good, methodical governor, didactic in all his actions, invariably says, that he will *consider* ; that he must *refer* to his council ; how of little affairs he makes great ones, and how happy a mortal he is when he has any to transact. Thus, in the two hemispheres, Paris alone excepted, ridicule must not imply inaptitude to govern ; since it is by the character men govern, and by the character men make themselves ridiculous.

I proposed leaving Lebanon the 7th at ten o'clock, but the weather was so bad that 1 staid till past one, expecting it to clear up ; I was obliged, however, to set out at last in a melting snow, the most continued, and the coldest I ever experienced. The bad weather urged me on so fast that I arrived at Voluntown about five o'clock. If the reader recollects what I have said at the beginning of my journal of Mr. D's. house, he will not be surprised at my returning to it with pleasure. Miss Pearce however was no longer there, but she was replaced by the youngest Miss D. a charming pretty girl, although not so regular a beauty as her friend. She has, like her, modesty, candour, and beauty in all her features ; and has besides, a serenity mixed with gaiety, which render her as amiable as the other is interesting. Her eldest sister had laid in since I was last at Voluntown ; she was in a great chair, near the fire, around which her family were seated. Her noble and commanding countenance seemed more changed by misfortune than by suffering ; yet every body about her was employed in consoling and taking care of her ; her mother, seated by her, held in her arms the infant, smiling at it, and caressing it ; but as for her, her eyes were sorrowfully fixed upon the little innocent, eyeing it with interest, but without pleasure, as if she were saying to it, *misero paragoletto il tuo destin, non sai.*† Never did a more interesting or more moral picture exercise the pencil of a Greuze, or the pen of a tender poet. May that man be banished from the bosom of society who could be so barbarous as to leave this amiable girl a prey to a misfortune which it is in his power to repair ; and may every benediction which heaven can bestow be showered on the being, generous and just enough to give her more legitimate titles

---

* The Hussars of Lauzun's Legion, and the Duke himself wore mustaches in America.—*Trans.*

† Unhappy child! thou knowest not the lot that is reserved for thee. *Metastasio. Demophoon.*

to the hallowed names of wife and mother, and thus restore her, to all that happiness, which nature had designed her.*

My journey henceforward affords nothing worthy of the smallest attention. I slept next day at Providence, and arrived the 9th at Newport; satisfied with having seen many interesting things, without meeting with any accident; but with a sorrowful reflection that the place I arrived at, after travelling so far, was still fifteen hundred leagues from that where I had left my friends; where I shall enjoy the little knowledge I have acquired, by sharing it with them: where I shall again be happy, if there still be any happiness in store for me ; the only place in short, *dove da longhi errori spero di reposar*.†

---

* *See* what is said on this subject, in a note at the commencement of this journal.

† I wish to recompense those who shall have the patience to complete the perusal of this journal, by laying before them the charming passage of *Metastasio* from whence these words are borrowed.

> L'Onda dal mar divisa
> Bagna la valla e il monte,
> Va passagiera in fiume
> Va prigioniera in fonte ;
> Mormora sempre e geme
> Fin che non torna al mar.
> Al mar dove ella nacque
> Dove acquisto' gli umori
> Dove da lunghi errori
> Spera di reposar.

The following is a free translation :

The wave once separated from the sea, strays over the mountains. or bathes the vallies : anon it travels with the rivers, &c. now is kept prisoner in the fountains ; but it never ceases to murmur and complain until it returns unto the sea.

To the sea its native abode, to the sea its last asylum, where fatigued after its long wanderings, it hopes at length to find some repose.

TRAVELS IN NORTH-AMERICA.

PART II.

JOURNAL OF A TOUR

IN UPPER VIRGINIA, IN THE APALACHIAN MOUNTAINS,

AND TO THE NATURAL BRIDGE.

TRAVELS IN NORTH-AMERICA.

CHAPTER I.

FROM the moment the French troops were established in the quarters they occupied in Virginia, I formed the project of travelling into the upper parts of that province, where I was assured that I should find objects worthy of exciting the curiosity of a stranger; and faithful to the principles, which from my youth I had lain down, never to neglect seeing every country in my power, I burned with impatience to set out. The season however, was unfavourable, and rendered travelling difficult and laborious ; besides, experience taught me that travelling in winter never offered the greatest satisfaction we can enjoy ; that of seeing nature, such as she ought to be, and of forming a just idea of the general face of a country ; for it is easier for the imagination to deprive a landscape of the charms of spring, than to clothe with them, the hideous skeleton of winter; as it is easier to imagine what a beauty at eighteen may be at eighty, than to conceive what eighty was at eighteen.—Monsieur de Rochambleau being absent likewise during the month of February, and Monsieur la Chevalier de la Luzerne having chosen the month of March to pay us a visit, politeness and my duty obliged me to wait till April, before I could begin my travels.—On the 8th of that month I set out with Mr. Lynch, then my aid-de-camp and Adjutant, now General ; Mr. Frank Dillon, my second aid-de-camp,* and Mr. le Chevalier d'Oyrè of the engineers : six servants and a led horse composed our train ; so that our little caravan consisted of four masters, six servants, and eleven horses. I regulated my journey by the spring, and gave it time sufficient to precede us. For though in the 37th degree of latitude, one might expect to find it in the month of April, I saw no trace of it in the wood through which we passed ; the verdure being hardly discoverable on the thorns, the sun notwithstanding was very ar-

---

* Monsieur le Baron de Montesquieu went to Europe after the siege of York, and did not return until the month of September following.

dent, and I regretted to find summer in the heavens, whilst
the earth afforded not the smallest appearance of the spring.
The eighteen miles through which we passed, before we baited
our horses at Bird's tavern, were sufficiently known to me, for
it was the same road I travelled last summer in coming from
Williamsburgh.   The remaining sixteen, which completed our
day's work and brought us to New-Kent court-house, offered
nothing curious; all I learnt by a conversation with Mr. Bird
was, that he had been pillaged by the English when they passed his house in their march to Westover, in pursuit of Monsieur
de la Fayette, and in returning to Williamsburgh, after endeavouring in vain to come up with him.   It was comparatively nothing to see their fruits, fowls, and cattle carried away by
the light troops which formed the vanguard,* the army collected what the vanguard had left, even the officers seized the
rum, and all kinds of provisions, without paying a farthing for
them ; this hurricane which destroyed every thing in its pass-

---

* It is with great reluctance that truth compels me to confirm the
horrid depredations committed by the English army in their progress
through many parts of America.   Much has been said on this subject,
both in and out of parliament, but I am sorry to say, that future historians of this unhappy war, will find the fact too well established to refuse a decisive verdict.   Happy if *the result* may tend henceforth to alleviate the miseries of mankind, and mitigate the horrors of a civil contest.   The wife of an Englishman, one of the principal merchants of
Philadelphia, having retired with her family to the neighbourhood of
Mountholsy in the Jerseys, assured me, that she found the country in
general well affected to the English, until the arrival of their army,
whose indiscriminate and wanton enormities soon alienated their most
zealous friends, for even the officers were contaminated with the insa-
tiable spirit of revenge and plunder.   Among various anecdotes, she
related to me the circumstance of the cruel treatment of a lady of her
acquaintance, who was devoted to the British interest, and gave up her
house with exultation to some officers of Clinton's army in their retreat from Philadelphia.   But not only was her zeal repaid with insult
and her own house plundered ; she had the mortification to see it
made the receptacle of the pillage of her poorer neighbours.   Observing
some of the officers make frequent excursions, and return, followed by
soldiers, laden with various articles, she had at length the curiosity to
pass into the garden, and looking through the window, saw four of
them, and *the Chaplain*, emptying a sack containing stockings, shirts,
shifts, counterpanes, sheets, spoons, and women's trinkets.   The
booty was regularly shared, and the distributor of these unhallowed
spoils, to her utter astonishment and horror, was no other than the
minister of virtue and religion.   The detail of this war is a history of
such iniquity : was it possible, therefore, to expect a more favourable
termination of it, either on the principle of a Divine Providence, or of
human conduct ?—*Trans.*

age, was followed by a scourge yet more terrible, a numerous rabble, under the title of Refugees and Loyalists, followed the army, not to assist in the field, but to partake of the plunder.* The furniture and clothes of the inhabitants were in general the sole booty left to satisfy their avidity ; after they had emptied the houses, they stript the proprietors ; and Mr. Bird repeated with indignation, that they had taken from him by force, the very boots from off his legs. In my way hither, I had the satisfaction however of recalling to mind the first punishment inflicted on these robbers. Six miles from Williamsburgh I passed near a place where two cross roads intersecting each other, leave an open space ; one leading to Williamsburgh, the other to Jamestown. On the 25th of June, Monsieur de la Fayette here ordered the vanguard to attack that of Lord Cornwallis ; Sincoe, who commanded it, was left behind to collect the cattle, whilst Lord Cornwallis was encamping at Williamsburgh, where he arrived the preceding evening. Monsieur de la Fayette's cavalry with some infantry mounted behind them, arrived soon enough to force Sincoe to an engagement, and was soon after joined by the rest of the American light infantry. Sincoe fought with disadvantage, till Lord Cornwallis marching to his assistance, the Americans retired,

---

* The Loyalists no doubt, no more merit indiscriminate censure than any other body of men ; the Translator, who thinks he understands the true principles of liberty, for which he has ever been a zealous and unshaken advocate, admits, however, and admires the virtue, honour, and steadfast attachment of many illustrious individuals to a cause, directly destructive of his own wishes ; but with every fair allowance for the violence inseparable from civil contests, he cannot help bearing his testimony to the wanton outrages committed by an unprincipled banditti who attached themselves to the royal cause, and branded it with ruin and disgrace. The root of this evil originated in the *Board of Loyalists* established by Lord George Germain at the instigation of skulking refugees, who flying themselves, from the scene of danger, took up their residence in London, and were in the incessant pursuit of personal and interested vengeance. He does not assert that their councils lost America, but it is now past doubt, that they formed a strong secondary cause of precipitating that event, and of embittering the separation. General Clinton, the whole army at New-York, can witness the insolence and indirect menaces of this incorporated rabble of marauders, in the affair of Captain Huddy, and the subsequent claim of the Congress. Had the war continued, this *imperium in imperio* must have been attended with the most fatal consequences ; this illiberal narrow minded set of men, became the spies and censors of British policy, and British conduct, and the commander-in-chief himself, was struck with horror at their unenlightened, blood-thirsty tribunal.—*Trans.*

after having killed or wounded near 150 men, with the loss
only of seven or eight.   Colonel Butler an American officer,
who commanded a battalion of light infantry, and Colonel
Galvan,* a French officer, who commanded another, distinguished themselves very much on this occasion.   The recollection of this event, the presage of that success which crowned our campaign, employed my thoughts so much the more
agreeably the whole evening, as we had taken up our lodgings
in a good inn, where we were served with an excellent supper,
composed chiefly of sturgeon, and I had two kinds of fish, at
least as good in Virginia as in Europe, but which make their
appearance only in the spring.

The next morning I had an enjoyment of another kind.   I
rose with the sun, and whilst breakfast was preparing, took a
walk round the house ; the birds were heard on every side, but
my attention was chiefly attracted by a very agreeable song,
which appeared to proceed from a neighbouring tree.   I approached softly, and perceived it to be a mocking bird, saluting the rising sun.   At first I was afraid of frightening it, but
my presence on the contrary gave it pleasure, for apparently
delighted at having an auditor, it sung better than before, and
its emulation seemed to increase, when it perceived a couple
of dogs, which followed me, draw near to the tree on which
it was perched.   It kept hopping incessantly from branch to
branch, still continuing its song, for this extraordinary bird is
not less remarkable for its agility, than its charming notes; it
keeps perpetually rising and sinking, so as to appear not less
the favourite of Terpsichore, than Polihymnia.   This bird cannot certainly be reproached with fatiguing its auditors, for nothing can be more varied than its song, of which it is impossible to give an imitation, or even to furnish any adequate idea.
As it had every reason to be contented with my attention, it
concealed from me no one of its talents ; and one would have
thought, that after having delighted me with a concert, it was
desirous of entertaining me with a comedy.   It began to counterfeit different birds ; those which it imitated the most naturally, at least to a stranger, were the jay, the raven, the cardi-
nal, and the lapwing.†   It appeared desirous of retaining me
near it, for after having listened for a quarter of an hour, on

---

* The same who afterwards shot himself at Philadelphia.   See previous notes.— *Trans.*

† Or rather the painted plover, which is the lapwing of America.
It differs from ours, by its plumage, mixt with grey, white and yellow
gilt; it differs also a little in its song, but it has the shape and manners, and is absolutely the same species.

my return to the house, it followed me, flying from tree to tree, always singing, sometimes its natural song, at others, those which it had learned in Virginia, and in its travels; for this bird is one of those which change climate, although it sometimes appears here during the winter. As the next day's journey was to be longer than that of the preceding one, we left New-Kent court-house before eight o'clock and rode twenty miles to Newcastle, where I resolved to give our horses two hour's repose; the road was not so level as that we had travelled the day before, and was rendered more agreeable by being diversified with some little hillocks. From the top of them you had a view to the distance of some miles, and at times one might perceive Pamunkey river, which runs at the bottom of a deep valley, covered with wood. As you approach Newcastle, the country becomes more gay. This little capital of a small district, contains twenty-five or thirty houses, some of which are pretty enough. When our horses were reposed, and the heat already troublesome in the middle of the day, was a little abated, we continued our journey, that we might arrive, before dark, at Hanover court-house, from which we were yet sixteen miles. The country through which we passed is one of the finest of lower Virginia. There are many well cultivated estates, and handsome houses, among others, one belonging to Mr. Jones, situated near the road, two miles from Newcastle, of a very elegant appearance, which, we were informed, was furnished with infinite taste, and what is still more uncommon in America, that it was embellished with a garden, laid out in the English style.* It is even pretended, that this kind of park, through which the river flows, yields not in beauty to those, the model of which the French have received from England, and are now imitating with such success.†

---

* The author has since seen this garden, which answers the description given, and is really very elegant.

† The gardens I have hitherto seen in France professedly laid out on the English model, are with great deference to the author, but very *unsuccessful imitations* of the English style; those of the Comte de Artois at Bagatelle, and of the Duke of Orleans at Mousseaux near Paris, are indeed no imperfect imitations of Mr. Sterling's in the comedy of the Clandestine Marriage, of the Spaniard's at Hampstead, of Bagnigge-wells, or a Common Councilman's retreat upon the Wandsworth road. They present a fantastic, and crowded groupe of Chinese pagodas, gothic ruins, immoveable windmills, molehill-mounts, thirty grass patches, dry bridges, pigmy serpentines, cockleshell cascades, and stagnant duck-pools. The gardens of the Thuilleries and Marly, with their undisguised, artificial labours, are at least noble,

Three miles from Hanover, there are two roads, that which we were to follow winds a little towards the north, and approaches the Pamunkey. We arrived before sunset and alighted at a tolerable handsome inn ; a very large saloon and a covered portico, are destined to receive the company who assemble every three months at the court-house, either on private or public affairs. This asylum is the more necessary, as there are no other houses in the neighbourhood. Travellers make use of these establishments, which are indispensable in a country so thinly inhabited, that the houses are often at the distance of two or three miles from each other. Care is generally taken to place the court-house in the centre of the county. As there are a great many counties in Virginia, they are seldom more than six or seven leagues diameter; thus every man can return home after he has finished his affairs.

The county of Hanover, as well as that of New-Kent, had still reason to remember the passage of the English. Mr. Tilghman, our landlord, though he lamented his misfortune in having lodged and boarded Lord Cornwallis and his retinue, without his Lordship's having made him the least recompense, could not yet help laughing at the fright which the unexpected arrival of Tarleton spread among a considerable number of gentlemen, who had come to hear the news, and were assembled in the court-house. A negro on horseback came full gallop, to let them know that Tarleton was not above three miles off. The resolution of retreating was soon taken, but the alarm was so sudden, and the confusion so great, that every one mounted the first horse he could find, so that few of those curious gentlemen returned upon their own horses. The English, who came from Westover, had passed the Chilkahominy at Button's bridge, and directed their march towards the South Anna, which M. de la Fayette had put between them and himself.

Mr. Tilghman having had time to renew his provisions since the retreat of Lord Cornwallis, we supped very well, and had the company of Mr. Lee, brother to Colonel Henry Lee ;*

---

magnificent, and useful ; their terraces are grand, and their lofty *Berceaus* beautiful, and well adapted to the climate.—*Trans.*

* Colonel Harry Lee is a smart, active young man, first cousin to Mr. Arthur Lee, and Mr. William Lee, late alderman of London. He rendered very essential services to his country, particularly in the southern war. His corps was mounted on remarkably fine, high-priced horses, mostly half blood English stallions, and officered principally by his own family and relations. Had the war continued, there is every reason to believe that the American cavalry would have taken some consistence, and have become very formidable in the field ; Mr.

who long commanded a legion, and often distinguished himself, particularly in Carolina.* We set out at nine the next morning, after having breakfasted much better than our horses, who had nothing but oats, the country being so destitute of forage, that it was not possible to find a truss of hay, or a few leaves of Indian corn, though we had sought for it two miles round. Three miles and a half from Hanover we crossed the South Anna on a wooden bridge. I observed that the river was deeply embanked, and from the nature of the soil concluded it was the same during a great part of its course : it appears to me therefore that would have been a good defence, if Monsieur de la Fayette, who passed it higher up, had arrived in time to destroy the bridge. On the left side of the river the ground rises, and you mount a pretty high hill, the country is barren, and we travelled almost always in the woods, till one o'clock, when we arrived at Offly, and alighted at General Nelson's, formerly governor of Virginia. I had got acquainted with him during the expedition to York, at which critical moment he was governor, and conducted himself with the courage of a brave soldier, and the zeal of a good citizen. At the time when the English armies were carrying desolation into the heart of his country, and our troops arrived unexpectedly to succour and revenge it, he was compelled to exert every means, and to call forth every possible resource, to assist Monsieur de la Fayette to make some resistance ; and furnish General Washington with horses, carriages, and provisions ; but I am sorry to add, what will do but little honour to Virginia, that the only recompense of his labours was the hatred of a great part of his fellow-citizens. At the first assembly of the province, held after the campaign, he experienced from them neither the satisfaction he had a right to expect, at being freed from servitude, nor that emulation which is the general consequence

---

Tarleton received many severe checks in his exploits from the corps under Colonel Washington, and that of Colonel Harry Lee. Towards the close of the war, he had to encounter an enemy very different from flying militia, and scattered bodies of broken, half disciplined infantry, of whom slaughter *may* be service, but conquest no honour.—*Trans*.

* Lord Cornwallis was unquestionably the English general whose courage, talents and activity, occasioned the greatest loss to the Americans ; it is not astonishing therefore he should not have inspired them with sentiments similar to those of his own troops, whose attachment, and admiration of his character, were unbounded. Yet they never accused him of rapine, nor even of interested views, and the complaints of Mr. Tilghman only prove the sad consequences of a war, in the course of which the English suffered more from want, in the midst of their

of success; but instead of these sentiments, so natural in such circumstances, a general discontent, arising from the necessity under which he had often laboured, of pressing their horses, carriages and forage. Those laws and customs which would have ceased to exist by the conquest of the province, were put in force against its defender, and General Nelson, worn out at length by the fatigues of the campaign, but still more by the ingratitude of his fellow-citizens, resigned the place of governor, which he had held for six months, but not without enjoying the satisfaction of justifying his conduct, and of seeing his countrymen pardon the momentary injuries he had done their laws, by endeavouring to save the state. If to the character I have just given of General Nelson, I should add, that he is a good and gallant man, in every possible situation of life, and has ever behaved with the utmost politeness to the French, you will be surprised that I should go to visit him in his absence, like Mathwin in the comedy of Rose and Colas, for though I knew he was not at home, as I had met him' near Williamsburgh, where he was detained by public business, the visit I intended to pay him formed a part of my journey I undertook —besides that I was desirous of seeing his family, particularly his younger brother, Mr. William Nelson, with whom I was intimately connected at Williamsburgh, where he passed the greatest part of the winter. Offly is far from corresponding with the riches of General Nelson, or with his high consideration in Virginia; it is but a moderate plantation, where he has contented himself with erecting such buildings as are necessary for the improvement of his lands, and for the habitation of his overseers; his general residence is at York, but that he was obliged to abandon: and Offly being beyond the South Anna, and situated far back in the country, he thought that this lonely house would be at least a safe retreat for his family; it was not secure however from the visits of Lord Cornwallis, who, in his peregrinations through Virginia, advanced even so far, though without doing much mischief. In the absence of the general, his mother and wife received us with all the polite-

---

success, than in their disasters; the former carrying them far from the fleet, and the latter obliging them to approach it. But the most painful of these consequences was the necessity which compelled a man of my Lord Cornwallis' birth and character, to conduct, rather than command, a numerous band of traitors and robbers, which English policy decorated with the name of *Loyalists*. This rabble preceded the troops in plunder, taking special care never to follow them in danger. The progress was marked by fire, devastation, and outrages of every kind; they ravaged some part of America it is true, but ruined England, by inspiring her enemies with an irreconcileable hatred.

ness, ease, and cordiality natural to his family. But as in America the ladies are never thought sufficient to do the honours of the house, five or six Nelsons were assembled to receive us; among others, the Secretary Nelson, uncle to the general, with his two sons, and two of the general's brothers. These young men were all married, and several of them were accompanied by their wives and children, all called Nelson, and distinguished only by their christian names,* so that during the two days which I passed in this truly patriarchal house, it was impossible for me to find out their degrees of relationship. When I say that we passed two days in this house, it may be understood in the most literal sense, for the weather was so bad, there was no possibility of stirring out. The house being neither convenient nor spacious, company assembled either in the parlour or saloon, especially the men, from the hour of breakfast, to that of bed-time, but the conversation was always agreeable and well supported. If you were desirous of diversifying the scene, there were some good French and English authors at hand. An excellent breakfast at nine in the morning, a sumptuous dinner at two o'clock, tea and punch in the afternoon, and an elegant little supper, divided the day most happily, for those whose stomachs were never unprepared. It is worth observing, that on this occasion, where fifteen or twenty people, (four of whom were strangers to the family or country,) were assembled together, and by bad weather forced to stay within doors, not a syllable was mentioned about play. How many parties would with us have been the consequence of such obstinate bad weather? But in America, music, drawing, public reading, and the work of the ladies, are resources as yet unknown, though it is to be hoped they will not long neglect to cultivate them; for nothing but study was wanting to a young Miss Tolliver who sung some airs, the words of which were English, and the music Italian. Her charming voice, and the artless simplicity of her singing, were a substitute for taste, if not taste itself; that natural taste, always sure, when confined within just limits, and when timid in its weakness, it has not been altered, or spoiled by false precepts and bad examples.

Miss Tolliver has attended her sister, Mrs. William Nelson, to Offly, who had just miscarried, and kept her bed. She was

---

* The French in general assume the surname, by which they choose to be distinguished in the world, so that the name which, with us, is a real bond of affection, is soon lost with them. I was long acquainted with four brothers in France, without knowing they were related to each other.—*Trans.*

brought up in the middle of the woods by her father, a great fox-hunter, consequently could have learned to sing from the birds only, in the neighbourhood, when the howling of the dogs permitted her to hear them. She is an agreeable figure, as well as Mrs. Nelson her sister, though less pretty than a third daughter, who remained with her father. These young ladies came often to Williamsburgh to attend the balls, where they appeared as well dressed as the ladies of the town, and always remarkable for their decency of behaviour. The young military gentlemen, on the other hand, had conceived a great affection for Mr. Tolliver their father, and took the trouble sometimes to ride over to breakfast and talk with him of the chase. The young ladies, who appeared from time to time, never interrupted the conversation. These pretty nymphs more timid and wild than those of Diana, though they did not conduct the chase, inspired the taste for it into the youth : they knew however how to defend themselves from fox-hunters, without destroying, by their arrows, those who had the presumption to look at them.

After this little digression, which requires some indulgence, I should be at a loss for a transition to an old magistrate, whose white locks, noble figure, and stature, which was above the common size, commanded respect and veneration. Secretary Nelson, to whom this character belongs, owes this title to the place he occupied under the English government. In Virginia the secretary, whose office it was to preserve the registers of all public acts, was, by his place, a member of the council, of which the governor was the chief. Mr. Nelson, who held this office for thirty years, saw the morning of that bright day which began to shine upon his country; he saw too the storms arise which threatened its destruction, though he neither endeavoured to collect, or to foment them.

Too far advanced in age to desire a revolution, too prudent to check this great event, if necessary, and too faithful to his countrymen to separate his interests from theirs, he chose the crisis of this alteration, to retire from public affairs. Thus did he opportunely quit the theatre, when new pieces demanded fresh actors, and took his seat among the spectators, content to offer up his wishes for the success of the drama, and to applaud those who acted well their part. But in the last campaign, chance produced him on the scene, and made him unfortunately famous. He lived at York, where he had built a very handsome house, from which neither European taste nor luxury was excluded; a chimney-piece and some bass-reliefs of very fine marble, exquisitely sculptured, were particularly admired, when fate conducted Lord Cornwallis to this town to be disarmed, as well as his till then victorious troops. Secretary Nelson did not think it necessary to fly from the English, to whom his conduct could not have made him disagreeable, nor have furnished any just motive of suspicion. He was well received by the general, who established his head-quarters in his house, which was built on an eminence, near the most important fortifications, and in the most agreeable situation of the town. It was the first object which struck the sight as you approached the town, but instead of travellers, it soon drew the attention of our bombardiers and cannoniers, and was almost entirely destroyed. Mr. Nelson lived in it at the time our batteries tried their first shot and killed one of his negroes at a little distance from him; so that Lord Cornwallis was soon obliged to seek another asylum. But what asylum could be found for an old man, deprived of the use of his legs by the gout? But, above all, what asylum could defend him against the cruel anguish a father must feel at being besieged by his own children; for he had two in the American army. So that every shot, whether fired from the town, or from the trenches, might prove equally fatal to him; I was witness to the cruel anxiety of one of these young men, when after the flag was sent to demand his father, he kept his eyes fixed upon the gate of the town, by which it was to come out, and seemed to expect his own sentence in the answer. Lord Cornwallis had too much humanity to refuse a request so just, nor can I recollect, without emotion, the moment in which I saw this old gentleman alight at General Washington's. He was seated, the fit of the gout not having yet left him; and whilst we stood around him, he related to us, with a serene countenance, what had been the effect of our batteries, and how much his house had suffered from the first shot.

The tranquillity which has succeeded these unhappy times, by giving him leisure to reflect upon his losses, has not embittered the recollection; he lives happily on one of his plantations, where, in less than six hours, he can assemble thirty of his children, grand-children, nephews, nieces, &c. amounting in all to seventy, the whole inhabiting Virginia. The rapid increase of his own family justifies what he told me of the population in general, of which, from the offices he has held all his life, he must have it in his power to form a very accurate judgment. In 1742 the people subject to pay taxes in the State of Virginia, that is to say, the white males above sixteen, and the male and female blacks of the same age, amounted only to the number of 63,000; by his account they now exceed 160,000.*

_____

* This calculation is much below that given by other writers, and I have reason to believe that it is considerably below the mark.—*Trans.*

After passing two days very agreeably with this interesting family, we left them the 12th at ten in the morning, accompanied by the secretary, and five or six other Nelsons, who conducted us to Little River Bridge, a small creek on the road about five miles from Offly. There we separated, and having rode about eleven miles farther through woods, and over a barren country, we arrived at one o'clock at Willis' inn or ordinary; for the inns which in the other provinces of America are known by the name of taverns, or public houses, are in Virginia called ordinaries. This consisted of a little house placed in a solitary situation in the middle of the woods, notwithstanding which we there found a great deal of company. As soon as I alighted, I inquired what might be the reason of this numerous assembly, and was informed it was a cock-match. This diversion is much in fashion in Virginia, where the English customs are more prevalent than in the rest of America. When the principal promoters of this diversion, propose to match their champions, they take great care to announce it to the public, and although there are neither posts, nor regular conveyances, this important news spreads with such facility, that the planters, for thirty or forty miles round, attend, some with cocks, but all with money for betting, which is sometimes very considerable. They are obliged to bring their own provisions, as so many people with good appetites could not possibly be supplied with them at the inn. As for lodgings, one large room for the whole company, with a blanket for each individual, is sufficient for such hearty countrymen, who are not more delicate about the conveniences of life, than the choice of their amusements.

Whilst our horses were feeding, we had an opportunity of seeing a battle. The preparation took up a great deal of time; they arm their cocks with long steel spurs, very sharp, and cut off a part of their feathers, as if they meant to deprive them of their armour. The stakes were very considerable; the money of the parties was deposited in the hands of one of the principal persons, and I felt a secret pleasure in observing that it was chiefly French.* I know not which is

---

* The prodigious quantity of French money brought into America by their fleets and armies, and the loans made to congress, together with the vast return of dollars from the Havana, and the Spanish, Portuguese, and English gold which found its way into the country from the British lines, rendered specie very plentiful towards the conclusion of the war; and the arrival of the army of the Comte de Rochambeau was particularly opportune, as it happened at the very distressing crisis of the death of the paper currency. The French money alone in circulation in the United States, in the year 1782 was estimated.

the most astonishing, the insipidity of such diversion, or the stupid interest with which it animates the parties.   This passion appears almost innate among the English, for the Virginians are yet English in many respects.   Whilst the interested parties animated the cocks to battle, a child of fifteen, who was near me, kept leaping for joy, and crying, Oh! it is a charming diversion.

We had yet seven or eight and twenty miles to ride, to the only inn where it was possible to stop, before we reached Mr. Jefferson's; for Mr. de Rochambeau, who had travelled the same road but two months before, cautioned me against sleep-

---

after very accurate calculations, at thirty-five millions of livres, or near a million and a half sterling.   Although it is impossible to ascertain with any degree of precision the quantity of British money circulating in the revolted part of the continent, under the forms of Spanish, Portugal, and English coin, yet some general idea may be entertained that the quantity was very considerable, from the following extract from the *seventh report of the commissioners of public accounts,* " We obtained by requisition from the office of the Paymaster-General of the forces, an account of the money issued to Messrs. Hartley & Drummond, pursuant to his Majesty's warrants, for the *extraordinary* services of his Majesty's forces serving in North-America *from the* 1st *of January,* 1776, *to the* 31st *of December,* 1781.   This sum amounts to 10,083,863l. 2s. 6d.—There are two ways by which this money goes from these remitters into the hands of their agents : the one is by bills drawn by them on the remitters, which bills they receive the value for in America, and the remitters discharge when presented to them in London ; the other is by sending out *actual cash,* whenever it becomes necessary to support the exchange, by increasing the quantity of current cash in the hands of the agents:"—Now the votes of parliament will show the reader, the vast sums *annually* granted to Messrs. Hartley & Drummond, for the specific purpose of purchasing Spanish and Portugal gold alone, to supply " this quantity of current cash."   Besides the vast exportation of English guineas ; nor is it to be doubted that a great proportion of this supply found its way into the heart of the United States, in return for provisions, in payment of their captive armies, &c. &c.   The British navy too is not included in this estimate.   Great sums, it is true, returned to Britain directly or indirectly for goods, &c., but much specie remained incontestibly in the country.   With respect to the Spanish dollars from the Havana and the West-Indies, no just calculation can be formed, but the amount must have been very considerable, as they appeared to me to circulate in the proportion of at least *three* or *four* to *one* of all the other coined specie.—When the translator added this note, he had not seen *Lord Sheffield's* observations on the subject.   In these, however, he thinks his lordship discovers *deep prejudices,* mixed with much excellent reasoning and a great deal of truth.—*Trans.*

ing at Louisa court-house, as the worst lodging he had found in all America. This public house is sixteen miles from Willis' ordinary. As he had given me a very forcible description not only of the house, but of the landlord, I had a curiosity to judge of it by my own experience. Under the pretence of inquiring for the road, therefore, I went in, and observed, that there was no other lodging for travellers than the apartment of the landlord. This man, called Johnson, is become so monstrously fat, that he cannot move out of his armchair. He is a good humoured fellow, whose manners are not very rigid, who loves good cheer, and all sorts of pleasure, insomuch that at the age of fifty he has so augmented his bulk, and diminished his fortune, that by two opposite principles he is near seeing the termination of both; but all this does not in the least affect his gaiety. I found him contented in his armchair, which serves him for a bed; for it would be difficult for him to lie down, and impossible to rise. A stool supported his enormous legs, in which were large fissures on each side, a prelude to what must soon happen to his belly. A large ham and a bowl of grog served him for company, like a man resolved to die surrounded by his friends. He called to my mind, in short, the country spoken of by Rabelais, where the men order their bellies to be hooped to prolong their lives, and especially the Abbé who having exhausted every possible resource, resolved to finish his days by a great feast, and invited all the neighbourhood to his *bursting*.

The night was already closed in, when we arrived at the house of Colonel Boswell, a tall, stout Scotsman, about sixty years of age, and who had been about forty years settled in America, where, under the English government, he was a colonel of militia. Although he kept a kind of tavern, he appeared but little prepared to receive strangers. It was already late indeed, besides that this road, which leads only to the mountains, is little frequented. He was quietly seated near the fire, by the side of his wife, as old, and almost as tall as himself, whom he distinguished by the epithet of "honey," which in French corresponds with *mon petit cœur*. These honest people received us cheerfully, and soon called up their servants, who were already gone to bed. Whilst they were preparing supper, we often heard them call Rose, Rose, which at length brought to view the most hideous negress I ever beheld. Our supper was rather scanty, but our breakfast the next morning better; we had ham, butter, fresh eggs, and coffee by way of drink: for the whiskey or corn-spirits we had in the evening, mixt with water, was very bad; besides that we were perfectly reconciled to the American custom of drinking coffee with meat, vegetables, or other food.

We set out the next morning at eight o'clock, having learned nothing in this house worthy of remark, except that notwithstanding the hale and robust appearance of Mr. and Mrs. Boswell, not one of fourteen of their children had attained the age of ten years. We were now approaching a chain of mountains of considerable height, called the South-West Mountains, because they are the first you meet in travelling westward, before you arrive at the chain known in France by the name of the Apalachians, and in Virginia by that of the Blue Ridge, North Ridge, and Allegany Mountains. As the country was much covered with woods, we had a view of them but very seldom; and travelled a long time without seeing any habitation, at times greatly perplexed to choose among the different roads, which crossed each other.* At last we overtook a traveller who preceded us, and served not only as a guide, but by his company helped to abridge our journey. He was an Irishman,†_who though but lately arrived in America, had made

---

* The difficulty of finding the road in many parts of America is not to be conceived except by those strangers who have travelled in that country. The roads, which are through the woods, not being kept in repair, as soon as one is in bad order, another is made in the same manner, that is, merely by felling the trees, and the whole interior parts are so covered, that without a compass it is impossible to have the least idea of the course you are steering. The distances too are so uncertain, as in every country where they are not measured, that no two accounts resemble each other. In the back parts of Pennsylvania, Maryland, and Virginia, I have frequently travelled thirty miles for ten, though frequently set right by passengers and negroes: but the great communications between the large towns, through all the well inhabited parts of the continent, are as practicable and easy as in Europe.—*Trans.*

† An Irishman, the instant he sets foot on American ground becomes, *ipso facto*, an American ; this was uniformly the case during the whole of the late war. Whilst Englishmen and Scotsmen were regarded with jealousy and distrust, even with the best recommendation, of zeal and attachment to their cause, a native of Ireland stood in need of no other certificate than his dialect ; his sincerity was never called in question, he was supposed to have a sympathy of suffering, and every voice decided as it were intuitively, in his favour. Indeed their conduct in the late revolution amply justified this favourable opinion ; for whilst the Irish emigrant was fighting the battles of America by sea and land, the Irish merchants, particularly at Charleston, Baltimore, and Philadelphia, laboured with indefatigable zeal, and at all hazards, to promote the spirit of enterprise, to increase the wealth, and maintain the credit of the country ; their purses were always open, and their persons devoted to the common cause. On more than one imminent occasion, Congress owed their existence, and America pos-

several campaigns, and received a considerable wound in his
thigh by a musket ball; which, though it could never be extracted, had not in the least affected either his health or gaiety.
He related his military exploits, and we inquired immediately
about the country which he then inhabited. He acquainted
us that he was settled in North-Carolina, upwards of eighty
miles from Catawbaw, and were then 300 from the sea. These
new establishments are so much the more interesting, as by
their distance from all commerce, agriculture is their sole resource; I mean that patriarchal agriculture which consists in
producing only what is sufficient for their own consumption,
without the hope of either sale or barter. These colonies
therefore must necessarily be rendered equal to all their wants.
It is easy to conceive that there is soon no deficiency of food,
but it is also necessary that their flocks and their fields should
furnish them with clothing, they must manufacture their own
wool, and flax, into clothes and linen, they must prepare the
hides to make shoes of them, &c. &c.;* as to drink, they are
obliged to content themselves with milk and water, until their
apple-trees are large enough to bear fruit, or until they have
been able to procure themselves stills, to distil their grain.
In these troublesome times we should scarcely imagine in Europe, that nails are the articles the most wanted in these new
colonies : for the axe and the saw can supply every other want.
They contrive however to erect huts, and construct roofs without nails, but the work is by this means rendered much more
tedious, and in such circumstances every body knows the value of time and labour. It was a natural question to ask such
a cultivator what could bring him four hundred miles from

---

sibly her preservation to the fidelity and firmness of the Irish. I had
the honour of dining with the Irish Society, composed of the steadiest
whigs upon the continent, at the City Tavern in Philadelphia, on St.
Patrick's day ; the members wear a medallion suspended by a riband,
with a very significant device, which has escaped my memory, but
was so applicable to the American revolution, that until I was assured
that it subsisted prior to that event, and had a reference only to the
oppression of Ireland by her powerful sister, I concluded it to be a
temporary illusion. General Washington, Mr. Dickinson, and other
leading characters are adopted members of this society, having been
initiated by the ceremony of an exterior application of a whole bottle
of claret poured upon the head, and a generous libation to liberty and
good living, of as many as the votary could carry off.—*Trans.*

* It is a natural supposition that workmen of all sorts (at least the
most necessary,) should form a part of every new colony, and follow
their particular trade as the most beneficial employment.—*Trans.*

home, and we learned from him that he carried on the trade of horse selling, the only commerce of which his country was susceptible,* and by which people in the most easy circumstances endeavoured to augment their fortunes. In fact these animals multiply very fast in a country where there is abundant pasture ; and as they are conducted without any expense, by grazing on the road, they become the most commodious article of exportation, for a country so far from any road or commerce. The conversation continued and brought us insensibly to the foot of the mountains. On the summit of one of them we discovered the house of Mr. Jefferson, which stands pre-eminent in these retirements ; it was himself who built it and preferred this situation ; for although he possessed considerable property in the neighbourhood, there was nothing to prevent him from fixing his residence wherever he thought proper. But it was a debt nature owed to a philosopher and a man of taste, that in his own possessions he should find a spot where he might best study and enjoy her. He calls his house Monticello, (in Italian, Little Mountain,) a very modest title, for it is situated upon a very lofty one, but which announces the owner's attachment to the language of Italy ; and above all to the fine arts, of which that country was the cradle, and is still the asylum. As I had no farther occasion for a guide, I separated from the Irishman ; and after ascending by a tolerably commodious road, for more than half an hour, we arrived at Monticello. This house, of which Mr. Jefferson was the architect, and often one of the workmen, is rather elegant, and in the Italian taste, though not without fault ; it consists of one large square pavillion, the entrance of which is by two porticos ornamented with pillars. The ground floor consists chiefly of a very large lofty saloon, which is to be decorated entirely in the antique style : above it is a library of the same form, two small wings, with only a ground floor, and attic story, are joined to this pavillion, and communicate with the kitchen, offices, &c. which will form a kind of basement story over which runs a terrace. My object in this short description is only to show the difference between this, and the other houses of the country ; for we may safely aver, that Mr. Jefferson is the first American who has consulted the fine arts to know how he should shelter himself from the weather. But it is on himself alone I ought to bestow my time. Let me describe to you a man, not yet forty, tall,

---

* Considerable quantities, of peltry are likewise brought from the back parts of North-Carolina ; and I have met with strings of horses laden with that article passing through Virginia to Philadelphia from the distance of six hundred miles.—*Trans.*

and with a mild and pleasing countenance, but whose mind and understanding are ample substitutes for every exterior grace. An American, who without ever having quitted his own country, is at once a musician, skilled in drawing, a geometrician, an astronomer, a natural philosopher, legislator, and statesman. A senator of America, who sat for two years in that famous Congress which brought about the revolution ; and which is never mentioned without respect, though unhappily not without regret: a governor of Virginia, who filled this difficult station during the invasions of Arnold, of Phillips, and of Cornwallis ; a philosopher, in voluntary retirement from the world, and public business, because he loves the world, inasmuch only as he can flatter himself with being useful to mankind ; and the minds of his countrymen are not yet in a condition either to bear the light, or to suffer contradiction. A mild and amiable wife, charming children, of whose education he himself takes charge, a house to embellish, great provisions to improve, and the arts and sciences to cultivate ; these are what remain to Mr. Jefferson, after having played a principal character on the theatre of the new world, and which he preferred to the honourable commission of Minister Plenipotentiary in Europe.* The visit which I made him was not unexpected, for he had long since invited me to come and pass a few days with him, in the centre of the mountains ; notwithstanding which I found his first appearance serious, nay even cold ; but before I had been two hours with him we were as intimate as if we had passed our whole lives together ; walking, books, but above all, a conversation always varied and interesting, always supported by that sweet satisfaction experienced by two persons, who in communicating their sentiments and opinions, are invariably in unison, and who understand each other at the first hint, made four days pass away like so many minutes.

This conformity of sentiments and opinions on which I insist, because it constitutes my own eulogium, (and self-love must somewhere show itself,) this conformity, I say, was so perfect, that not only our taste was similar, but our predilections also, those partialities which cold methodical minds ridicule as en-

---

* Mr. Jefferson having since had the misfortune to lose his wife, has at last yielded to the intreaties of his country, and accepted the place of Minister Plenipotentiary at the court of France, and is now at Paris. It is necessary to observe that Mr. Jefferson, who justly stands in the highest situation in America, was one of the five Ministers Plenipotentiary for concluding a peace in Europe, named by Congress full two years before it took place ; Messrs. Franklin, Adams, Laurens, and Jay, were the other four.—*Trans.*

thusiastic, whilst sensible and animated ones cherish and adopt the glorious appellation. I recollect with pleasure that as we were conversing one evening over a bowl of punch, after Mrs. Jefferson had retired, our conversation turned on the poems of Ossian. It was a spark of electricity which passed rapidly from one to the other; we recollected the passages in those sublime poems, which particularly struck us, and entertained my fellow travellers, who fortunately knew English well, and were qualified to judge of their merit, though they had never read the poems. In our enthusiasm the book was sent for, and placed near the bowl, where, by their mutual aid, the night far advanced imperceptibly upon us. Sometimes natural philosophy, at others politics or the arts, were the topics of our conversation, for no object had escaped Mr. Jefferson; and it seemed as if from his youth he had placed his mind, as he has done his house, on an elevated situation, from which he might contemplate the universe.

CHAPTER II.

THE only stranger who visited us during our stay at Monticello, was Colonel Armand, whom I have mentioned in the
first part of my Journal; he had been in France the preceding
year with Colonel Laurens, but returned soon enough to be
present at the siege of York, where he marched as a volunteer at the attack of the redoubts. His object in going to
France, was to purchase clothing and accoutrements complete
for a regiment he had already commanded, but which had
been so roughly handled in the campaigns to the southward,
that it was necessary to form it anew: he made the advance
of the necessaries to Congress, who engaged to provide men
and horses. Charlotteville, a rising little town, situated in a
valley two leagues from Monticello, being the quarter assigned
for assembling this legion, Colonel Armand invited me to dine
with him the next day, where Mr. Jefferson and I went, and
found the legion under arms. It is to be composed of 200
horse and 150 foot. The horse was almost complete and very
well mounted; the infantry was still feeble, but the whole
were well clothed, well armed, and made a very good appearance. We dined with Colonel Armand, all the officers of his
regiment, and a *wolf* he amuses himself in bringing up, which
is now ten months old, and is as familiar, mild, and gay as a
young dog; he never quits his master, and has constantly the
privilege of sharing his bed. It is to be wished that he may
always answer so good an education, and not resume his natural character as he advances to maturity. He is not quite of the
same kind with ours, his skin is almost black, and very glossy;
he has nothing fierce about the head, so that were it not for his
upright ears and pendent tail, one might readily take him for
a dog. Perhaps he owes the singular advantage of not exha-
ling a bad smell, to the care which is taken of his toilet; for I
remarked that the dogs were not in the least afraid of him, and
that when they crossed his trace, they paid no attention to it.
But it appears improbable, that all the neatness in the world
can deceive the instinct of those animals, which have such a
dread of wolves, that they have been observed, in the King's
garden at Paris, to raise their coats and howl at the smell only

of two mongrels, engendered by a dog and a she-wolf. I am inclined therefore to believe, that this peculiarity belongs to the species of black wolf, for they have our species also in America; and in Europe we may possibly have the black kind, for so it may be conjectured at least from the old proverb: "He is as much afraid of me as of a *grey* wolf," which implies that there are also black ones.

Since I am on the subject of animals, I shall mention here some observations which Mr. Jefferson enabled me to make upon the wild beasts which are common in this country. I have been a long time in doubt whether to call them roebucks, stags, or deer, for in Canada they are known by the first name, in the eastern provinces by the second, and in the southern by the third. Besides, in America, their nomenclatures are so inaccurate, and their observations so slight, that no information can be acquired by examining the people of the country. Mr. Jefferson amused himself by raising a score of these animals in his park; they are become very familiar, which happens to all the animals of America; for they are in general much easier to tame than those of Europe. He amuses himself by feeding them with Indian corn, of which they are very fond, and which they eat out of his hand. I followed him one evening into a deep valley, where they are accustomed to assemble towards the close of the day, and saw them walk, run, and bound: but the more I examined their paces, the less I was inclined to annex them to any particular species in Europe; they are absolutely of the same colour as the roebuck, and never change even when they are tamed, which often happens to deer. Their horns, which are never more than a foot and a half long, and have more than four branches on each side, are more open and broader than those of the roebuck; they take an oblique direction in front; their tails are from eight to ten inches long, and when they leap they carry them almost vertical like the deer; resembling those animals not only in their proportions, but in the form of their heads which are longer and less frizzled than those of the roebuck. They differ also from that species, as they are never found in pairs. From my own observations, in short, and from all I have been able to collect on the subject, I am convinced that this kind is peculiar to America, and that it may be considered something betwixt the deer and roebuck.* Mr. Jefferson being no sportsman, and not having crossed the seas, could have no decided

---

* I have been lately assured, that when these animals grow old, their horns are as large as those of the stag, but their flesh has certainly the same taste with that of the deer in England.

opinion on this part of natural history; but he has not neglected the other branches. I saw with pleasure that he had
applied himself particularly to meteorological observation,
which, in fact, of all the branches of philosophy, is the most
proper for the Americans to cultivate, from the extent of their
country, and the variety of their situations, which give them
in this point a great advantage over us, who in other respects
have so many over them. Mr. Jefferson has made, with Mr.
Maddison, a well informed professor of mathematics, some cor-
respondent observations on the reigning winds at Williamsburgh, and Monticello; and although these two places are at
the distance only of fifty leagues, and not separated by any
chain of mountains, the difference of their results was, that
for 127 observations on the northeast wind at Williamsburgh,
there were only 32 at Monticello, where the northwest wind
in general supplies the place of the northeast. This latter
appears to be a sea-wind, easily counteracted by the slightest
obstacle, insomuch that twenty years since it was scarcely ever
felt beyond West-Point; that is to say beyond the conflux of
the Pawmunkey and the Matapony, which unite and form York
river, near thirty-five miles from its mouth.* Since the progress of population and agriculture has considerably cleared
the woods, it penetrates so far as Richmond, which is thirty
miles farther. It may hence be observed, first, that the winds
vary infinitely in their obliquity, and in the height of their region. Secondly, That nothing is more essential than the
manner in which we proceed in the clearing of a country, for
the salubrity of the air, nay even the order of the seasons,
may depend on the access which we allow the winds, and the

---

* The rapid changes of the temperature of the air in America, and
particularly to the southward, are apt to destroy the best European
constitutions. In the middle of the hottest day in July and August,
when the heat was so intolerable as almost to prevent respiration, I
have frequently known the wind shift suddenly round to the northwest,
attended with a blast, so cold and humid, as to make it immediately
necessary to shut all the doors and windows, and light large fires. It
is impossible to conceive any thing more trying for the human body,
relaxed and open at every pore, from a continuance of burning heat,
than this raw, piercing wind which blows over such immense bound-
less tracts of lakes and forests; but the melioration of the climate,
even from the partial and comparatively inconsiderable destruction of the woods in many parts of the continent, is so rapid as
to be strikingly perceptible even in the course of a very few years;
and its salubrity in proportion to the progress of these improvements,
will probably approach much nearer to those of Europe under the
same latitudes.—*Trans.*

direction we may give them. It is a generally received opinion at Rome, that the air is less healthy since the felling of a large forest situated between that city and Ostia, which defended it from the winds known in Italy by the names of the *Scirocco* and the *Libico*. It is believed in Spain also, that the excessive droughts, of which the Castilians complain more and more, are occasioned by the cutting down of the woods, which used to attract and break the clouds in their passage. There is yet a very important consideration upon which I thought it my duty to fix the attention of the learned in this country, whatever diffidence I may have of my own knowledge in philosophy, as well as on every other subject. The greatest part of Virginia is very low and flat, and so divided by creeks and great rivers, that it appears absolutely redeemed from the sea, and an entire new creation; it is consequently very swampy, and can be dried only by the cutting down a great quantity of wood; but as on the other hand it can never be so drained as not still to abound with mephitical exhalations; and of whatever nature these exhalations may be, whether partaking of fixed or inflammable air, it is certain that vegetation absorbs them equally, and that trees are the most proper to accomplish this object.* It appears equally dangerous either to cut down or to preserve a great quantity of wood; so that the best manner of proceeding to clear the country, would be to disperse the settlements as much as possible, and to leave some groves of trees standing between them. In this manner the ground inhabited would be always healthy; and as there yet remain considerable marshes which they cannot drain, there is no risk of admitting the winds too easily, as they would serve to carry off the exhalations.

But I perceive my journal is something like the conversation I had with Mr. Jefferson; I pass from one object to another, and forget myself as I write, as it happened not unfrequently in his society. I must now quit the friend of nature, but not nature herself, who expects me in all her splendour at the end of my journey; I mean the famous *Bridge of Rocks*, which unites two mountains, the most curious object I ever yet beheld, as its construction is the most difficult of solution. Mr. Jefferson would most willingly have conducted me thither, although this wonder is upwards of eighty miles from him, and he had often seen it; but his wife being expected every moment to lie-in, and himself as good a husband, as he is an excellent philosopher and a virtuous citizen, he only acted as my guide for about sixteen miles, to the passage of the little river

---

* This discovery the world owes to Doctor Franklin.

Mechum, where we parted, and I presume, to flatter myself, with mutual regret.

We walked our horses seventeen miles farther in the defiles of the western mountains, before we could find a place to bait them; at last we stopped at a little lonely house, a Mr. Mac Donnell's, an Irishman, where we found eggs, bacon, chickens, and whiskey, on which we made an excellent repast. He was an honest, obliging man; and his wife, who had a very agreeable and mild countenance, had nothing rustic either in her conversation or her manner. For in the centre of the woods, and wholly occupied in rustic business, a Virginian never resembles an European peasant: he is always a freeman, participates in the government, and has the command of a few negroes. So that uniting in himself the two distinct qualities of citizen and master, he perfectly resembles the bulk of individuals who formed what were called *the people* in the ancient republics; a people very different from that of our days, though they are very improperly confounded, in the frivolous declamations of our half philosophers, who, in comparing ancient with modern times, have invariably mistaken the word *people*, for mankind in general; and believing themselves its defenders, have bestowed their praises on the oppressors of humanity. How many ideas have we still to rectify? How many words, the sense of which is yet vague and indeterminate? The dignity of man has been urged a hundred times, and the expression is universally adopted. Yet after all, the dignity of man is relative; if taken in an individual sense, it is in proportion to the inferior classes; the plebeian constitutes the dignity of the noble, the slave that of the plebeian, and the negro that of his white master. If taken in a general acceptation, it may inspire man with sentiments of tyranny and cruelty, in his relative situation with respect to other animals; destroying thus the general beneficence, by counteracting the orders and the views of nature. What then is the principle on which reason, escaped from sophists and rhetoricians, may at last rely? The equality of rights; the general interest which actuates all; private interest, connected with the general good; the order of society; as necessary as the symmetry of a beehive, &c. if all this does not furnish matter for eloquence, we must console ourselves, and prefer genuine morality to that which is fallacious.* We had

---

* The Marquis de Chastellux has distinguished himself very honourably in the literary world by several productions, but particularly by his treatise *De la Felicité Publique*, wherein he breathes the generous, enlightened language of philanthropy and freedom. He was chosen a member of the French academy at a very early age, by dint of his own merit, and not by a court mandate, or intrigue, and was, *if I mistake*

reason to be contented with that of Mr. MacDonnell ; he presented us with the best he had, did not make us pay too dear, and gave us every instruction necessary to continue our journey ; but not being able to set out until half past four o'clock, and having twelve miles to go before we passed the Blue Ridges, we were happy in meeting on the road with an honest traveller, who served us for a guide, and with whom we entered into conversation. He was an inhabitant of the county of Augusta, who had served in Carolina as a common *rifleman*,* notwithstanding which, he was well mounted, and appeared much at his ease. In America the militia is composed of all the inhabitants without distinction, and the officers are elected by them without respect either to service or experience. Our fellow-traveller had been at the battle of *Cowpens*, where General *Morgan*, with eight hundred militia, entirely defeated the famous *Tarleton*, at the head of his legion, a regiment of regular troops, and of different pickets drawn from the army, forming near twelve hundred men, of whom upwards of eight hundred were killed or made prisoners.† This event, the most

---

not, when very young, in correspondence with, and a favourite of, the illustrious Pope Ganganelli. He has lately translated into French, Colonel Humphrey's poem, *The Campaign*, mentioned in the notes to the previous part of this work.—*Trans.*

* The riflemen are a Virginian militia, composed of the inhabitants of the mountains, who are all expert hunters, and make use of rifle guns. Towards the end of the war little use was made of them, as it was found that the difficulty of loading their pieces more than equalled the advantages derived from their exactness. The Americans had great numbers of riflemen in small detachments on the flanks of General Burgoyne's army, many of whom took post on high trees *in the rear of their own line*, and there was seldom a minute's interval of smoke without officers being taken off by single shot. Captain Green of the 31st regiment, aid-de-camp to General Philips, was shot through the arm by one of those marksmen as he was delivering a message to General Burgoyne. After the convention, the commanding officer of the riflemen informed General Burgoyne that the shot was meant for him ; and as Captain Green was seen to fall from his horse, it was for some hours believed in the American army that General Burgoyne was killed. His escape was owing to the captain's having lace furniture to his saddle, which made him to be mistaken for the general. General Burgoyne says, in his narrative, that not an Indian could be brought within the sound of a rifle shot.—*Trans.*

† Lord Cornwallis, in his answer to Sir Henry Clinton's narrative, published in 1783, gives the following state of his army before the defeat of Tarleton, and subsequent to that event, from which we may

extraordinary of the whole war, had always excited my curiosity. The modesty and simplicity with which General Morgan gave the account of it, have been generally admired. But

---

authenticate the loss of men, and deduce the importance of Morgan's victory to America.

January 15th, 1781, the rank and file of his Lordship's army was,

Guards,	690
7th regiment,	167
16th, three companies,	41
23d regiment,	286
33d regiment,	328
71st, 1st battalion,	249
71st, 2d battalion,	237
71st light company,	69
German regiment of Bose,	347
Yagers,	103
Tarleton's legion,	451
N. Carolina volunteers,	256
Total before the battle,	3224

February 1st, 1781, after the defeat of Tarleton,

Guards,	690
7th regiment,	
16th regiment,	
23d regiment,	279
33d regiment,	334
71st, 1st battalion,	
71st, 2d battalion,	234
71st light company,	
German regiment of Bose,	345
Yagers,	97
Tarleton's legion,	174
N. Carolina volunteers,	287
Total after the defeat of Tarleton,	2440

Total loss with the detachment of artillery 800 out of 1050 men, the real number of Tarleton's force.

The names of the regiments that have no numbers annexed to them in the last column are those which were totally destroyed, that is, killed, wounded, or taken, in the battle of Cowpens, on the 17th of January, between Morgan and Tarleton. Lord Cornwallis in his Gazette account, immediately after the affair, stated the loss only at 400, but the truth at length appears, when the purposes of misrepresentation are at an end, and the detail becomes necessary to the general's own honour.

Lord Cornwallis in his account of Tarleton's defeat, mentions a very honourable circumstance for the corps of artillery, but which was by no means unexamined by this brave body of men, in several actions

one circumstance in this relation had always astonished me. Morgan drew up his troops in order of battle, in an open wood, and divided his riflemen upon the two wings, so as to form, with the line, a kind of *tenaille*, which collected the whole fire, both directly and obliquely, on the centre of the English. But after the first discharge, he made so dangerous a movement, that had he commanded the best disciplined troops in the world, I should be at a loss to account for it. He ordered the whole line to wheel to the right, and after retreating thirty or forty paces, made them halt, face about, and recommence the fire. I begged this witness, whose deposition could not be suspected, to relate what he had seen, and I found his account perfectly conformable to Morgan's own relation. But as he could assign no reason for this retrograde motion, I inquired if the ground behind the first position was not more elevated and advantageous, but he assured me it was absolutely the same ; so that if it was this action which tempted the English (whose attack is not hot, but consists in general of a brisk fire, rather than in closing with the enemy) to break their line, and advance inconsiderately into a kind of focus of shot poured from the centre and the wings, it depended on General Morgan alone to have claimed the merit, and to have boasted of one of the boldest stratagems ever employed in the art of war. This is a merit however he never claimed, and the relation of this rifleman leaves no doubt with me, that the general, dreading the superiority of the English, had at first designed to give up gradually the field of battle, and retreat to covered ground, more advantageous for inferior forces ; but finding himself closely pressed, he had no other resource but to risk every thing and give battle on the spot. Whatever was the motive of this singular manœuvre, the result of it was the defeat of Tarleton, whose troops gave way on all sides, without a possibility of rallying them. Fatigued by a very long march, they were soon overtaken by the American militia, who, assisted by sixty horse under Colonel Washington, made upwards of five hundred prisoners, and took two pair of colours and two pieces of cannon.

It is natural to inquire how Tarleton's cavalry were employed during the engagement, and after the defeat ; whilst the infantry were engaged, they endeavoured to turn the flanks of General Morgan's army, but were kept in awe by some rifle-

---

in America : he says, " In justice to the detachment of royal artillery, I must here observe that no terrors could induce tham to abandon their guns, and they were *all* either killed or wounded in defence of them." —*Trans.*

men, and by the American horse detached by Colonel Washington, to support them, in two little squadrons.   After the
battle, they fled full gallop, without ever thinking of the infantry, or taking the least precaution to cover their retreat.   As
to the English general, God knows what become of him.   And
this is that Tarleton who with Cornwallis was to finish the conquest of America ; who with Cornwallis had received the thanks
of the House of Commons, and whom all England ,admired as
the hero of the army and the honour of the nation.*

In reflecting on the fate of war, let us recollect, that two
months after this victory gained by the militia† over 1200 veteran troops, General Greene, after having assembled near 5000
men, half militia, half continentals, made choice of an excellent position, and employed all the resources of military art,
was beaten by 1800 men, abandoned by his militia,‡ and forced

---

* Colonel Tarleton has given so many proofs not only of courage
but of great bravery and firmness, that every soldier ought to approve
the eulogiums bestowed upon his valour.   It were to be wished that
he had always made good use of those qualities, and that he had shown
himself as humane and sensible, as brave and determined.   The design of these reflections is to show, how much the English, in this war,
have been obliged to swell their successes, and diminish their defeats.
The more rare they became, the more they were disposed to solemn-
ize the former.   Howe and Burgoyne were disgraced for not conquering America, whilst others have obtained promotion for gaining
some trifling advantages.

† Earl Cornwallis in his letter in the London Gazette of March 31st,
1781, says that Morgan had with him, " By the best accounts he
could get, about 500 men, Continental and Virginia state troops, 103
cavalry under Colonel Washington, and 6 or 700 militia ; but that body is so fluctuating, that it is impossible to ascertain its number within some hundreds, for three days following."   This account seems to
have been intended to qualify the defeat of Tarleton, who was a great
favourite ; but the fact is nearly as the Marquis de Chastellux states
it, for Morgan had very few continentals with him, and his whole body
did not exceed 800 men.

‡ The returns of Lord Cornwallis' army taken a fortnight before
the battle, were 2213 : the returns seventeen days after it, 1723 ; his
loss consequently may be stated at about the difference, 490.
Several attempts have been likewise made to prove that General
Greene had with him at Guildford an army of 9 or 10,000 men, but
Lord Cornwallis himself, in his letter to Lord Rawdon, dated Camp
at Guildford, March 17, 1781, and published in the London Gazette
of May 10, 1781, expressly says, " General Greene having been very
considerably reinforced from Virginia by eight months' men and militia, and having collected all the militia of this province, advanced with
an army of about 5 or 6000 men, and 4 six pounders, to this place."

to limit all his glory to the making the English pay dear for the field of battle, which the rest of his troops defended foot by foot, and yielded with reluctance.* Our conversation on

---

From this *unexpected* account we may collect pretty clearly the indifferent composition of General Greene's force, and must render justice to the fairness of the French General's detail which calls them 5000 men, *half* militia, *half* continentals ; and states the conquering army *only* at 1800 men. The translator hopes the reader will not find these comparisons superfluous, as such scrutinies tend to elucidate the interesting events of an ever memorable revolution, and to enlighten history. General Gates showed me, at his house in Virginia, a letter from General Greene, wherein he took occasion in the most liberal manner to reconcile him to the unfortunate affair of *Camden*, by a detail of the bad conduct of *the same militia*, at the battle of *Guildford*, the *Eutaws*, &c. He touched upon the matter with a delicacy and candour which did equal honour to his sensibility and judgment. Such a tribute of justice from the officer who had superseded him in his command could not but be highly grateful to General Gates, possessing, as he does, in the most eminent degree, the warlike virtues, a pure disinterested attachment to the cause of freedom, and all the generous susceptibility of an amiable private gentleman. Whilst under a cloud himself, I heard him with admiration uniformly expatiate with all the distressed warmth of public virtue on the successes of other generals, and instead of jealous repining and disgust, pay his tribute of applause to the merits even of those he could not love, and prognosticate, with confidence, the final success of America. It was with real joy therefore, that I saw his honour vindicated by the deliberate voice of Congress, himself restored to his former rank, and that harmony which never should have been disturbed, renewed between this true patriot and General Washington, under whom I left him second in command at the camp at Verplank's on the North River in October, 1782.—*Trans.*

* Since the journal was written, the author has had an opportunity of seeing General Morgan ; he is a man about fifty, tall, and of a very martial appearance. The services he rendered the state during the war, were very numerous, and his promotion rapid. It is pretended that he was formerly *a carter*, and from the same unacquaintance with the customs and language of the country, another general is said to have been *a farmer*, because he employed himself in cultivation, and a third to have been *a butcher*, because he dealt in cattle. General Morgan was formerly engaged in waggons, undertook the transport of goods sent by land, and often put himself at the head of these little convoys. The Marquis de Ch———, the first time he had an opportunity of seeing him, commanded the French troops in the absence of the Comte de Rochambeau at Philadelphia, during the march from Williamsburgh to Baltimore. The Marquis de Ch——— was then at Colchester, with the first division of the troops, after passing in boats the river which runs near the town. The carriages and artillery had taken another road, to gain an indifferent ford.

war and battles brought us to the foot of the *gap*, or, as it is called, the neck of Rock-Fish, which, in an extent of more than fifty miles is the only passage to cross the Blue Ridges, at least in a carriage. We ascended very commodiously, for about two miles, and on arriving at the top of the mountain, were surprised to find a little cottage lately built and inhabited by white people. I inquired of my fellow-traveller what could engage them to settle in so barren and desert a place, he told me they were poor people who expected to get some assistance from passengers.

General Morgan met them when they were engaged in a very narrow passage, and finding the carters did not understand their business, he stopped, and showed them how they ought to drive. Having put every thing in order, he alighted at the Marquis', and dined with him. The simplicity of his deportment, and the nobleness of his behaviour, recalled to mind the ancient Gallic and German chiefs, who, when in peace with the Romans, came to visit and offer them assistance. He expressed a great attachment to the French nation, admired our troops, and never ceased looking at them ; often repeating, that the greatest pleasure of his life would be, to serve in numerous and brilliant armies. It will easily be conjectured that his host asked him many questions, particularly respecting the affair of Cowpens. His answer confirmed what the rifleman had said ; he owned also very candidly that the retrograde movement he had made, was not premeditated. His troops were intimidated, when the English, with more confidence than order, advanced to the attack : observing them keep their ranks, he suffered them to retreat a hundred paces, and then commanded them to halt and face the enemy, as if the retrograde movement had been really preconcerted.* Though this account, which is more recent and surer than in the text, might render those reflections useless, it was thought proper to preserve them, because on one hand they are not uninteresting to the soldier, and on the other, they may teach philosophers and critics to suspect those who have written history, above all, those who, like Titus Livius, Dionÿsius of Halicarnassus, and all the copious and elegant historians, delight in multiplying and varying the descriptions of battles; or, what is yet more reprehensible, who like Frontin, Pollien, and other compilers, borrow from historians the events and stratagems of war, which they endeavour to collect.

General Morgan has not served since the affair of Cowpens ; he lives in the county of Fairfax and on the estate which he had either purchased or increased, waiting till opportunity shall present him with some command.

* General Morgan by thus dexterously availing himself of the circumstances of his very critical position, has perhaps more real merit, than if he had really preconceived the manœuvre which has given him so much fame ; a manœuvre, from which, unless justified by a necessity such as his, he had no right to expect success, in the face of a *skilful* enemy ; but Tarleton never was a *commander.—Trans.*

I expected this answer, and was sorry to find in a new country, where the earth wants inhabitants, and agriculture hands, white people under the necessity of begging. I stopped a moment to view the wild but uninteresting prospect of the western mountains, from the summit of the Blue Ridges. But as the sun was near setting, I hastened to reach the only inn where lodgings could be had, on the other side of the mountains. Notwithstanding which, I stopped once more, nor had I any reason to regret it. My servant always followed me with a fowling-piece, and as it frequently happened that I was obliged to alight to fire at a partridge, or some other game, our conversation did not prevent me from being always upon the watch. I perceived a large bird which crossed the road, and by the instinct of a sportsman, I concluded it to be what the inhabitants of the mountains call a pheasant, but which resembles much more a woodhen. To alight, call my dog, and take my gun, was the work of a moment; as I was preparing to follow the woodhen among the bushes, one of my servants pointed out to me two others, perched upon a tree behind him, and which looked at me with great tranquillity. I fired at the one nearest to me, nor did it require much address to kill it. Except that it was perhaps a little bigger, it resembled the one I had seen at Newport, where the Americans carry them sometimes to market, in winter, when they descend from the mountains, and are more easily killed. This one, before it was plucked, was of the size of a capon; its plumage on the back and wings resembled that of a hen pheasant, and, on the belly and thighs, the large winter thrush. It was booted like the rough footed pigeon, to its feet, and the plumage of its head formed a kind of aigrette: take it altogether, it is a beautiful bird, and good eating; but when stript of its feathers, it was not larger than the red-footed partridge, or bartavelle. After ordering the woodhen I had killed, for supper, I tried to find the first I had seen run into the underwood. I raised it once, and although I ran immediately, and had an excellent dog, it was impossible to find it; these birds running very fast, like the pheasant and the rayl. The mode which the inhabitants of the mountains make use of to kill them, is to walk in the woods at sunrising and sunsetting, to attend to the noise they make in beating their sides with their wings, which may be heard above a mile; they then approach softly, and usually find them sitting upon the trunk of some old tree. It was perhaps lucky that my shooting did not continue with more success; for it was almost night when we arrived at the ford of South River, and the waters, considerably augmented by the late rains, were very high. I was proud of fording the famous

Potomac, which had taken me an hour in a boat, at the ferry of Alexandria.*

South river in fact is only a branch of the Potomac, the source of which is in the mountains, and like all other rivers is humble in its rise; but it may be looked upon as the proudest of its branches, as at the distance of thirty leagues, it is above a mile broad, and resembles more an arm of the sea, than a river. Two hundred paces from the ford, but more than forty miles from the place from which I set out, I found the inn which Mr. Jefferson had described to me; it was one of the worst in all

---

* In travelling from Fredericktown to Leesburgh, in a single-horse chaise for one person, called in America *a sulky*, the shafts of my carriage broke about a mile from the Potomac, on the Maryland side, and I was reduced to the necessity, having no servant, of leaving it with all my papers, money, fire-arms, &c. and of mounting my horse in search of assistance. Night was coming on in a most difficult country, to which I was an utter stranger, and not even a negro hut was to be met with. In these circumstances I approached the Potomac, on the other side of which I discovered a smoke in the woods, which gave me hopes of its proceeding from a house, but the river was near a mile broad, and my horse barely fourteen hands high. Whilst I was thus standing in suspense, two travellers arrive on horseback and push into the river, a little higher up. I flew to follow them, but scarcely had they advanced one hundred yards before they returned, declaring it not fordable, and, to add to my distress, they assured me that I was at a great distance from any house on that side, but, on the other, I should find an ordinary kept by a Scotsman. They excused themselves from assisting me on the plea of urgent business, and left me with the consoling assurance that the river might possibly be fordable, though they who were inhabitants of the country, did not choose to venture it. Perceiving the bottom of a good gravel, and free from rocks, I attempted the passage as soon as they left me, and in about twenty dangerous and irksome minutes reached the other side, where I obtained the cheerful aid of two native negroes at the Scotsman's hut, for it was no better, and recrossing the river, went in search of my broken carriage, which we found in security. It was ten o'clock before I passed the river a third time, always up to my waist, and reached my quarters for the night, where at least I met with as hospitable a reception as the house afforded; but the consequence of this adventure, wherein I was successively wet and dry three times, in the hot month of July, was a fever and ague which tormented me for five months. At Alexandria, about fifty miles lower down, the Potomac rolls its majestic stream with sublimity and grandeur, sixty-gun ships may lie before the town, which stands upon its lofty banks, commanding, to a great extent, the flatter shore of Maryland. This town, which stands above 200 miles from the sea, is rapidly on the increase, and from the lavish prodigality of nature, cannot fail of becoming one of the first cities of the new world.—*Trans.*

America. Mrs. Teaze, the mistress of the house, was some time since left a widow; she appears also to be in fact the widow of her furniture, for surely never was house so badly furnished. A solitary tin vessel was the only bowl for the family, the servants and ourselves; I dare not say for what other use it was proposed to us on our going to bed.* As we were four masters, without reckoning the rifleman, who had followed us, and whom I had engaged to supper, the hostess and the family were obliged to resign to us their beds. But at the moment we were inclined to make use of them, a tall young man entering the chamber, where we were assembled, opened a closet, and took out of it a little bottle. I inquired what it was; it is, said he, something which the doctor in the neighbourhood has ordered me to take every day. And for what complaint, said I? Oh! not much, he replied, only a *little itch!* I own his confession was ingenuous, but I was by no means sorry that I had sheets in my portmanteau. It may easily be imagined we were not tempted to breakfast in this house. We set out therefore very early on the 18th, in hopes (as we had been told,) that we should find a better inn, at the distance of ten miles, but those hopes were vain. Mr. Smith, a poor planter, to whom we were recommended, had neither forage for our horses, nor any thing for ourselves. He only assured us, that eight miles farther we should find a mill, the proprietor of which kept a public-house, and we found accordingly the mill and the miller. He was a young man, twenty-two years of age, whose charming face, fine teeth, red lips, and rosy cheeks, recalled to mind the pleasing portrait which Marmontel gives of *Lubin.* His walk and carriage did not however correspond with the freshness of his looks, for he appeared sluggish and inactive. I inquired the reason, and he told me he had been in a languishing state ever since the battle of Guildford, in which he had received fifteen or sixteen wounds with a hanger. He had not, like the Romans, a crown to attest his valour; nor,

---

* The Marquis' distress on this occasion, reminds me naturally of a similar, but still worse situation in which I found myself on my return from America towards the end of the war, with four officers of the army of the Comte de Rochambeau. Our captain being obliged suddenly to take advantage of one of those violent north-westers which blow in December, to get clear of the coast, beset with New-York Privateers, forgot all his crockery ware, so that in default of plates, mugs, &c. we were obliged, during a winter's voyage of seven weeks, to apply two tin jugs we had purchased to drink our cider, to every use; and, in spite of my representations, even to some purposes I am unwilling to repeat; for in bad weather, these excellent *land-officers* could not be prevailed upon to look on deck.—*Trans.*

like the French, either pension or certificate of honour : instead of them, he had a piece of his skull, which his wife brought to show me. I certainly little thought of finding, amidst the solitudes of America, such lamentable traces of European steel ; but I was the most touched to learn that it was after he had received his first wound, and was made prisoner, that he had been thus cruelly treated. This unhappy young man acquainted me, that overcome with wounds, and wallowing in his blood, he yet retained his presence of mind, and imagining his cruel enemies would not leave existing a single witness or victim of their barbarity, there remained no other way of saving his life, than by appearing as if he had lost it.

The all-seeing eye of Divine Justice alone can discover and make known the authors of such a crime ; but, if discovered —Oh ! for the voice of a Stentor, and the trumpet of Fame, to devote the vile perpetrators to present and future horror ! And to announce to all sovereigns, generals, and chiefs, that the enormities which they tolerate, or leave unpunished, will accumulate upon their heads, and, at some future time, render them the execration of a posterity still more sensible, and more enlightened than we yet are !

Even if Mr. Steel, our landlord, had been more active, and his wife, who was young and handsome, more industrious, they could not have supplied the total want in which they then were, of bread, and of every thing to drink ; the bread was just kneaded, but not yet put into the oven ; and as for liquors, the house made use of none ; the same stream which turned the mill, was the only cellar of the young couple, so that we might apply to Mrs. Steel those verses of Guarini,

> Quel fonte on d'ella beve
> Quel solo aneo la bagna, e la configlia.

But these pastoral manners are but ill suited to travellers. A few cakes, however, baked upon the cinders, excellent butter, good milk, and above all, the interest with which Mr. Steel inspired us, made us pass agreeably the time which was necessary to put our horses in a condition to perform a long and difficult day's journey. About five o'clock in the evening, after we had travelled thirty-eight miles, we found some houses, where we learned that we were yet six miles from Praxton's tavern, where we intended to sleep ; that we had two fords to pass, the last of which was impracticable on account of the late rains ; but that we should not be stopped, as we should find a canoe to take us across, and our horses would swim behind. The night, and a black storm which was brewing, made us hasten our steps. Notwithstanding which, we were obliged to mount and descend a very high mountain ; scarcely was there remaining the least twilight when we arrived at the second river, which is as large as James', but near its source, and at a place where it descends from the mountains under the name of the Fluvanna. The difficulty was to pass ten men and as many horses with the help of a single canoe, such as is made use of by the savages, which at most could contain only four or five persons and a single negro, armed with a paddle instead of an oar. We put into the canoe our saddles and baggage, and made several trips, at each of which two horses were swam across, held by the bridle. It was night, and very dark before this business was finished. But after we had, not without great trouble, resaddled and reloaded our horses, the difficulty was to reach the inn, which was half a mile from the place where we landed; for the river flows between two precipices, and as the canoe could not land us at the ford, nor consequently at the road, we were obliged to climb up the mountain, by a path but little used, and very difficult even by daylight; nor should we ever have found our way had I not engaged the waterman to conduct us. We clambered up as well as we could, every one leading his horse through the trees and branches, which we could not perceive, from the obscurity of the night, until they struck us on the face. At last we arrived at Praxton's tavern; but it was ten o'clock, and the house already shut up, or more properly the houses, for there are two. I approached the first that offered, and knocked at the door, which they opened, and we saw five or six little negroes lying upon a mat before a large fire. We then went to the other, and there found five or six white children lying in the same manner; two or three grown up negroes presided over each of these little troops.* They told us that Mr. Praxton, his wife, and all his family, were invited to a wedding, but not far off, and that they would go and fetch them. As for us, we were invited to supper by a very voracious appetite, after a long journey and a great deal of fatigue, and were very differently situated from the new married couple and their company, and had no small apprehensions of

---

* It was a singular sight for an European to behold the situation of the negroes in the southern provinces during the war, when clothing was extremely scarce. I have frequently seen in Virginia, on visits to gentlemen's houses, young negroes and negresses running about or basking in the court-yard naked as they came into the world, with well characterized marks of perfect puberty; and young negroes from sixteen to twenty years old, with not an article of clothing, but a loose shirt, descending half way down their thighs, waiting at table where were ladies, without any apparent embarrassment on one side, or the slightest attempt at concealment on the other.—*Trans.*

seeing our host and hostess return completely drunk. But in this we were deceived; they arrived perfectly sober, were polite and desirous to please, and a little after midnight we had an excellent supper. Though the apartments and beds were not exactly what we wished, they were better than at Mrs. Teaze's, and we had no right to complain. Besides, we enjoyed the satisfaction of having accomplished the object of our journey; for the *Natural Bridge* was not above eight miles off, and we had obtained every information necessary to find the road. The next morning our breakfast was ready betimes, and served by the daughters of Captain Praxton; they had not appeared to advantage the preceding evening, notwithstanding which, so far as the obscurity of the room we supped in, our appetites, and the immense caps in which they were muffled up for the marriage, had permitted us to judge of them, we thought them tolerably handsome; but when we saw them by daylight, with their hair only turned up, without any other head-dress, the repose of the night their sole ornament, and for every grace, their natural simplicity, we were confirmed in the opinion we had already formed, that the people of the mountains are, in general, handsomer and healthier than those on the sea coast.* There was in the house a young man also, tolerably well dressed, and of an agreeable countenance, whom I concluded to be an intended match for one of our young hostesses. But I soon discovered that he was come for matches of another kind. In fact, one of my fellow-travellers inviting me to go and see a very fine horse, which stood alone in a little stable, I was informed it was a stallion, which this young man had brought upwards of eighty miles, to dispose of his favours to the mares of the country.† His price

---

* The South-Carolina gentlemen with whom I was acquainted, assured me, that the inhabitants of the back parts of that state, which is one of the most unhealthy on the continent, are a vigorous and beautiful race of people, and possess all that hale ruddiness which characterises the natives of northern climates.—*Trans.*

† Great attention is paid to the breed of blood horses to the southward, and particularly in Virginia, and many second rate race horses are annually sent from England to serve as stallions. There were two or three in the stables of one Bates, near Philadelphia, which I had seen win plates in England. This Bates is a native of Morpeth in Northumberland, and went to America before the war to display feats of horsemanship, but he had the good fortune to marry a widow possessed of five hundred pounds a year, and is now master of a most beautiful villa on the banks of the Delaware, four or five miles from Philadelphia, still following, however, the occupation of breeding and selling horses, and keeping stallions, for there are no resources for idleness in that country.—*Trans.*

was twenty shillings Virginia currency,* or eighteen livres of our money, (about fifteen shillings sterling,) for each visit, or the double if the connection was of longer duration: which is much less than is paid in the other parts of Virginia.   These details, which may appear trifling, will however serve to make the reader acquainted with a country, the inhabitants of which, dispersed in the woods, are separated only for the purposes of domestic comfort, which renders them independent of each other, but who readily communicate for the general interest, or their mutual wants.   But I am too near the Natural Bridge to stop at other objects.

---

* The difference of currency is one of the most puzzling and disagreeable circumstances for a stranger in America, the value of *the pound* varying in every state ; an inconvenience which existed under the British government, and, I am afraid, is still likely to subsist.—*Trans.*

CHAPTER III.

We set out at nine o'clock in the morning, and to say the truth, rather heedlessly; for in these mountains, where there are either too many or too few roads, people always think they have given sufficient directions to travellers, who seldom fail to go astray. This is the common fault of those who instruct others in what they themselves are well acquainted with, nor are the roads to science exempt from this inconvenience. After riding about two miles however, we luckily met a man who had just got his horse shod, at a neighbouring forge, and was returning home followed by two or three couple of hounds.* We soon entered into conversation with him, and what seldom happens in America, he was curious to know who I was, and whither I was going.† My quality of a general officer in the

---

* Stopping one day at a smith's shop near Winchester, in the interior of Virginia, I found one of the workmen to be a Scotch Highlander in his Gaelic dress, and soon saw several more returning from harvest; these men had been soldiers, and were then prisoners, but they were all peaceable industrious labourers, and I could not find that any of them thought of returning to the barren hills of Caledonia. General Gates had several of them in his employ, and they were dispersed over the whole country, where they appeared completely naturalized and happy. I afterwards saw many of them working at mills, and as quarry-men on the picturesque banks of that sublime river the Susquehannah, a circumstance which transported my imagination to the well known borders of the Tay, and of Loch Lomond.—*Trans.*

† I am apt to think that the experience of every person who has visited North-America, as well as my own country, will rise in judgment against this observation of the author; for my part, were I searching for a general characteristic of that part of the Continent, I should not scruple to distinguish it by the name of *the country of the curious.* Wherever you bend your course, to whomsoever you address yourself, you are indispensably subject to a good humoured, inoffensive, but *mighty* troublesome inquisition. Do you inquire your road? you are answered by a question, " I suppose you come from the eastward, don't you?" Oppressed with fatigue, hunger, and thirst, and drenched per-

French service, and the desire I expressed of seeing the wonders of his country, inspiring him with a kind of affection for
me, he offered to be our conductor, leading us sometimes
through little paths, at others through woods, but continually
climbing or descending mountains, so that without a guide,
nothing short of witchcraft could have enabled us to find
the road.   Having thus travelled for two hours, we at last descended a steep declivity, and then mounted another; during
which time he endeavoured to render the conversation more
interesting.   At last, pushing his horse on briskly, and stopping
suddenly, he said to me, "You desire to see the *Natural
Bridge*, don't you Sir? You are now upon it, alight and go
twenty steps either to the right or left, and you will see this
prodigy."   I had perceived that there was on each side a considerable deep hollow, but the trees had prevented me from
forming any judgment, or paying much attention to it.   Approaching the precipice, I saw at first two great masses or
chains of rocks, which formed the bottom of a ravine, or rather
of an immense abyss; but placing myself, not without precaution, upon the brink of the precipice, I saw that these two
buttresses were joined under my feet, forming a vault, of which
I could yet form no idea, but of its height.   After enjoying
this magnificent but tremendous spectacle, which many persons could not bear to look at, I went to the western side, the
aspect of which was not less imposing, but more picturesque.
This *Thebais*, these ancient pines, these enormous masses of

---

haps with rain, you answer shortly in the affirmative, and repeat your
inquiry—"Methinks you are in a mighty haste—What news is there to
the eastward?"   The only satisfaction you can obtain till you have
opened your real, or pretended budget of news, and gratified the de-
mander's curiosity.   At an inn, the scrutiny is more minute; your
name, quality, the place of your departure, and object of your journey,
must all be declared to the good family in some way or other, (for their
credulity is equal to their curiosity,) before you can sit down in comfort to the necessary refreshment.   This curious spirit is intolerable
in the eastern states, and I have heard Dr. Franklin, who is himself a
Bostonian, frequently relate with great pleasantry, that in travelling
when he was young, the first step he took for his tranquillity, and to
obtain immediate attention at the inns, was to anticipate inquiry, by
saying, " My name is Benjamin Franklin, I was born at Boston, am a
printer by profession, am travelling to Philadelphia, shall return at such
a time, and have no news—Now what can you give me for dinner?"
The only cause which can be assigned for the author's error in this
respect, is the state in which he travelled, his being a foreigner, and
the facility of obtaining information from the persons of his retinue.—
Trans.

rocks, so much the more astonishing as they appear to possess a wild symmetry, and rudely to concur, as it were, in forming a certain design; all this apparatus of rude and shapeless nature, which art attempts in vain, attacks at once the senses and the thoughts, and excites a gloomy and melancholy admiration. But it is at the foot of these rocks, on the edge of a little stream which flows under this immense arch, that we must judge of its astonishing structure; there we discover its immense spurs, its back-bendings, and those profiles which architecture might have given it. The arch is not complete, the eastern part of it not being so large as the western, because the mountain is more elevated on this than on the opposite side. It is very extraordinary that at the bottom of the stream there appear no considerable ruins, no trace of any violent laceration, which could have destroyed the kernel of the rock, and have left the upper part alone subsisting; for that is the only hypothesis that can account for such a prodigy. We can have no possible recourse either to a volcano or a deluge, no trace of a sudden conflagration, or of a slow and tedious undermining by the water.

The rock is of the calcareous kind, and its different strata are horizontal; a circumstance which excludes even the idea of an earthquake, or subterraneous cavern. It is not, in short, for a small number of travellers to give a decided opinion for the public on this phenomenon of nature. It belongs to the learned of both worlds to judge of it, and they will now be enabled to attempt the discussion. The necessary steps are taken to render it as public as its singularity deserves; an officer of the engineers, the Baron de Turpin, an excellent mathematician and an accurate draughtsman, is gone to take the principal aspects and dimensions. His labours will supply the deficiency of my description. Though unacquainted with the powers of nature, we may at least have some idea of our own. I shall therefore leave to more able hands the care of finishing this picture, of which I have given only an imperfect sketch, and continue the relation of our journey, which, though the principal object be already accomplished, is not near being terminated, for the Natural Bridge is more than two hundred and fifty miles from Williamsburgh.

Whilst I was examining on all sides, and endeavouring to take some drawings, my fellow-travellers had learned from our conductor that he kept a public-house, about seven or eight miles from the place where we were, and not more than two from the road which must be taken next day to leave the mountains. Mr. Grisby, (the name of our guide,) had expressed his wishes to receive us, assuring us we should be as well as at the tavern recommended by Mr. Praxton; but had this been otherwise, we had too many obligations to Mr. Grisby not to give him the preference. We renewed our journey therefore, under his guidance, through the woods, which were very lofty; strong robust oaks, and immense pines sufficient for all the fleets of Europe, here grow old, and perish on their native soil; from which they have never yet been drawn even by the hand of industry.* One is surprised to find every where in these immense forests, the traces of conflagrations. These accidents are sometimes occasioned by the imprudence of travellers, who light a fire when they go to sleep, and neglect afterwards to extinguish it. Little attention is paid them when the woods alone are the victims, but as there are always some cultivated parts, the fire often reaches the fences, by which the fields are surrounded, and sometimes the houses themselves, which is inevitable ruin to the cultivators.

I recollect that during my stay at Monticello, from which one may discover an extent of thirty or forty leagues of wood, I saw several conflagrations three or four leagues distant from each other, which continued burning until a heavy rain fell luckily and extinguished them.† We arrived at Mr. Grisby's a little before five o'clock, having met with nothing on the road but a wild turkey, which rose so far off, that it was impossible to find it again. The house was not large, but neat and commodious; we found it already taken up by other travellers, to whom we assuredly owed every token of respect, if

---

* The quality of the American oak is found by repeated experience to be by no means equal to, or so durable as that of Britain. A general survey of the American woods was taken by order of the government of England, previous to the war, and the different qualities ascertained by the surveyors, who, on their general report, gave the preference to the southern oak on the Apalachians, and in the interior of Georgia and Florida; but in the English yards, even the Dantzick plank, which grows in Silesia, and that of Stettin is still preferred to the American.—*Trans.*

† Conflagrations which take their rise in this manner sometimes spread to a prodigious extent in America, in the morasses, as well as in the woods; in travelling from Easton on the Delaware over the Musconetgung mountains in the Upper Jersey, in 1782, I saw immense tracts of country lying in ashes from one of these accidental fires; and, during the same summer, Philadelphia was sometimes covered with smoke, from a vast morass which had taken fire in the Jerseys, and kept burning to a great depth from the surface, and for an extent of many miles around, for several months; the progress of which could not be stopped by the large trenches dug by the labour of the whole country, nor until it was extinguished by the autumnal rains.—*Trans.*

pre-eminence betwixt travellers were to be measured by the length of their respective journies.

The other guests were a healthy good humoured young man of eight and twenty, who set out from Philadelphia with a pretty wife of twenty, and a little child in her arms, to settle five hundred miles beyond the mountains, in a country lately inhabited, bordering on the Ohio, called the country of Kentucky. His whole retinue was a horse, which carried his wife and child. We were astonished at the easy manner with which he proceeded on his expedition, and took the liberty of mentioning our surprise to him. He told us that the purchase of good land in Pennsylvania was very extravagant, that provisions were too dear, and the inhabitants too numerous, in consequence of which he thought it more beneficial to purchase for about fifty guineas the grant of a thousand acres of land in Kentucky. This territory had been formerly given to a colonel of militia, until the king of England thought proper to order the distribution of those immense countries; part of which was sold, and the other reserved to recompense the American troops who had served in Canada.* But, said I,

---

* The author means the soldiers who served in Canada against the French in the war before the last. Kentucky is at present peopled by above fifty thousand settlers, and is on the point of being admitted into the union, as an independent state. Kentucky is a settlement on the creek, or rather river of that name, which falls into the Ohio, and is 627¾ miles distant from Fort Pitt ; but is extending in every direction over a tract of the finest and most fertile country in the world ; and as it is from the interior settlements of this vast country, that America will derive her future greatness, and establish new empires to rival, and perhaps outdo the ancient world, I hope I shall be pardoned for transcribing the following short but interesting account of the banks of the Ohio from Captain Hutchin's Topographical Description of that country, accompanying his maps—" The lands upon the Ohio, and its branches, are differently timbered according to their quality and situation. The high and dry lands are covered with red, white, and black oak, hickory, walnut, red and white mulberry, and ash trees, grape vines, &c. The low and meadow lands are filled with sycamore, poplar, red and white mulberry, cherry, beech, elm, aspen, maple, or sugar trees, grape vines, &c. And below, or southwardly of the *rapids*, are several large cedar and cypress swamps, where the cedar and cypress trees grow to a remarkable size, and where also is great abundance of canes, such as grow in South-Carolina. There is a great variety of game, viz. buffaloes, bear, deer, &c. as well as ducks, geese, swans, turkeys, pheasants, partridges, &c. which abound in every part of this country. The Ohio, and the rivers emptying into it, afford green, and other turtle, and fish of various sorts ; particularly carp, sturgeon, perch and catfish ; the two latter of an uncommon

where are the cattle? The implements of husbandry with which you must begin to clear the land you have purchased? In the country itself, replied he. I carry nothing with me,

---

size; viz. perch from eight to twelve pounds weight, and catfish from fifty to one hundred pounds weight. The country on both sides of the Ohio, extending south-easterly and south-westerly from Fort Pitt to the Mississippi, and watered by the Ohio river and its branches, contains at least a million of square miles, and it may with truth be affirmed, that no part of the globe is blessed with a more healthful air or climate; watered with more navigable rivers, and branches communicating with the Atlantic ocean, by the rivers Potomac, James, Rappahannock, Mississippi, and St. Lawrence; or capable of producing, with less labour and expense, wheat, Indian corn, buckwheat, rye, oats, barley, flax, hemp, tobacco, rice, silk, pot-ash, &c. than the country under consideration; and it may be added, that no soil can yield larger crops of red and white clover, and other useful grass, than this does." Colonel Gordon, in his journal, gives the following description of this soil and climate: " The country on the Ohio, &c. is every where pleasant, with large level spots of rich land, remarkably healthy. One general remark of this nature may serve for the whole tract comprehended between the western skirts of the Allegany mountains, beginning at Fort Ligonier, thence bearing south-westerly to the distance of 500 miles opposite to the Ohio falls, then crossing them northerly to the heads of the rivers that empty themselves into the Ohio; thence east along the ridge that separates the lakes and Ohio's streams to French creek, which is opposite to the above mentioned Fort Ligonier northerly. This country may, from a proper knowledge, be affirmed to be the most healthy, the most pleasant, the most commodious, and most fertile spot of earth *known to European people.*" To which may be added the following extract of a letter addressed to the Earl of Hillsborough, in the year 1772, then Secretary of State for the North American department.

" No part of North America will require less encouragement for the production of naval stores, and raw materials for manufactures in Europe, and for supplying the West-India islands with lumber, provisions, &c., than the country of the Ohio, and for the following reasons: First, the lands are excellent, the climate temperate, the native grapes, silk-worms and mulberry-trees abound every where; hemp, hops, and rye grow spontaneously in the vallies and low lands; lead and iron ore, coal also, are plenty in the hills; salt and fresh springs are innumerable; and no soil is better adapted to the culture of tobacco, flax, and cotton, than that of the Ohio. Secondly, the country is well watered by several navigable rivers communicating with each other; by which, and a short land carriage, the produce of the lands of the Ohio can *even now* (in the year 1772) be sent cheaper to the sea-port town of Alexandria, on the Potomac, in Virginia, than any kind of merchandize is sent from Northampton to London. Thirdly, the Ohio is, at all seasons of the year, navigable with large boats like the west coun-

but I have money in my pocket, and shall want for nothing.
I began to relish the resolution of this young man, who was
active, vigorous, and free from care; but the pretty wo-

---

try barges, rowed only by four or five men ; and from the month of
February to April, large ships may be built on the Ohio, and sent to
sea, laden with hemp, iron, flax, silk, rice, tobacco, cotton, pot-ashes,
&c. Fourthly, corn, beef, ship-plank, and other useful articles can
be sent down the stream of Ohio to West-Florida, and from thence to
the West-Indies, much cheaper, and in better order than from New-
York, or Philadelphia. Fifthly, hemp, tobacco, iron, and such bulky
articles may also be sent down the Ohio to the sea, at least 50 per cent.
cheaper than these articles were ever carried by a land carriage of only
sixty miles in Pennsylvania where waggonage is cheaper than in any
other part of North-America. Sixthly, the expense of transporting
European manufactures from the sea to the Ohio, will not be so much
as is now paid, and must ever be paid, to a great part of the counties
of Pennsylvania, Virginia, and Maryland, as there is scarce a place
between Fort Pitt and the rapids, a distance of 705 computed miles,
where good roads may not be made, on the banks which are not liable
to crumble away, and horses employed in drawing up large barges,
as is done on the margin of the Thames in England, and the Seine in
France, against a stream remarkably gentle, except in high freshets.
Whenever the farmers or merchants of Ohio shall properly understand
the business of transportation, they will build schooners, sloops, &c.
on the Ohio, suitable for the West-India or European markets ; or, by
having black walnut, cherry-tree, oak, &c. properly sawed for foreign
markets, and formed into rafts, as is now practised by the settlers near
the upper parts of the Delaware river, and thereon stow their
hemp, tobacco, &c. and proceed with them to New-Orleans. It may
not be amiss perhaps, to observe, that large quantities of flour are
made in the distant (western) counties of Pennsylvania, and
sent by an expensive land carriage to the city of Philadelphia, and
from thence shipped to South-Carolina, and to East and West-Florida,
there being little or no wheat raised in these provinces. The river
Ohio seems kindly designed by nature as the channel through which
the two Floridas may be supplied with flour, not only for their own
consumption, but for the carrying on an extensive commerce with Jamaica [the Floridas were then in the possession of England] and the
Spanish settlements in the Bay of Mexico. Millstones in abundance
are to be obtained in the hills near the Ohio, and the country is every
where well watered with large and constant springs, and streams for
grist and other mills. The passage from Philadelphia to Pensacola,
is seldom made in less than a month, and sixty shillings sterling per ton
freight (consisting of sixteen barrels) is usually paid for flour, &c. thither.
Boats carrying from 800 to 1000 barrels of flour may go in about the
same time from the Ohio, (even from Pittsburgh,) as from Philadelphia to Pensacola, and for half the above freight ; the Ohio merchants would be able to deliver flour, &c. there in much better order

man, twenty years of age only, I doubted not but she was in despair at the sacrifice she had made; and I endeavoured to discover, in her features and looks the secret sentiments of her soul. Though she had retired into a little chamber, to make room for us, she frequently came into that where we were; and I saw, not without astonishment, that her natural charms were even embellished by the serenity of her mind. She often caressed her husband and her child, and appeared to me admirably disposed to fulfil the first object of every infant colony—" to increase and multiply." Whilst supper was preparing, and we were talking of travels, and examining on the map the road our emigrants were to follow, I recollected that we had as yet an hour's daylight, and that it was just the time I had seen the wood-hens, of which, they assured me, there was plenty in the neighbourhood, and that there is a critical moment in hunting as well as love. I took my fowling-piece, therefore, and proceeded to the woods; but instead of wood-hens, I found only a rabbit, which I wounded, but it rolled down into a bottom, where I lost sight of it, till it was discovered by Mr. Grisby's dogs, which, accustomed to the report of a gun, found it in a hollow tree, to the top of which it would have scrambled had its leg not been broken. The rabbits of America differ from those of Europe; they do not burrow, but take refuge in hollow trees, which they climb like cats, and often to a very considerable height. Content with my victory, I returned to the house, but stopped some time to hear, at sunset, two thrushes, which seemed to challenge each other to the song, like the

---

than from Philadelphia, and without incurring the damage and delay of the sea, the charges of ensurance, and risk in time of war, &c. or from thence to Pensacola. This is not mere speculation; for it is a fact, that about the year 1746, there was a great scarcity of provisions at New-Orleans; and the French settlements at the Illinois, small as they then were, sent thither, in one winter, upwards of eight hundred thousand weight of flour." Mr. Lewis Evans, in the Analysis to his Map of the Middle Colonies of North-America, in the year 1755, says, that " Vessels from 100 to 200 tons burthen, by taking advantage of the spring floods, may go from Pittsburgh to the sea with safety, as then the falls, rifts, and shoals are covered to an equality with the rest of the river." To which Captain Hutchins, the present Geographer-General to the United States, adds, " And though the distance is upwards of *two thousand miles* from Fort Pitt to the sea, yet as there are *no obstructions* to prevent vessels from proceeding both day and night, I am persuaded that this extraordinary inland voyage may be performed, during the season of the floods, by rowing, in sixteen or seventeen days."—Here surely is a rational and ample field for the well regulated imagination of the philosopher and politician!!!—*Trans.*

shepherds of Theocritus. This bird ought, in my opinion, to be considered as the nightingale of America; it resembles those of Europe in its form, colour, and habits; but is twice as large. Its song is similar to that of our thrush, but so varied and so much more perfect, that, if we except the uniform plaintive notes of the European nightingale, they might be taken for each other. It is a bird of passage, like the mocking-bird, and like it, also, sometimes remains through the winter.

At my return to the house, supper was the sole object; about which Mr. and Mrs. Grisby took great pains, whilst their daughters, about sixteen or seventeen, who were perfect beauties, were laying the cloth. I asked Mr. Grisby to sup with us, but he excused himself, by assuring us that he was yet employed in our service; nor was his attention useless, for we had an excellent supper; and though whiskey was our only drink, we contrived to convert it into tolerable toddy. Breakfast was ready betimes the next morning, and corresponded with our supper. Mr. Grisby, who had nothing to do, sat down to table with us. He had a horse saddled, that he might accompany us as a guide as far as Greenly Ferry, where we were to repass the Fluvanna; but I was informed that one of the servant's horses was so much wounded in the withers, that it was impossible to mount him. This accident was the more inconvenient, as I had already been obliged to leave one at Mr. Jefferson's, so that I had no fresh horse to substitute. On applying to Mr. Grisby, he told me that the only horse he had which could answer my purpose, was the one he generally rode, and which he was going to make use of to conduct us, but that he would willingly oblige me with it, and take mine in its place. On my assuring him that I would give him any thing he thought proper in return, he went to look at my horse, and when he came back told me, that when cured, he thought he might be worth his own, and that he left the difference entirely to myself. As each of them might be worth ten or twelve guineas, I gave him two in exchange, and he was perfectly contented. I had just before asked for the bill, and when he declined letting me have it, I gave him four guineas. He received them with satisfaction, assuring me it was double the sum he could have charged. At last we were obliged to take our leave of this good house, but not of Mr. Grisby, who had taken another horse to accompany us. On the road he showed us two plantations which he had occupied successively, before he settled on the one he at present cultivates. He had left them in good condition, and sold them at the rate of twelve or thirteen shillings, Virginia currency, an acre, about ten livres of our money (8s.$\frac{1}{4}$ English.) We saw several other settlements in the woods, all of which were situated on the banks of some stream, whose source was not far distant. The peach trees, which they take care to plant, and the Judas tree (or *filiquastrum*, but different from that which produces the balm of Mecca) which grows naturally at the water's edge, were both in flower, and made a charming contrast to the immense firs and oaks, in the centre of which were situated these new plantations.

It was near ten o'clock when we arrived at the ferry, and as we approached, still following the course of the river, I saw an animal, to which I was a stranger, returning from the side of the river, and endeavouring to reach the wood. I pushed my horse towards it, hoping to frighten and make it climb a tree, for I took it for a racoon ; in fact it mounted the nearest tree, but very slowly and awkwardly. I had no great difficulty in killing it, for it did not even endeavour to hide itself, like the squirrel, behind the large branches. When I had taken it from the dogs, among which it struggled hard, and had bitten them pretty sharply ; on examining it with attention, I discovered it to be the monax, or the marmoset of America. In its form, fur, and colour it resembled very much the musk-rat ; but it is larger and differs essentially in the tail, which is short and rough. Like the musk-rat, however, its ribs are so short and flexible, that they might be mistaken for gristles, so that though it is much bulkier than a hare, it can pass through a hole of not above two inches in diameter.

Greenly Ferry derives its name from the proprietor, and is situated between two steep banks. We passed it in three trips, and parting with Mr. Grisby, depended entirely on our own industry to find the road to a very steep, but little frequented gap, the only passage by which we could get out of the mountains. They told us, at the ferry, that we should find but one house, three miles from thence, and at the foot of the very mountain we were to climb. A little path conducted us to this house : after asking new instructions, we followed another path, and began to ascend, not without difficulty, for in general the acclivity was so rapid, that we were obliged to stop our horses to give them breath. This ascent, which formed the road, is at least three miles long, by which you may judge of the height of these mountains ; for in the space of an hundred miles, this is the least steep of any which compose what are called the Blue Ridges. Arrived at the summit, we enjoyed the reward generally bestowed on such labours. A magnificent, but savage prospect, presented itself to our eyes ; we saw the mountains which form the North Ridge, and those which, crossing from one chain to the other, sometimes unite the Blue Ridges. In one of these traverses of mountains, the Natural Bridge is placed. It is to be observed, that I speak here only of the view to the north, for we had not the advantage of enjoying the double prospect; some neighbouring summits, and the height of trees, prevented us from extending our view to the southward. The descent was not less rapid than the ascent; its length was also three miles. We judged it necessary, for the relief of our horses and our own safety, to alight and walk; though the stones, which rolled under our feet, rendered it very incommodious. The dogs, which were not so fatigued by this inconvenience as ourselves, beat the woods, while we walked slowly on, and two hundred paces from us they sprang five wild turkeys; but as these birds directed their flight towards a steep hill behind us, we did not thing proper to follow them. We were almost at the bottom of the mountain when we began to perceive the horizon; but this horizon discovered nothing but woods and mountains, far less elevated than those we were leaving, if we except three summits known by the name of the Peaks of Otter, which are very lofty, and advance from the Blue Ridges as a kind of counter-guard. In general, all the country from the Blue Ridges to the sources of the Apamatock, may be considered as a glacis composed of little mountains, beginning at the foot of the Blue Ridges, and continually diminishing. Of this the best charts of Virginia give not the least indication, so that it is impossible, by the inspection of them, to form a just idea of the nature of this country.

It was half past one o'clock, and we had rode sixteen miles in very bad roads, when we arrived at the first house at the foot of the gap; but as it was an indifferent hut, we were obliged to proceed two miles farther, to a planter's of the name of Lambert, who received us with every mark of politeness. He gave us cakes and milk, for he had neither bread nor biscuit; and, whilst our horses were feeding, he entertained us with gay, joyous conversation. Mr. Lambert is a kind of phenomenon in America, where longevity is very rare; he is eighty-three years of age, and scarcely appears to be fifty-five; he is well known in the country, for there is hardly a trade he has not followed, nor a part of it he has not lived in. He is now a husbandman, and resides at a very fine plantation, which he has cleared, at the foot of the mountains. His wife, who is only sixty-five, looks much older than he does; his sons are yet young; one is a captain in the Virginia Legion, and formed his company himself in the beginning of the war. It was then composed of sixty-three men, all enlisted in the neighbourhood; and at the end of six campaigns all the sixty-three are living, some few of them only having been wounded. At five we mounted again to proceed ten miles farther, to the house of a Captain Muller, who, like Mr. Lambert, does not keep a public house, but willingly receives the few travellers who pass by this unfrequented road. Although they assured us we could not possibly miss the road, they would more properly have said it was impossible to find it; for we deemed it very fortunate to lose ourselves but twice, and at length, after dark, we arrived at Mr. Muller's. He is a man about sixty, six feet high, and bulky in proportion, very loquacious, but a good kind of man, attached to his country; and a great news-monger. He told us he would do his best to give us something for supper, but that he could offer us no other lodging than the room in which he received us, where he would order them to place our beds. The room was spacious and clean, but already occupied by a sick person, whom he could not disturb, and whom he begged us to leave in the little corner he possessed. This was an unfortunate old man of eighty, who, two days before, travelling in the neighbourhood, had been half devoured by a great bitch, whose whelps he had imprudently approached; she had lacerated one of his arms and thighs. Mr. Muller bestowed on him every possible care, and Mrs. Muller herself dressed his wounds. This poor man slept all the evening, but in the night he complained much, and sometimes awakened us. On my asking him, the next morning, how he found himself, he answered mighty weak.* Before we went away I desired to have the bill, but Mr. Muller not choosing to present any, I begged him to accept of a couple of guineas, desiring, at the same time, to know if it was enough. "Too much," replied he, "you come from France to my country to support and defend it; I ought to receive you better and take nothing, but I am only a poor countryman, and not in a condition to demonstrate my gratitude. If I were not ill, (and indeed he was asthmatic,) I would mount my horse and attend you to the field of battle."

The little resource we had found in this house, and the necessity of dividing the long journey we had to make, determined us to set out very early, and breakfast at New-London, a little town, two miles from hence. The difficulty of finding the road still remaining, I luckily met a man in the court-yard, just ready to mount, who relieved us from this anxiety. He was an old captain of the Virginia Legion, whom I had seen arrive in the evening in company with two tall young ladies, in huge gauze bonnets, covered with ribands, and dressed in such a manner as formed a perfect contrast to the simplicity

---

* Mighty little, mighty few, mighty weak, &c. are favourite expressions in America.—*Trans.*

of the house in which they were.* These, I understood, were Mr. Muller's daughters, returned from supping in the neighbourhood ; but I was careful not to speak to them, as I doubted not but we had taken possession of the beds destined for these fine ladies and their company, and was in great terror least French gallantry should compel us to resign them. I know not how they managed, but they appeared again in the morning and were far from handsome.

The Captain had been to sleep a mile from hence, at a sister's of Mr. Muller, and was mounting his horse to return to New-London, whither he offered to conduct us, and to provide our breakfast as he kept a tavern. I accepted both his proposals, and we travelled the distance of ten miles very agreeably ; the country, like that through which we passed the preceding evening being diversified with very pretty plantations. New-London, where we arrived at ten in the morning, is an infant town, but already pretty considerable, for there are at least seventy or eighty houses. There is likewise a military magazine established here, and several workshops for repairing arms. Its situation, in the middle of the woods, far distant from the seat of war, as well as commerce, does not require it should be fortified, but nature has prepared every thing to make it a strong place. Situated upon a little platform, surrounded by a glacis, the declivity of which is exactly what could be wished, this little town might be fortified at a small expense, and defended

---

* The rage for dress among the women in America, in the very height of the miseries of war, was beyond all bounds ; nor was it confined to the great towns, it prevailed equally on the sea-coasts, and in the woods and solitudes of the vast extent of country, from Florida to New-Hampshire. In travelling into the interior parts of Virginia I spent a delicious day at an inn, at the ferry of Shenandoah, or the Catacton Mountains, with the most enchanting, accomplished and voluptuous girls, the daughters of the landlord, a native of Boston, transplanted thither ; who, with all the gifts of nature, possessed the art of dress not unworthy of Parisian milliners, and went regularly three times a week to the distance of seven miles, to attend the lessons of one de Grace, a French dancing-master, who was making a fortune in the country. In one of my journies, too, I met with a young Frenchman, who was travelling on the business of the celebrated M. de Beaumarchais, and was uncommonly successful in his amours, of which I speak from personal knowledge. On my inquiring the secret of his success, he assured me, and put it beyond a doubt, that his *passe-partout*, or master key, consisted in a fashionable assortment of ribands, and other small articles contained in a little box, from which, in difficult cases he opened an irresistible and never failing battery.—*Trans.*

by a trifling garrison; we left it about twelve o'clock, and
had twenty-four miles to go to the only house where we could
find a good lodging.   It was not a tavern, but the proprietor,
Mr. Hunter, received strangers with pleasure.   The difference
between a real tavern, and a hospitable house of reception, is
greatly to the advantage of the traveller ; for in America, as
in England, publicans pay heavy taxes, and indemnify themselves by their exorbitant charges.   Mr. Hunter received us
well, and in a very clean house.   We set out early the next
morning, and after riding eight miles, always in dry, arid
woods, we stopped to breakfast at Mr. Pattison's.   He is a fat
man, about forty-five, disabled in his legs since he was two
years old, and so helpless that he cannot transport himself from
one place to another, but by pushing his chair.   One would
hardly think that a man afflicted with such an infirmity should
choose to live in the midst of woods, where he has no company
but one white man servant, and negroes of each sex.   I believe
him impotent in more than one respect, for he has lived in a
constant state of celibacy, and his ostensible imbecility would
have been no obstacle in a country where every body marries.

After we had proceeded twenty miles farther, we stopped, at
four o'clock, at a Scotsman's of the name of Johnson, who is
the most ridiculous personage imaginable.   He pronounces
English in so unintelligible a manner, that Mr. Dillon asked
him, very ingenuously, what language he was speaking.   As
Mr. Johnson was an ill-tempered fellow, and a little drunk, I
foresaw that this question could not succeed, and would turn
out to our disadvantage, on quitting this sort of tavern.   It
happened as I imagined ; for after a stay of only three-quarters
of an hour, he was not ashamed to ask seven dollars for about
twenty pounds weight of the leaves of Indian corn for our
horses, and two bowls of toddy for the servants.   I consoled
myself, like Monsieur de Pourceaugnac in Moliere, with the
satisfaction only, on paying him, of telling him my sentiments
of his behaviour, and went twelve miles farther to seek hospitality at another Scotsman's, where we arrived at the close of
day.   But this was a very different character from the other.
He was an old man of seventy-two, called Hodnett, who has
been established in America above forty years, though but
lately fixed in the plantation where he now lives.   He was
eager to please, polite, and even inclined to compliment, proud
of being born in Europe, and having past some time at Cork,
where he missed, he told me, a fine opportunity of learning
French ; for he had lived with several French merchants, whose
names he yet remembered, although it was upwards of fifty
years ago.   He inquired at least twenty times of me if I knew

them, and brought me an old book, the only one he had in the house, which was a bad treatise of geography. It was doubled in at the article of Cork, and one might see that he often read this chapter, as the paper was more thumbed there than else-where. Whilst he presented me with this book, he observed, with an air of importance, that in his opinion it was the best geographical work existing, nor was it difficult to perceive that it was the only one he ever heard of. I amused myself how-ever with assuring him that he possessed a real treasure, and that he ought carefully to preserve it. He went immediately to lock it up, and returned with a scrap of illuminated paper, which represented the arms and mottos of the family of the Hodnetts. I made him happy by declaring they were known all over Europe, and surely it was not paying too dear for a good supper and good beds; for the next morning he would not give us any bill. I thought proper, however, to pay him handsomely; hoping, at the same time, that the family of the Hodnetts would know nothing of it, nor think themselves under the necessity of adding the sign of an ale-house to their armorial bearings.

It was on the 23d, but the heat was already very trouble-some, when we arrived to breakfast at nine o'clock at Cumber-land court-house. This is the chief manor-house of a very considerable country; it is situated in a plain of about a mile diameter, sixteen miles from Hodnett's. Besides the court-house, and a large tavern, its necessary appendage, there are seven or eight houses inhabited by gentlemen of fortune. I found the tavern full of people, and understood that the judges were assembled to hold a court of claims, that is to say, to hear and register the claims of sundry persons, who had furnished provisions for the army. We know, that in general, but par-ticularly in unexpected invasions, the American troops had no established magazines, and as it was necessary to have subsist-ence for them, provisions and forage were indiscriminately laid hold of, on giving the owners a receipt, which they call a cer-tificate. During the campaign, whilst the enemy was at hand, little attention was given to this sort of loans, which accumu-lated incessantly, without the sum total being known, or any means taken to ascertain the proofs. Virginia being at length loaded with these certificates, it became necessary, sooner or later, to liquidate these accounts. The last assembly of the State of Virginia, had accordingly thought proper to pass a bill, authorising the justices of each county to take cognizance of these certificates, to authenticate their validity, and to regis-ter them, specifying the value of the provisions in money, ac-cording to the established tariff. I had the curiosity to go to the court-house, to see how this affair was transacted, and saw it was performed with great order, and simplicity. The judges wore their common clothes, but were seated on an elevated tribunal, as at London in the Court of King's Bench or Common Pleas. One of them seeing me standing at the door of the hall, descended from the bench, and invited me to go and take some refreshment at his house, where the family would entertain me till the sessions were finished. I told him I was obliged to proceed on my journey, and really we had no time to lose, for there yet remained twenty-eight miles to travel, and on a road so unprovided with every necessary for travellers, that though we intended giving our horses another bait, we could not find forage nearer than at a smith's shop, at twenty miles distance. As I intended therefore staying only half an hour at most, I seated myself under some trees; but Monsieur D'Oyré having gone into the house, returned and told me there was a company of four or five young girls, all pretty and very well dressed. Curiosity inducing me to see them, my attention was soon fixed upon a young woman of eighteen, who was suckling her child. Her features were so regular, and there was such decency and modesty in her behaviour, that she recalled to my mind those beautiful virgins of Raphael, the model, or example of the beau ideal. As I no longer permit myself to consider beauty but with a philosophic eye,* I shall here make an observation which has occurred to me in foreign countries, particularly in England and America; it is, that the beauty of forms and of features, the beauty independent of grace, motion, and expression, is oftener found among the people of the north, or among their descendants, than in France, or towards the south. If I were to assign the cause of this difference, I should say, that from some unaccountable reason, unconnected, doubtless, with the temperature of the climate, the youth of both sexes are more forward, and more ripe, among them than with us, from which it results, that young people, particularly young girls of twelve, or thirteen, unite that roundness of form, freshness of complexion, and regularity of features, before they are modified by passions and habits.

In France it is quite different; children are there very pretty to the age of seven or eight years; but it is seldom that girls

---

* The reader will here, doubtless, be apt to picture to himself the author as a grey-headed worn out veteran, or an unimpassioned, stoical member of the French Academy, barely remembering " the days when he was young;" but it is my duty to undeceive him : the Marquis de Chastellux is a well made, handsome man, of about four and forty, with eyes full of intelligence and fire, the carriage and deportment of a man of rank, and with a disposition extremely remote from an indifference to beauty.—*Trans.*

preserve their beauty to the age of puberty. This is the epoch, however, when we must form our opinion of what they may be ; but even these prognostics are often deceitful. This period is a kind of chrysalis, a state of probation, in which the handsome become ugly, and the ugly handsome. It is from the age of twenty to twenty-five that the features develop and declare themselves, and that nature completes her work, if not diverted from her course by sickness, but especially by the moral and natural consequences of marriage. On the other hand, our women, this danger once over, retain their beauty longer than in any other country. It appears as if their very souls were identified in their features, and watched over their preservation ; not a movement without a grace, no grace without expression ; the desire of pleasing improves and perpetuates the means ; and nature, rather aided than counteracted by art, is never absolutely abandoned to a domestic life, nor lavished by an unlimited fecundity.* Thus useful trees may serve to decorate our gardens, if the too great quantity of fruit does not prevent the reproduction of their blossoms. These reflections prove, that the French women have no reason to envy strangers ; that their beauty, in fact, though longer in coming to maturity, and less perfect, is more bewitching and more durable ; that if others furnish better models for the painter, they will stand the test of a longer examination, and that, in short, if they are not always those we most admire, they are certainly those we must love the most and the longest.

But let me return from this dangerous excursion, and resume my journey. We had rode forty-four miles, and night was closing fast upon us, when we arrived at Powhatan court-house ; this is a more recent, and more rustic settlement than that of Cumberland. It consists only of two mean huts, one for the purpose of holding the sessions, the other by way of public-house ; but which hitherto is scarcely fit for the recep-

---

* It is certain that population is not the main object of marriage in France among the higher classes. Among the nobility, in particular, the parties are generally contracted, when very young, by their respective parents, who bring them together to make an heir, or two, for the family ; which object, once completed, they part with as little affection as when they met, but with less passion, and pass the remainder of their lives in perfect freedom. Whilst family duty is performing for family purposes, their conduct is dictated, in general, by the nicest honour, and their noble blood is transmitted tolerably pure and free from contamination ; but " unlimited fecundity," as it is checked by some on principles of economy and prudence, is deemed *vulgar* and *barbarous* by all, except the lower classes, who are strangers to this system of refinement.—*Trans.*

tion of travellers. It is kept by a young man who has just settled here; his wife is a tall, handsome woman, his sister-in-law not quite so pretty. We had a good supper and good beds, but our horses were obliged to do without forage. The county of Powhatan takes its name from a king of the savages, famous in the history of Virginia, who reigned at the commencement of the last century; when the colony formed its first establishment at Jamestown, it was often necessary to treat, and sometimes to wage war with him. He is represented as a profound, but perfidious, politician. He had conquered all the country betwixt the Apamatock and Bay of Chesapeake, and was dreaded by the neighbouring nations.

CHAPTER IV.

WE left Powhatan the 24th, early in the morning, and, after having stopped twice, the first time to breakfast in a poor little house, eight miles from Powhatan, and the last, twenty-four miles farther, at a place called Chesterfield court-house, where we saw the ruins of the barracks formerly occupied by Baron Steuben, since burnt by the English, arrived in good time at Petersburgh. This day's journey was also forty-four miles. The town of Petersburgh is situated on the right bank of the Apamatock; there are some houses on the opposite shore, but this kind of suburb is a district independent of Petersburgh, and called Pocahunta. We passed the river in a ferry-boat, and were conducted to a little public-house about thirty steps from thence, which had an indifferent appearance; but, on entering, we found an apartment very neatly furnished; a tall woman, handsomely dressed, and of a genteel figure, who gave the necessary orders for our reception, and a young lady, equally tall, and very elegant, at work. I inquired their names, which I found were not less entitled to respect than their appearance. The mistress of the house, already twice a widow, was called Spencer, and her daughter, by her first husband, Miss Saunders. I was shown my bed-chamber; and the first thing which struck me was a large magnificent harpsichord, on which lay also a guitar. These musical instruments belonged to Miss Saunders, who knew very well how to use them; but as we stood more in need of a good supper, than a concert, I was apprehensive at first of finding our landladies too good company, and that we should have fewer orders to give than compliments to make. Mrs. Spencer, however, happened to be the best woman in the world; a gay, cheerful creature, no common disposition in America; and her daughter, amidst the elegance of her appearance, was mild, polite, and easy in conversation. But to hungry travellers all this could, at the best, be considered but as a good omen for the supper, for which we had not long to wait; for scarcely had we time to admire the neatness and beauty of the table-cloth, before it was covered with plenty of good dishes, particularly some very large and excellent fish. We were very good friends with our charming landladies before we went to bed, and breakfasted with them the next morning. We were just going out to take a walk, when we received a visit from Mr. Victor, whom I had seen at Williamsburgh; he is a Prussian, who had formerly been in the army, and, after having travelled a great deal in Europe, came and settled in this country, where by his talents, he first made his fortune; and, like every body else, finished by turning planter. He is an excellent musician, and plays every kind of instrument, which makes his company in great request by the whole neighbourhood. He told us he was come to pass a few days with Mrs. Bowling, one of the greatest landholders in Virginia, and proprietor of half the town of Petersburgh. He added, that she had heard of our arrival, and hoped we would come and dine with her, which invitation we accepted, and put ourselves under the guidance of Mr. Victor, who first took us to the ware-houses or magazines of tobacco. These ware-houses, of which there are numbers in Virginia, though, unfortunately, great part of them has been burned by the English, are under the direction of public authority. There are inspectors nominated to prove the quality of the tobacco brought by the planters, and if found good, they give a receipt for the quantity. The tobacco may then be considered as sold, these authentic receipts circulating as ready money in the country. For example: suppose I have deposited twenty hogsheads of tobacco at Petersburgh, I may go fifty leagues thence to Alexandria or Fredericksburgh, and buy horses, cloths, or any other article, with these receipts, which circulate through a number of hands before they reach the merchant who purchases the tobacco for exportation. This is an excellent institution, for by this means tobacco becomes not only a sort of bank-stock, but current coin. You often hear the inhabitants say, "This watch cost me ten hogsheads of tobacco; this horse fifteen hogsheads; or, I have been offered twenty," &c. It is true that the price of this article, which seldom varies in peace, is subject to fluctuations in time of war; but then, he who receives it in payment, makes a free bargain, calculates the risks and expectations, and runs the hazard; in short, we may look on this as a very useful establishment; it gives to commodities value and circulation, as soon as they are manufactured, and, in some measure, renders the planter independent of the merchant.

The warehouses at Petersburgh belong to Mrs. Bowling. They were spared by the English, either because the Generals Phillips and Arnold, who lodged with her, had some respect for her property, or because they wished to preserve the tobacco contained in them in expectation of selling it for their profit. Phillips died in Mrs. Bowling's house, by which event the supreme command devolved upon Arnold; and I heard it said, that Lord Cornwallis, on his arrival, found him at great variance with the navy, who pretended that the booty belonged to them. Lord Cornwallis terminated the dispute, by burning the tobacco; but not before Mrs. Bowling, by her interest, had time sufficient to get it removed from her warehouses. She was lucky enough, also, to save her valuable property in the same town, consisting of a mill, which turns such a number of mill-stones, bolting machines, cribbles, &c. and, in so simple and easy a manner, that it produces above 800l. a year sterling. I passed upwards of an hour in examining its various parts, and admiring the carpenter's work, and the construction. It is turned by the waters of the Apamatock, which are conveyed to it by a canal excavated in the rock. Having continued our walk in the town, where we saw a number of shops, many of which were well stocked, we thought it time to pay our respects to Mrs. Bowling, and begged Mr. Victor to conduct us to her. Her house, or rather houses, for she has two on the same line resembling each other, which she proposes to join together, are situated on the summit of a considerable slope, which rises from the level of the town of Petersburgh, and corresponds so exactly with the course of the river, that there is no doubt of its having formerly formed one of its banks. This slope, and the vast platform on which the house is built, are covered with grass, which afford excellent pasturage, and are also her property. It was formerly surrounded with rails, and she raised a number of fine horses there; but the English burned the fences, and carried away a great number of the horses. On our arrival we were saluted by Miss Bowling, a young lady of fifteen, possessing all the freshness of her age; she was followed by her mother, brother, and sister-in-law. The mother, a lady of fifty, has but little resemblance to her countrywomen; she is lively, active, and intelligent; knows perfectly well how to manage her immense fortune, and what is yet more rare, knows how to make good use of it. Her son and daughter-in-law I had already seen at Williamsburgh. The young gentleman appears mild and polite, but his wife, of only seventeen years of age, is a most interesting acquaintance, not only from her face and form, which are exquisitely delicate, and quite European, but from her being also descended from the Indian Princess, Pocahontas, daughter of king Powhatan, of whom I have already spoken. We may presume that it is rather the disposition of that amiable American woman, than her exterior beauty, which Mrs. Bowling inherits.

Perhaps they who are not particularly acquainted with the history of Virginia, may be ignorant, that Pocahontas was the protectress of the English, and often screened them from the cruelty of her father. She was but twelve years old when Captain Smith, the bravest, the most intelligent, and the most humane of the first colonists, fell into the hands of the savages; he already understood their language, had traded with them several times, and often appeased the quarrels between the Europeans and them ; often had he been obliged also to fight them, and to punish their perfidy. At length, however, under the pretext of commerce, he was drawn into an ambush, and the only two companions who accompanied him, fell before his eyes ; but, though alone, by his dexterity he extricated himself from the troop which surrounded him, until, unfortunately, imagining he could save himself by crossing a morass, he stuck fast, so that the savages, against whom he had no means of defending himself, at last took and bound him, and conducted him to Powhatan. The king was so proud of having Captain Smith in his power, that he sent him in triumph to all the tributary princes, and ordered that he should be splendidly treated, till he returned to suffer that death which was prepared for him.*

---

* Dr. Robertson, Mr. Adair, and a number of writers have given an account of the cruel mode by which the Indians torture their prisoners of war, before they put them to death. During my residence near Alexandria, in Virginia, in 1782, I had the following relation of their barbarous treatment, from a gentleman who had just escaped out of the hands of these infernal furies. Colonel Crawford, and his son, two great land surveyors, and most respectable planters in Virginia, in heading a party against the Indians and Tories, aided by some light horse from the British frontiers, who had spread horror and devastation through the infant back settlements of the United States, were defeated and made prisoners. The gentleman, from whom I had this account, was surgeon to the party, and was conducted with Mr. Crawford and his son, to be sacrificed in his turn, at one of the Indian villages, to the manes of their people slain in battle. The bloody business commenced with Mr. Crawford, the father, who was delivered over to the women, and being fastened to a stake, in the centre of a circle formed by the savages and their allies, the female furies, after the preamble of a war song, began by tearing out the nails of his toes and fingers, then proceeded, at considerable intervals, to cut off his nose and ears ; after which they stuck his lacerated body full of pitch pines ; to all of which they set fire, and which continued burning, amidst the inconceivable tortures of the unhappy man, for a considerable time. After thus glutting their revenge, by acts of the most horrible barbarity, the success of which was repeatedly applauded by the surrounding demons, they rushed in upon him, finished his misery with their tomahawks, and hacked his body limb from limb. This dreadful scene passed in the presence of the son of the unhappy sufferer, and the surgeon, who were to be conveyed to different villages to undergo the

The fatal moment at last arrived, Captain Smith was laid upon the hearth of the savage king, and his head placed upon a large stone to receive the stroke of death, when Pocahontas, the youngest and darling daughter of Powhatan, threw herself upon his body, clasped him in her arms, and declared, that if the cruel sentence were executed, the first blow should fall on her. All savages, (absolute sovereigns and tyrants not excepted,) are invariably more affected by the tears of infancy, than the voice of humanity. Powhatan could not resist the tears and prayers of his daughter : Captain Smith obtained his life, on condition of paying for his ransom a certain quantity of muskets, powder, and iron utensils; but how were they to be obtained? They would neither permit him to return to Jamestown, nor let the English know where he was, lest they should demand him sword in hand. Captain Smith, who was as sensible as courageous, said, that if Powhatan would permit one of his subjects to carry to Jamestown a little board which he would give him, he should find under a tree, at the day and hour appointed, all the articles demanded for his ransom. Powhatan consented, but without having much faith in his promises, believing it to be only an artifice of the captain's to prolong his life. But he had written on the board a few lines sufficient to give an account of his situation. The messenger returned. The King sent to the place fixed upon, and was greatly astonished to find every thing which had been demand-

---

same fate. The next day, accordingly, young Crawford was sacrificed with the same circumstances of horror ; after which, the surgeon, being entrusted to the care of four of the savages, who fortunately got drunk with some rum, given them as a recompense by their European friends, escaped from them in the woods, and, bound as he was, wandered for four or five and twenty days, subsisting on leaves and berries, before he reached the neighbourhood of Winchester, whence he got down to Alexandria. Among these wretches was one Simon Girty, a native of Virginia, who was formerly well acquainted with Colonel Crawford, and had been employed by the assembly of Virginia to conciliate the savages, and obtain their neutrality ; but who having been detected by the Governor in some malversations of the public money entrusted to him, and his duplicity discovered, went over to the British and became more merciless than the worst of these infernal hell-hounds. Mr. Crawford in the midst of his tremendous sufferings, seeing Girty standing in the circle, with a gun, called to him by his name, and implored him as an old friend, a Christian, and a countryman, to shoot him, and by that act of mercy relieve him from his misery ; but the inhuman monster tauntingly replied, " No, Crawford, I have got *no powder*, your assembly did not choose to trust me, and you must now pay for it," and continued to feast his eyes with the bloody sacrifice.—*Trans.*

ed. Powhatan could not conceive this mode of transmitting
thoughts, and Captain Smith was henceforth looked upon as a
great magician, to whom they could not show too much respect. He left the savages in this opinion, and hastened to
return home. Two or three years after, some fresh differences arising amidst them and the English, Powhatan, who no
longer thought them sorcerers, but still feared their power,
laid a horrid plan to get rid of them altogether. His project
was to attack them in profound peace, and cut the throats of
the whole colony. The night of this intended conspiracy,
Pocahontas took advantage of the obscurity, and in a terrible
storm which kept the savages in their tents, escaped from her
father's house, advised the English to be upon their guard, but
conjured them to spare her family, to appear ignorant of the
intelligence she had given, and terminate all their differences
by a new treaty. It would be tedious to relate all the services
which this angel of peace rendered to both nations. I shall
only add, that the English, I know not from what motives, but
certainly against all faith and equity, thought proper to carry
her off. Long and bitterly did she deplore her fate, and the
only consolation she had was Captain Smith, in whom she
found a second father. She was treated with great respect, and
married to a planter of the name of Rolle, who soon after
took her to England. This was in the reign of James the
First; and, it is said, that this monarch, pedantic and ridiculous in every point, was so infatuated with the prerogatives of
royalty, that he expressed his displeasure, that one of his subjects should dare to marry the daughter even of a savage king.
It will not perhaps be difficult to decide on this occasion, whether it was the savage king who derived honour from finding
himself placed upon a level with the European prince, or the
English monarch, who by his pride and prejudices reduced
himself to a level with the chief of the savages. Be that as
it will, Captain Smith, who had returned to London before the
arrival of Pocahontas, was extremely happy to see her again,
but dared not to treat her with the same familiarity as at Jamestown. As soon as she saw him, she threw herself into his
arms, calling him her father; but finding that he neither returned her caresses with equal warmth, nor the endearing title
of daughter, she turned aside her head and wept bitterly, and
it was a long time before they could obtain a single word from
her. Captain Smith inquired several times what could be the
cause of her affliction.—"What!" said she, "did I not save
thy life in America? When I was torn from the arms of my
father, and conducted among thy friends, didst thou not promise to be a father to me? Didst thou not assure me, that if
I went into the country thou wouldst be my father, and that I

should be thy daughter? Thou hast deceived me, and behold me, now here, a stranger and an orphan." It was not difficult for the captain to make his peace with this charming creature, whom he tenderly loved. He presented her to several people of the first quality, but never dared take her to court, from which however she received several favours. After a residence of several years in England, an example of virtue and piety, and attachment to her husband, she died, as she was on the point of embarking on her return to America. She left an only son, who was married, and left only daughters; these daughters, others; and thus, with the female line, the blood of the amiable Pocahontas now flows in the veins of the young and charming Mrs. Bowling.

I hope I shall be pardoned this long digression, which may be pleasing to some readers. My visit to Mrs. Bowling and her family, having convinced me, that I should pass part of the day with them agreeably, I continued my walk, with a promise of returning at two o'clock. Mr. Victor conducted me to the camp formerly occupied by the enemy, and testified his regret that I could not take a nearer view of Mr. Bannister's handsome country-house, which was in sight; there being no other obstacle however than the distance, about a mile and a half, and the noonday heat, we determined that this should not stop us; and walking slowly, we reached, without fatigue, this house, which is really worth seeing. It is decorated rather in the Italian, than the English or American style, having three porticos at the three principal entries, each of them supported by four columns.* It was then occupied by an inhabitant of

---

* The Italian architecture, that of porticos in particular, is admirably adapted to all hot climates, and of course to the southern states of America. The same motives, therefore, which induced the invention of this mode of building in ancient Greece and Rome, and in general throughout the Eastern world, would naturally give rise to the same inventions of convenience in similar climates; and, in fact, though the richer and more polished descendants of Britain, in the New World, may be supposed to adopt these porticos from Italy, as the cultivated mind of the author imagines; the very poorest settler, nay even the native Indian, invariably attempts some kind of substitute for this necessary protection from the sun and weather. Every tavern or inn is provided with a covered portico for the convenience of its guests, and this evidently from the necessity of the case. We have only to examine the resources of the savage islander in the Pacific ocean, and recur to the origin of all architecture, from the fluted Corinthian in the hall of empire, to the rustic prop of the thatched roof, to discover the natural progress of the human mind, and the similarity of human genius.—*Trans.*

Carolina, called Nelson, who had been driven from his country by the war, which followed him to Petersburgh. He invited me to walk in, and whilst he made me, according to custom, drink a glass of wine, another Carolinian, of the name of Bull, arrived to dine with him. The latter was a militia general, and came from General Greene's army, where his time of service was expired. The history of Mr. Bull, which is not long, will give a general idea of the state of the southern provinces. Possessed of a great number of negroes, large personal property, particularly in plate, previous to, and during the war, he did not think proper, after the capture of Charleston, to expose his wealth to the rapacity of the English. He set off therefore with two hundred negroes, followed by a great number of wagons laden with his effects, and provisions for his little army, and travelled, in this manner, through South and North-Carolina, and part of Virginia, pitching his camp every evening in the most commodious situations. At length he arrived at Tukakoe, on James river, the seat of his old friend Mr. Randolph, a rich planter of Virginia, who gave him a spot of ground near his house, on which his negroes built one for himself. Here he lived in tranquillity, surrounded by his slaves and his flocks, until Arnold and Phillips invaded Virginia, and approached his new asylum. Mr. Bull once more departed with his wealth, his flocks, and negroes, to retire into the upper country near Fredericksburg. On my asking him what he would have done, had we not opportunely arrived to expel the English, who intended to complete the conquest of Virginia, "I should have retired to Maryland," he replied,— and if they had gone thither?—" I should have proceeded to Pennsylvania, and so on, even to New-England." Does not this recall to mind the ancient patriarchs emigrating with their family and flocks, with a certainty of finding every where a country to receive and nourish them?* General Bull was

---

* I have already said, that I had the happiness of a particular acquaintance with many of the principal gentlemen of South-Carolina. The reflection on the pleasing hours I passed with them in their exiled situation at Philadelphia, and the warm friendship with which they honoured me, whilst it reconciles me to the world, and soothes the memory of past sufferings, touches the tenderest affections of a sensible and grateful heart. My bosom beat high with genuine ardour in the cause for which they sacrificed every personal consideration, but I had frequently the opportunity of appreciating that sacrifice. Seeing what I saw, I want no instances of Greek or Roman virtue to stimulate my feelings, or excite my emulation ; and it will ever be matter of congratulation with me, to have witnessed in the principal inhabitants of Carolina, all the blandishments of civilized

preparing to return to Carolina in hopes, henceforth, of passing happier days.   After putting many questions to him respecting affairs to the southward, which he answered with
great frankness and good sense, I returned to Mrs. Bowling's,
where I was not disappointed in finding a good dinner, the honours of which she did with much cordiality, without restraint
or ceremony.   After dinner, Miss Bowling played on the harpsichord, and sung like an adept in music, although her voice
was not agreeable; whilst the descendant of Pocahontas touched a guitar, and sung like a person unskilled in music, but with
a charming voice.   On my return home, I had another concert; Miss Saunders singing some airs, which she accompanied sometimes with the harpsichord, and sometimes with the
guitar.·

Next day we were obliged to quit this good house and agreeable company; but before I left Petersburgh, I observed that
it was already a flourishing town, and must become more so,
every day, from its favourable situation with respect to commerce.   First, because it is placed immediately below the Falls,
or Rapids of the Apamatock, and the river can here float vessels of fifty or sixty tons burthen.   Secondly, because the productions of the southern part of Virginia have no other outlet,
and those even of North-Carolina are gradually taking this
way, the navigation of the Roanöke and Albemarle Sound being by no means so commodious as that of the Apamatock and
James river.   But these advantages are unfortunately balanced
by the insalubrity of the climate; for I have been assured, that
of all the inhabitants of the three little burghs of Pocahunta,
of Blandford and Petersburgh, which may be considered as
forming one town, not two persons are to be found who are
natives of the country.   Commerce and navigation, notwith-

society, the love of life and all its blessings, a humanity void of re-
proach, an hospitality not exceeded in the patriarchal ages, contrary
to the paradoxes of systematic writers, blended with the inflexible virtue which distinguished the best and purest ages of the world.   From
the number, I shall only select the brilliant examples of Major Pierce
Butler, and Mr. Arthur Middleton.   Wealth, honour, interest, domestic happiness, their children, were nothing in the eyes of such
men, though calculated to enjoy, and communicate happiness in every
sphere, when put in competition with the great objects of universal
public happiness, and sacred Freedom's holy cause.   How painful is
it to be compelled to add, that such was the cold, selfish spirit of too
many of the inhabitants of Philadelphia towards their Carolina brethren, who had every claim upon their sympathy and good offices, as
to merit the indignation of every feeling mind, and to fix an indelible
stain upon their character as men and citizens.— *Trans.*

standing, produce a concourse of strangers. The situation, besides, is agreeable, and the climate may probably be rendered more salubrious by draining some morasses in the neighbourhood.

Five miles from Petersburgh, we passed the small river of Randolph, over a stone bridge; and travelling, through a rich and well peopled country, arrived at a fork of roads, where we were unlucky enough precisely to make choice of that which did not lead to Richmond, the place of our destination. But we had no reason to regret our error, as it was only two miles about and we skirted James river to a charming place called Warwick, where a groupe of handsome houses form a sort of village, and there are several superb ones in the neighbourhood; among others, that of Colonel Carey, on the right bank of the river, and Mr. Randolph's on the opposite shore. One must be fatigued with hearing the name of Randolph mentioned in travelling in Virginia, (for it is one of the most ancient families in the country,) a Randolph being among the first settlers, and is likewise one of the most numerous and rich. It is divided into seven or eight branches, and I am not afraid of exaggerating, when I say, that they possess an income of upwards of a million of livres. It is only twenty-five miles from Petersburgh to Richmond, but as we had lost our way, and travelled but slowly, it was near three o'clock when we reached Manchester, a sort of suburb to Richmond, on the right bank of the river, where you pass the ferry. The passage was short, there being two boats for the accommodation of travellers. Though Richmond be already an old town, and well situated for trade, being built on the spot where James river begins to be navigable, that is, just below the Rapids, it was, before the war, one of the least considerable in Virginia, where they are all, in general, very small; but the seat of government having been removed from Williamsburgh, it is become a real capital, and is augmenting every day. It was necessary, doubtless, to place the legislative body at a distance from the sea-coast, where it was exposed to the rapid and unexpected inroads of the English; but Williamsburgh had the still farther inconvenience of being situated at the extremity of the state, which obliged a great part of the delegates to make a long journey to the assembly; besides, that from its position between James and York rivers, it has no port nor communication with them but by small creeks very difficult for navigation, whilst vessels of 200 tons come up to Richmond. This new capital is divided into three parts, one of which is on the edge of the river, and may be considered as the port; the two others are built on two eminences, which are separated by a little valley. I was conducted to that on the west, where I found a good inn, and my lodgings and dinner ordered by a servant whom I had sent on two days before, with a lame horse. We were served, therefore, immediately, but with such magnificence and profusion, that there would have been too much for twenty persons. Every plate that was brought us produced a burst of laughter, but not without considerable alarm for the bill of the next day ; for I had been apprized that the inns at Richmond were uncommonly extravagant. I escaped, however, for seven or eight Louis d'or, which was not enormous, considering our expenditure. A short time before Mr. de Rochambeau had paid five and twenty Louis, at another inn, for some horses which remained there for four or five days, although he neither ate nor slept in it himself. Mr. Formicalo, my landlord, was more honest ; his only error was the exalted idea he had formed of the manner in which French General Officers must be treated. He is a Neapolitan, who came to Virginia with Lord Dunmore, as his *Maitre d'Hotel*, but he had gone rather round about, having been before in Russia. At present he has a good house, furniture, and slaves, and will soon become a man of consequence in his new country. He still, however, recollects his native land with pleasure, and I have no doubt that my attention in addressing him only in Italian, saved me a few Louis.

After dinner I went to pay a visit to Mr. Harrison, then Governor of the State. I found him in a homely, but spacious enough house, which was fitted up for him. As the assembly was not then sitting, there was nothing to distinguish him from other citizens. One of his brothers, who is a Colonel of Artillery, and one of his sons, who acts as his Secretary, were with him. The conversation was free and agreeable, which he was even desirous of prolonging ; for on my rising in half an hour, lest I might interrupt him, he assured me that the business of the day was at an end, and desired me to resume my seat. We talked much of the first Congress in America, in which he sat for two years, and which, as I have already said, was composed of every person distinguished for virtue and capacity on the continent. This subject led us naturally to that which is the most favourite topic among the Americans, the origin and commencement of the present revolution. It is a circumstance peculiar to Virginia, that the inhabitants of that country were certainly in the best situation of all the colonists under the English government. The Virginians were planters, rather than merchants, and the objects of their culture were rather valuable than the result of industry. They possessed, almost exclusively, the privileged article of tobacco, which the English came in quest of into the very heart of the country, bringing in exchange every article of utility, and even of luxury.

They had a particular regard and predilection for Virginia, and favoured accordingly the peculiar disposition of that country, where cupidity and indolence go hand-in-hand, and serve only as boundaries to each other. It was undoubtedly no easy matter therefore, to persuade this people to take up arms, because the town of Boston did not choose to pay a duty upon tea, and was in open rupture with England. To produce this effect, it was necessary to substitute activity for indolence, and foresight for indifference. That idea was to be awakened at which every man, educated in the principles of the English constitution, shudders, at the idea of a servile submission to a tax to which he has not himself consented. The precise case however relative to them, had not yet occurred, though every enlightened mind foresaw that such was the object, and would be the inevitable consequence of the early measures of the government : but how were the people to be convinced of this ? By what other motive could they be brought to adopt decisive measures, if not by the confidence they reposed in their leaders ? Mr. Harrison informed me, that when he was on the point of setting out with Mr. Jefferson and Mr. Lee to attend the first Congress at Philadelphia, a number of respectable, but uninformed inhabitants, waited upon, and addressed them as follows : " You assert that there is a fixed intention. to invade our rights and privileges ; we own that we do not see this clearly, but since you assure us that it is so, we believe the fact. We are about to take a very dangerous step, but we confide in you, and are ready to support you in every measure you shall think proper to adopt." Mr. Harrison added, that he found himself greatly relieved by a speech made by Lord North soon after, in which he could not refrain from avowing, in the clearest manner, the plan of the British government.* This speech was

---

* I cannot here resist transcribing a passage from Mr. Payne's celebrated letter to the Abbé Raynal, which merits preservation, and may serve to illustrate the ideas of America respecting the general views of Britain, in hopes that every reflecting Englishman is at length dispassionate enough to bear the observation. " I shall now take my leave of this passage of the Abbé, with an observation, which until something unfolds itself to convince me of the contrary, I cannot avoid believing to be true ; which is, that it was the fixed determination of the British cabinet to quarrel with America at all events. They (the members who compose the cabinet,) had no doubt of success, if they could once bring it to the issue of a battle ; and they expected from a conquest, what they could neither propose with decency, nor hope for by negotiation. The charters and constitutions of the colonies were become to them matters of offence, and their rapid progress in property and population were beheld with disgust, as the growing

printed in the public papers, and all America rang with its
contents. Returning afterwards to Virginia, he saw the same
persons who had thus addressed him on his departure, who now
confessed that he had not deceived them, and that henceforward they were resolutely determined upon war. These particular details cannot but be useful to such Europeans as are
desirous of forming a just idea of those great events, in which
they took so deep an interest ; for they would be much deceived in imagining that all the Thirteen States of America were
invariably animated by the same spirit, and affected by the
same sentiments. But they would commit a still greater error,
did they imagine, that these people resembled each other in
their forms of government, their manners and opinions. One
must be in the country itself; one must be acquainted with the
language, and take a pleasure in conversing, and in listening,
to be qualified to form, and that slowly, a proper opinion and
a decisive judgment.* After this reflection, the reader will

---

and natural means of independence. They saw no way to retain them
long, but by reducing them in time. A conquest would at once have
made them lords and landlords ; and put them in possession both of
the revenue and the rental. The whole trouble of government would
have ceased in a victory, and a final end been put to remonstrance and
debate. The experience of the stamp act had taught them how to
quarrel, with the advantages of cover and convenience, and they had
nothing to do but to renew the scene, and put contention into motion.
They hoped for a rebellion, and they made one. They expected a
declaration of independence, and they were not disappointed. But
after this, they looked for victory, and they obtained a defeat. If this
be taken as the generating cause of the contest, then is every part of
the conduct of the British ministry consistent, from the commencement of the dispute, until the signing the treaty of Paris, (the American and French alliance,) after which, conquest becoming doubtful,
they had recourse to negotiation, and were again defeated. If we
take a review of what part Britain has acted, we shall find every thing
which ought to make a nation blush. The most vulgar abuse, accompanied by that species of haughtiness which distinguishes the hero of
a mob from the character of a gentleman ; it was as much from her
manners, as from her injustice, that she lost the colonies. By the latter she provoked their principles, by the former she exhausted their patience. And it ought to be held out to the world, to show, how necessary it is to conduct the business of government with civility."—*Trans.*

* The same ingenious author of *Common Sense*, makes another observation, in his answer to the very ignorant, or very prejudiced work
of the Abbé Raynal on the revolution of America, to which, however
it may militate against the utility of the present publication, or the
notes of the translator, he cannot avoid perfectly subscribing, viz.: " I
never yet saw an European description of America that was true.

not be surprised at the pleasure I took in conversing with Mr. Harrison. Besides that I was particularly happy to form an acquaintance with a man of so estimable a character in every respect, and whose best eulogium it is to say, that he is the intimate friend of Dr. Franklin.* He pressed me to dine with him next day, and to pass another day at Richmond; but as there was nothing to excite curiosity in that town, and I was desirous of stopping at Westover before I returned to Williamsburgh, where I was anxious to arrive, we set out the 27th at eight in the morning, under the escort of Colonel Harrison, who accompanied us to a road from which it was impossible to go astray. We travelled six and twenty miles without halting, in very hot weather, but by a very agreeable road, with magnificent houses in view at every instant; for the banks of James river form the garden of Virginia. That of Mrs. Bird, to which I was going, surpasses them all in the magnificence of the buildings, the beauty of its situation, and the pleasures of society.†

---

neither can any person gain a just idea of it, but by coming to it.—*Trans*.

* The illustrious and amiable character of Dr. Franklin is far beyond my praise. To have known him; to have been a frequent witness to the distinguished acts of his great mind; to have been in a situation to learn, and to admire his comprehensive views, and benevolent motives; to have heard the profound maxims of wise philosophy and sound politics, drop from his lips with all the unaffected simplicity of the most indifferent conversation; to have heard him deviate from the depths of reason, and adopt his instructive discourse to the capacity and temper of the young and the gay; to have enjoyed in short, the varied luxuries of his delightful society, is a subject of triumph and consolation, of which nothing can deprive me. He too as well as the envious and interested enemies of his transcendent merit, must drop from off the scene, but his name, *ære perennius*, is inscribed in indelible characters on the immortal roll of philosophy and freedom, for the *ardentia verba* of the most honest advocate of freedom, of the present age, the late Serjeant Glynn, on a great occasion; the action against Lord Halifax for the false imprisonment of Mr. Wilkes, may with peculiar justice be applied to this great man. " Few men in whole revolving ages can be found, who dare oppose themselves to the force of tyranny, and whose single breasts contain the spirit of nations."—*Trans*.

† The most perfect ease and comfort characterize the mode of receiving strangers in Virginia, but no where are these circumstances more conspicuous than at the house of General Washington. Your apartments are your home, the servants of the house are yours, and whilst every inducement is held out to bring you into the general society in the drawing-room, or at the table, it rests with yourself to be served or not with every thing in your own chamber.—*Trans*.

Mrs. Bird is the widow of a Colonel who served in the war of 1756, and was afterwards one of the council under the British government. His talents, his personal qualities, and his riches, for he possessed an immense territory, rendered him one of the principal personages of the country ; but being a spendthrift and a gambler, he left his affairs, at his death, in very great disorder. He had four children by his first wife, who were already settled in the world, and has left eight by his second, of whom the widow takes care. She has preserved his beautiful house, situated on James river, a large personal property, a considerable number of slaves, and some plantations which she has rendered valuable. She is about two and forty, with an agreeable countenance, and great sense. Four of her eight children are daughters, two of whom are near twenty, and they are all amiable and well educated. Her care and activity have in some measure repaired the effects of her husband's dissipation, and her house is still the most celebrated, and the most agreeable of the neighbourhood. She has experienced however, fresh misfortunes ; three times have the English landed at Westover, under Arnold and Cornwallis; and though these visits cost her dear, her husband's former attachment to England, where his eldest son is now serving in the army, her relationship with Arnold, whose cousin german she is, and perhaps too, the jealousy of her neighbours, have given birth to suspicions, that war alone was not the object which induced the English always to make their descents at her habitation. She has been accused even of connivance with them, and the government have once put their seal upon her papers ; but she has braved the tempest, and defended herself with firmness ; and though her affair be not yet terminated, it does not appear as if she was likely to suffer any other inconvenience than that of being disturbed and suspected. Her two eldest daughters passed the last winter at Williamsburgh, where they were greatly complimented by M. de Rochambeau and the whole army.* I had also received them in the best

---

* The prudent conduct of the French officers, and the strict discipline of their troops in a country with different manners, language, and religion, full of inveterate prejudices, and wherein they had very lately been regarded as natural enemies, must ever be considered as an epocha and a phenomenon, in the history of policy and subordination. Whilst all ranks of officers were making it their study successfully to conciliate the good opinion of the higher classes, nothing could exceed the probity, and urbanity of the common soldiers ; not only did they live with the American troops in a harmony, hitherto unknown to allied armies, even of kindred language, interest, and religion, but their conduct was irreproachable, and even delicate to the inhabitants of the

manner I could, and received the thanks of Mrs. Bird, with a
pressing invitation to come and see her ; I found myself in
consequence, quite at home. I found here also my acquaintance the young Mrs. Bowling, who was on a visit.to Mr. Mead,
a friend and neighbour of Mrs. Bird's, who had invited him and
his company to dinner. I passed this day therefore very agreeably, and Mr. and Mrs. Mead, whom I had also known at
Williamsburgh, engaged the company to dine with them the
next day. The river alone separates the two houses, which
are notwithstanding, upwards of a mile distant from each other ;
but as there is very little current, the breadth of the water between them does not prevent it from being soon passed. Mr.
Mead's house is by no means so handsome as that of Westover,
but it is extremely well fitted up within, and stands on a charming situation ; for it is directly opposite to Mrs. Bird's, which,
with its surrounding appendages, has the appearance of a small
town, and forms a most delightful prospect. Mr. Mead's garden, like that of Westover, is in the nature of a terrace on the
bank of the river, and is capable of being made still more beautiful, if Mr. Mead preserves his house, and gives some attention
to it ; for he is a philosopher of a very amiable but singular
turn of mind, and such as is particularly uncommon in Virginia, since he rarely attends to affairs of interest, and cannot prevail upon himself to make his negroes work.* He is even so
disgusted with a culture wherein it is necessary to make use of
slaves, that he is tempted to sell his possessions in Virginia and
remove to New-England. Mrs. Bird, who has a numerous
family to provide for, cannot carry her philosophy so far ; but

---

country. They who predicted discord on the introduction of a French
army, had reason and experience on their side, but the spirit of policy
and wisdom which presided in the French councils had gone forth,
and diffusing itself through every subordinate class of men, persuaded
even the meanest actors in the war, and baffled foresight. Nor was
this one of the least extraordinary circumstances of this wonderful
revolution.—*Trans.*

* Whilst the Translator was employed in this passage, he read in
the public prints, the exultation of a friend to his fellow-creatures,
that a Mr. Pleasants, a quaker on James river in Virginia, had libera-
ted his slaves, and made a sacrifice of 3000*l.* sterling to this noble act
of humanity. The Translator knows the country too well not to feel
the force of the Author's subsequent reasoning on the difficulty and
danger of a general emancipation of the negroes, nor after mature reflection now, and on the spot, is he able to overcome his objections.
But God, in his divine providence, forbid that so splendid an example
of active virtue, should clash with the unavoidable policy, or the necessary welfare of society !—*Trans.*

she takes great care of her negroes, makes them as happy as their situation will admit, and serves them herself as a doctor in time of sickness. She has even made some interesting discoveries on the disorders incident to them, and discovered a very salutary method of treating a sort of putrid fever which carries them off commonly in a few days, and against which the physicians of the country have exerted themselves without success.

The 29th, the whole of which day I spent at Westover, furnishes nothing interesting in this journal, except some information I had the opportunity of acquiring respecting two sorts of animals, of very different species, the sturgeon and the humming-bird. As I was walking by the river-side, I saw two negroes carrying an immense sturgeon, and on my asking them how they had taken it, they told me at this season, they were so common as to be taken easily in a seine (a sort of fishing-net,) and that fifteen or twenty were found sometimes in the net; but that there was a much more simple method of taking them, which they had just been using. This species of monsters, which are so active in the evening as to be perpetually leaping to a great height above the surface of the water, usually sleep profoundly at mid-day.* Two or three negroes then proceed

---

* From General Washington's house, which stands on the lofty banks of the Potomac, in a situation more magnificent than I can paint to an European imagination, I have seen for several hours together, in a summer's evening, hundreds, perhaps I might say thousands of sturgeon, at a great height from the water at the same instant, so that the quantity in the river must have been inconceivably great; but notwithstanding the rivers in Virginia abound with fish, they are by no means plentiful at table, such is the indolence of the inhabitants!

Mr. Lund Washington, a relation of the General's, and who managed all his affairs during his nine years' absence with the army, informed me that an English frigate having come up the Potomac, a party was landed who set fire to and destroyed some gentlemen's houses on the Maryland side in sight of Mount Vernon, the General's house; after which the Captain, (I think Captain Graves of the Acteon) sent a boat on shore to the General's, demanding a large supply of provisions, &c. with a menace of burning it likewise in case of a refusal. To this message Mr. Lund Washington replied, " that when the General engaged in the contest he had put all to stake, and was well aware of the exposed situation of his house and property, in consequence of which he had given him orders by no means to comply with any such demands, for that he would make no unworthy compromise with the enemy, and was ready to meet the fate of his neighbours." The Captain was highly incensed on receiving this answer, and removed his frigate to the Virginia shore; but before he commenced his operations, he sent another message to the same purport, offering likewise a passport

in a little boat furnished with a long cord, at the end of which
is a sharp iron crook, which they hold suspended like a log line.
As soon as they find this line stopped by some obstacle, they
draw it forcibly towards them, so as to strike the hook into the
sturgeon, which they either drag out of the water, or which,
after some struggling, and losing all its blood, floats at length
upon the surface, and is easily taken.

As for the humming-birds, I saw them for the first time, and
was never tired of beholding them.   The walls of the garden
and the house were covered with honeysuckles, which afforded
an ample harvest for these charming little animals.   I saw
them perpetually flying over the flowers, on which they feed
without ever alighting, for it is by supporting themselves on
their wings that they insinuate their beaks into the calix of the
flowers.   Sometimes they perch, but it is only for a moment;
it is then only one has an opportunity of admiring the beauty
of their plumage, especially when opposite to the sun, and
when in removing their heads, they display the brilliant ena-
mel of their red necks, which almost rival the splendour of the
ruby or the diamond.   It is not true that they are naturally
passionate, and that they tear to pieces the flowers in which they
find no honey.   I have never observed any such circumstance
myself, either at Westover or Williamsburgh; and the inhabitants of the country assured me, that they had never made any
such observation.   These birds appear only with the flowers, with
which likewise they disappear, and no person can tell what

---

to Mr. Washington to come on board : he returned accordingly in
the boat, carrying with him a small present of poultry, of which he
begged the Captain's acceptance.   His presence produced the best effect, he was hospitably received notwithstanding he repeated the same
sentiments with the same firmness.   The Captain expressed his personal respect for the character of the General, commending the conduct of Mr. Lund Washington, and assured him nothing but his having
misconceived the terms of the first answer could have induced him for a
moment to entertain the idea of taking the smallest measure offensive
to so illustrious a character as the General, explaining at the same
time the real or supposed provocations which had compelled his severity on the other side of the river.   Mr. Washington, after spending
some time in perfect harmony on board, returned, and instantly despatched sheep, hogs, and an abundant supply of other articles as a present to the English frigate.   The Translator hopes that in the present
state of men and measures in England, Mr. Graves, or whoever the
Captain of that frigate was, will neither be offended at this anecdote,
nor be afraid to own himself the actor in this generous transaction.
Henry IVth supplied Paris with provisions whilst he was blockading it !
—*Trans.*

becomes of them.   Some are of opinion that they hide themselves, and remain torpid the remainder of the year.   In fact, it is difficult to conceive how their wings, which are so slight and slender as to be imperceptible if not in motion, could possibly resist the winds, and transport them to distant climates. They are not intractable, for I have seen one of them, which was taken a few days before, in no wise frightened at the persons who looked at it, but flew about the room, as in a garden, and sucked the flowers which they presented to it ; but it did not live above a week.   These birds are so fond of motion, that it is impossible for them to live without the enjoyment of the most unrestrained liberty.   It is difficult even to catch them, unless they happen, as was the case with that I am speaking of, to fly into the chamber, or be driven there by the wind. An inhabitant of the country, who amused himself in preserving them for his cabinet, has discovered a very ingenious method of killing, without disfiguring them.   This is a very difficult undertaking ; for a single grain of small shot is a cannon bullet for, so small a creature.   This method is to load his gun with a bladder filled with water.   The explosion of this water is sufficient to knock down the humming-bird, and deprive it of motion.

CHAPTER V.

THE reader will certainly not accuse me of playing the orator, and reserving objects of the greatest magnitude for the end of my discourse; for I shall here conclude my journal. It is unnecessary to speak of my return to Williamsburgh, unless it be worthy of remark, that the Chickahoming, which is only a secondary river, since it falls into that of James, is yet so wide, six miles from its conflux, that I was three quarters of an hour in passing it. But if he will still favour me with his attention, I shall terminate this long narrative of a short journey, by some observations on a country I have travelled through, and inhabited long enough to know it thoroughly.

The Virginians differ essentially from the inhabitants to the north and eastward of the bay, (of Chesapeake) not only in the nature of their climate, that of their soil, and the objects of cultivation peculiar to it, but in that indelible character which is imprinted on every nation at the moment of its origin, and which by perpetuating itself from generation to generation, justifies the following great principles, that every thing which is, partakes of that which has been. The discovery of Virginia dates from the end of the sixteenth century, and the settlement of the colony took place at the commencement of the seventeenth. These events passed in the reigns of Elizabeth and James the first. The republican and democratical spirit was not then common in England; that of commerce and navigation was scarcely in its infancy; and the long wars with France and Spain had perpetuated, under another form, the same military cast given to the nation by William the Conqueror, Richard, Coeur de Lion, Edward the third, and the Black Prince. There were no longer any Knights Errant, as in the time of the Crusades, but in their place rose a number of adventurers who served indifferently their own country, and foreign powers, and gentlemen, who disdaining agriculture and commerce, had no other profession but that of arms; for at that period the military spirit maintained the prejudices favourable to that nobility, from which it was long inseparable; besides that the dignity of the peerage, from being less common in England, gave more eclat and more consistence to those who possessed it by hereditary right. The first colonists of Virginia were composed, in a great measure, of such soldiers, and such gentlemen, some of whom went in search of fortune, and others, of adventures. And in fact, if the establishment of a colony requires all the industry of the merchant and the cultivator, the discovery, and conquest of unknown countries seems more peculiarly adapted to the ideas of the warlike and romantic. Accordingly the first company which obtained the exclusive property of Virginia, was principally composed of men the most distinguished by their rank or birth ; and though all these illustrious proprietors did not actually become colonists, several of them were not afraid to pass the seas ; and a Lord Delaware was among the first Governors of Virginia. It was natural therefore for these new colonists, who were filled with military principles, and the prejudices of nobility, to carry them into the midst even of the savages whose lands they were usurping ; and of all our European ideas, these were what the unpolished tribes most readily conceived. I know that there now remains but an inconsiderable number of these ancient families, but they have retained a great estimation, and the first impulse once given, it is not in the power of any legislator, nor even of time itself, wholly to destroy its effect. The government may become democratic, as it is at the present moment ; but the national character, the spirit of the government itself, will be always aristocratic. Nor can this be doubted, when we take into consideration another cause, co-operating with the former ; I mean to speak of slavery ; not that it is any mark of distinction, or peculiar privilege to possess negroes, but because the empire men exercise over them cherishes vanity and sloth, two vices which accord wonderfully with the already established prejudices. It will, doubtless, be asked, how these prejudices have been brought to coincide with a revolution founded on such different principles. I shall answer that they have even perhaps contributed to produce it. That whilst the revolt of New-England was the result of reason and calculation, pride possibly had no inconsiderable share in dictating the measures of Virginia. I shall add, what I have above hinted, that in the beginning, even the indolence of this people may have been useful to them, as it obliged them to rely upon a small number of virtuous and enlightened citizens, who led them farther than they would have proceeded, without a guide, had they consulted only their own dispositions. For it must be allowed, that Virginia stepped forth with a good grace, at the very commencement of the troubles ; that she was the first to offer succours to the Bostonians, and the first also to set on foot a considerable body of troops. But it may likewise be observed, that as soon as the new legislature was

established, and when, instead of leaders, she had a govern
ment, the mass of citizens was taking part in that government,
the national character prevailed, and every thing went worse
and worse.   Thus, states, like individuals, are born with a particular complexion, the bad effects of which may be corrected
by regimen and habits, but can never be entirely changed.
Thus, legislators, like physicians, ought never to flatter themselves that they can bestow, at pleasure, a particular tempera-
ment on bodies politic, but strive to discover what they already
have, and thence study to remedy the inconveniences, and multiply the advantages resulting from it.

   A general glance at the different States of America will
serve to justify this opinion.   The people of New-England had
no other motive for settling in the new world, than to escape
from the arbitrary power of their monarchs, who, at once, sovereigns of the state, and heads of the church, exercised at that
period the double tyranny of despotism and intolerance.   They
were not adventurers, they were men who wished to live in
peace, and who laboured for their subsistence.   Their principles taught them equality, and disposed them to industrious
pursuits.   The soil, naturally barren, affording them but scanty
resources, they attached themselves to fishing and navigation ;
and at this hour, they are still friends to equality and industry ; they are fishermen and navigators.   The states of New-
York, and the Jerseys, were peopled by necessitous Dutchmen
who wanted land in their own country, and occupied themselves more about domestic economy than the public government.   These people have preserved the same character ; their
interests, their efforts, so to speak, are personal ; their views
are concentered in their families, and it is only from necessity
that these families are formed into a state.   Accordingly, when
General Burgoyne was on his march to Albany, the New-Eng-
landmen chiefly contributed to impede his progress ; and, if
the inhabitants of the State of New-York and the Jerseys have
often taken arms, and displayed courage, it is because the former were animated by an inveterate hatred against the savages,
which generally preceded the English armies,* and the latter

---

* The employing the Indians, independent of the measure, it is now
pretty generally admitted, produced consequences directly opposite to
the interest of Great-Britain ; uniting the inhabitants of all the countries liable to their incursions as one man against them and their allies,
and producing such bloody scenes of inveterate animosity and vengeance as make human nature shudder.   The following narrative will
prove how far men of all casts, colours, and religions, resemble each
other in similar situations, and to what lengths even the christians of

were excited to take personal vengeance for the excesses committed by the troops of the enemy, when they over-ran the country.* If you go farther to the south, and pass the Delaware, you will find that the government of Pennsylvania, in its origin, was founded on two very opposite principles; it was a government of property, a government in itself feudal, or, if you will, patriarchal, but the spirit of which was the greatest toleration, and the most complete liberty. Penn's family at

---

an enlightened age can go, when compelled to act under the guidance of the worst passions. The inhabitants of the back frontiers of Pennsylvania, goaded to fury by the ravages committed on them by the Indians, and by the murder of their families and kindred, collected the militia in the beginning of 1782, and took the field against their savage intruders. In one of their excursions they fell in with a small tribe of christian Indians, called the *Muskingums*, who being suspected of attachment to the Americans, had been for some time confined at Detroit, and were released only on condition of observing a strict neutrality, since they could not be persuaded to take arms. These unhappy wretches, to the number of about two hundred, returning to their habitations, were employed in putting their seed-corn into the ground, when they were surprised by the American militia. In vain did they urge their situation, and their sufferings from the British ; they were Indians, and their captors, men who had lost sons, brothers, fathers, wives, or children in this horrid war ; no other plea was necessary to palliate their meditated vengeance. The Indians were shut up in a barn, and ordered to prepare for death, but with this barbarous consolation, that, as they were christian converts, they should be allowed a respite till the next morning. The innocent victims spent the night in singing Moravian hymns, and in other acts of christian devotion ; and in the morning, men, women, and children, were led to the slaughter, and butchered by their fellow worshippers of the meek Jesus ! The Moravians at Bethlehem and Nazareth, whose missionaries had converted them, made strong representations to Congress on the subject. I was at Philadelphia when the news arrived ; and it is but justice to say, that horror was painted on every countenance, and every mind was at work to devise expedients for avenging this atrocious murder ; but after various efforts, both Congress and the Assembly of the State were found unequal to the punishment of these assassins, who were armed, distant from the seat of government, the only safeguard and protection of the frontiers, and from their own savage nature alone fit to cope with the dreadful enemy brought into action by the British.

* The murder committed on Mrs. Maxwell, the wife of a respectable and popular clergyman in the Jerseys, and afterwards on himself, with similar acts of cruelty perpetrated by a licentious soldiery, and unprincipled refugees, inflamed the minds of a great body of the inhabitants, particularly of the Dutch and their descendants, who, as the Marquis observes, were certainly disposed at least to a neutrality.— *Trans.*

first formed the vain project of establishing a sort of Utopia, or perfect government, and afterwards of deriving the greatest possible advantage from their immense property, by attracting foreigners from all parts. Here it arises that the people of Pennsylvania have no characteristic assimilation, that they are intermingled and confounded, and more actuated to individual, than to public liberty, more inclined to anarchy than to democracy.* Maryland, subjected in the first instance to a proprietary government, and considered only as a private domain, remained long in a state of the most absolute dependence. This is the first time she merits to be regarded as a state ; but this state seems to be forming under good auspices ; she may become of great weight after the present revolution, because she was formerly of no significance. The two Carolinas and Georgia are next to be considered ; but I am not sufficiently acquainted with these three states to hazard on them any observations, which may not be so just in fact as they appear to me ; but which are at least of a delicate nature, and require more than a superficial examination. I only know, that North-Carolina, peopled by Scotsmen, brought thither by poverty, rather than by industry, is a prey to acts of pillage, and to inter-

---

* The Irish and the Germans form the most numerous part of the inhabitants of Pennsylvania. The latter, if I am not mistaken, constitutes a fifth, if not a fourth, of the whole number, and are a most useful, industrious body of men, well versed in the mechanic arts and agriculture. I have travelled several days in the interior parts of that state, and heard scarcely any other language than German, the acts of Congress, and the State are promulgated in that language, German Gazettes are published at Philadelphia, and in general they proved themselves true friends to the revolution. Congress availing themselves of this circumstance, very politically encamped the Brunswick, and other German troops taken with Burgoyne, near the town of Reading, where I saw them. The neighbourhood abounding with their countrymen, the men had permission to work at harvest, and other trades, and soon formed connexions with the females of the country. Calculating their market price, and the obligation they lay under to restore them, or their prime cost, they took every measure to prevent them from remaining in the country ; for which purpose, they transmitted but small sums at a time by their commissaries from New-York, taking care to keep large arrears in their hands, as a temptation for their return. But all these precautions were, as may naturally be imagined, but of a partial effect, with men habituated to a country of freedom, wherein they felt themselves restored to their natural rights, and animated by the example of their countrymen, enjoying the full comforts of their honest industry ; contrasted too with the degraded state of a wretched mercenary, held up to sale by his arbitrary master.—*Trans.*

nal dissensions :* that South-Carolina, possessing a commerce, wholly of exportation, owes its existence to its sea-ports, especially to that of Charleston, which has rapidly increased, and is become a commercial town, in which strangers abound, as at

---

* It is true that a great number of Scotsmen are settled in North-Carolina, but that they were not even the majority of the inhabitants, is very apparent from the events of the late revolution ; for the Scots, though loyalists nearly to a man, were repeatedly defeated, and finally crushed by the militia of the country. Notwithstanding her efforts appeared less concentered, and more vaguely directed, owing to the local circumstances of the province, and the dispersed state of the inhabitants, rather than disinclination to the cause, North-Carolina rendered most essential services, by her exertions in the field, and the delegates she sent to Congress. Her constitution of government, contracted as it is, is not perhaps inferior to many in the confederacy, and bespeaks the wisdom of " the enlightened few," to which the Marquis attributes the wise councils of Virginia.   It was the North-Carolina militia which gave the first turn to the ruined affairs of America to the southward, by their spirited attack and defeat of Colonel Ferguson at King's Mountain.   The translator, who was then in England, received, by a private channel, the first intelligence of that important event, which he communicated to the public ; but the circumstances of the surprise of a large body of British troops, flushed with the capture of Charleston, and the victory at Camden, by a body of 1600 *horsemen*, from the back country of North-Carolina, appeared so extraordinary, that he could not obtain credit for the fact, either with the friends to America, or the ministerial party in that country.   The Ministers had no intelligence of the matter, and the easterly winds then happening to prevail for a period of six weeks, it was treated as a fiction, both in and out of Parliament, and the translator as an enthusiast or a fabricator of false news.   Time, however, verified the fact, which he knew to be authentic, to its full extent, viz. that Colonel Ferguson, with eight hundred British troops, had been surprised ; himself slain, and his whole force defeated by sixteen hundred Carolina militia, mounted on horseback, hastily collected, and commanded by a few militia Colonels ! This spirited and successful enterprise, with its consequences, merits certainly a conspicuous place in the history of this great revolution ; for, like the surprise at Trenton, it changed the whole face of affairs, and restored energy to the friends of America in that important seat of war.

North-Carolina is a very fine country, beautifully diversified with pleasant hills, large valleys, and noble rivers, though none of them is navigable for vessels above 80 tons, except the rivers Fear and Clarendon ; yet as they intersect the country in every direction, they are admirably calculated for inland navigation.   There are, for this reason, no large towns ; but, from the various produce of this state, and the rapid increase of population, the white inhabitants, now amounting to near two hundred thousand, there is every reason to believe that it will

Marseilles and Amsterdam :* that the manners there are consequently polished and easy : that the inhabitants love pleasure, the arts, and society ; and that this country is more European in its manners than any in America.

Now, if there be any accuracy in this sketch, let me desire the reader to compare the spirit of the American States with their present government. I desire him to form the comparison at the present moment, in twenty, or in fifty years hence, and I am persuaded, that since all these governments resemble each other, as they are all democratical, he will still discover the traces of that original character, of that spirit which presides at the formation of people, and at the establishment of nations.

Virginia will retain this discriminating character longer than the other states; whether it be that prejudices are more durable, the more absurd, and the more frivolous they are, or that those which injure a part only of the human race, are more subject to remark than those which affect all mankind. In the present revolution, the ancient families have seen, with pain, new men occupying distinguished situations in the army, and in the magistracy; and the tories have even hence drawn advantages, to cool the ardour of the less zealous of the whigs. But the popular party have maintained their ground, and it is only to be regretted that they have not displayed the same activity in combating the English, as in disputing precedences. It is to be apprehended, however, that circumstances becoming less favourable to them, on a peace, they may be obliged entirely to give way, or to support themselves by factions, which must necessarily disturb the order of society. But if reason ought to blush at beholding such prejudices so strongly established among a new people, humanity has still more to suffer from the state of poverty, in which a great number of white people live in Virginia. It is in this country that I saw poor persons, for the first time, after I passed the sea ; for, in the midst of those rich plantations, where the negro

---

become not one of the least considerable on the continent, nor will the philosopher view the circumstances which forbid the formation of large towns as an evil, either in this country or in Virginia.—*Trans.*

* The author here refers to the former situation of the province ; but as I have already mentioned, the interior of this extensive state is daily peopling with a race of healthy, industrious planters, and is highly susceptible of every species of improvement. As for sea-ports, there are none worth mentioning but Charleston ; and as for Georgia, its position is in every respect similar to that of South-Carolina.— *Trans.*

alone is wretched, miserable huts are often to be met with, inhabited by whites, whose wane looks, and ragged garments.
bespeak poverty. At first I was puzzled to explain to myself,
how, in a country where there is still so much land to clear,
men who do not refuse to work, should remain in misery; but
I have since learned, that all these useless territories, these immense estates, with which Virginia is covered, have their proprietors. Nothing is more common than to see some of them
possessing five or six thousand acres of land, who clear out
only as much as their negroes can cultivate; yet will they not
give, nor even sell the smallest portion of them, because
they form a part of their possessions, and they are in
hopes of one day augmenting the number of their negroes. These white men, without fortune, and frequently
without industry, are straitened, therefore, on every side, and
reduced to the small number of acres they are able to acquire.
Now, the land not being good in general in America,* especially in Virginia, a considerable number of them is necessary,
in order to clear it with success, because they are the cattle
from which the cultivator derives his aid and his subsistence.
To the eastward are a great number of cleared grounds, but the
portions of land which are easily purchased there, and for almost nothing, consist always of at least two hundred acres;
besides, that to the southward, the climate is less healthy, and
the new settlers, without partaking of the wealth of Virginia,
share all the inconveniencies of the climate, and even the
indolence it inspires.†

---

* The land, *within the mountains*, in the hitherto settled parts of
North-America, are not in general very good, and it is of these only
that the Marquis speaks; but as the authors of the *Nouvelle Encyclopedie* observe, in their *new article* of the *United States*, this must have
been the case in almost every new-country, the soil of Europe having
been meliorated by the progress of population, the quantity of manure,
and the means by which the earth is protected from the effects of heavy
rains, &c. by care and cultivation. Abbé Raynal's remarks on this
subject, in his last work, called the Revolution of America, discover so
much ignorance as scarcely to merit the elaborate discussion bestowed on them by the ingenious authors of the *Encyclopedie*, who have
likewise transcribed from him several important passages, which have
been ably and fully refuted by Mr. Payne.—*Trans.*

† The indolence and dissipation of the middling and lower classes
of white inhabitants of Virginia, are such as to give pain to every reflecting mind. Horse-racing, cock-fighting, and boxing-matches, are
standing amusements, for which they neglect all business; and in the
latter of which they conduct themselves with a barbarity worthy of
their savage neighbours. The ferocious practice of stage-boxing in
England, is urbanity, compared with the Virginian mode of fighting.

Beneath this class of inhabitants, we must place the negroes, whose situation would be still more lamentable, did not their natural insensibility extenuate, in some degree, the sufferings annexed to slavery.   On seeing them ill lodged, ill clothed, and often oppressed with labour, I concluded that their treatment was as rigorous as elsewhere.   I have been assured, however, that it is extremely mild, in comparison with what they suffer in the sugar colonies ; and, in truth, you do not usually hear, as at Saint Domingo, and Jamaica, the sound of whips, and the cries of the unhappy wretches whose bodies they are

---

In their combats, unless specially precluded, they are admitted (to use their own term,) " to bite and goudge," which operations, when the first onset with fists is over, consists in fastening on the nose or ears of their adversaries with their teeth, and dexterously scooping out an eye ; on which account it is no uncommon circumstance to meet men in the prime of youth, deprived of one of those organs.   This is no traveller's exaggeration, I speak from knowledge and observation.   In the summer months it is very common to make a party on horseback to a limestone spring, near which there is usually some little hut with spirituous liquors, if the party are not themselves provided, where their debauch frequently terminates in a boxing-match, a horse-race, or perhaps both.   During a day's residence at Leesburgh, I was myself accidentally drawn into one of these parties, where I soon experienced the strength of the liquor, which was concealed by the refreshing coolness of the water.   While we were seated round the spring, at the edge of a delightful wood, four or five countrymen arrived, headed by a veteran cyclops, the terror of the neighbourhood, ready on every occasion to risk his remaining eye.   We soon found ourselves under the necessity of relinquishing our posts, and making our escape from these fellows, who evidently sought to provoke a quarrel.   On our return home, whilst I was rejoicing at our good fortune, and admiring the moderation of my company, we arrived at a plain spot of ground by a wood side, on which my horse no sooner set foot, than taking the bit between his teeth, off he went at full speed, attended by the whoops and hallooings of my companions.   An Englishman is not easily thrown off his guard on horseback ; but at the end of half a mile my horse stopped short, as if he had been shot, and threw me with considerable violence over his head ; my buckle, for I was without boots, entangled me in the stirrup, but fortunately broke into twenty pieces.   The company rode up, delighted with the adventure ; and it was then, for the first time, I discovered that I had been purposely induced, by one of my *friends*, to change horses with him for the afternoon ; that his horse had been accustomed to similar exploits on the same *race ground ;* that the whole of the business was neither more nor less than a Virginian piece of pleasantry ; and that my friends thought they had exhibited great moderation in not exposing me, at the spring, to the effects of " *biting and goudging.*"—*Trans.*

tearing to pieces.* This arises from the general character of the Virginians, which is more mild than that of the inhabitants of the sugar islands, who consist almost entirely of rapacious men, eager and pressing to make fortunes to return to Europe. Another reason is, that the produce of their culture not being of so much value, labour is not urged on them with so much severity ; and to do justice to both, it is because the negroes, on their side, are not so much addicted to cheating and thieving as in the islands. For the propagation of the black species being very rapid, and very considerable here, the greatest part of the negroes are born in the country ; and it is remarked that they are generally less depraved than those imported from Africa. I must likewise do the Virginians the justice to declare that many of them treat their negroes with great humanity. I must add, likewise, a still more honourable testimony, that in general they seem afflicted to have any slavery, and are constantly talking of abolishing it, and of contriving some other means of cultivating their estates. It is true that this opinion, which is almost generally received, is inspired by different motives. The philosophers and the young men, who are almost all educated in the principles of a sound philosophy, regard nothing but justice, and the rights of humanity. The fathers of families and such as are principally occupied with

---

* During the Translator's residence in the West-Indies, he took considerable pains to inform himself of the different modes of treatment of the negroes, by the principal European nations, possessing colonies in that quarter of the globe, the result of which was, that the Dutch are the most cruel ; the English more humane ; the French still more so ; and the Spaniards the most indulgent masters. He was greatly struck with this gradation, the truth of which seemed to be confirmed by his own observations ; but he leaves it to others to decide what influence the various forms of government, and the religious principles or prejudices of each of these nations, may have in the operation of this seeming paradox. A lover of truth will never shrink from the discussion of any question interesting to humanity, whatever be his political or religious bias. The Translator, from impulse, and from reason, is a strenuous assertor of the rights and original equality of mankind ; but it is an old remark, that the republicans are the worst masters, a position which pursued through the above succession, seems in some measure to receive a confirmation ; yet to him appears unaccountable from any given principles, unless it be the aristocratic principles, which to the misfortune of mankind, have hitherto uniformly taken possession of all the republican governments, and baffled the foresight of the virtuous and good. But there is reason to hope that the democracies of America will form a brilliant and consoling exception to the triumphant reproaches of the idolators of regal power.—*Trans.*

schemes of interest, complain that the maintenance of their negroes is very expensive ; that their labour is neither so productive nor so cheap, as that of day labourers, or white servants ; and, lastly, that epidemical disorders, which are very common, render both their property and their revenue extremely precarious. However this may be, it is fortunate that different motives concur in disgusting men with that tyranny which they exercise upon their fellow creatures at least, if not people entirely of the same species ; for the more we regard the negroes, the more must we be persuaded that the difference between them and us, consists in something more than complexion. As for the rest, it cannot be denied that it is a very delicate point to abolish slavery in America. The negroes in Virginia amount to two hundred thousand. They equal at least, if they do not exceed the number of white men. Necessarily united by interest, by the conformity of their situation, and the similarity of colour, they would unquestionably form a distinct people, from whom neither succour, virtue, nor labour, could be expected. Sufficient attention has not been paid to the difference between slavery, such as it exists in our colonies, and the slavery which was generally established among the ancients. A white slave had no other cause of humiliation, than his actual state ; on his being freed, he mixed immediately with free men, and became their equal. Hence that emulation among the slaves to obtain their liberty, either as a favour, or to purchase it with the fruit of their labour. There were two advantages in this ; the possibility of enfranchising them without danger, and that ambition, which almost generally took place among them, and turned to the advantage of morals and of industry. But in the present case, it is not only the slave who is beneath his master, it is the negro who is beneath the white man. No act of enfranchisement can efface this unfortunate distinction ; accordingly we do not see the negroes very anxious to obtain their freedom, nor much pleased when they have obtained it. The free negroes continue to live with the negro slaves, and never with the white men, insomuch that interest alone makes them desirous of quitting slavery, when they are endowed with a particular industry, of which they wish to reap the profits. It appears, therefore, that there is no other method of abolishing slavery, than by getting rid of the negroes, a measure which must be very gradually adopted. The best expedient would be to export a great number of males, and to encourage the marriage of white men with the females. For this purpose the law must be abrogated which transmits slavery by the side of the mother ; or it might be enacted, that every female slave shall become, *ipso facto*, free, by marrying a freeman. From respect to property, perhaps it

might be just to require of the latter, a compensation to be fixed by law, to be paid either in labour or in money, as an indem-
nity to the proprietors of the negress ; but it is certain, at all
events, that such a law, aided by the illicit, but already well
established commerce between the white men and negresses,
could not fail of giving birth to a race of mulattoes, which
would produce another of *Quarterons*, and so on until the colour
should be totally effaced.

But I have enlarged sufficiently on this subject, which has
not escaped the policy and philosophy of the present age. I
have only to apologise for not having treated it with *declama-
tion ;* but it has always been my opinion that eloquence can influence only the resolutions of the moment, and that every
thing which can only be effected by time alone, must be the
result of reason ; it is not difficult, however, to add ten or a
dozen pages to these reflections, which are to be considered as
a symphony composed only of the principal parts, *con corni ad
libitum.*

We have seen the inconveniencies of slavery, and of the too
extensive possession of territory in Virginia ; let us now examine the inconsiderable number of advantages arising from
them. The Virginians have the reputation, and with reason,
of living nobly in their houses, and of being hospitable; they
give strangers not only a willing, but a liberal reception. This
arises, on one hand, from their having no large towns, where
they may assemble, by which means they are little acquainted
with society, except from the visits they make ; and, on the
other, their lands and their negroes furnishing them with every
article of consumption, and the necessary service, this renown-
ed hospitality costs them very little. Their houses are spacious, and ornamented, but their apartments are not commodious ; they make no ceremony of putting three or four persons
into the same room;* nor do these make any objection to their
being thus heaped together ; for being in general ignorant of
the comfort of reading and writing, they want nothing in their
whole house but a bed, a dining-room, and a drawing-room for
company. The chief magnificence of the Virginians consists

---

* Throughout America, in private houses, as well as in the inns,
several people are crowded together in the same room ; and in the
latter it very commonly happens, that after you have been some time
in bed, a stranger of any condition, (for there is little distinction,) comes
into the room, pulls off his clothes, and places himself, without ceremony, between your sheets.*—*Trans.*

* This was probably the ease at the time the translator wrote; but at the present day there is no country in which travellers can be more retired, or better
accommodated than in the United States.

in furniture, linen, and plate; in which they resemble our ancestors, who had neither cabinets nor wardrobes in their castles, but contented themselves with a well-stored cellar, and a handsome buffet. If they sometimes dissipate their fortunes, it is by gaming, hunting, and horse-races;* but the latter are of some utility, inasmuch as they encourage the breed of horses, which are really very handsome in Virginia. We see that the women have little share in the amusements of the men; beauty here serves only to procure them husbands; for the most wealthy planters, giving but a small fortune with their daughters, their fate is usually decided by their figure. The consequence of this is, that they are often pert and coquettish before, and sorrowful helpmates after marriage. The luxury of being served by slaves still farther augments their natural indolence; they are always surrounded by a great number of them, for their own service, and that of their children, whom they content themselves with suckling only. They, as well as their husbands, pay attention to them when young, and neglect them when grown up. We may say in general of the Americans, as of the English, that they are very fond of their *infants*, and care little for their *children*. It would be a delicate discussion, perhaps, to inquire, whether this be really a natural sentiment, and whether our conduct, which is very different, be not the result of self-love, or of ambition; but we may safely affirm, that the care we take of ours, is a means of attaching ourselves to them, and of ensuring their reciprocal attachment; a sentiment the nobleness and utility of which cannot be contested.†

I was desirous of celebrating the virtues peculiar to the Virginians, and in spite of my wishes, I am obliged to limit myself to their magnificence and hospitality. It is not in my power to add generosity; for they are strongly attached to their interests; and their great riches, joined to their pretensions, gives more deformity to this vice. I ought, in the first

---

* I have already spoken of horse-races, but it is with regret I add, that the general spirit of gaming is prevalent in this as well as in all the United States, but more particularly throughout the southern ones, which has already been attended with suicide, and all its baneful consequences.—*Trans.*

† I confess myself at a loss to discover from what source of observation the author has derived the fact on which he reasons so ingeniously. Perhaps it is the secret spirit of national prejudice that has led me, who was born an Englishman, to reverse the remark, as applied to the two countries of France and England; but I leave the fact and the discussion to more acute observers.—*Trans.*

instance, to have treated of the article of religion ; but there is nothing remarkable respecting it in this country, except the facility with which they dispense with it. The established religion, previous to the revolution, was that of the Church of England, which we know requires Episcopacy, and that every priest must be ordained by a bishop. Before the war, persons destined to the church, went to England, to study and to be ordained. It is impossible, therefore, in the present circumstances, to supply the vacancies of the pastors who drop off. What has been the consequence of this? That the churches have remained shut; the people have done without a pastor, and not a thought has been employed towards any settlement of an English church, independent of England.* The most complete toleration is established; but the other communions have made no acquisition from the losses of the former ; each sect has remained in its original situation ; and this sort of religious interregnum, has been productive of no disorder. The clergy have besides received a severe check in the new constitution, which excludes them from all share in the government, even from the right of voting at elections. It is true that the judges and lawyers are subjected to the same exclusion, but that is from another motive; to prevent the public interest from falling into competition with that of individuals. The legislature dreaded the reaction of these interests; it has been thought proper, in short, to form a sort of separate body in the state, under the name of the Judicial Body. These general

---

* During the war there was a great scarcity of ministers of the Episcopal church, on account of the numbers of that body who attached themselves to England, which was pretty generally the case ; but after the peace, many young Americans, distinguished for the gown, finding a repugnance on the part of the English bishops, got ordained by the nonjuring bishops in Scotland. An act has at length passed, however, to authorise the ordination of foreign clergy by the English bishops, which is evidently intended to promote the cause of the hierarchy in the United States. I shall here take the opportunity of mentioning, that on account of the great scarcity of bibles, a new edition was published by one Aikin, a printer, of Philadelphia, by order of Congress, under the inspection of the reverend Mr. White, brother-in-law to Mr. Morris, and the other chaplain to that body ; but such are ancient prejudices, that very few of the zealous followers either of Luther or of Calvin, could be brought to look upon it as the genuine old book. The wary devotees, dreaded, no doubt, similar errors to that for which the company of stationers were mulcted in the time of king Charles ; the omission of the *negative* in one of the commandments, by printing " Thou *shalt* do murder."—*Trans.*

views are perhaps salutary in themselves; but they are attended with an inconvenience at the present moment; for the lawyers, who are certainly the most enlightened part of the community, are removed from the civil councils, and the administration is entrusted either to ignorant, or to the least skilful men. This is the principal objection made in the country to the present form of government, which to me appears excellent in many respects. It is every where in print, and easily to be procured; but I shall endeavour to give a sketch of it in a few words. It is composed, 1st. Of the Assembly of Deputies, named by the cities and counties, a body corresponding with the House of Commons. 2d. Of a Senate, the members of which are elected by several united counties, in a greater or less number, according to the population of the counties, which answers to the House of Peers. 3d. Of an Executive Council, of which the governor is president, and the members chosen by the two Chambers; a substitute for the executive power of the king in England.*

It is not by accident that I have postponed the consideration of every thing respecting the progress of the arts and sciences in this country, until the conclusion of my reflections on Virginia; I have done it expressly because the mind, after bestowing its attention on the variety of human institutions, reposes itself with pleasure on those which tend to the perfection of the understanding, and the progress of information; and above all, because having found myself under the necessity of speaking less advantageously of this state than I wished to have done, I am happy to conclude with an article, which is wholly in their commendation. The college of William and Mary, whose founders are announced by the very name, is a noble establishment which embellishes Williamsburgh, and does honour to Virginia. The beauty of the edifice is surpassed by the richness of its library, and that still farther by the distinguished merit of several of the professors, such as the Doctors Madison, Wythe, Bellini, &c. &c., who may be regarded as living books, at once affording precepts and examples. I must likewise add, that the zeal of these professors has been crowned with the most distinguished success, and that they have already formed many distinguished characters, ready to serve their country in the various departments of government. Among these, it is with

---

* See the constitutions of the different states, republished in England by the reverend Mr. Jackson, and the excellent translation from the original, with notes, published in Paris by the *Duke de la Rochefoucault—Trans.*

pleasure I mention Mr. Short, with whom I was particularly connected. After doing justice to the exertions of the University of Williamsburg, for such is the college of William and Mary ; if it be necessary for its farther glory to cite miracles, I shall only observe that they created me a Doctor of Laws.

Williamsburgh, 1st of May, 1782.

TRAVELS IN NORTH-AMERICA.

PART III.

JOURNAL OF A TOUR

IN NEW-HAMPSHIRE, THE STATE OF MASSACHUSETTS,

AND UPPER PENNSYLVANIA.

TRAVELS IN NORTH-AMERICA.

CHAPTER I.

THE Baron de Viomenil having joined the army in the beginning of October, I ought to have resigned to him of course
the command of the first division, so that I had now no necessary occupation, unless I had chosen to take the command of
the second division, in which case I must have superseded the
Comte de Viomenil, which was far from my intention ; it depended upon myself, therefore, to return to Philadelphia, to
wait for Mr. de Rochambeau, who was expected there, after
marching his troops to the eastward ; but my departure would
have too plainly discovered the intention of embarking them,
which it was wished to keep a secret, at least until they had
reached Hartford. The Comte de Viomenil, on the other hand,
being desirous of visiting Saratoga, the Baron de Viomenil requested me to retain the command of the first, whilst he took that
of the second division. I consented, therefore, to sacrifice another listless and fatiguing fortnight, and marched with the troops
to Hartford.* I submitted also not to return to the southward,

---

* The Translator attended the French army on their march, nearly
the whole way, from Alexandria to the North river, and was a witness
to their strict discipline, and the surprising harmony between them
and the people of the country, to whom they gave not the slightest
reason of complaint. He insists the more on this fact, as it appears to
him no less singular than interesting. On their arrival at their quarters
on the march, the whole country came to see them, and it was a general scene of gaiety and good humour. When they encamped at Alexandria, on the ground formerly occupied by Braddock, the most elegant and handsome young ladies of the neighbourhood danced with the
officers on the turf, in the middle of the camp, to the sound of military
music ; and, (a circumstance which will appear singular to European
ideas,) the circle was in a great measure composed of soldiers, who,
from the heat of the weather, had disengaged themselves from their
clothes, retaining not an article of dress except their shirts, which

before M. de Rochambeau, and to accompany him thither after seeing them embarked. I determined, however, to avail myself of these circumstances to visit the upper part of the state of Massachusetts, and New-Hampshire, which I had not yet seen. With this view, I set out from Hartford the 4th of November, the very day the Comte de Rochambeau marched with the first division to encamp at Bolton.* It was two in the afternoon when I got on horseback; my companions were Messieurs Lynch, de Montesquieu, the Baron de Taleyrand, and Mr. de Vaudreuil. We followed the Bolton route to a cross road about three miles beyond the Meeting-house, where there is a stone for the traveller's direction. We here took to the left, to reach Mr. Kendal's tavern, in the township of Coventry, seventeen miles from Bolton, and four from the cross-roads. In a quarter of an hour we met Mr. Kendal, who was on horseback, carrying letters to Mr. de Rochambeau, from the Marquis de Vaudreuil, our Admiral; for this route, which is the shortest between Bolton and Hartford, was preferred for the chain of expresses between the fleet, the army, and Philadelphia. Mr. de Montesquieu returned with him to Bolton, to know whether these letters contained any interesting intelligence. As we travelled slowly, he rejoined us in half an hour, and informed us, that they were only answers to those he had received from the army, with the state of the troops to be embarked. Before we reached Mr. Kendal's, we passed a hut which scarcely merited the name of a *hoghouse*, and was only half covered, but which was inhabited by a man who accosted us in French; he was a labourer from Canada, who had frequently changed habitations, and had seven children. We were all lodged and treated at Mr. Kendal's, who is above the common class, and is more occupied in commerce than in farming; he sat down to table with us, and we were pleased with his conversation.

---

in general were neither extremely long, nor in the best condition; nor did this occasion the least embarrassment to the ladies, many of whom were of highly polished manners, and the most exquisite delicacy; or to their friends or parents; so whimsical and arbitrary are manners.—*Trans*.

* The French army, at the time the Marquis speaks of, had been for some time encamped at Crompont, near Cortland's manor, a few miles from that of General Washington's, and between which there was a daily intercourse. The Translator dined, in October, 1782, in General Washington's tent, with the Marquis de Laval, the Baron de Viomenil, and several French officers, within hearing of the British guns, which were at that period happily become a *brutum fulmen*.—*Trans*.

We set out at half past eight in the morning of the 5th, and travelled through a very agreeable and variegated country, presenting us every moment with the view of handsome habitations. The face of the country is unequal, but the hills are neither high nor steep. We stopped to bait our horses at Mr. Clark's tavern, in Ashford township, by the side of the rivulet of Mounthope, on this side of a river marked in the chart by the name of Monchoas, and of a branch of that river called Bigslack. We left this place at two o'clock, the country still continuing to be pleasant. I was particularly struck with the position of Woodstock meeting-house, which is placed on an eminence, commanding a very gay and well-peopled country. There are several inns around this meeting-house, but we went three miles and a half farther, to Mrs. Chandler's. Our journey this day, was thirty-three miles, it being seventeen from Clark's to Chandler's tavern. This house is kept by a widow, who was from home, and Mr. Lynch, who had preceded us, was very ill received by an old servant maid. We found him in great distress, because she would make no preparation of even killing a few chickens, before she received the orders of her mistress. Fortunately, however, the latter arrived in a quarter of an hour, in a sort of single horse chaise, and we found her very polite and obliging, she gave us a tolerable supper, and we were neatly lodged.*

The 6th we set out at ten o'clock, having been apprized that on reaching Oxford, it would be necessary to inquire the road at a tavern kept by Mr. Lord, at twelve miles distance; but the weather being bad when we got there, we determined to stop a couple of hours until the rain ceased, which had continued the whole morning. We had two roads to choose; that which goes through Shrewsbury would have led us more directly to Portsmouth; but I preferred that by Grafton, which leads to Concord; that celebrated spot, where the first blood was shed, which commenced the civil war. The rain abating a little, we resumed our journey at two, and passed through Salton, a pretty enough place, where there are several well-built houses; but the rain redoubling, we were obliged to halt seven miles farther on, at Baron's tavern, where we were well received. We dried ourselves by a good fire, in a very handsome apartment, adorned with good prints, and handsome mahogany furniture; and finding the useful correspond with the agreeable in this house, we reconciled ourselves to the bad weather, which had forced us into such good quarters.

We left this place at nine the next morning, the road lead-

---

* This is one of the best houses I met with in America.—*Trans.*

ing us through Grafton, after which we passed Blackstone
river, and arrived at Gale's tavern, fifteen miles from Baron's,
after a journey through a very pleasant country. I remarked
that the meadows, of which there are a great number, were in
general intersected and watered by trenches cut on purpose.
Mr. Gales informed me that these meadows were worth from
ten to twenty dollars an acre ; from one of which, in his possession, he reaped four tons of hay an acre. The after-grass
is for the cattle, to produce butter and cheese, principally
of this country. The price of meat is here about twopence-
halfpenny the pound of fourteen ounces. After baiting our
horses, we continued our journey by Marlborough, where
there are handsome houses, and more collected than in the
other towns or townships. We at length entered a wood,
which conducted us to the river of Concord, or Billerika, over
which we passed by a bridge about a mile from the Meeting-
house, and at the same distance from Mr. John's, where it was
near nine o'clock before we arrived. This is an excellent inn,
kept by a most determined whig, who acted his part in the affair of Concord.* Major Pitcairn, who commanded the English on this occasion, had lodged frequently at his house, in
travelling through the country in disguise ; a method he had
sometimes taken, though very dangerous, of gaining information to communicate to General Gage. The day on which he
headed the English troops to Concord, he arrived at seven in
the morning, followed by a company of grenadiers, and went
immediately to Mr. John's tavern, the door of which being
shut, he knocked several times, and on the refusal to open it,
ordered his grenadiers to force it. Entering it himself the
first, he pushed Mr. John with such violence as to throw him
down, and afterwards placed a guard over him, frequently in-
sisting on his pointing out the magazines of the rebels. The

---

* It took place on the 19th of April, 1775. General Gage had
detached from Boston all his grenadiers, light infantry, and some other
troops, amounting together to 900 men, under the orders of Lieutenant-Colonel Smith, and Major Pitcairn. At Lexington they fell in
with a company of militia, whom they found under arms. The English, in a haughty tone, ordered the Americans to disperse, which
they refused, and whilst the conversation was confined to words, the
English fired without giving notice, and at that discharge killed seven
or eight Americans, who had made no disposition to shelter themselves
from the fire ; they were compelled to give way to numbers. The
English advanced to Concord, where they paid dearly for their violence,
and this first act of hostility, for which they were alone responsible,
cost them near 300 men. Major Pitcairn was slain at the battle of
Bunker's Hill, a short time after the affair of Concord.

Americans had in fact collected some cannon and warlike stores at Concord, but having received timely notice in the night, they had removed every thing into the woods, except three twenty-four pounders, which remained in the prison yard, of which Mr. John was the keeper. Major Pitcairn carrying his violence so far as to clap a pistol to his throat, Mr. John, who had himself been in a passion, grew calm, and tried to pacify the English commander. He assured him that there were only the above three pieces at Concord, and that he should see them, if he would follow him. He conducted him to the prison, where the English entered, he says, in a rage at seeing the *Yankees* so expert in mounting cannon, and in providing themselves with every thing necessary for the service of artillery, such as sponges, rammers, &c. Major Pitcairn made his men destroy the carriages, and break the trunnions; then ordered the prison to be set open, where he found two prisoners, one of whom being a tory, he released.

The first moments of trouble being over, Major Pitcairn returned to Mr. John's, where he breakfasted, and paid for it. The latter resumed his station of innkeeper; numbers of the English came to ask for rum, which he measured out as usual, and made them pay exactly. In the mean time, the Americans, who had passed the river in their retreat, began to rally, and to unite with those, who, apprised by the alarum bells, and various expresses, were coming to their assistance. The disposition Major Pitcairn had to make for his security, whilst he was employed in searching for, and destroying the ammunition, was by no means difficult; it was only necessary to place strong guards at the two bridges to the north and south, which he had done. Towards ten o'clock in the morning, the firing of musketry was heard at the north bridge, on which the English rallied at the place appointed, on a height, in a church-yard situated to the right of the road, and opposite the town-house. Three hundred Americans, who were assembled on the other side of the river, descended from the heights by a winding road which leads obliquely to the bridge, but which, at sixty paces from the river, turns to the left, and comes straight upon it. Until they had reached this angle, they had their flank covered by a small stone wall; but when they came to this point, they marched up boldly to the bridge, which they found the enemy employed in breaking down. The latter fired the first, but the Americans fell upon them, and they easily gave way, which appears rather extraordinary. Mr. John affirms that the English at first imagined the Americans had no ball, but that they soon found their error, on seeing several of their soldiers wounded. They even speak here of an officer, who informed his men that they had nothing to fear, for that *the Americans fired only with powder;* but a drummer who was near him receiving at the moment a musket shot, replied, *take care of that powder, Captain.* The English had three men killed here, and several wounded, two of them were officers. The Americans now passed the bridge, and formed immediately on a small eminence, to the left of the road, as they were situated, and at short cannon shot from that on which the English were collected. There they remained some time watching each other; but the sight of some houses on fire irritated the Americans, and determined them to march towards the English, who then retreated by the Lexington road, which forming an elbow, the Americans, who knew the country, took the string of the bow, and got up with them before they advanced a mile. It was here the retreating fight began, of which every body has seen the accounts, and which continued to Lexington, where the English were joined by the reinforcement under the command of Earl Percy.

It was on the morning of the 8th that I examined the field of battle at Concord, which took me up till half past ten, when I resumed my journey. Ten miles from Concord is Billerika, a pretty considerable township; the country here was less fertile, and the road rather stony. We halted at South-Andover, five miles beyond Billerika, at a bad inn, kept by one Forster; his wife had some beautiful children, but she appeared disordered, and I thought her rather drunk. She showed me, with much importance, a book her eldest daughter was reading, and I found it, to my no small surprise, to be a book of prayers in Italian. This daughter, who was about seventeen, repeated also a prayer in the Indian language, of which she understood not a word, having learnt it accidentally from an Indian servant; but her mother thought all this admirable. We contented ourselves with baiting our horses in this wretched alehouse, and set out at half past one, travelled through South and North-Andover. North Parish, or North Andover, is a charming place, where there are a great number of very handsome houses, a quantity of meadows, and fine cattle. Almost on quitting this long township, you enter Bradford, where night overtook us, and we travelled two or three miles in the dark before we reached Haverhill ferry. It was half past six before we had crossed it, and got to Mr. Harward's inn, where we had a good supper, and good lodgings. At Haverhill, the Merrimack is only fit for vessels of thirty tons, but much larger ones are built here, which are floated down empty to Newbury. Three miles above Haverhill are falls, and higher up the river is only navigable for boats. The trade of this town formerly consisted in timber for ship-building, which has been suspended since the war. It is pretty considerable, and tolerably well built; and its situation, in the form of an amphitheatre on the left shore of the Merrimack, gives it many agreeable aspects.

We left this place the 9th, at nine in the morning, our road lying through Plastow, a pretty considerable township; after which we met with woods, and a wild and horrid country. We saw a great number of pines and epicias; there are also several large lakes, some of which are traced upon the chart. Since we quitted the confines of Connecticut, I have in general observed a great number of these ponds, which contributed to increase the resemblance between this country and that of the Bourbonnois, and the Nivernois, in France. Twelve miles from Haverhill is Kingston, a township inferior to those we had observed upon the route; and at the end of eighteen miles is Exeter, at present the capital of New-Hampshire, that is to say, the place where the President or Governor resides, and the members of the state assemble. It is rather a handsome town, and is a sort of port; for vessels of seventy tons can come up, and others as large as three or four hundred tons are built here, which are floated down Exeter river into the bay of that name, and thence to Piscataqua. We stopped at a very handsome inn kept by Mr. Ruspert, which we quitted at half past two; and though we rode very fast, night was coming on when we reached Portsmouth. The road from Exeter is very hilly. We passed through Greenland, a very populous township, composed of well built houses, Cattle here are abundant, but not so handsome as in Connecticut, and the state of Massachusetts. They are dispersed over fine meadows, and it is a beautiful sight to see them collected near their hovels in the evening. This country presents, in every respect, the picture of abundance and of happiness. The road from Greenland to Portsmouth is wide and beautiful, interspersed with habitations, so that these two townships almost touch. I alighted at Mr. Brewster's, where I was well lodged; he seemed to me a respectable man, and much attached to his country.

In the morning of the 10th I went to pay a visit to Mr. Albert de Rioms, captain of the Pluton,* who had a house on shore, where he resided for his health; he invited me to dinner, which he advised me to accept, as the Comte de Vaudreuil was in great confusion on board his ship, the mizen mast of which had been struck by lightning five days before, and which

---

* The Marquis de Vaudreuil's squadron was then at Boston, and some of his ships were refitting, and taking in masts at Portsmouth. M. de Albert de Rioms is the officer who commanded the evolutions of the French squadron, on the late visit of the king to Cherbourg.—*Trans.*

penetrated to his first battery; but he offered me his boat to
carry me on board the Auguste.   In returning for my cloak, I
happened to pass by the meeting, precisely at the time of service, and had the curiosity to enter, where I remained above
half an hour, that I might not interrupt the preacher, and to
show my respect for the assembly ; the audience were not numerous on account of the severe cold, but I saw some handsome women, elegantly dressed.   Mr. Barkminster, a young
minister, spoke with a great deal of grace, and reasonably
enough for a preacher.   I could not help admiring the address
with which he introduced politics into his sermon, by comparing the christians redeemed by the blood of Jesus Christ, but
still compelled to fight against the flesh and sin, to the thirteen
United States, who, notwithstanding they have acquired liberty
and independence, are under the necessity of employing all
their force to combat a formidable power, and to preserve those
invaluable treasures.   It was near twelve when I embarked in
Mr. Albert's boat, and saw on the left, near the little Island of
Rising Castle, the America,* (the ship given by Congress to
the king of France,) which had been just launched, and appeared to me a fine ship.   I left on the right the Isle of Wash-

---

* The America is the vessel given by Congress to the king of
France, to replace the Magnifique, lost on Lovel's-Island in Boston
harbour, when the French fleet entered that port some months after
the defeat of the Comte de Grasse.   This ship was designed for the
well known *Paul Jones*, who by his command of the little squadron
on the coasts of England, had acquired the title of commodore, and
was sighing after that of admiral of America, which Congress, no bad
appreciators of merit, thought proper to refuse him.   The Translator
met him at a public table at Boston, on his return from Portsmouth,
where he told the company, that notwithstanding the reason he had to
be discontented, he had given his advice in the construction and launch-
ing of the vessel, in which latter operation, however, the ship struck
fast on the slip, but without any material damage.   This accident is
not intended by any means as an imputation on Mr. Jones, who certainly was fortunate enough, at one time, to render considerable service to
America.   He is said to have acquired a considerable property by the
prizes he made in that cruise, but his officers and crews complain (the
Translator does not say with what justice) that there has never been
any distribution of the prize money, and that numbers of his maimed
and mutilated sailors were reduced to beg for a subsistence in France,
and elsewhere, to the discredit of America.   Mr. Jones read some
pretty enough verses in his own honour to the same company, at
Brackett's tavern in Boston, extracted from a London newspaper, and
said to be written by Lady Craven.   The America is now at Brest,
and is esteemed one of the handsomest ships in the French navy.—
Trans.

ington, on which stands a fort of that name.   It is built in the
form of a star, the parapets of which are supported by stakes,
and was not finished.   Then leaving Newcastle on the right,
and Bittery on the left, we arrived at the anchoring ground,
within the first pass.   I found Mr. Vaudreuil on board, who presented me to the officers of his ship, and afterwards to those
of the detachment of the army, among whom were three officers of my former regiment of Guienne, at present called
Viennois.   He then took me to see the ravages made by the
lightning, of which M. de Biré, who then commanded the ship,
M. de Vaudreuil having slept on shore, gave me the following
account: at half past two in the morning, in the midst of a
very violent rain, a dreadful explosion was heard suddenly, and
the sentinel, who was in the gallery, came in a panic into the
council chamber, where he met with M. Biré, who had leaped
to the foot of his bed, and they were both struck with a strong
sulphureous smell.   The bell was immediately rung, and the
ship examined, when it was found that the mizen mast was cut
short in two, four feet from the forecastle; that it had been
lifted in the air, and fallen perpendicularly on the quarter-
deck, through which it had penetrated, as well as the second
battery.   Two sailors were crushed by its fall, two others, who
never could be found, had doubtless been thrown into the sea
by the commotion, and several were wounded.

At one o'clock we returned on shore to dine with M. Albert
de Rioms, and our fellow guests were M. de Biré, who acted
as flag captain, though but a lieutenant; M. de Mortegues,
who formerly commanded the Magnifique (lost at the same
period on Lovel's-Island in Boston harbour) and was destined
to the command of the America; M. de Siber, lieutenant *en
pied* of the Pluton; M. d'Hizeures, captain of the regiment of
Viennois, &c.; after dinner we went to drink tea with Mr. Langdon.   He is a handsome man, and of a noble carriage; he
has been a member of Congress, and is now one of the first people of the country; his house is elegant and well furnished, and
the apartments admirably well wainscotted; he has a good manuscript chart of the harbour of Portsmouth.   Mrs. Langdon, his
wife, is young, fair, and tolerably handsome, but I conversed less
with her than with her husband, in whose favour I was prejudiced, from knowing that he had displayed great courage and
patriotism at the time of Burgoyne's expedition.   For repairing to the council chamber, of which he was a member, and
perceiving that they were about to discuss some affairs of little
consequence, he addressed them as follows: " Gentlemen, you
may talk as long as you please, but I know that the enemy is
on our frontiers, and that I am going to take my pistols, and
mount my horse, to ·combat with my fellow-citizens;" the

greatest part of the members of the council and assembly followed him, and joined General Gates at Saratoga. As he was marching day and night, reposing himself only in the woods, a negro servant who attended him says to him, " Master, you are hurting yourself, but no matter, you are going to fight for liberty; I should suffer also patiently if I had liberty to defend." " Don't let that stop you," replied Mr. Langdon, " from this moment you are free." The negro followed him, behaved with courage, and has never quitted him. On leaving Mr. Langdon's, we went to pay a visit to Colonel Wentworth, who is respected in this country, not only from his being of the same family with Lord Rockingham, but from his general acknowledged character for probity and talents. He conducted the naval department at Portsmouth, and our officers are never weary in his commendation. From Mr. Wentworth's, M. de Vaudreuil and M. de Rioms took me to Mrs. Whipple's, a widow lady, who is, I believe, sister-in-law to General Whipple; she is neither young nor handsome, but appeared to me to have a good understanding, and gaiety. She is educating one of her nieces, only fourteen years old, who is already charming. Mrs. Whipple's house, as well as that of Mr. Wentworth's, and all those I saw at Portsmouth, are very handsome and well furnished.

I proposed, on the morning of the 11th, to make a tour among the islands in the harbour, but some snow having fallen, and the weather being by no means inviting, I contented myself with paying visits to some officers of the navy, and among others to the Comte de Vaudreuil, who had slept on shore the preceding night ; after which we again met at dinner at Mr. Albert's, a point of union which was always agreeable. M. d'Hizeures had ordered the music of the regiment of Viennois to attend, and I found with pleasure, that the taste for music, which I had inspired into that corps, still subsisted, and that the ancient musicians had been judiciously replaced.* After dinner, we again drank tea at Mr. Langdon's, and then paid a visit to Dr. Brackett, an esteemed physician of the country, and afterwards to Mr. Thompson. The latter was born in England ; he is a good seamen, and an excellent shipbuilder, and is besides a sensible man, greatly attached to his new country, which it is only fifteen years since he adopted. His wife is an American, and pleases by her countenance, but still more by her amiable and polite behaviour. We finished

---

* The Marquis de Chastellux, among his various accomplishments, is distinguished not only in the character of an amateur, but for his scientific knowledge of music.— *Trans.*

the evening at Mr. Wentworth's, where the Comte de Vaudreuil lodged ; he gave us a very handsome supper, without ceremony, during which the conversation was gay and agreeable.

The 12th I set out, after taking leave of M. de Vaudreuil, whom I met as he was coming to call on me, and it was certainly with the greatest sincerity that I testified to him my sense of the polite manner in which I had been received by him, and by the officers under his command.

The following are the ideas which I had an opportunity of acquiring relative to the town of Portsmouth. It was in a pretty flourishing state before the war, and carried on the trade of ship timber, and salt fish. It is easy to conceive that this commerce must have greatly suffered since the commencement of the troubles, but notwithstanding, Portsmouth is, perhaps, of all the American towns, that which will gain the most by the present war. There is every appearance of its becoming to *New*-England, what the other Portsmouth is to the *Old* ; that is to say, that this place will be made choice of as the depôt of the continental marine. The access to the harbour is easy, the road immense, and there are seven fathoms water as far up as two miles above the town ; add to this, that notwithstanding its northern situation, the harbour of Portsmouth is never frozen, an advantage arising from the rapidity of the current. This circumstance, joined to its proximity to the timber for ship-building, especially for masts, which can only be balanced by the harbour of Rhode-Island, will doubtless determine the choice of Congress. But if a naval establishment be thought necessary at Portsmouth, the quays, the rope-walks, the arsenals, &c. must be placed in the islands, and not on the continent ; for it would be easy for an enemy's army to land there, and take possession of the town, the local situation of which would require too considerable a developement of fortification to shelter it from insult. I imagine, however, that a good entrenched camp might be formed between the two creeks, but I am only able to judge of that from a slight observation, and from charts.

It has happened in New-Hampshire, as in the state of Massachusetts, that the losses of commerce have turned to the advantage of agriculture ; the capitals of the rich, and the industry of the people having flowed back from the coasts towards the interior of the country, which has profited rapidly by the reflux. It is certain that this country has a very flourishing appearance, and that new houses are building, and new farms are settling every day.

New-Hampshire hitherto has no permanent constitution, and its present government is no more than a simple convention ;

it much resembles that of Pennsylvania, for it consists of one legislative body, composed of the representatives of the people, and the executive council; which has for its chief, a President, instead of Governor. But during my stay at Portsmouth, I learnt that there was an assembly at Exeter, for the purpose of establishing a constitution, the principal articles of which were already agreed on. This constitution will be founded on the same principles as those of New-York and Massachusetts. There will be, as in the former, an executive power vested in the hands of the Governor, the Chancellor and the Chief Justices ; the latter of whom will be perpetual, at least *quam diu se bene gesserint*, during good behaviour, but the members of the senate will be annually changed, and the requisite qualification of a senator, very inconsiderable, which I think is a great inconvenience.* Mr. Langdon observes, and perhaps with reason that the country is as yet too young, and the materials wanting to give this senate all the weight and consistence it ought to have, as in Maryland, where the senators are elected for three years, and must possess at least five hundred pounds.

When I was at Portsmouth the necessaries of life were very dear, owing to the great drought of the preceding summer. Corn costs two dollars a bushel, (of sixty pounds weight) oats almost as much, and Indian corn was extremely scarce. I shall hardly be believed when I say, that I paid eight livres ten sols (about seven shillings and three pence) a day for each horse. Butcher's meat only was cheap, selling at two-pence halfpenny a pound. That part of New-Hampshire bordering on the coast is not fertile ; there are good lands at forty or fifty miles distance from the sea, but the expense of carriage greatly augments the price of articles, when sold in the more inhabited parts. As for the value of landed property it is dear enough for so new a country. Mr. Ruspert, my landlord, paid seventy pounds currency per annum, (at eighteen livres, or fifteen shillings the pound) for his inn. Lands sell at from ten to sixteen dollars an acre. The country produces little fruit, and the cider is indifferent.

The road from Portsmouth to Newbury passes through a barren country. Hampton is the only township you meet with, and there are not such handsome houses there as at Greenland. As we had only twenty miles to go, I was unwilling to stop, and desired the Vicomte de Vaudreuil only, to go on a little before us to dinner. It was two o'clock when we reached Merrimack ferry, and from the shore we saw the open-

---

* A new form of government has been established since the peace.—*Trans.*

ing of the harbour, the channel of which passes near the northern extremity of Plumb-Island, on which is a small fort, with a few cannon and mortars. Its situation appears to me well chosen, at least as far as I was capable of judging from a distance. At the entrance of the harbour is a bar, on which there are only eighteen feet water in the highest tides, so that although it be a very commercial place, it has always been respected by the English. Several frigates have been built here ; among others, the Charlestown, and the Alliance.* The har-

---

* The privateers which so greatly molested the British trade were chiefly from the ports of Newbury, Beverley, and Salem, in which places large fortunes were made by this means : and such must ever be the case in any future war, from the peculiarity of their position, whence they may run out at any season of the year, and commit depredations on any of the maritime powers to which America is hostile, with little fear of retaliation. Newfoundland, Nova-Scotia, the Gulfs of St. Lawrence, and of Florida, and the whole trade of the West-India Archipelago, are in a manner at their doors. However Great Britain may affect to despise America, she is perhaps, even in her present infant state, from various circumstances, the most formidable enemy she can have to cope with, in case of a rupture ; for, as nations ought collectively to be dispassionate, though individuals are not, it behooves her to reflect, where, and in what manner she can return the blow. Mr. Jefferson, the present Minister of the United States at Versailles, among other excellent observations on this subject has the following, which I extract with pleasure from his Notes on Virginia, a most interesting work, with which I have just privately been favoured. " The sea is the field on which we should meet an European enemy, on that element it is necessary we should possess some power. To aim at such a navy as the greater nations of Europe possess would be a foolish and wicked waste of the energies of our countrymen. It would be to pull on our heads that load of military expense which makes the European labourer go supperless to bed, and moistens his bread with the sweat of his brow. It will be enough if we enable ourselves to prevent insult from those nations of Europe which are weak on the sea, because *circumstances exist which render even the stronger ones weak as to us. Providence has placed their richest and most defenceless possessions at our door; has obliged their most precious commerce to pass as it were in review before us.* To protect this, or to assail us, *a small part* only of their naval force will ever be risked across the Atlantic. The dangers to which the elements expose them here are too well known, and the greater danger to which they would be exposed at home, were any general calamity to involve their whole fleet. They can attack us by *detachment only;* and it will suffice to make ourselves equal to what they may detach. Even a smaller force than they may detach will be rendered equal or superior *by the quickness with which any check may be repaired with us,* while losses with them will be irreparable till too late. A small naval force then is ne-

bour is extensive, and well sheltered. After passing the ferry
in little flat boats, which held only five horses each, we went to
Mr. Davenport's inn, where we found a good dinner ready. I
had letters from Mr. Wentworth to Mr. John Tracy, the most
considerable merchant in the place ; but, before I had time to
send them, he had heard of my arrival, and, as I was rising
from table, entered the room, and very politely invited me to
pass the evening with him. He was accompanied by a Colonel, whose name is too difficult for me to write, having never
been able to catch the manner of pronouncing it ; but it was
something like Wigsleps. This Colonel remained with me till
Mr. Tracy finished his business, when he came with two handsome carriages, well equipped, and conducted me and my aid-
de-camp to his country-house. This house stands a mile from
the town, in a very beautiful situation ; but of this I could myself form no judgment, as it was already night. I went however, by moonlight, to see the garden, which is composed of
different terraces. There is likewise a hot-house and a number of young trees. The house is very handsome and well-
finished, and every thing breathes that air of magnificence accompanied with simplicity, which is only to be found among
merchants. The evening passed rapidly by the aid of agreeable conversation and a few glasses of punch. The ladies we
found assembled were Mrs. Tracy, her two sisters, and their
cousin, Miss Lee. Mrs. Tracy has an agreeable and a sensible countenance, and her manners correspond with her appearance. At ten o'clock an excellent supper was served, we
drank good wine, Miss Lee sung, and prevailed on Messieurs
de Vaudreuil and Taleyrand to sing also : towards midnight

---

cessary for us, and a small one is really needful. What this should be I
will not undertake to say. I will only say it should by no means be
so great as we are able to make it. Supposing the million of dollars,
or £300,000 sterling, which Virginia would annually spare without
distress, be applied to the creating a navy. A single year's contribution would build, equip, man, and send to sea a force which should
carry 300 guns. The rest of the confederacy exerting themselves in
the same proportion would equip 1500 guns more. So that one year's
contribution would set up a navy of 1800 guns. The British ships of
the line average 76 guns ; their frigates 38—1800 guns then would
form a fleet of 30 ships, 18 of which might be of the line, and 12 frigates. Allowing eight men, the British average, for every gun, their
annual expense, including subsistence, clothing, pay, and ordinary repairs, would be about 1280 dollars for every gun; or 2,304,000 dollars for the whole. I state this only as one year's possible exertion,
without deciding whether more or less than a year's exertion should
be thus applied."—*Trans.*

the ladies withdrew, but we continued drinking Madeira and
Xery. Mr. Tracy, according to the custom of the country, offered us pipes, which were accepted by M. de Taleyrand, and
M. de Montesquieu, the consequence of which was that they
became intoxicated, and were led home, where they were happy to get to bed. As to myself, I remained perfectly cool,
and continued to converse on trade and politics with Mr. Tracy,
who interested me greatly with an account of all the vicissi-
tudes of his fortune since the beginning of the war. At the
end of 1777, his brother and he had lost one and forty ships,
and with regard to himself, he had not a ray of hope but in a
single letter-of-marque of eight guns, of which he had received no news. As he was walking one day with his brother,
and they were reasoning together on the means of subsisting
their families (for they were both married) they perceived a
sail making for the harbour. He immediately interrupted the
conversation, saying to his brother, " Perhaps it is a prize for
me." The latter laughed at him, but he immediately took a
boat, went to meet the ship, and found that it was in fact a
prize belonging to him, worth five and twenty thousand pounds
sterling. Since that period, he has been almost always fortunate, and he is at present thought to be worth near £120,000
sterling. He has my warmest wishes for his prosperity ; for he
is a sensible, polite man, and a good patriot. He has always
assisted his country in time of need, and in 1781 lent five thousand pounds to the state of Massachusetts for the clothing of
their troops, and that only on the receipt of the Treasurer, yet
his quota of taxes in that very year amounted to six thousand
pounds. One can hardly conceive how a simple individual
can be burthened so far ; but it must be understood, that besides the duty of five per cent. on importation, required by
Congress, the state imposed another tax of the same value on
the sale of every article, in the nature of an excise, on rum,
sugar, coffee, &c. These taxes are levied with great rigour :
a merchant who receives a vessel is obliged to declare the cargo, and nothing can go out of the ship or warehouse without
paying the duty. The consequence of this restraint is, that the
merchants, in order to obtain free use of their property, are
obliged themselves to turn retailers, and pay the whole duty,
the value of which they must recover from those to whom they
sell. Without this, they could neither draw from their stores
what is necessary for their own consumption, nor the small articles which they are in the way of selling, at the first hand ;
they are consequently obliged to take out licenses, like tavern-
keepers and retailers, thus supporting the whole weight of the
impost both as merchants and as shop-keepers. Patriot as he
is, Mr. Tracy cannot help blaming the rigour with which com-

merce is treated; a rigour arising from the preponderance of
the farmers or landholders, and also from the necessity which
the government is under of finding money where it can; for
the farmers easily evade the taxes; certificates, receipts, al-
leged grievances, reduce them almost to nothing.   Thus has
a state, yet in its infancy, all the infirmities of age, and taxa-
tion attaches itself to the very source of wealth, at the risk of
drying up its channels.   [This observation appears rather forced, as applied generally, the Marquis admitting that these im-
positions were the result of a critical and immediate want.
Trans.]

CHAPTER II.

NEWBURYPORT—IPSWICH—BEVERLY—SALEM—CAMBRIDGE—BUN-
KER'S HILL—BOSTON.

I LEFT Newburyport the 13th at ten in the morning, and often stopped before I lost sight of this pretty little town, for I had great pleasure in enjoying the different aspects it presents. It is in general well built, and is daily increasing in new buildings. The warehouses of the merchants, which are near their own houses, serve by way of ornament, and in point of architecture resemble not a little our large green-houses. You cannot see the ocean from the road to Ipswich; and the country to the eastward is dry and rocky. Toward the west it is more fertile; but in general the land throughout the country, bordering on the sea, is not fruitful. At the end of twelve miles is Ipswich, where we stopped to bait our horses, and were surprised to find a town between Newbury and Salem, at least as populous as these two sea-ports, though indeed much less opulent. But mounting an eminence near the tavern, I saw that Ipswich was also a sea-port; I was told, however, that the entrance was difficult, and that at some times of the year there were not five feet upon the bar. From this eminence you see Cape Anne, and the south side of Plumb-Island, as well as a part of the north. The bearing of the coast, which trends to the eastward, seems to me badly laid down in the charts; this coast trends more southerly above Ipswich, and forms a sort of bay. Ipswich at present has but little trade, and its fishery is also on the decline; but the ground in the neighbourhood is pretty good, and abounds in pasturage, so that the seamen having turned farmers, they have been in no want of subsistence,* which may account likewise for the very considerable

---

* The activity and enterprise of the inhabitants of the eastern states are unremitted. The seaman when on shore immediately applies himself to some handicraft occupation, or to husbandry, and is always ready at a moment's warning to accompany the captain his neighbour, who is likewise frequently a mechanic, to the fisheries. West-India voyages are the most perilous expeditions, so that it is no uncommon circumstance to find in a crew of excellent New-England mariners, not a single seaman, so to speak, by profession. Hence arise that zeal.

population of this place, where you meet with upwards of two hundred houses, in about two miles square. Before you arrive at Salem, is a handsome rising town called Beverly. This is a new establishment produced by commerce, on the left shore of the creek which bathes the town of Salem on the north side. One cannot but be astonished to see beautiful houses, large warehouses, &c. springing up in great numbers, at so small a distance from a commercial town, the prosperity of which is not diminished by it.* The rain overtook us just as we were passing near the lake which is three miles from Beverly. We crossed the creek in two flat-bottomed boats, containing each

---

sobriety, industry, economy and attachment for which they are so just-ly celebrated, and which cannot fail of giving them, sooner or later, a decided superiority at least in the seas of the new world. This edu-cation and these manners are the operative causes of that wonderful spirit of enterprise and perseverance, so admirably painted by Mr. Ed-mund Burke, in his wise, eloquent, and immortal speech of March 22, 1775, on his motion for conciliation with the colonies. "Pray, sir," says he, "what in the world is equal to it? Pass by the other parts (of America,) and look at the manner in which the people of New-England have of late carried on the whale fishery. Whilst we follow them among the tumbling mountains of ice, and behold them penetra-ting into the deepest recesses of Hudson's Bay, and Davis' Straits, whilst we are looking for them beneath the arctic circle, we hear that they have pierced into the opposite region of polar cold, that they are at the antipodes, and engaged under the frozen serpent of the south. Falkland's-Island which seemed too remote and romantic an object for the grasp of national ambition, is but a stage and resting place in the pro-gress of their victorious industry. Nor is the equinoctial heat more discouraging to them than the accumulated winter of both the poles. We know that whilst some of them draw the line and strike the har-poon on the coast of Africa, others run the longitude, and pursue their gigantic game along the coast of Brazil. No sea but what is vexed by their fisheries. No climate that is not witness to their toils. Nei-ther the perseverance of Holland, nor the activity of France, nor the dexterous and firm sagacity of English enterprise, ever carried this most perilous mode of hardy industry to the extent to which it has been pushed by this recent people; a people who are still, as it were, but in the gristle, and not yet hardened into the bone of manhood."—*Trans.*

* The town of Beverley began to flourish greatly towards the con-clusion of the war by the extraordinary spirit of enterprise, and great success of the Messieurs Cobbets, gentlemen of strong understandings and the most liberal minds, well adapted to the most enlarged commer-cial undertakings, and the business of government. Two of their privateers had the good fortune to capture in the European seas, a few weeks previous to the peace, several West-Indiamen to the value of at least £100,000 sterling.—*Trans.*

six horses.   It is near a mile wide ; and in crossing, we could
very plainly distinguish the opening of the harbour, and a castle situated on the extremity of the neck, which defends the
entrance.   This neck is a tongue of land running to the eastward, and connected with Salem only by a very narrow sort of
causeway.   On the other side of the neck, and of the causeway, is the creek that forms the true port of Salem, which has
no other defence than the extreme difficulty of entering without a good practical pilot.   The view of these two ports, which
are confounded together to the sight ; that of the town of Salem, which is embraced by two creeks, or rather arms of the
sea, the ships and edifices which appear intermingled, form a
very beautiful picture, which I regret not having seen at a better season of the year.   As I had no letters for any inhabitant
of Salem, I alighted at Goodhue's tavern, now kept by Mr.
Robinson, which I found very good, and was soon served with
an excellent supper.   In this inn was a sort of club of merchants, two or three of whom came to visit me ; and among
others, Mr. De la Fille, a merchant of Bordeaux, who had been
established five years at Boston ; he appeared a sensible man,
and pretty well informed respecting the commerce of the country, the language of which he speaks well.*

The 14th in the morning, Mr. De la Fille called upon me to
conduct me to see the port and some of the warehouses.   I
found the harbour commodious for commerce, as vessels may
unload and take in their lading at the quays ; there were about
twenty in the port, several of which were ready to sail, and
others which had just arrived.   In general, this place has a
rich and animated appearance.   At my return to the inn I
found several merchants who came to testify their regret at not
having been apprised more early of my arrival, and at not having it in their power to do the honours of the town.   At eleven,
I got on horseback, and taking the road to Boston, was surprised to see the town, or suburb of Salem, extending near a mile
in length to the westward.   On the whole, it is difficult to conceive
the state of increase, and the prosperity of this country, after so
long and so calamitous a war.   The road from Salem to Boston passes through an arid, and rocky country, always within
three or four miles of the sea, without having a sight of it ; at
length, however, after passing Lynn,† and Lynn creek, you get

---

* The translator, who was residing at this time at Salem, regretted
exceedingly his accidental absence on the day the Marquis spent there,
which he learnt, to his great mortification, on his return to the inn
which the Marquis had just quitted.—*Trans.*

† Lynn is a very populous little place, and is celebrated for the ma

a view of it, and find yourself in a bay formed by Nahant's-Point, and Pulling's-Point.   I got upon the rocks to the right of the roads, in order to embrace more of the country, and form a better judgment.   I could distinguish not only the whole bay but several of the islands in Boston road, and part of the peninsula of Nantucket, near which I discovered the masts of our ships of war.   From hence to Winisimmet ferry, we travel over disagreeable roads, sometimes at the foot of rocks, at others across salt marshes.   It is just eighteen miles from Salem to the ferry, where we embarked in a large *scow*, containing twenty horses ; and the wind, which was rather contrary, becoming more so, we made seven tacks, and were near an hour in passing.   The landing is to the northward of the port, and to the east of Charlestown ferry.   Although I knew that Mr. Dumas had prepared me a lodging, I found it more convenient to alight at Mr. Brackett's, the Cromwell's head, where I dined.*   After dinner I went to the lodgings prepared for me at Mr. Colson's, a glover in the main street.   As I was dressing to wait on the Marquis de Vaudreuil, he called upon me, and after permitting me to finish the business of the toilet, we went together to Dr. Cooper's, and thence to the association ball, where I was received by my old acquaintance Mr. Brick, who was one of the managers.   Here I remained till ten o'clock ; the Marquis de Vaudreuil opened the ball with Mrs. Temple.†

---

nufacture of women's shoes, which they send to all parts of the continent.   The town is almost wholly inhabited by shoemakers.—*Trans.*

* This is a most excellent inn, and Mr. Brackett a shrewd and active friend to the true principles of the revolution.   His sign of Cromwell's head gave great umbrage to the British under General Gage, who would not suffer it to remain.   This circumstance alone could have induced Mr. Brackett to restore it after they were expelled the town, as reflection might have convinced him, that in the actual position of America, there was much more to be apprehended from a Cromwell than a Charles.—*Trans.*

† The reader will observe that the author in speaking of this lady, of Mr. Bowdoin, her father, and the rest of the family, disdains to mention her husband, Mr. John Temple, so celebrated for political duplicity on both sides of the water.   This gentleman was, however, at this very time at Boston, abusing Gov. Hancock, Dr. Cooper, and the most tried friends to America, in the public prints, and endeavouring to sow dissensions among the people.   Every newspaper into which he could obtain admission, was stuffed with disgusting encomiums on Mr. John Temple, whom Mr. John Temple himself held forth as the paragon of American patriotism, as the most active and inveterate enemy to England, and a victim to British vengeance, which he endeavoured to prove by instances taken from the English prints, of

M. de l'Aiguille the elder, and Mr. Trueguet danced also, each of them a minuet, and did honour to the French nation, by their noble and easy manner; but I am sorry to say, that the contrast was considerable between them and the Americans, who are in general very awkward, particularly in the minuet. The prettiest women dancers were Mrs. Jarvis, her sister, Miss Betsy Broom, and Mrs. Whitmore. The ladies were all well dressed, but with less elegance and refinement than at Philadelphia.* The assembly room is superb, in a good style of architecture, well decorated, and well lighted; it is admirably well calculated for the coup d'oeil, and there is good order, and every necessary refreshment. This assembly is much superior to that of the City tavern at Philadelphia.

The 15th, in the morning, M. de Vaudreuil, and M. le Tombes, the French Consul, called on me the moment I was going out to visit them. After some conversation, we went first to wait on Governor Hancock,† who was ill of the gout, and un-

---

his treachery to England, and by boasting of his dexterity in outwitting the ministry of that country. Yet no sooner did peace take place, than to the astonishment of every sensible and honest man in Europe and America, this very person, equally detested by, and obnoxious to, both countries, was despatched as the sole representative of England to that country, of which he is also a sworn citizen, and whose father-in-law is the present Governor of Massachusetts. It is impossible to add to the folly and infamy of such a nomination. The choice of an ambassador to Congress would have fallen with more propriety on Arnold. His was a bold and single act of treachery; the whole political life of Mr. Temple has been one continued violation of good faith. For farther particulars of this gentleman's conduct, see the Political Magazine for 1780, p. 691, and 740; but volumes might be written on this subject. The translator is sorry to add, that whilst he lives and flourishes, the virtuous, the amiable Dr. Cooper is in his grave, and Mr. Hancock, that illustrious citizen, he fears, not far removed from it. —*Trans.*

* The translator was present at this assembly at Boston, which was truly elegant, where he saw Mr. J. Temple standing behind the crowd, eyeing, like Milton's devil, the perfect harmony and good humour subsisting between the French officers and the inhabitants, not as a friend to Britain, for that would have been pardonable. but to discord, for he was at this very instant boasting of his inveteracy to Britain.—*Trans.*

† I had seen Mr. Hancock eighteen months before, on my former journey to Boston, and had a long conversation with him, in which I easily discovered that energy of character which had enabled him to act so distinguished a part in the present revolution. He formerly possessed a large fortune, which he has almost entirely sacrificed in the defence of his country, and which contributed not a little to main-

able to receive us; thence we went to Mr. Bowdoin's, Mr.
Brick's, and Mr. Cushing's, the deputy Governor. I dined
with the Marquis de Vaudreuil, and after dinner drank tea at
Mr. Bowdoin's who engaged us to supper, only allowing M. de
Vaudreuil and myself half an hour to pay a visit to Mrs. Cushing. The evening was spent agreeably, in a company of
about twenty persons, among whom was Mrs. Whitmore, and
young Mrs. Bowdoin, who was a new acquaintance for me, not
having seen her at Boston when I was there the preceding year.
She has a mild and agreeable countenance, and a character
corresponding with her appearance.

The next morning I went with the Marquis de Vaudreuil to
pay some other visits, and dined with Mr. Brick, where were
upwards of thirty persons, and among others, Mrs. Tudor, Mrs.
Morton, Mrs. Swan, &c. The two former understood French;
Mrs. Tudor, in particular, knows it perfectly, and speaks it tolerably well. I was very intimate with her during my stay at
Boston, and found her possessed, not only of understanding,
but of grace and delicacy, in her mind and manners. After
dinner, tea was served, which being over, Mr. Brick in some
sort insisted, but very politely, on our staying to supper. This
supper was on table exactly four hours after we rose from dinner; it may be imagined, therefore, that we did not eat much,
but the Americans paid some little compliments to it; for, in
general, they eat less than we do, at their repasts, but as often
as you choose, which is in my opinion a very bad method. Their
aliments behave with their stomachs, as we do in France on
paying visits; they never depart, until they see others enter.
In other respects we passed the day very agreeably. Mr. Brick
is an amiable man, and does the honours of his table extremely
well; and there reigned in this society a *ton* of ease and freedom, which is pretty general at Boston, and cannot fail of being
pleasing to the French.

The day following I waited at home for M. de Vaudreuil,
who called on me to conduct me to dinner on board the Souverain. This ship, as well as the Hercule, was at anchor about
a mile from the port. The officer who commanded her, gave
us a great and excellent dinner, the honours of which he did,
both to the French and Americans, with that noble and benevolent spirit which characterizes him. Among the latter, was
a young man of eighteen, of the name of Barrel, who had been
two months on board, that by living continually with the French,

---

tain its credit. Though yet a young man, for he is not yet fifty, he is
unfortunately very subject to the gout, and is sometimes, for whole
months, unable to see company.

he might accustom himself to speak their language, which cannot fail of being one day useful to him.* For this is far from being a common qualification in America, nor can it be conceived to what a degree it has hitherto been neglected ; the importance of it however begins to be felt, nor can it be too much encouraged for the benefit of both nations. It is said, and certainly with great truth, that not only individuals, but even nations, only quarrel for want of a proper understanding ; but it may be affirmed in a more direct and positive sense, that mankind in general are not disposed to love those to whom they cannot easily communicate their ideas and impressions. Not only does their vivacity suffer, and their impatience become inflamed, but self-love is offended as often as they speak without being understood ; instead of which, a man experiences a real satisfaction in enjoying an advantage not possessed by others, and of which he is authorised constantly to avail himself. I have remarked during my residence in America, that those among our officers, who spoke English, were much more disposed to like the inhabitants of the country, than the others who were not able to familiarize themselves with the language. Such is in fact the procedure of the human mind, to impute to others the contrarieties we ourselves experience, and such, possibly, is the true origin of that disposition we call *humeur*, which must be considered as a discontent of which we cannot complain ; an interior dissatisfaction which torments us, without giving us the right of attributing the cause of it to any other person. *Humeur* or *peevishness*, seems to be to anger, what melancholy is to grief; both one and the other are of longer duration, because they have no fixed object, and do not carry, so to speak, their *compliment* with them ; so that never attaining that excess, that *maximum* of sensibility, which brings on that repose, or change of situation which nature wills, they can neither be completely gratified, nor exhale themselves entirely. As for the Americans, they testified more surprise than peevishness, at meeting with a foreigner who did not understand English. But if they are indebted for this opinion to a prejudice of education, a sort of national pride, that pride suffered not a little from the reflection, which frequently occurred, of the language of the country being that of their oppressors. Accordingly they avoided these expressions, " you speak English ; you understand English well ;" and I have

---

* This is a very amiable young gentleman, and his father a great connoisseur in prints and paintings. He was happy to have the opportunity of purchasing a complete collection of Hogarth's prints from the Translator. then on his return to Europe.—*Trans.*

often heard them say—" you speak American well ; the American is not difficult to learn." Nay, they have carried it even so far, as seriously to propose introducing a new language ; and some persons were desirous, for the convenience of the public, that the Hebrew should be substituted for the English. The proposal was, that it should be taught in the schools, and made use of in all public acts. We may imagine that this project went no farther ; but we may conclude from the mere suggestion, that the Americans could not express in a more energetic manner, their aversion for the English.

This digression has led me far from the Souverain, where I would return, however, with pleasure, were it not to take leave of the Commander de Glanderes, and to experience a thick fog, which compelled me to renounce an excursion I proposed making in the harbour, and to get back to Boston as fast as possible, without visiting Castle-Island, and Fort William. On landing, the Marquis de Vaudreuil and I went to drink tea at Mr. Cushing's, who is Lieutenant-Governor of the State ; whence we went to Mr. Tudor's, and spent a very agreeable evening. M. de Parois, nephew of M. de Vaudreuil, had brought his harp, which he accompanied with great taste and skill ; this was the first time, however, for three years, that I had heard truly vocal and national music : It was the first time that my ear had been struck with those airs, and those words which reminded me of the pleasures, and agreeable sentiments, which employed the best era of my life. I thought myself in heaven, or which is the same thing, I thought myself returned to my country, and once more surrounded by the objects of my affection.

On the 17th, I breakfasted with several artillery officers, who had arrived with their troop ; that corps having greatly preceded the rest of the infantry, in order to have time to embark their cannon, and other stores. At eleven I mounted my horse, and went to Cambridge, to pay a visit to Mr. Willard. the President of that University. My route though short, it being scarce two leagues from Boston to Cambridge, required me to travel both by sea and land, and to pass through a field of battle and an intrenched camp. It has been long said that the route to Parnassus is difficult, but the obstacles we have there to encounter, are rarely of the same nature with those which were in my way. A view of the chart of the road, and town of Boston, will explain this better than the most elaborate description. The reader will see that this town, one of the most ancient in America, and which contains from twenty to five and twenty thousand inhabitants, is built upon a peninsula in the bottom of a large bay, the entrance of which is difficult, and in which lie dispersed a number of islands; that serve still farther for its defence; it is only accessible one way on the land side, by a long neck or tongue of land, surrounded by the sea on each side, forming a sort of causeway. To the northward of the town is another peninsula, which adheres to the opposite shore by a very short rock, and on this peninsula is an eminence called Bunker's hill, at the foot of which are the remains of the little town of Charlestown. Cambridge is situated to the northwest, about two miles from Boston, but to go there in a right line, you must cross a pretty considerable arm of the sea, in which are dangerous shoals, and upon the coast, morasses difficult to pass, so that the only communication between the whole northern part of the continent, and the town of Boston, is by the ferry of Charlestown, and that of Winissimmet. The road to Cambridge lies through the field of battle of Bunker's hill. After an attentive examination of that post, I could find nothing formidable in it ;* for the Americans had scarcely time to form a breastwork, that is, a slight retrenchment without a ditch, which shelters the men from musket shot as high as the breast. Their obstinate resistance, therefore, and the prodigious loss sustained by the English on this occasion, must be attributed solely to their valour. The British troops were repulsed on all sides, and put in such disorder, that General Howe is said to have been at one time left single in the field of battle, until General Clinton arrived with a reinforcement, and turned the left of the American position which was weaker and more accessible on that side. It was then that General Warren, who was formerly a physician, fell, and the Americans quitted the field, less perhaps from the superiority of the enemy, than from knowing that they had another position as good, behind the neck which leads to Cambridge ; for, in fact, that of Bunker's hill was useful only in as much as it commanded Charlestown ferry,† and allowed them to raise batteries against the town of Boston. But was it necessary to expose themselves to the destruction of their own houses, and the slaughter of their fellow-citizens, only that they might harass the English in an asylum which sooner or later they must abandon? Besides that, the Ameri-

---

* Bunker's hill is an eminence neither more steep, nor more difficult of access than Primrose hill near Hampstead, in the neighbourhood of London.—*Trans.*

† A bridge of 1503 feet in length, and 42 in breadth, is just completed (in 1786) between Boston and Charlestown, well lighted at night with 40 lamps. This important work was executed by subscription. The greatest depth of the water is 46 feet nine inches, and the least is 14 feet.—*Trans.*

cans could only occupy the heights of Bunker's hill, the sloops
and frigates of the enemy taking them in flank the instant they
descended from them. Such, however, was the effect of this
memorable battle, in every respect honourable for our allies.
that it is impossible to calculate the consequences of a complete victory.* The English who had upwards of eleven hundred men killed and wounded, in which number were seventy
officers, might possibly have lost as many more in their retreat:
for they were under the necessity of embarking to return to
Boston, which would have been almost impracticable, without
the protection of their shipping; the little army of Boston
would in that case have been almost totally destroyed, and the
town must of course have been evacuated. But what would have
been the result of this? Independence was not then declared, and the road to negociation was still open; an accommodation might have taken place between the mother country
and her colonies, and animosities might have subsided. The
separation would not have been completed, England would
not have expended one hundred millions; she would have preserved Minorca and the Floridas; nor would the balance of
Europe, and the liberty of the seas have been restored. For it
must in general be admitted, that England alone has reason to
complain of the manner in which the fate of arms has decided
this long quarrel.

Scarcely have you passed the neck which joins the peninsula
to the Continent, and which is hemmed in on one side by the
mouth of the Mystick, and on the other by a bay called Milk
pond, than you see the ground rising before you, and you distinguish on several eminences the principal forts which defended the entrenched camp of Cambridge. The left of this camp
was bounded by the river, and the right extended towards the
sea, covering this town which lay in the rear. I examined
several of these forts, particularly that of Prospect hill. All
these entrenchments seemed to me to be executed with intelligence; nor was I surprised that the English respected them
the whole winter of 1776. The American troops, who guarded this post, passed the winter at their ease, in good barracks,
well flanked, and well covered; they had at that time abundance of provisions, whilst the English, notwithstanding their
communication with the sea, were in want of various essential
articles, particularly fire-wood and fresh meat. Their government, not expecting to find the Americans so bold and obsti-

---

* This attack on Bunker's hill took place in the time of the hay harvest, and much execution was done among the British by some field-
pieces, and musketry concealed behind the cocks of hay.—*Trans.*

nate, provided too late for the supply of the little army at Boston. This negligence, however, they endeavoured to repair, and spared nothing for that purpose, by freighting a great number of vessels, in which they crowded a vast number of sheep, oxen, hogs, and poultry of every kind; but these ships, sailing at a bad season of the year, met with gales of wind in going out of port, and were obliged to throw the greatest part of their cargoes into the sea, insomuch that, it is said, the coast of Ireland, and the adjoining ocean, were for some time covered with herds, which, unlike those of Proteus, were neither able to live amidst the waves, nor gain the shore. The Americans, on the contrary, who had the whole continent at their disposal, and had neither exhausted their resources, nor their credit, lived happy and tranquil in their barracks, awaiting the succours promised them in the spring. These succours were offered and furnished with much generosity by the southern provinces; provinces, with which, under the English government, they had no connexion whatever, and which were more foreign to them than the mother country. It was already a great mark of confidence, therefore, on the part of the New-Englanders, to count upon that aid which was offered by generosity alone:* but who could foresee that a citizen of Virginia, who, for the first time, visited these northern countries, not only should become their liberator, but should even know how to erect trophies, to serve as a base to the great edifice of liberty? Who could foresee that the enterprise, which failed at Bunker's hill, at the price even of the blood of the brave Warren, and that of a thousand English sacrificed to his valour, attempted on another side and conducted by General Washington, should be the work only of one night, the effect of a simple manœuvre, of a single combination? Who could foresee, in short, that the English would be compelled to evacuate Boston, and to abandon their whole artillery and all their ammunition, without costing the life of a single soldier?

To attain this important object, it was only necessary to occupy the heights of Dorchester, which formed another peninsula, the extremity of which is within cannon shot of Boston, and in a great measure commands the port: but it required the eye of General Washington to appreciate the importance of this post; it required his activity and resolution to undertake to steal a march upon the English, who surrounded it with their

---

* Surely good policy had some share in the alacrity of these proffered succours, nor does this supposition, whilst it does credit to the discernment, derogate from the generosity of the Virginians. *Tua res agitur, paries cum proximus ardet!—Trans.*

shipping, and who could transport troops thither with the greatest facility. But it required still more : nothing short of the power, or rather the great credit he had already acquired in the army, and the discipline he had established, were requisite to effect a general movement of the troops encamped at Cambridge, and at Roxbury, and carry his plan into execution, in one night, with such celerity and silence, as that the English should only be apprised of it, on seeing, at the break of day, entrenchments already thrown up, and batteries ready to open upon them. Indeed he had carried his precautions so far, as to order the whips to be taken from the wagoners, lest their impatience, and the difficulty of the roads might induce them to make use of them, and occasion an alarm. It is not easy to add to the astonishment naturally excited by the principal, and above all, by the early events of this memorable war; but I must mention, that whilst General Washington was blockading the English in Boston, his army was in such want of powder as not to have three rounds a man ; and that if a bomb-ketch had not chanced to run on shore in the road, containing some tons of powder, which fell into the hands of the Americans, it would have been impossible to attempt the affair of Dorchester; as without it, they had not wherewithal to serve the batteries proposed to be erected.

I apprehend that nobody will be displeased at this digression ; but should it be otherwise, I must observe, that in a very short excursion I had made to Boston, eighteen months before, having visited all the retrenchments at Roxbury and Dorchester, I thought it unnecessary to return thither, and I was the less disposed to it from the rigour of the season, and the short time I had to remain at Boston. But how is it possible to enter into a few details of this so justly celebrated town, without recalling the principal events which have given it renown ? But how, above all, resist the pleasure of retracing every thing which may contribute to the glory of the Americans, and the reputation of the illustrious Chief? Nor is this straying from the temple of the Muses, to consider objects which must long continue to constitute their theme. Cambridge is an asylum worthy of them ; it is a little town inhabited only by students, professors, and the small number of servants and workmen whom they employ. The building destined for the university is noble and commanding, though it be not yet completed ; it already contains three handsome halls for the classes, a cabinet of natural philosophy, and instruments of every kind, as well for astronomy, as for the sciences dependant on mathematics; a vast gallery, in which the library is placed, and a chapel corresponding with the grandeur and magnificence of the other parts of the edifice. The library, which is already numerous, and which contains handsome editions of the best authors, and well bound books, owes its richness to the zeal of several citizens, who, shortly before the war, formed a subscription, by means of which they began to send for books from England. But as their fund was very moderate, they availed themselves of their connexions with the mother country, and, above all, of that generosity which the English invariably display whenever the object is, to propagate useful knowledge in any part of the world. These zealous citizens not only wrote to England, but made several voyages thither in search of assistance, which they readily obtained. One individual alone made them a present to the amount of £500 sterling; I wish I could recollect his name, but it is easy to discover it.* It is inscribed in letters of gold over the compartment containing the books which he bestowed, and which form a particular library. For it is the rule, that each donation to the university shall remain as it was received, and occupy a place apart; a practice better adapted to encourage the generosity of benefactors, and to express gratitude, than to facilitate the librarian's labour, or that of the students. It is probable therefore, that as the collection is augmenting daily, a more commodious arrangement will be adopted.

The professors of the university live in their own houses, and the students board in the town for a moderate price. Mr. Willard, who was just elected President, is also a member of the academy of Boston, to which he acts as Secretary of the foreign correspondence. We had already had some intercourse with each other, but it pleased me to have the opportunity of forming a more particular acquaintance with him; he unites to great understanding and literature, a knowledge of the abstruse sciences, and particularly astronomy. I must here repeat, what I have observed elsewhere, that in comparing our universities and our studies in general, with those of the Americans, it would not be our interest to call for a decision of

---

* The Translator is happy in being able to supply this deficiency, by recording the respected name of the late THOMAS HOLLIS, Esq.; a truly eminent citizen of England, who, in every act of his public and private life, did honour to his illustrious name, to his country, and to human nature. One of his ancestors too, of the same name, founded, in this same college, a professorship for the mathematics and natural philosophy, and ten scholarships for students in these and other sciences, with other benefactions, to the amount of little less than £5000 sterling. Public virtue, and private accomplishments seem to be hereditary in this family; Mr. Thomas Brand Hollis, the inheritor of this fortune, pursuing the footsteps of his excellent predecessors—*passibus œquis.*—*Trans.*

the question, which of the two nations should be considered
as an infant people.

The short time I remained at Cambridge allowed me to see
only two of the professors, and as many students, whom I either
met with, or who came to visit me at Mr. Willard's. I was
expected to dine with our Consul, Mr. de le Tombes, and I was
obliged to hurry, for they dine earlier at Boston than at Philadelphia. I found upwards of twenty persons assembled, as
well French officers, as American gentlemen, in the number of
whom was Doctor Cooper, a man justly celebrated, and not
less distinguished by the graces of his mind, and the amiable-
ness of his character, than by his uncommon eloquence, and
patriotic zeal. He has always lived in the strictest intimacy
with Mr. Hancock, and has been useful to him on more than one
occasion. Among the Americans attached by political interest to France, no one has displayed a more marked attention
to the French, nor has any man received from nature a character more analogous to their own. But it was in the sermon he
delivered, at the solemn inauguration of the new constitution
of Massachusetts, that he seemed to pour forth his whole soul,
and develop at once all the resources of his genius, and every
sentiment of his heart. The French nation, and the monarch
who governs it, are there characterized and celebrated with
equal grace and delicacy. Never was there so happy, and so
poignant a mixture of religion, politics, philosophy, morality,
and even of literature. This discourse must be known at Paris, where I sent several copies, which I have no doubt will be
eagerly translated. I hope only that it will escape the avidity of those hasty writers, who have made a sort of property of
the present revolution ; nothing, in fact, is more dangerous
than these precipitate traders in literature, who pluck the fruit
the moment they have any hopes of selling it, thus depriving
us of the pleasure of enjoying it in its maturity. It is for a
Sallust and a Tacitus alone to transmit in their works, the actions and harangues of their contemporaries ; nor did *they*
write till after some great change in affairs had placed an immense interval between the epocha of the history they transmitted, and that in which it was composed ; the art of printing
too, being then unknown, they were enabled to measure, and
to moderate, at pleasure, the publicity they thought proper to
give to their productions.

Doctor Cooper, whom I never quitted without regret, propo-
sing to me to drink tea with him, I accepted it without difficulty. He received me in a very small house, furnished in the
simplest manner, every thing in it bore the character of a modesty which proved the feeble foundation of those calumnies so
industriously propagated by the English, who lost no occasion

of insinuating that his zeal for the Congress and their allies had a very different motive from patriotism and the genuine love of liberty.* A visit to Mrs. Tudor, where Mr. de Vaudreuil and I had again the pleasure of an agreeable conversation, interrupted from time to time by pleasing music, rapidly brought round the hour for repairing to the club. This assembly is held every Tuesday, in rotation, at the houses of the different members who compose it; this was the day for Mr. Russel,† an honest merchant, who gave us an excellent reception. The laws of the club are not straitening, the number of dishes for supper alone are limited, and there must be only two of meat, for supper is not the American repast. Vegetables, pies, and especially good wine, are not spared. The hour of assembling is after tea, when the company play at cards, converse and read the public papers, and sit down to table between nine and ten. The supper was as free as if there had been no strangers, songs were given at table, and a Mr. Stewart sung some which were very gay, with a tolerable good voice.

The 19th the weather was very bad, and I went to breakfast with Mr. Broom, where I remained some time, the conversation being always agreeable and unrestrained. Some officers who called upon me, having taken up the rest of the morning, I at length joined Mr. de Vaudreuil to go and dine with Mr. Cushing. The Lieutenant-Governor, on this occasion, perfectly supported

---

* Mr. John Temple finding himself detected, and ill received at Boston, was the undoubted author of these calumnies against Doctor Cooper, who had nobly dared to warn his countrymen against his insidious attempts to disunite the friends to liberty, under the mask of zeal and attachment to America. He dared, contrary to the decisive evidence of a long series of pure disinterested public conduct in the hour of danger, when Mr. Temple was a skulking, pensioned refugee in England, more than to insinuate, that Doctor Cooper, and Mr. Hancock, that martyr to the public cause, were actually in pay of the French court; but if ever there could be a doubt entertained of such characters, founded on the assertions of such a man, his subsequent conduct has irrefragably proved, that as the calumny was propagated by him, so the suggestion must have originated in his own heart. Let not the Anglo-American Consul-General to the United States complain. Historical justice will overtake both him and Arnold. It is a condition in the indenture of their bargain.—*Trans.*

† The translator had the pleasure of being acquainted with the son of Mr. Russel and his friend Winthrop, in France and Holland. He had the good fortune likewise to meet with the latter at Boston. He takes a pride in mentioning these amiable young men, as they cannot fail of becoming valuable members of a rising country, which attracts the attention of the world.—*Trans.*

the justly acquired reputation of the inhabitants of Boston, of being friends to good wine, good cheer, and hospitality. After dinner he conducted us into the apartment of his son, and his daughter-in-law, with whom we were invited to drink tea. For though they inhabited the same house with their father, they had a separate household, according to the custom in America; where it is very rare for young people to live with their parents, when they are once settled in the world. In a nation which is in a perpetual state of increase, every thing savours of that general tendency; every thing divides and multiplies. The sensible and amiable Mrs. Tudor was once more our centre of union, during the evening, which terminated in a familiar and very agreeable supper at young Mrs. Bowdoin's. Mr. de Parois, and Mr. Dumas sung different airs and duets, and Mrs. Whitmore undertook the pleasure of the eyes, whilst they supplied the gratification of our ears.

The 20th was wholly devoted to society. Mr. Broom gave me an excellent dinner, the honours of which were performed by Mrs. Jarvis and her sister, with as much politeness and attention as if they had been old and ugly. I supped with Mr. Bowdoin, where I still found more handsome women assembled. If I do not place Mrs. Temple, Mr. Bowdoin's daughter, in the number, it is not from want of respect, but because her figure is so distinguished as to make it unnecessary to pronounce her truly beautiful; nor did she suffer in the comparison with a girl of twelve years old, who was formed however to attract attention. This was neither a handsome child nor a pretty woman, but rather an angel in disguise of a young girl; for I am at a loss otherwise to express the idea which young persons, of that age, convey in England and America; which, as I have already said, is not, among us, the age of beauty and the graces. They made me play at whist, for the first time since my arrival in America. The cards were English, that is, much handsomer and dearer than ours, and we marked our points with louis-d'ors, or six-and-thirties; when the party was finished, the loss was not difficult to settle; for the company was still faithful to that voluntary law established in society from the commencement of the troubles, which prohibited playing for money during the war. This law, however, was not scrupulously observed in the clubs, and parties made by the men among themselves. The inhabitants of Boston are fond of high play,*

---

* It is with real concern the translator adds, that gaming is a vice but too prevalent in all the great towns, and which has been already attended with the most fatal consequences, and with frequent suicide. —*Trans.*

and it is fortunate, perhaps, that the war happened when it did, to moderate this passion which began to be attended with dangerous consequences.

On Thursday the 21st there fell so much snow as to determine me to defer my departure, and Mr. Brick, who gave a great dinner to Mr. d'Aboville, and the French artillery officers, understanding that I was still at Boston, invited me to dine, whither I went in Mr. de Vaudreuil's carriage. Mr. Barrel came also to invite me to tea, where we went after dinner; and, as soon as we were disengaged, hastened to return to Mrs. Tudor's. Her husband,* after frequently whispering to her, at length communicated to us an excellent piece of pleasantry of her invention, which was a petition to the queen, written in French, wherein, under the pretext of complaining of Mr. de Vaudreuil and his squadron, she bestowed on them the most delicate and most charming eulogium. We passed the remainder of the evening with Mr. Brick, who had again invited us to supper, where we enjoyed all the pleasures inseparable from his society. I had a great deal of conversation with Doctor Jarvis, a young physician, and also a surgeon, but what was better, a good whig, with excellent views in politics. When Mr. D'Estaing left Boston, the sick and wounded were entrusted to his care, and he informed me, that the sick, who were recovering fast, in general relapsed, on removing them from the town of Boston, where they enjoyed a good air, to Roxbury, which is an unhealthy spot, surrounded with marshes. The physicians in America pay much more attention than ours to the qualities of the atmosphere, and frequently employ change of air as an effectual remedy.

---

* Mr. Tudor is the gentleman who has so frequently distinguished himself by animated orations on the annual commemoration of some of the leading events of this civil war.

CHAPTER III.

THE 22d I set out at ten o'clock, after taking leave of Mr. Vaudreuil, and having had reason to be satisfied with him, and the town of Boston. It is inconceivable how the stay of the squadron has contributed to conciliate the two nations, and to strengthen the connections which unite them. The virtue of Mr. de Vaudreuil, his splendid example of good morals, as well as the simplicity and goodness of his manners, an example followed, beyond all hope and belief, by the officers of his squadron, have captivated the hearts of a people, who though now the most determined enemies to the English, had never hitherto been friendly to the French. I have heard it observed a hundred times at Boston, that in the time even of the greatest harmony with the mother country, an English ship of war never anchored in the port without some violent quarrels between the people and the sailors ; yet the French squadron had been there three months without occasioning the slightest difference.

The officers of our navy were every where received, not only as allies, but brothers ; and though they were admitted by the ladies of Boston to the greatest familiarity, not a single indiscretion, not even the most distant attempt at impertinence ever disturbed the confidence, or innocent harmony of this pleasing intercourse.

The observations I have already made on the commerce of New-England, render it unnecessary to enter into any particular details on that of the town of Boston. I shall only mention a vexation exercised towards the merchants ; a vexation still more odious than that I have spoken of relative to Mr. Tracy, and of which I had not the smallest suspicion, until Mr. Brick gave me a particular account of it. Besides the excise and license duties mentioned above, the merchants are subject to a sort of tax on wealth, which is arbitrarily imposed by twelve assessors, named indeed by the inhabitants of the town ; but as the most considerable merchant has only one vote any more than the smallest shopkeeper, it may be imagined how the interests of the rich are respected by this committee. These twelve assessors having full power to tax the people according to their ability, they estimate, on a view, the business transacted by each merchant, and his probable profits. Mr. Brick, for example, being agent for the French navy, and interested besides in several branches of commerce, among others in that of ensurance, they calculate how much business he may be supposed to do, of which they judge by the bills of exchange he endorses, and by the policies he underwrites, and according to their valuation, in which neither losses nor expenses are reckoned, they suppose him to gain so much a day ; and he is consequently subjected to a proportionable daily tax. During the year 1781, Mr. Brick paid no less than *three guineas and a half per day.* It is evident that nothing short of patriotism, and above all, the hope of a speedy conclusion to the war, could induce men to submit to so odious and arbitrary an impost ; nor can the patience with which the commercial interest in general, and Mr. Brick in particular, bear this burthen, be too much commended.

The 22d I went, without stopping, to Wrentham, where I slept, and reached Providence to dinner the 23d ; where I found our infantry assembled, and waiting till the vessels were ready to receive them. Here I remained six days, during which I made an excursion of four and twenty hours to visit my old friends at Newport.

The 30th I left Providence, with Messrs. Lynch, Montesquieu, and de Vaudreuil, and slept at Voluntown. The next day Mr. Lynch returned to Providence,* and we separated with mutual regret. The same day, the 1st of December, we stopped at Windham to rest our horses, and slept at White's tavern at Andover, near Bolton. The 2d I got to breakfast at Hartford where I staid two or three hours, as well to arrange many particulars relative to the departure of my baggage, as to pay a visit to Mrs. Wadsworth. Mr. Frank Dillon, who had come to me at Providence, where he remained a day longer than me, joined me here. From hence we went to Farmington, where we arrived as night was coming on, and alighted at an inn kept by a Mr. Wadsworth, no relation of the Colo-

---

* Mr Lynch, who was aid-Major-General, and designed to be employed under the orders of the Baron de Viomenil, embarked with the troops. Mr. de Taleyrand was determined to follow them as a simple volunteer, and, assuming the uniform of a soldier in the regiment of Soissonnois, he marched into Boston in the ranks of the company of Chasseurs. This company embarked in the same vessel with the Comte de Segur, then Colonel *en second* of the Soissonnois ; and Mr. de Talevrand remained attached to it till his return to Europe.

nel's; but with whom I had lodged a month before, when ou
the march with my division. Mrs. Lewis hearing of my arrival,
sent her son to offer me a bed at her house, which I declined
with a promise of breakfasting with her the next morning; but
in a quarter of an hour, she called on me herself, accompanied
by a militia Colonel, whose name I have forgot, and supped with
us. The 3d, in the morning, I visited Mr. Pitkin the minister,
with whom I had lodged the preceding year, when the French
army was on its march to join General Washington on the
North river. He is a man of an extraordinary turn, and rather
an original, but is neither deficient in literature nor information. His father was formerly Governor of Connecticut; he
professes a great regard for the French, and charged me, half
joking, and half in earnest, to give his compliments to the king,
and tell him that there was one Presbyterian minister in America on whose prayers he might reckon. I went to breakfast
with Mrs. Lewis, and at ten set out for Litchfield. The roads
were very bad, but the country is embellished by new settlements, and a considerable number of houses newly built, several of which were taverns. It was four when we arrived at
Litchfield, and took up our quarters at Shelding's tavern, a
new inn, large, spacious, and neat, but indifferently provided.
We were struck with melancholy on seeing Mr. Shelding send
a negro on horseback into the neighbourhood to get something
for our supper, for which, however, we did not wait long, and
it was pretty good.

The 4th we set out at half past eight, and baited at Washington, after admiring a second time the picturesque prospect
of the two *falls*, and the furnaces, half way between Litchfield
and Washington. Nor was it without pleasure that I observed
the great change two years had produced in a country at that
time wild and desert. On passing through it two years before,
there was only one miserable alehouse at this place; at present we had the choice of four or five inns, all clean and fit to
lodge in. Morgan's passes for the best, but through mistake
we alighted at another, which I think is not inferior to it. Thus
has the war, by stopping the progress of commerce, proved
useful to the interior of the country; for it has not only obliged several merchants to quit the coasts, in search of peaceable habitations in the mountains, but it has compelled commerce to have recourse to inland conveyance, by which means
many roads are now frequented which formerly were but little
used. It was five in the afternoon when I arrived at Moorhouse's tavern. In this journey, I passed the river at Bull's
works, and having again stopped to admire the beauty of the
landscape, I had an opportunity of convincing myself that my
former eulogium is not exaggerated. The river, which was

swelled by the thaw, rendered the cataract still more sublime ; but a magazine of coals having fallen down, in some measure destroyed the prospect of the furnaces. On this occasion I had not much reason to boast of the tavern. Colonel Moorhouse, after whom it was named, no longer kept it, but had resigned it to his son, who was absent, so that there were none but women in the house. Mr. Dillon, who had gone on a little before, had the greatest difficulty in the world to persuade them to kill some chickens ; our supper was but indifferent, and as soon as it was over, and we had got near the fire, we saw these women, to the number of four, take our place at table, and eat the remainder of it, with an American dragoon, who was stationed there. This gave us some uneasiness for our servants, to whom they left in fact a very trifling portion. On asking one of them, a girl of sixteen, and tolerably handsome, some questions the next morning, I learnt that she, as well as her sister, who was something older, did not belong to the family ; but that having been driven by the savages from the neighbourhood of Wyoming, where they lived, they had taken refuge in this part of the country, where they worked for a livelihood, and that being intimate with Mrs. Moorhouse, they took a pleasure in helping her, when there were many travellers ; for this road is at present much frequented. Observing this poor girl's eyes filled with tears in relating her misfortune, I became more interested, and on desiring farther particulars, she told me that her brother was murdered, almost before her eyes, and that she had barely time to save herself on foot, by running as fast as she could ; that she had travelled in this manner fifty miles, with her feet covered with blood, before she found a horse. In other respects she was in no want, nor did she experience any misery. That is a burthen almost unknown in America. Strangers and fugitives, these unfortunate sisters had met with succours. Lodgings, and nourishment, are never wanting in this country ; clothing is more difficult to procure, from the dearness of stuffs ; but for this they strive to find a substitute by their own labour. I gave them a Louis to buy some articles of dress with ; my aid-de-camp, to whom I communicated the story, made them a present likewise ; and this little act of munificence being soon made known to the mistress of the house, obtained us her esteem, and she appeared very penitent for having shown so much repugnance to kill her chickens.

The 5th we set out at nine, and rode without stopping, to Fishkill, where we arrived at half past two, after a four and twenty miles journey through very bad roads. I alighted at Boerorn's tavern, which I knew to be the same I had been at two years before, and kept by Mrs. Egremont. The house was changed for the better, and we made a very good supper. We

passed the North river as night came on, and arrived at six
o'clock at Newburgh, where I found Mr. and Mrs. Washington, Colonel Tilgham, Colonel Humphreys, and Major Walker.
The head quarters of Newburgh consist of a single house,
neither vast nor commodious, which is built in the Dutch fashion. The largest room in it (which was the proprietor's parlour for his family, and which General Washington has converted into his dining room) is in truth tolerably spacious, but
it has seven doors, and only one window. The chimney, or
rather the chimney back, is against the wall; so that there is
in fact but one vent for the smoke, and the fire is in the room
itself. I found the company assembled in a small room which
served by way of parlour. At nine supper was served, and
when the hour of bedtime came, I found that the chamber, to
which the General conducted me, was the very parlour I speak
of, wherein he had made them place a camp-bed. We assembled at breakfast the next morning at ten, during which interval my bed was folded up, and my chamber became the sitting-
room for the whole afternoon; for American manners do not
admit of a bed in the room in which company is received, especially when there are women. The smallness of the house,
and the difficulty to which I saw that Mr. and Mrs. Washington had put themselves to receive me, made me apprehensive
lest Mr. Rochambeau, who was to set out the day after me, by
travelling as fast, might arrive on the day that I remained there.
I resolved therefore to send to Fishkill to meet him, with a request that he would stay there that night. Nor was my precaution superfluous, for my express found him already at the
landing, where he slept, and did not join us till the next morning as I was setting out. The day I remained at head-quarters
was passed either at table or in conversation. General Hand,
Adjutant-General, Colonel Reed of New-Hampshire, and Major Graham dined with us. On the 7th I took leave of General
Washington, nor is it difficult to imagine the pain this separation gave me; but I have too much pleasure in recollecting
the real tenderness with which it affected him, not to take a
pride in mentioning it. Colonel Tilghman got on horseback
to show me, in the road, the barracks that serve as winter
quarters for the American army, which were not quite finished,
though the season was already far advanced, and the cold very
severe. They are spacious, healthy, and well-built, and consist in a row of log-houses containing two chambers, each inhabited by eight soldiers when complete, which makes commonly from five to six effectives; a second range of barracks
is destined for the non-commissioned officers. These barracks
are placed in the middle of the woods, on the slope of the hills,
and within reach of water; as the great object is a healthy and

convenient situation ; the army are on several lines, not exactly parallel with each other. But it will appear singular in Europe, that these barracks should be built without a bit of iron,
not even nails, which would render the work tedious and difficult, were not the Americans very expert in putting wood together. After viewing the barracks, I regained the high road;
but passing before General Gates' house, the same that General Knox inhabited in 1780, I stopped some time to make a
visit of politeness. The remainder of the day I had very fine
weather, and I stopped and baited my horses at an inn in the
township of Chester. In this inn I found nothing but a woman,
who appeared good and honest, and who had charming children. This route is little peopled, but new settlements are
forming every day. Before we reached Chester we passed by
a bridge of wood, over a creek, called *Murderer's* river, which
falls into the North river, above New-Windsor, on the other
side of Chester; I still kept skirting the ridge of mountains
which separates this country from the Clove. Warwick, where
I slept, a pretty large place for so wild a country, is twelve
miles from Chester, and twenty-eight from Newburgh ; I lodged here in a very good inn kept by Mr. Smith, the same at
whose house I had slept two years before at Ckeat, which was
much inferior to this. The American army having, for two
years past, had their winter quarters near West-Point, Mr.
Smith imagined, with reason, that this road would be more frequented than that of Paramus, and he had taken this inn of a
Mr. Beard, at whose house we stopped next day to breakfast.
The house had been given up to him with some furniture, and
he had upwards of one hundred and fifty acres of land belonging to it, for the whole of which he paid seventy pounds, (currency) making about one hundred pistoles. I had every reason to be content both with my old acquaintance and the new
establishment.

The next morning, the 7th, we set out before breakfast, and
the snow began to fall as soon as we got on horseback, which
did not cease till we got to Beard's tavern. This house was
not near so good as the other, but the workmen were busy in
augmenting it. On inquiring of Mr. Beard, who is an Irishman,
the reason of his quitting his good house at Warwick to keep
this inn, he informed me, that it was a settlement he was forming for his son-in-law, and that as soon as he had put it in order, he should return to his house at Warwick. This Mr.
Beard had long lived as a merchant at New-York, and even
sold books, which I learnt from observing some good ones at
his house, among others, Human Prudence, which I purchased
of him. It ceased snowing at noon, and the weather modera-
ted ; but in the afternoon it returned in blasts, for which, how-

ever, I was indemnified by the beautiful effect produced by the setting sun amidst the clouds, its rays being reflected on the east, and forming a sort of parhelion. Towards the evening the weather became very cold, and we reached Sussex an hour before dark, and took up our lodgings at Mr. Willis'. The fire being not well lighted in the room intended for me, I stepped into the parlour where I found several people who appeared to be collected together upon business; they had, according to custom, drank a good quantity of grog, one of them, called Mr. Archibald Stewart, smelt pretty strong. A conversation took place among us, and Mr. Poops, formerly aid-de-camp to General Dickinson, and at present a rich landholder in the Jerseys, having learnt that I was going to Bethlehem,* or imagining so from the questions I asked about the roads, very obligingly invited me to come the next day and sleep at his house. His house is on the banks of the Delaware, twenty-six miles from Sussex, thirteen from Easton, and twenty-four from Bethlehem. At first I had some difficulty in accepting his offer, from the apprehension one naturally has of being straitened oneself, or of straitening others. He insisted, however, so strongly, and assured me so often that I should find no inn, that I partly promised to lie at his house the following night. These gentlemen, and he in particular, gave me every necessary information; and, as I was desirous of seeing Moravian Mill,† a village situated near Easton, four miles above Sussex, he directed me to Mr. Calver, who keeps a sort of an inn there. The company went away, and we passed a very agreeable evening by a good fire, hugging ourselves at not being exposed to the severe cold we experienced on stirring out of the house. We were also well content with our landlord, Mr. Willis, who seemed to be a gallant man, and very conversible. He was born at Elizabethtown, but has been sixteen years settled at Sussex. Thus does population advance into the interior parts, and go in search of new countries.

I set out the 8th a little before nine, the weather being extremely cold, and the roads covered with snow and ice; but on quitting the Ridge, and turning towards the west, by descending from the high mountains to lower ground, we found the temperature more mild, and the earth entirely free. We

---

* Bethlehem is a sort of colony founded by the *Moravian brethren*, frequently called *Herrenhuter*. It was to see this establishment, and the town of Easton and the Upper Delaware that I quitted the ordinary route, which leads from New-Windsor to Philadelphia.

† This is a property they have purchased in the neighbourhood of Bethlehem.

arrived at half past eleven at the Moravian Mill, and, on stopping at Mr. Calver's, found that Mr. Poops had announced our coming, and that breakfast was prepared for us.* This fresh attention on his part, encouraged me to accept his offer for the evening. As soon as we had breakfasted, Mr. Calver, who had treated us with an anxiety and respect, more German than American, served us by way of conductor, and led us first to see the saw-mill, which is the most beautiful, and the best contrived I ever saw. A single man only is necessary to direct the work, the same wheels which keep the saw in motion, serve also to convey the trunks of trees from the spot where they are deposited to the workhouse, a distance of twenty-five or thirty toises; they are placed on a sledge, which sliding on a groove, is drawn by a rope which rolls and unrolls on the axis of the wheel itself. Planks are sold at six shillings, Pennsylvania currency (about three shillings and four-pence sterling) the hundred; if you find the wood, it is only half the money, and the plank in that case is sawed for one farthing per foot.† This

---

* The Moravian sect is pretty generally known in Europe. They are the followers of the famous Count *Zinzendorff*,* whose picture they have at Bethlehem ; they have several establishments in Europe, similar to those the Marquis is about to speak of, one of which I have seen at Ziest, near Utrecht, where Louis the XIVth took up his quarters, but America seems to be the promised land of sectaries. Even the despised, ill-treated Jews, are well received in the United States, and begin to be very numerous ; many of them were excellent citizens during the severe trial of the war, and some even lost their lives as soldiers, gallantly fighting for the liberties of their country. One family, in particular, I believe of the name of Salvador, at Rhode-Island, was most eminently distinguished. What a glorious field is this for unprejudiced philanthrophic speculation !—*Trans.*

† It is remarked, that on the lands within reach of the Moravian settlements, the cultivation is superior, and every branch of husbandry

* The following account of the Moravians is taken from a translation from the German, of an account of that body, by the Reverend B. La Trobe.—'' The sect of the Unitas fratrum, more commonly known by the names of Herrenhuters and Moravians, was at first formed by Nicholas Lewis, Count of Zinzendorff, at Bartheldorf in Upper Lusatia, in the year 1722. Finding his followers increase, particularly from Moravia, he built a house in a wood near Bartheldorf for their public meetings : and, before the end of the year 1732, this place grew into a village, which was called Herrenhuth, and contained about six hundred inhabitants, all of them following Zinzendorff, and leading a kind of monastic life. From this time the sect has spread its branches from Germany, through all the Protestant states in Europe, made considerable establishments on the continent of America, and Western Isles, and extended itself to the East-Indies, and into Africa. In England, Moravian congregations are formed at London, Bedford. Oakbrook near Derby, Pudsey near Leeds, Dunkerfield in Cheshire, Leominster, Haverford West, Bristol, Kingswood, Bath, and Tetherton.'' Their settlements are becoming very numerous too, but not their population, in all the different states in the American union.—*Trans.*

mill is near the fall of a lake which furnishes it with water. A
deep cut is made in a rock to form a canal for conducting the
waters to the corn-mill, which is built within musket-shot of the
former; it is very handsome, and on the same plan with that
of Mrs. Bowling at Petersburgh, but not so large. From the
mill I went to the church, which is a square building, containing the house of the minister. The place where the duty is
performed, and which may properly be called the church, is on
the first floor, and resembles the Presbyterian meeting-houses,
with this difference, that there is an organ and some religious
pictures.* This house of prayer, so singularly placed, reminded me of a story I heard at Boston. Divine service was formerly celebrated there in one of their places of worship, where
the faithful were not assembled, it is true, on the first floor, but
which, like this, contained the minister's house, below which

---

is better carried on, first, from the emulation excited by these industrious people, and secondly, from the supply the countryman procures
from them of every necessary implement of husbandry, &c. fabricated
in these settlements. Besides those the Marquis speaks of, I visited
some others, not far from Bethlehem, at one of which, called Nazareth, is a famous gunsmith, from whom my friend Major Pierce Butler,
bought a pair of pistols, many of which I saw there of the most perfect workmanship. Nothing can be more enchanting than these establishments ; out of the sequestered wilderness they have formed well
built towns, vast edifices all of stone, large orchards, beautiful and regular shaded walks in the European fashion, and seem to combine with
the most complete separation from the world, all the comforts and even
many of the luxuries of polished life. At one of their cleared-out settlements, in the midst of a forest between Bethlehem and Nazareth,
possessing all the advantages of mills and manufactures, I was astonished with the delicious sounds of an Italian concerto, but my surprise was
still greater on entering a room where the performers turned out to be
common workmen of different trades, playing for their amusement.
At each of these places, the brethren have a common room, where vio-
lins and other instruments are suspended, and always at the service of
such as choose to relax themselves, by playing singly, or taking a part
in a concert.—*Trans.*

* The Moravians appear to me to be a sect between the Methodists
and the Catholics ; at Nazareth, I met with an old Gloucestershire
man, who came to America with the late Mr. Whitfield, with whom I
had much conversation, and who told me that that gentleman was
much respected, both living and dead, by the Moravians ; but, indeed,
besides that, their hymns resemble much those of our Methodists, by
spiritualizing even the grossest carnal transactions ; I found that they
all spoke of him as one of their own sect, but utterly disclaimed Mr.
Wesley. They are very fond of pictures representing *the passion*, to
which they pay a respect little short, if at all, of idolatry. Their car-

were cellars.   The pastor, a very learned man in other respects, besides his spiritual functions, carried on a trade in wine ; that is to say, a great deal of it went out of his cellar, but not a drop ever entered it.   A simple negro servant he had, used to say, that his master was a great saint, for that he employed him every year in rolling into his cellar a number of casks of cider, over which, when he had preached and prayed a few Sundays, they were converted into wine.

On coming out of church I perceived Mr. Poops, who had taken the trouble to come and meet me.   We mounted on horse back together, and after passing through a tolerably fertile valley, in which are some beautiful farms, chiefly Dutch, and well cultivated fields, we arrived in the evening at his house. It is a charming settlement, consisting of a thousand acres of land, the greatest part of which is in tillage, with a fine corn-mill, a saw-mill, and distillery.   The manor house is small, but neat and handsome.   He conducted us into a parlour, where we found Mrs. Poops his wife, Mrs. Scotland his mother-in-law, and Mr. Scotland his brother-in-law.   Mrs. Poops has a pleasing countenance, somewhat injured by habitual bad health, her behaviour is that of an accomplished woman, and her conversation amiable.   The evening was spent very agreeably, partly in conversation, and partly at play.   I had some conversation also with Mr. Scotland, a young man who though but six and twenty, has made three campaigns, as Captain of artillery, and is now a lawyer of great practice.   I have already observed that this is the most respectable, and most lucrative profession in America.   He told me that he usually received, for a simple consultation, four dollars, and sometimes *half a joe;* (thirty-six shillings sterling) and when the action is commenced, so much is paid for every writ, and every deed, for in America lawyers act likewise in the capacity of notaries and attornies.   I had much pleasure in conversing with Mr. Poops, who is a man of good education, well informed, and active, and concerned in a variety of business, which he conducts

---

nal allusions are fully verified in the following hymn taken from one of their books in the Moravian chapel at Pudsey in England, in 1773, an allusion than which nothing can be more infamous and shocking.

> " And she so blessed is,
> She gives him many a kiss :
> Fix'd are her eyes on him ; .
> Thence moves her every limb ;
> And since she him so loves,
> She only with him moves :
> His matters and his blood ●
> Appear her only good."—*Trans.*

with great intelligence.   He had been employed in the commissary's department when General Green* was Quarter-Master-General, and made extraordinary exertions to supply the
army, which rendered him so obnoxious to the tories, that he
was for a long time obliged to remain armed in his house, which
he barricaded every night.   The supper was as agreeable as
the preceding part of the evening ; the ladies retired at eleven,
and we remained at table till midnight.   Mr. Poops' brother
arrived as we were at the desert ; he appeared to me a sensible man, he had married in Virginia the daughter of Colonel
Fims, who had espoused one of his sisters.   He was now a
widower.

The next day, the 10th of December, we breakfasted with
the ladies, and set out at half past ten ; Mr. Poops accompanying me to Easton, where he had sent to prepare dinner.   I
should have preferred my usual custom of making my repast
at the end of my day's journey, but it was necessary for a little
complaisance to return the civilities I had received.   Two
miles from the house of Mr. Poops, we forded a small river, and
travelled through an agreeable and well cultivated country.
Some miles before we came to Easton, we passed over a height
from whence one discovers a vast tract of country, and among
others, a chain of mountains which Mr. Poops desired us to remark.   It forms a part of that great chain which traverses all
America from south to north.†   He pointed out to us two *hiatus*, or openings, resembling two large doors or windows,
through one of which flows the river Delaware ; the other is a
gap leading to the other side of the mountains, and is the road
to *Wyoming*, a pass become celebrated by the march of General Sullivan in 1779.‡   Before we got to Easton, we passed in

---

* The Gazettes have just announced the death of General Green.
In him America has lost one of her best citizens, and most able soldiers.   It is his greatest eulogium to say, that he stood high with General Washington, who recommended him to Congress, and that he
amply justified the opinion entertained of him by that great, good man.
—*Trans.*

† These are called the Kittatinny mountains.   For an account of
this *hiatus*, or gap, see Mr. Charles Thompson's Observations on Mr.
Jefferson's Notes on Virginia, under the account of the National
Bridge.—*Trans.*

‡ See the first part of this Journal, where the author gives an account of his conversations with General Schuyler.   In whatever manner this expedition was set on foot, which took place in 1779, after the
evacuation of Philadelphia, and the diversion made by d'Estaing's
squadron, the greatest difficulty to surmount was, the long march to be

ferry boats, the eastern branch of the Delaware ; for this town is situated on the fork formed by the two branches of that river. It is a handsome though inconsiderable town, but which will probably enlarge itself on a peace, when the Americans no longer under apprehensions from the savages, shall cultivate anew the fertile lands between the Susquehannah and the Delaware. Mr. Poops took us to the tavern of Mr. Smith, who is at once an innkeeper and lawyer. He has a handsome library, and his son, whom Mr. Poops presented to me on my arrival, appeared to be a well educated and well informed young man. I invited him to dinner, as well as another youth who boarded with him, a native of Dominica, who had come to complete his studies among the Americans, to whom he seemed much more attached than to the English. He had made choice of Easton as more healthy, and more peaceable than the other towns of America, and found all the necessary instruction in the lessons and the books of Mr. Smith. As they knew of my coming, we did not wait long for dinner, and at half past three we got on horseback, Mr. Poops being still so good as to accompany me a mile or two, to obtain my permission for which, he pretended that there was a cross road where I might lose myself. At length we parted, leaving me penetrated with gratitude for his numerous civilities. Before I lost sight of Easton I stopped

---

made through woods, deserts, and morasses, conveying all their provisions on beasts of burthen, and being continually exposed to the attacks of the savages. The instructions given by General Sullivan to his officers, the order of march he prescribed to the troops, and the discipline he had the ability to maintain, would have done honour to the most experienced among ancient or modern Generals. It may safely be asserted, that the Journal of this expedition would lose nothing in a comparison with the famous retreat of the ten thousand, which it would resemble very much, if we could compare the manoeuvres, the object of which is attack, with those which have no other than the preservation of a forlorn army. General Sullivan, after a month's march, arrived without any check, at the entrenched camp, the last refuge of the savages ; here he attacked them, and was received with great courage, insomuch that the victory would have remained undecided, had not the Indians lost many of their Chiefs in battle, which never fails to intimidate them, and retreated during the night. The General destroyed their houses and plantations, since which they have never shown themselves in a body. However slight and insufficient the idea may be that I have given of this campaign, it may, nevertheless, astonish our European military men, to learn that General Sullivan was only a lawyer in 1775, and that in the year 1780 he quitted the army to resume his profession. and is now civil Governor of New-Hampshire.

upon a hill, from whence I admired, for some time, the pictu-- resque *coup d'œil* presented by the two branches of the Dela- ware,* and the confused and whimsical form of the mountains, through which they pursue their course. When I was satisfi- ed with the spectacle, it was necessary to push forward to reach Bethlehem before night, and we travelled the eleven miles in two hours, but not before the day was closed.† We had no difficulty in finding the tavern, for it is precisely at the entrance of the town.

This tavern was built at the expense of the Society of Mo- ravian Brethren, to whom it served formerly as a magazine, and is very handsome and spacious.‡ The person who keeps it is

---

* In travelling over this hill, the Translator stopped near an hour to view this noble and enchanting prospect, with which it is impossible to satiate the eye. Nothing can be more delightful than the town and neighbourhood of Easton.—*Trans.*

† The first time I visited Bethlehem was from Philadelphia, and after travelling two days through a country alternately diversified with sa- vage scenes and cultivated spots, on issuing out of the woods at the close of the evening, in the month of May, found myself on a beautiful extensive plain, with the vast eastern branch of the Delaware on the right, richly interspersed with wooded islands, and at the distance of a mile in the front of the town of Bethlehem, rearing its large stone edi- fices out of a forest, situated on a majestic, but gradually rising emi- nence, the back ground formed by the setting sun. So novel and un- expected a transition filled the mind with a thousand singular and sub- lime ideas, and made an impression on me, never to be effaced. The romantic and picturesque effect of this glorious display of natural beau- ties, gave way to the still more noble and interesting sensations, arising from a reflection on the progress of the arts and sciences, and the sub- lime anticipation of the " populous cities," and " busy hum of men," which are one day to occupy, and to civilize the vast wildernesses of the new world.—*Trans.*

‡ This inn, for its external appearance, and its interior accommo- dations, is not inferior to the best of the large inns in England, which, indeed, it very much resembles in every respect. The first time I was at Bethlehem, in company with my friends Major Pierce Butler, Mr. Thomas Elliot, and Mr. Charles Pinkney, Carolina gentlemen, we re- mained here two or three days, and were constantly supplied with ve- nison, moor game, the most delicious red and yellow bellied trout, the highest flavoured wild strawberries, the most luxuriant asparagus, and the best vegetables, in short, I ever saw ; and notwithstanding the diffi- culty of procuring good wine and spirits at that period, throughout the continent, we were here regaled with rum and brandy of the best quality, and exquisite old Port and Madeira. It was to this house that the Marquis de la Fayette retired, to be cured of the first wound

only the cashier, and is obliged to render an account to the administrators. As we had already dined, we only drank tea. but ordered a breakfast for the next morning at ten o'clock. The landlord telling me there was a *growse*, or heath bird, in the house, I made him bring it, for I had long had a great desire to see one. I soon observed that it was neither the *Poule de Pharaon*, nor the heath cock ; it was about the size of a pheasant, but had a short tail, and the head of a capon, which it resembles also in the form of its body, and its feet were covered with down. This bird is remarkable for two large transverse feathers below his head : the plumage of his belly is a mixture of black and white, the colour of his wings of a red grey, like our grey partridges. When the growse is roasted, his flesh is black like that of a heath cock, but it is more delicate, and has a higher flavour.*

I could not derive much information from my landlord on the origin, the opinions, and manners of the society, but he informed me that I should next day see the ministers and administrators, who would gratify my curiosity, The 11th, at half past eight, I walked out with a Moravian, given me by the landlord, but who was likewise ill informed, and only served me as a guide.† He was a seaman, who imagines he has some talents for drawing, and amuses himself with teaching the young peo-

---

he received in fighting for America ; an accident, which I am well assured gave this gallant young nobleman more pleasure than most of our European *petits maitres* would receive from the most flattering proofs of the favour of a mistress. Mr. Charles Pinkney, whom I have above mentioned, is a young gentleman at present in Congress for South Carolina, and who, from the intimate knowledge I have of his excellent education and strong talents, will, I venture to predict, whenever he pleases to exert them, stand forth among the most eminent citizens of the new confederation of Republics. It is my boast and pride to have co-operated with him, when he was only at the age of twenty, in the defence of the true principles of liberty, and to have seen productions from his pen, which, in point of composition, and of argument, would have done honour to the head and heart of the most experienced and most virtuous politician. Should the present work ever fall into his hands, let him recognize in this just tribute to his worth, an affectionate friend, who, knowing his abilities, wishes to excite him to exertion, in the noble, but arduous field before him.—*Trans.*

* This bird must be what we call the black or grey game, and not what is known by the name of *growse* in England.—*Trans.*

† Our company was much more fortunate, Major Butler having obtained letters from Philadelphia to Mr. Van Vleck, a man of property. living here. but formerly of New-York.—*Trans.*

ple, having quitted the sea since the war, where, however, he had no scruple in sending his son.* He subsists on a small estate he has at Reading, but lives at Bethlehem, where he and his wife board in a private family. We went first to visit the house for *single women.* This edifice is spacious, and built with stone. It is divided into several large chambers, all heated with stoves, in which the girls work, some coarse work, such as spinning cotton, hemp, and wool, others works of taste and luxury, such as embroidery, either in thread, or silk, and they excel particularly in working ruffles, little pocket-books, pincushions, &c. like our French nuns. The superintendent of the house came to receive us. She is a woman of family, born in Saxony; her name is Madame de Gastorff; but she does not presume upon her birth, and appeared surprised at my giving her my hand, as often as we went up and down stairs.† She conducted us to the first floor, where she made us enter a large vaulted apartment, kept perfectly clean, in which all the women sleep, each having a bed apart, in which is plenty of feathers.‡ There is never any fire in this room, and though it be very high and airy; a ventilator is fixed in the roof like those in our play-houses The kitchen is not large, but it is clean, and well arranged; in it there are immense earthen pots, upon furnaces, as in our hospitals. The inhabitants of the house dine in the refectory, and are served every day with meat and

---

* It is remarkable enough, that the son of this Moravian, whose name is Garrison, should have served on board a vessel with me, and was, without exception, the most worthless profligate fellow we had in a mixed crew of English, Scotch, Irish, and Americans, to all of whom his education had been infinitely superior. Neither bolts nor bars could prevent, nor any chastisement correct, his pilfering disposition. In a long winter's voyage of thirteen weeks, with only provisions and water for five, this fellow was the bane and pest of officers, passengers, and seamen. Whilst every other man in the ship, even the most licentious in prosperity, submitted to regulations laid down to alleviate our dreadful sufferings, and preserve our lives, this hardened, unreflecting wretch, ignorant of every feeling of sympathy and human nature, seemed to take a savage delight in diffusing misery around him, and adding to the distresses of his fellow sufferers. He had been well educated in the humane principles of the Moravians, but he truly verified the just adage of *Corruptio optimi pessima.*—*Trans.*

† When the Translator visited Bethlehem, the superintendent, or at least her deputy, was a Mrs. Langley, a very mild pretty behaved English woman, who had been a follower of George Whitfield.—*Trans.*

‡ The Americans in general are remarkably fond of very large soft feather beds, even in the hottest climates, and we suffered greatly in this particular. at the inn at Bethlehem.—*Trans.*

vegetables; they have three shillings and sixpence currency per week, about fourpence per day, to the common stock, but they have no supper, and I believe the house furnishes only bread for breakfast. This expense, and what they pay for fire, and candle deducted, they enjoy the produce of their labour, which is more than sufficient to maintain them. This house also has a chapel, which serves only for evening prayer, for they go to their church on Sundays. There is an organ in this chapel, and I saw several instruments suspended upon nails. We quitted Madame de Gastorff well pleased with her reception, and went to the church, which is simple, and differs little from that we had seen at Moravian mill. Here also are several religious pictures. From hence we went to the house of the *single men*. I entered the intendant's apartment, whom I found employed in copying music. He had in his room an indifferent *forte piano*, made in Germany. I talked with him on music, and discovered that he was not only a performer, but a composer. So that on his accompanying us to the chapel, and being asked to touch the organ, he played some voluntaries, in which he introduced a great deal of harmony, and progressions of base. This man, whose name I have forgot, is a native of New-York, but resided seven years in Germany, whence he had lately arrived. I found him better informed than those I had yet met with, yet it was with some difficulty that I got from him the following details: The Moravian brethren, in whatever quarter of the world they live, are under the discipline of their metropolitans, who reside in Germany,* from whence commissaries are sent to regulate the different establishments. The same metropolitans advance the sums necessary for forming them, which are paid in proportion as these colonies prosper; thus the revenue of the mills I have spoken of, as well as the farms and manufactures of Bethlehem, are employed in the first instance to pay the expenses of the community, and afterwards to reimburse the sums advanced in Europe. Bethlehem, for example, possesses a territorial property, purchased by the Moravians in Europe, which consists of fifteen hundred acres of land, forming a vast farm, which is managed by a steward, who accounts for it to the community. If an individual wants a lot of land, he must purchase it of the public, but under this restriction, that in case of defection from the

---

* The Moravians maintain a constant intercourse with Germany in particular, of which country those in America are chiefly natives, and think nothing of a voyage to Europe. Governor Joseph Reed, of Philadelphia, had a son here, learning the German language, when I was at Bethlehem.—*Trans*.

sect, or emigration from the place, he shall restore it to the community, who will reimburse him the original payment. As to their opinions, this sect resembles more the Lutherans, than the Calvinists ; differing, however, from the latter, by admitting music, pictures, &c. into their churches, and from the former, by having no bishops, and being governed by a Synod.* Their police, or discipline, is of the monastic kind, since they recommend celibacy, but without enjoining it, and keep the women separate from the men. There is a particular house also, for the widows, which I did not visit. The two sexes being thus habitually separated, none of those familiar connexions exist between them, which lead to marriage; nay, it is even contrary to the spirit of the sect, to marry from inclination. If a young man finds himself sufficiently at his ease to keep house for himself, and maintain a wife and children, he presents himself to the commissary, and asks for a girl, who (after consulting with the superintendent of the women) proposes one to him, which he may, in fact, refuse to accept; but it is contrary to the custom to choose a wife for himself. Accordingly, the Moravian colonies have not multiplied, in any proportion, to the other American colonies. That at Bethlehem is composed of about six hundred persons, more than half of whom live in a state of celibacy; nor does it appear that it has increased for several years. Every precaution is taken to provide for the subsistence of their brethren, and in the houses destined for the unmarried of both sexes, there are masters who teach them different trades.

The house of the single men which I saw in detail, does not differ from that of the women; I shall only take notice of a very convenient method they have of awakening those who wish to be called up at any given hour; all their beds are numbered, and near the door is a slate, on which all the numbers are registered. A man who wishes to be awakened early, at five o'clock in the morning for example, has only to write a figure of 5 under his number; the watchman who attends the chamber, observes this in going his rounds, and at the hour appointed, the next morning goes straight to the number of the bed without troubling himself about the name of the sleeper.

Before I left the house, I mounted on the roof, where there is a Belvidere, from whence you see the little town of Bethlehem, and the neighbourhood; it is composed of seventy or eighty houses, and there are some others belonging to the co-

* I do not speak with confidence, but am inclined to think that they have bishops, at least a person was pointed out to us at Bethlehem, under that denomination.——*Trans.*

lony at the distance of a mile or two ; they are all handsome
and built with stone.* Every house has a garden cultivated
with care. In returning I was curious to see the farm-house,
which is kept in good order, but the inside was neither so clean,
nor so well kept as in the English farm-houses, because the
Moravians are still more barbarous than their language. At
length at half past ten I returned to the inn, where I was expected by my moor fowl, two woodhens, and many other good
things, so that I was still better satisfied with my breakfast
than with my walk.† At twelve we set out to travel twenty
miles farther, to Kalf's tavern, a German house very poor and
filthy. We had passed the eastern branch of the Delaware
a mile from Bethlehem ;‡ there is neither town nor village on
the road, but the burghs to which the scattered houses we saw,
belonged, are called Socconock and Springfield. The 12th I
breakfasted at Montgomery, twelve miles from Kalf's tavern,
and passing Whitemarsh and Germantown, we arrived towards
five at Philadelphia.

---

* From this Belvidere the view is beautifully romantic, and among
other objects on the eastern side of the Delaware, you see a cultivated farm formed out of an immense wood and near the summit of a
lofty mountain, which I likewise visited, and every step of which gives
you the idea of enchanted ground. Besides the particular gardens to
each private house, there is a large public walk belonging to the community, nay, the church-yard itself is a gay scene of beauty and regularity, the verdant turf being clad in summer with strawberries and
flowers.—*Trans.*

† Notwithstanding the good cheer at the tavern, the author, and I
hope the reader, will pardon me for not crediting this declaration.—
Trans.

‡ The eastern branch of the Delaware which passes by Bethlehem,
and forms a junction with the western at Easton, is here called the
Lecha. There is an excellent ferry over this rapid stream, of which I
have spoken in the first volume. The Moravians among an infinity of
other ingenious inventions, have a large hydraulic machine in the middle of the town which is at a great height from the river for raising
the water to supply the inhabitants.—*Trans.*

Description of the Natural Bridge, called in Virginia, Rocky Bridge.

ON my return from my journey in Upper Virginia, I regretted not having been able to take the dimensions of the Natural Bridge.* I was anxious that some person, who was at once a

---

* So interesting an object could not escape the curiosity and observations of Mr. Jefferson.* He had measured the height and breadth of the Natural Bridge, of which he speaks in an excellent memoir. composed in 1781, a few copies of which he printed under the modest title of Notes upon Virginia, or rather without any title, for this work has never been made public. We hope, however, that the precious documents on natural philosophy, as well as politics, contained in that work, will not be lost to the public. A well known man of letters† has made use of them, and we recommend the perusal of a work, which will speedily make its appearance under the title of Observations on Virginia.

* The following is Mr. Jefferson's account of the Natural Bridge alluded to in this note, which I am happy in being able to lay before the reader :—" The Natural Bridge, the most sublime of nature's works, is on the ascent of a hill, which seems to have been cloven through its length by some great convulsion. The fissure, just at the bridge, is by some admeasurements 270 feet deep, by others only 205. It is about 45 feet wide at the bottom, and 90 feet at the top; this of course determines the length of the bridge, and its height from the water. Its breadth in the middle is about 60 feet, but more at the ends, and the thickness of the mass at the summit of the arch, about 40 feet. A part of this thickness is constituted by a coat of earth, which gives growth to many large trees. The residue, with the hill on both sides, is one solid rock of limestone. The arch approaches the semi-elliptical form ; but the larger axis of the ellipses, which would be the chord of the arch, is many times longer than the transverse. Though the sides of the bridge are provided in some parts with a parapet of fixed rocks, yet few men have resolution to walk to them, and look over into the abyss. You involuntarily fall on your hands and feet, creep to the parapet, and look over it. Looking down from this height about a minute, gave me a violent head-ache. If the view from the top be painful and intolerable, that from below is delightful in the extreme. It is impossible for the emotions arising from the sublime to be felt beyond what they are here : on the sight of so beautiful an arch, so elevated, so light, and springing as it were up to heaven, the rapture of the spectator is really indescribable ! The fissure continuing narrow, deep, and strait for a considerable distance above and below the bridge, opens a short but very pleasing view of the North Mountain on one side, and Blue Ridge on the other, at the distance each of them of about five miles. This bridge is in the county of Rockbridge, to which it has given name, and affords a public and commodious passage over a valley, which cannot be crossed elsewhere for a considerable distance. The stream passing under it is called Cedar creek. It is a water of James' river, and sufficient, in the dryest seasons, to turn a grist mill, though its fountain is not more than two miles above."—*Trans.*

† Monsieur De Meunier, in his new article of Etats Unis in the last Livraison of La Nouvelle Encyclopedie, and the Abbe de Morlaix, who is translating them into French.—*Trans.*

designer and geometrician, should undertake an expedition to the Apalachians for that sole object, and that he should be provided with the instruments necessary for accomplishing it with accuracy. No man was more capable of this than the Baron de Turpin, Captain in the royal corps of Génie; for in him were united all those branches of knowledge, which are carried to so great a height in the corps to which he belongs, with the talent of designing with as much facility as precision; besides which, he was well enough acquainted with the English language to dispense with an interpreter. I proposed, therefore, to the Comte de Rochambeau, to charge him with this commission, which I was confident he would acquit with pleasure. The general thought that it would be rendering a fresh service to the Americans, to make them acquainted with one of the wonders which render their country celebrated, and that it would be pleasant enough for Frenchmen to be the first to give them a precise idea and a correct plan of it. The Baron de Turpin set out, therefore, in the beginning of May, and in three weeks brought me back five plans. Two of them present perspectives, taken from the two sides of the Natural Bridge, and from the bottom of the valley from whence it springs. The third, a bird's-eye view, and represents a part of the country in which it is. The two others being supposed sections of this bridge where it holds by the bank, and which may be considered as its abutment. As to the dimensions, they are as follows, as given me by M. de Turpin:

"The Natural Bridge forms an arch of fifteen toises (six feet English) in length, of that species we denominate the cow's horn: the chord of this arch is seventeen toises at the head of Amont, and nine at that of Aval, and the right arch is the segment of an ellipse, so flat that the small axis is only a twelfth of the large one. The mass of rock and stone which loads this arch is forty-nine feet solid on the key of the great centre, and thirty-seven on that of the small one; and as we find about the same difference in taking the level of the hill, it may be supposed that the roof is on a level, the whole length of the key. It is proper to observe, that the live rock continues also the whole thickness of the arch, and that on the opposite side it is only twenty-five feet wide, in its greatest breadth, and becomes gradually narrower.

"The whole arch seems to be formed of one and the same stone, for the joints which one remarks at the head of Amont, are the effect of lightning, which struck this part in 1779; the other head has not the smallest vein, and the intrados is so smooth, that the martins, which fly round it in great numbers, cannot fasten on it. The abutments, which have a gentle

slope, are entire ; and, without being absolute planes, have all
the polish which a current of water would give to unhewn stone
in a certain time. The four rocks adjacent to the abutments
seem to be perfectly homogeneous, and to have a very trifling
slope. The two rocks on the right bank of the rivulet are two
hundred feet high above the surface of the water, the intrados
of the arch one hundred and fifty, and the two rocks on the left
bank one hundred and eighty.

" If we consider this bridge simply as a picturesque object,
we are struck with the majesty with which it towers in the valley. The white oaks, which grow upon it, seem to rear their
lofty summits to the clouds ; whilst the same trees, which bor-
der on the rivulet, appear like shrubs. As for the naturalist,
he must content himself with such observations as may guide
a more hardy philosopher to form some probable conjecture on
the origin of this extraordinary mass.

" From every part of the arch, and of its supporters, cubic
pieces of three or four lines dimension were taken, and placed
successively in the same aqua fortis ; the former were dissolved in less than half an hour ; the others required more time,
but this must be attributed to the diminution of strength of the
aqua fortis, which lost its activity in proportion as it became
saturated.

" We see that these rocks being of a calcareous nature, ex-
clude every idea of a volcano, which besides cannot be reconciled with the form of the bridge and its adjacent parts. If it
be supposed that this astonishing arch is the effect of a current
of water, we must suppose likewise that this current has had
the force to break down, and carry to a great distance, a mass of
5000 cubic fathoms, for there remains not the slightest trace of
such an operation. The blocks found under the arch, and a
little below it, have their interior positions marked on the col-
lateral pendants on the side of *Aval*, and are occasioned by no
other demolition than that of the bridge itself, which is said
to have been one-third wider.

" The excavation of eight or ten inches, formed in the *pied
droit*, or supporter, on the left bank of the stream, under the
spring of the arch, lengthens it into the form of a crow's beak.
This decay, and some other parts which are blown up, give
reason to presume that this surprising edifice will one day become a victim of that time which has destroyed so many
others."

Such are the observations, the Baron de Turpin brought
back with him, and with which he was pleased to favour me.
As their accuracy may be relied on, perhaps it would be sufficient to transcribe them here, and leave the reader to exercise
his thoughts on the causes which could produce this sort of

prodigy. This was in fact the resolution I had taken, when, abandoned to my own powers, of which I was justly diffident, I was writing at Williamsburgh, and for myself alone, the journal of my late expedition. A Spanish work, however, which fell into my hands, confirmed me in the opinion I at first had entertained, that it was to the labour only of the Creator that we owe the magnificent construction of the Natural Bridge. The opinion of the Count de Buffon, whom I have since consulted, has left me no doubt upon the subject. His sublime conceptions of the different epochs of nature should have been sufficient to put me in the way; but the disciple, who knows how to do justice to himself, is timid, even in the application of. his master's principles. But, whoever has travelled in America, becomes a witness entitled to depose in favour of that genius whose oracles frequently meet with too many opposers. If it be necessary to justify what the Montesquieus, the Humes, the Voltaires have said on the fatal effects heretofore produced by superstition, by ignorance, and prejudice, we might still, in surveying Europe, find whole nations which would present to us the picture of what we were 300 years ago. Nations, which are, so to speak, the contemporaries of past ages, and the truth of historical facts would be demonstrated by those to which we ourselves are witnesses. It is the same in America with respect to the epoch of nature, and all the documents of natural history. In visiting this part of the world, you think yourself removed back a whole epoch; the lower grounds, the plains are watered by such large rivers, and intersected by so many creeks; the coasts are so frequently divided by gulfs, and arms of the sea, which seem to conduct the waves to the very heart of the country, and to the very foot of the mountains, that it is impossible not to be persuaded that all this part of the continent is not of new creation, and produced entirely by successive ebbings of the water. On the other hand, if we observe that all the high mountains form long chains parallel with each other, and almost in a direction north and south; that the greatest part of the rivers, which fall into the ocean, take their origin in the narrow vallies which separate these mountains, and that after following their direction for a considerable space, they turn suddenly towards the east, pierce the mountains, and at length reach the sea, acquiring magnitude as they proceed; we shall be apt to think ourselves, if not contemporaries, at least not far removed from that epoch of nature, when the waters collected to an extraordinary height in hollow vallies, were striving to break down their dykes, still uncertain of the means to be adopted for making their escape; we shall be led to think that the motion of the earth on its axis, or the westerly winds, which in North-

America correspond with the trade winds of the Tropics, and of which they are possibly the effect, have at length determined the motion of the waters towards the east. In which case, one of 'these two circumstances might happen ; either that the waters having exceeded the heights of the least lofty summits which opposed their passage, formed a sort of gutters, by which the superfluity escaped ; or that unable to attain the height of these mountains, they met with some softer parts of the greater mass itself, which they first sapped, and then entirely penetrated. In the first case, if the declivity was very steep, and the rock which served by way of apron was very hard, they would form a cataract, but where the declivity was less rapid, and the soil less compact, the waters not only will have formed the gutter which served them as a passage, but have overthrown and hurried along with them the lands, forming them into long *glacis*, which would lose themselves finally in the plains. Thus Hudson river, the Delaware, the Potomac, James river, and many others, have opened ways for themselves to the sea, by piercing the mountains at angles, more or less approaching to right angles, and forming, more or less, spacious vallies. In the second case, the waters unable to pass the mountains, unless below their summits, must have left above them a sort of *calotte*, or arch, similar to that of the Natural Bridge. But how many chances are there, both that these arches must fall down after a certain time, especially when the beds of the rivers becoming deeper and deeper, the burthen becomes too weighty, and they have lost their bases !*

---

* Mr. Jefferson, in his excellent Notes on Virginia, seems to lean to the system of Buffon, in the following sublime and animated description :

" The courses of the following great rivers of Virginia, says he, are at right angles with the long chain of mountains, known in the European maps by the name of the Apalachian Mountains. James and Potama penetrate through all the ridges of mountains eastward of the Alleghany. That is, broken by no watercourse, it is in fact the spine of the country between the Atlantic on one side, and the Mississippi and St. Lawrence on the other. The passages of the Potomac through the Blue Ridge is perhaps one of the most stupendous scenes in nature ; you stand on a very high point of land. On your right comes up the Shenandoah, having ranged along the foot of the mountains an hundred miles to seek a vent. On your left approaches the Potomac, in quest of a passage also. In the moment of their junction they rush together against the mountain, rend it asunder, and pass off to the sea. The first glance of this scene hurries our senses into the opinion that this earth had been created in time, that the mountains were formed first, that the rivers began to flow afterwards, that in this place particu-

Do we still doubt of the probability of this hypothesis? Do we wish for more striking tokens, more evident traces of the operation of the waters, let us continue to travel in America;

larly they have been dammed up by the Blue Ridge of mountains, and have formed an ocean which filled the whole valley; that continuing to rise, they have at length broken over at this spot, and have torn the mountain down from its summit to its base. The piles of rock on each hand, but particularly on the Shenandoah, the evident marks of their disrupture evulsion from their beds, by the most powerful agents of nature, corroborate the impression. But the distant finishing which nature has given to the picture, is of a very different character. It is a true contrast to the fore ground. It is as placid and delightful as that is wild and tremendous. For the mountain being cloven asunder, she presents to your eye, through the cleft, a small catch of smooth blue horizon, at an infinite distance in the plain country, inviting you, as it were, from the riot and tumult roaring around, to pass through the breach, and partake of the calm below. Here the eye ultimately composes itself; and that way too the road happens actually to lead. You cross the Potomac above the junction, pass along its side through the base of the mountain for three miles, its terrible precipices hanging in fragments over you, and within about twenty miles reach Frederictown, and the fine country round it. This scene is worth a voyage across the Atlantic. Yet here, as in the neighbourhood of the Natural Bridge, are people who have passed their lives within half a dozen miles, and have never been to survey these monuments of a war between rivers and mountains, which must have shaken the earth itself to its centre."

Mr. Charles Thompson, Secretary to Congress, in an appendix to Mr. Jefferson's work, adds the following remarks on the same subject. The reader will pardon, I am confident, the length of these extracts from a work so highly interesting, and which is not yet given to the public.

" The reflections," says Mr. Thompson, " I was led into on viewing this passage of the Potomac through the Blue Ridge were, that this country must have suffered some violent convulsion, and that the face of it must have been changed from what it was probably some centuries ago : that the broken and ragged faces of the mountain on each side the river, the tremendous rocks which are left with one end fixed in the precipice, and the others jutting out, and seemingly ready to fall for want of support; the bed of the river for several miles below obstructed and filled with the loose stones carried from this mound; in short, every thing on which you cast your eye, evidently demonstrates a disrupture and breach in the mountain, and that, before this happened, what is now a fruitful vale was formerly a great lake or collection of water, which possibly might have here formed a mighty cascade, or had its vent to the ocean by the Susquehanna, where the Blue Ridge seems to terminate. Besides this, there are other parts of this country which bear evident traces of a like convulsion. From the best ac-let us go into the vicinity of the Ohio, on the banks of the river Kentucky ; we may there observe what follows, or rather

counts I have been able to obtain, the place where the Delaware now flows through the Kittatinny mountain, which is a continuation of what is called the North Ridge or Mountain, was not its original course, but that it passed through what is now called, " The Wind Gap," a place several miles to the westward, and above an hundred feet higher than the present bed of the river. This Wind Gap is about a mile broad, and the stones in it such as seem to have been washed for ages by water running over them. Should this have been the case, there must have been a large lake behind that mountain, and by some uncommon swell of the waters, or by some convulson of nature. the river must have opened its way through a different part of the mountain, and meeting there with less obstruction, carried away with it the opposing mounds of earth, and deluged the country below with the immense collection of waters to which this passage gave vent. There are still remaining, and daily discovered, innumerable instances of such a deluge on both sides of the river, after it passed the hills above the falls of Trenton, and reached the Champaign. On the New-Jersey side, which is flatter than the Pennsylvania side, all the country below Cresswick hills seems to have been overflowed to the distance of from ten to fifteen miles back from the river, and to have acquired a new soil by the earth and clay brought down and mixed with the native sand. The spot on which Philadelphia stands evidently appears to be made ground. The different strata through which they pass in digging to water, the acorns, leaves, and sometimes branches which are found above twenty feet below the surface, all seem to demonstrate this.* I am informed that at Yorktown in Virginia, in the bank of York river, there are different strata of shells and earth, one above another, which seem to point out that the country there has undergone several changes, that the sea has for a succession of ages occupied the place where dry land now appears, and that the ground has been suddenly raised at various periods. What a change would it make in the country below, should the mountains at Niagara, by any accident be cleft asunder, and a passage suddenly opened to drain off the waters of lake Erie and the upper lakes! While ruminating on these subjects, I have often been hurried away by fancy, and led to imagine that what is now the bay of Mexico was once a champaign country, and that from the point or cape of Florida, there was a continued range of mountains through Cuba, Hispaniola, Porto Rico, Martinique, Guadaloupe, Barbadoes and Trinidad, till it reached the coast of America, and formed the shores which bounded the ocean and guarded the

* From an accurate topographical observation of the mountainous parts of England, and other countries, on these principles, might we not be able to solve various phenomena which present themselves in the plains bordering upon rivers, that is to say, within reach of such a supposed overflow of waters; the quantity of large solid oak timber, for example, found in Walker Colliery near Newcastle, on the banks of the river Tyne, at the prodigious depth of 120 fathoms !—*Trans.*

what the recent historian of that country* has written. " Among the natural curiosities of this territory, the winding banks, or rather the precipice of Kentucky, and of the river Dick, merit the first rank. The astonished eye beholds, almost on every side, three or four hundred feet of a calcareous rock, perpendicularly cut; in some places a beautiful white marble, curiously shaped in arches or in columns, or piled upon a fine stone for building. These precipices, as I have already observed, resemble the sides of a deep trench, or a canal, the earth around being level, except in the course of the rivulets, and covered with groves of red cedar; you can only cross this river at certain places, one of which is worthy of admiration : it is a highway formed by the buffaloes, and wide enough for wagons, in a gentle slope, from the summit to the foot of a very steep eminence, close to the river above Leestown."

But let us consult Don Joseph d'Ulloa, already so celebrated by his voyages; he is the author of the above-mentioned Spanish book, entitled, Noticias Americanas, in which he gives very curious and minute descriptions of all Spanish America. In the article I am going to translate, he begins by remarking a very sensible difference between the mountains in America, situated under the torrid zone, and those we observe in other parts of the globe; for although the height of the latter be often very considerable, as the ground rises gradually, and their combined summits form immense countries, they who inhabit them may be ignorant of their elevation above the level of the sea; whereas those of America being separated, and, so to speak, cloven their whole height, give incessantly the idea, and even the measure of their prodigious altitude. " In this part of the world, adds he, the earth is intersected by profound trenches (*quebradas*) of a very considerable width, since they form the separation of the mountains from each other, and form frequently an opening, of more than two leagues, at the upper part of them. This space becomes contracted in proportion as they are more or less profound; and it is in the bot-

country behind : that by some convulsion or shock of nature the sea had broken through these mounds and deluged that vast plain till it reached the foot of the Andes ; that being there heaped up by the trade winds, always blowing from one quarter, it had found its way back, as it continues to do, through the gulf between Florida and Cuba, carrying with it the loom and sand which it may have scooped from the country it had occupied, part of which it may have deposited on the shores of North America, and with part formed the banks of the Newfoundland. But these are only the visions of fancy." The Translator adds, but they are the sublime visions of a great and enlightened mind.—*Trans.*

* Mr. Filson, whose work is lately translated into French—*Trans.*

tom of this kind of valleys that the rivers flow, which almost regularly occupy the middle, leaving an equal extent of level ground on each side of them. But what is most remarkable, is, that the angles or sinuosities formed by these rivers, correspond perfectly with those we observe to the right and left in the segments of these mountains; so that if we could at once bring together the two sides of these valleys, we should have a solid mass, without any interruption. The rivers pursue their course in these embankments, until they reach the plain, and from thence the ocean. In this latter part of their career, their bed is not deep, and their bottom is nearly on a level with the sea. Thus it may in general be remarked, that the more lofty the mountains of the Cordelliers, the more profound is the bed of the rivers which flow through their valleys.

"In the province of Angaras, among the *lusus naturæ*, with which these countries abound, there is one which merits particular attention. This province, which is a dependency of Guancavelica, is divided into several departments; in one of these departments, called Conaica, is the small village of Vinas, situated at nine leagues distance from Conaica. About midway between them, is a mountain known by the name of Corosunta: on arriving at the foot of this mountain, you enter into a cleft, or if you will, an opening, through which flows the rivulet of Chapllancas; this rivulet enters an embankment the breadth of which is from twenty to five and twenty feet, and its height upwards of forty; without being perceptibly wider at the superior than the inferior part. This gap, which is occupied in its whole width by the stream, forms the only communication that exists between Vinas and Conaica. You can only cross the river in those places where, as I have already said, the opening is twenty feet broad, and you are obliged to cross it nine times, taking advantage of those places where it departs a little from the rock, which only happens where it has formed some sinuosities; for when its course is direct, it exactly fills the opening through which it passes. This trench is formed out of the live rock, and with so much regularity, that all the prominent parts of one side, correspond perfectly with the recipient parts or indentures of the other in its whole height; insomuch that it might be taken for a canal cut expressly for the passage of the water, and which had been executed with so complete a symmetry, as that the two sides might exactly fit each other, without leaving the smallest interstice between them. There is no danger in travelling this road, for the rock is too solid to give any apprehension of its crumbling, and the small river is not rapid enough to endanger boats; yet it is difficult to suppress a sentiment of terror, on finding yourself engaged in this narrow gap, the two sides of which, from their perfect correspondence, present the idea of a box half opened for a moment, and always ready to close upon you.

"The cavity I have been describing is so much the more worthy our observation, as it may be looked upon as a model, or example of what the valleys of the Cordilleras have been, when in their origin they did not exceed the depth of this; for their sides, which now form a gentle slope, were then doubtless perpendicularly cut, and it was not until the waters undermined them to a great depth, that the upper parts being overloaded, have successively crumbled down. This analogy is even confirmed by the decay to be observed in the embankment formed by the Chapllancas; a waste occasioned by the slow and successive effect of the rains and frost, and the crevices produced by the sun, but which are less sensible there than elsewhere, because the rock is harder, more solid, and more continuous, not being interrupted by any bed of earth, or other matter easily to be dissolved or crumbled. Every thing, therefore, leads to a conclusion, that the waters alone have formed this canal in the form we now see it, and that they will continue to augment its depth, since we know that time alone is sufficient to reduce the hardest stone to a fine and almost imperceptible sand, and that this progress is already discoverable from the little fragments of stone visible at the bottom of the river, as well as from those it carries to the plain; when, finding a more extensive range, it begins to enlarge its surface.

"Whether we attribute the origin of this canal to the friction of the waters which have gradually deepened it, or whether we suppose the mountain to have been rent asunder by an earthquake, so as to open a new passage for this river which flowed antecedently in another direction; it is still certain that such an aperture cannot have existed at the epocha immediately subsequent to the deluge. It is the same with respect to the larger embankments of this kind, known by the name of quebradas, and which are frequently to be met with in the upper part of South-America. It is evident that they have been formed equally by the labour of the waters; for on the one hand, we know that the rapidity of their current is capable of wrenching off stones of an extraordinary size; and on the other, we have manifest proofs of the continual effort made by them to deepen their bed, an effort the traces of which are discovered in the huge blocks they have formed into the shape of dice, or cubes, as often as the rocks oppose too much resistance to them to admit of their dividing and clearing away the whole extent of the bottom on which they exercise their activity. In the river of Isuchaca, near the village of that name, is a large mass of stone, of a regular square form, and each side of which may be above five and thirty or forty feet. When the waters are low,

it rises five and twenty feet above their level. But to account
for the form of these large cubic masses, as well as of other
smaller ones, which are often to be found in the bed of rivers,
and which are all regularly shaped, we must suppose that the
waters have successively torn and wrenched off the rocks by which
they were surrounded, thus leaving them single, and isolated,
in their present form ; but this only until the beds of the rivers
becoming deeper and deeper, the waters meet at their bases
with some veins of earth or other matter easy of dissolution ;
for in that case you will undermine and unset them, (so to speak)
so as one day to displace them entirely and hurry them along.
These masses, once in motion, will shock either those on the
banks, those they meet with in the bed even of the river, which
breaking and being reduced to various masses of less dimension,
will be the more easily drifted.   Such is without doubt the origin of all those stones we see under the water, or on the banks,
some of which are very small, and others so enormous, that no
human effort is able to remove them.   As to the extraordinary
profundity of those valleys or quebradas, one example will be
sufficient to give an idea of it.   The town of Guanvelica is
built in a valley formed by different chains of mountains ; the
barometer there stands at eighteen inches, one line and a half
(this mean term is taken between eighteen inches and a quarter, and eighteen inches one third, which form the greatest va-
riation of the barometer at that place ;) according to this height
of the mercury, the elevation above the level of the sea should
be 1949 toises.   On the summit of the mountain in which is
the mine of Asoguès, a spot still habitable, and which is itself
as much lower than other adjacent heights, as it is higher than
the town of Guanvelica, the mercury only stands at sixteen
inches just, which gives 2337 toises above the level of the sea,
and about 500 toises for the depth of the quebrada, or valley
of Guanvelica, which seems to be no other than the deepened
bed of the river we now see flowing through the middle of it."
     After so many observations on the extraordinary effects of the
waters, have we not some foundation for supposing that the
Natural Bridge is also their production, and ought we not to
regard it as a sort of quebrada?   When the valleys of the Apalachians were only vast lakes, in which the waters were retained prisoners, this little valley, whose depth they traverse, may
have served as a partial reservoir, wherein they have remained
even after those of the large valleys made their escape.   The
mass of the rock out of which the Natural Bridge is excavated,
may have served them as a barrier, but whether it be that they
have not risen to the summit of the rock, or whether they succeeded more easily in sapping the lower part of it, they will in
either case have left subsisting that immense gap which form

the arch such as we now see it.   It would be useless, and perhaps rash, to endeavour minutely to explain the manner in which
the bending of this vault has been so regularly traced out; but
the cause once understood, all the effects, however varied, and
however astonishing they may appear, must have the same origin.   We may observe besides, that the greatest bend of this
vault corresponds with the angle formed by the valley in this
place, insomuch that the rock seems to have been the more
worked upon, as the effort of the waters have been more considerable.   However this may be, I leave every one at liberty
to form such conjectures as he pleases,* and as I have said
above, my design has been less to explain this prodigy of nature,
than to describe it with such accuracy as to enable the learned
to form a judgment on the subject.

---

* Mr. Jefferson, after speaking of the above passage of the Spanish
author, differs from him and from the Marquis de Chastellux, in their
reasoning on the probable causes of its production, as follows: " Don
Ulloa inclines to the opinion, that this channel has been effected by the
wearing of the water which runs through it, rather than that the mountain should have been broken open by any convulsion of nature.   But
if it had been worn by the running of the water, would not the rocks,
which form the sides, have been worn plane ? or if, meeting in some
parts with veins of harder stone, the water had left prominences on one
side, would not the same cause have sometimes, or perhaps generally,
occasioned prominences on the other side also ?   Yet Don Ulloa tells
us, that on the other side there are always corresponding cavities, and
that these tally with the prominences so perfectly, that were the two
sides to come together, they would fit in all their indentures, without
leaving any void.   I think that this does not resemble the effect of running water, but looks rather as if the two sides had parted asunder.
The sides of the break, over which is the Natural Bridge of Virginia,
consists of a veiny rock which yields to time, the correspondence between the satient and re-entering inequalities, if it existed at all, has
now disappeared.   This break has the advantage of the one described
by Don Ulloa in its finest circumstance, no portion in that instance
having held together, during the separation of the other parts, so as to
form a bridge over the abyss."—*Trans.*

PART IV.

CORRESPONDENCE.

CHASTELLUX TO MADISON.—WASHINGTON TO

CHASTELLUX.

CORRESPONDENCE.

LETTER I.

FROM THE MARQUIS DE CHASTELLUX, TO MR. MADISON,* PROFESSOR
OF PHILOSOPHY, IN THE UNIVERSITY OF WILLIAMSBURGH.

I HAVE not forgot, Sir, the promise I made you on leaving
Williamsburgh ; it reminds me of the friendship with which you
were pleased to honour me, and the flattering prejudices in
my favour, which were the consequences of it. I am afraid
that I have undertaken more than I am able to perform ; but I
shall at least address you in the language of sincerity, in the
sort of literary bankruptcy I am now about to make.—By putting you in full possession of my feeble resources, however,
I may perhaps obtain a still further portion of that indulgence,
to which you have so frequently accustomed me. The subject
on which I rather thought of asking information from you, than
of offering you my ideas, would require long and tranquil me-
ditation, and since I quitted Virginia, I have been continually
travelling, some times from duty with the troops, at others to
gratify my curiosity in the eastern parts of America, as far even
as New-Hampshire. But even had my time been subject to
less interruption, I am not sure that I should have been more

---

* Mr. Madison's son is a member of the Assembly, and has served in
Congress for Virginia. This young man, who at the age of 30 asto-
nishes the new Republics by his eloquence, his wisdom, and his genius,
has had the humanity and the *courage*, (for such a proposition requires
no small share of courage) to propose a general emancipation of the
slaves, at the beginning of this year, 1786 : Mr. Jefferson's absence at
Paris, and the situation of Mr. Whythe, as one of the judges of the
state, which prevented them from lending their powerful support, occasioned it to miscarry for the moment, but there is every reason to
suppose that the proposition will be successfully renewed. As it is,
the assembly have passed a law declaring that there shall be no more
slaves in the Republic but those existing the first day of the session of
1785-6, and the descendants of female slaves.—*Trans.*

capable of accomplishing your wishes. My mind, aided and excited by yours, experienced an energy it has since lost ; and if in our conversation, I have chanced to express some sentiments which merited your approbation, it is not to myself that they belonged, but to the party that spoke with Mr. Madison. At present I must appear in all my weakness, and with this farther disadvantage, that I want both time and leisure, not only to rectify my thoughts, but even to throw them properly on paper. No matter ; I venture on the task, persuaded that you will easily supply my unavoidable omissions, and that the merit of this essay, if there will be any, will be completed by yourself.

The most frequent object of our conversations was the progress that the arts and sciences cannot fail of making in America, and the influence they must necessarily have on manners and opinions. It seems as if every thing relative to government and legislation ought to be excluded from such discussions, and undoubtedly a stranger, should avoid as much as possible, treating matters of which he cannot be a competent judge. But in the physical, as in the moral world, nothing stands isolated, no cause acts single and independent. Whether we consider the fine arts, and the enjoyments they produce, as a delicious ambrosia the gods have thought proper to partake with us, or whether we regard them as a dangerous poison ; that liquor, whether beneficent or fatal, must always be modified by the vessel into which it is infused. It is necessary therefore, to fix our attention for a moment on the political constitution of the people of America, and in doing this, may I be permitted to recall a principle, I have established, and developed elsewhere ;* which is, that the character, the genius of a people, is not solely produced by the government they have adopted, but by the circumstances under which they were originally formed. Locke, and after him, Rousseau have observed that that the education of man should commence from the cradle, that is to say, at the moment when he is contracting his first habits ; it is the same with states. Long do we discover in the rich and powerful Romans, the same plunderers collected by Romulus to live by rapine ; and in our days the French, docile and polished, possibly to excess, still preserve the traces of the feudal spirit ; whilst the English amidst their clamours against the royal authority, continue to manifest a respect for the crown, which recalls the epoch of the conquest, and the Norman government. Thus every thing that is, partakes of what has been ; and to attain a thorough know-

---

* See the author's work—*de la felicité publique.*

ledge of any people, it is not less necessary to study their history than their legislation. If then we wish to form an idea of the American Republic, we must be careful not to confound the Virginians, whom warlike as well as mercantile, and whose ambitious as well as speculative genius, brought upon the continent, with the New-Englanders, who owe their origin to enthusiasm ; we must not expect to find precisely the same men in Pennsylvania, where the first colonists thought only of keeping and cultivating the deserts, and in South-Carolina, where the production of some exclusive articles fixes the general attention on external commerce, and establishes unavoidable connexions with the old world. Let it be observed, too, that agriculture which was the occupation of the first settlers, was not an adequate means of assimilating the one with the other, since there are certain species of culture which tend to maintain the equality of fortune, and others to destroy it.

These are sufficient reasons to prove that the same principles, the same opinions, the same habits, do not occur in all the thirteen United States, although they are subject nearly to the same force of government. For, notwithstanding that all their constitutions are not similar, there is through the whole a democracy, and a government of *representation*, in which the people give their suffrage by their delegates. But if we choose to overlook those shades, which distinguish this confederated people from each other ; if we regard the thirteen states only as one nation, we shall even then observe that she must long retain the impression of those circumstances, which have conducted her to liberty. Every philosopher acquainted with mankind, and who has studied the springs of human action, must be convinced that, in the present revolution, the Americans have been guided by two principles, whilst they imagined they were following the impulse of only one. He will distinguish, a *positive* and a *negative* principle, in their legislation, and in their opinions. I call that principle, positive, which in so enlightened a moment as the present, reason alone could dictate to a people making choice of that government which suited them the best ; I call that a negative principle which they oppose to the laws and usages of a powerful enemy for whom they had contracted a well founded aversion. Struck with the example of the inconveniences offered by the English government, they had recourse to the opposite extreme, convinced that it was impossible to deviate from it too much. Thus a child who has met with a serpent in his road, is not contented with avoiding it, but flies far from the spot where he would be out of danger of his bite. In England, a septennial parliament invites the king to purchase a majority on which he may reckon for a long period; the American assemblies *therefore*, must be annual ; on the other side of the water, the executive power, too uncontrolled in its action, frequently escapes the vigilance of the legislative authority ; on this continent, each officer, each minister of the people must be under the immediate dependence of the assemblies, so that his first care on attaining office, will be to court the popular favour for a new election. Among the English, employments confer, and procure rank and riches, and frequently elevate their possessors to too great a height: among the Americans, offices neither conferring wealth, nor consideration, will not, it is true, become objects of intrigue or purchase, but they will be held in so little estimation as to make them avoided rather than sought after, by the most enlightened citizens, by which means every employment will fall into the hands of new and untried men, the only persons who can expect to hold them to advantage.

In continuing to consider the thirteen United States under one general point of view, we shall observe still other circumstances which have influenced as well the principles of the government, as the national spirit. These thirteen states were at first colonies ; now, the first necessity felt in all rising colonies is population ; I say in rising colonies, for I doubt much whether that necessity exists at present, so much as is generally imagined. Of this, however, I am very sure, that there will still be a complaint of want of population, long after the necessity has ceased ; America will long continue to reason as follows : we must endeavour to draw foreigners among us, for which purpose it is indispensably necessary to afford them every possible advantage ; every person once within the state, shall be considered, therefore, as a member of that state, as a real citizen. Thus one year's residence in the same place shall suffice to establish him an inhabitant, and every inhabitant shall have the right of voting, and shall constitute a part of the sovereign power ; from whence it will result that this sovereignty will communicate and divide itself without requiring any pledge, any security from the person who is invested with it. This has arisen from not considering the possibility of other emigrants than those from Europe,* who are supposed to fix themselves in

---

* There are various opinions in America on the subject of encouraging emigration. Mr. Jefferson, for example, a man of profound thought, and great penetration, is of opinion that emigrants from Europe are not desirable, lest the emigrants bringing with them not only the vices, but the corrupt prejudices of their respective ancient governments, may be unable to relish that bold universal system of freedom and toleration which is a novelty to the old world : but I venture to think, and trust,

the first spot where they may form a settlement; we shall one day, however, see frequent emigrations from state to state; workmen will frequently transplant themselves, many of them will be obliged even to change situations from the nature of their employments, in which case it will not be singular to see the elections for a district of Connecticut, decided by inhabitants of Rhode-Island or New-York.

Some political writers, especially the more modern, have advanced, that property alone should constitute the citizen. They are of opinion that he alone whose fortune is necessarily connected with its welfare has a right to become a member of the state. In America, a specious answer is given to this reasoning; among us, say they, landed property is so easily acquired, that every workman who can use his hands, may be looked upon as likely soon to become a man of property. But can America remain long in her present situation? And can the regimen of her infant state agree with her, now she has assumed the virile robe?

The following, Sir, is a delicate question which I can only propose to a philosopher like you. In establishing among themselves a purely democratic government, had the Americans a real affection for a democracy? And if they have wished all men to be equal, is it not solely, because, from the very nature

---

that such emigrations will be attended with no bad consequences; for who will be the emigrants to a country where there are neither gold nor silver mines, and where subsistence is alone to be obtained by industry? Men of small, or no fortunes, who cannot live with comfort, nor bring up a family in Europe; labourers and artizans of every kind; men of modesty and genius, who are cramped by insurmountable obstacles in countries governed by cabal and interest; virtuous citizens compelled to groan in silence under the effects of arbitrary power; philosophers who pant after the liberty of thinking for themselves, and of giving vent, without danger, to those generous maxims which burst from their hearts, and of contributing their mite to the general stock of enlightened knowledge; religious men, depressed by the hierarchical establishments of every country in Europe; the friends to freedom; in short, the liberal, generous, and active spirits of the whole world. To America, then, I say with fervency, in the glowing words of Mr. Payne, who is himself an English emigrant—" O! receive the fugitives and prepare in time an asylum for mankind." The history of the late revolution, too, may justify our hopes, for it is an observation, for the truth of which I appeal to fact, that the Europeans settled in America were possessed of *at least as much* energy, and served that country with as much zeal and enthusiasm in the cabinet, and in the field, as the native Americans, and to speak with the late Lord Chatham, who said many absurd, but more wise things than most statesmen, " they infused a portion of new health into the constitution."—*Trans.*

of things, they were themselves nearly in that situation? For to preserve a popular government in all its integrity, it is not sufficient, not to admit either rank or nobility, riches alone never fail to produce marked differences, by so much the greater, as there exist no others. Now, such is the present happiness of America that she has no poor, that every man in it enjoys a certain ease and independence, and that if some have been able to obtain a smaller portion of them than others, they are so surrounded by resources, that the future is more looked to than their present situation. Such is the general tendency to a state of equality; that the same enjoyments which would be deemed superfluous in every other part of the world, are here considered as necessaries. Thus the salary of the workman must not only be equal to his subsistence and that of his family, but supply him with proper and commodious furniture for his house, tea and coffee for his wife, and the silk gown she wears as often as she goes from home; and this is one of the principal causes of the scarcity of labour so generally attributed to the want of hands. Now, sir, let us suppose that the increase of population may one day reduce your artizans to the situation in which they are found in France and England. Do you, in that case, really believe that your principles are so truly democratical, as that the landholders and the opulent, will still continue to regard them as their equals? I shall go still farther, relying on the accuracy of your judgment to testify every thing you may find too subtle or too speculative in my idea. I shall ask you then, whether under the belief of possessing the most perfect democracy, you may not find that you have insensibly attained a point more remote from it, than every other republic. Recollect, that when the Roman senate was compelled to renounce its principles of tyranny, the very traces of it were supposed to be effaced, by granting to the people a participation of the consular honours. That numerous and oppressed class found themselves exalted by the prospect alone which now lay open to a small number of their body, the greatest part of them remained necessitous, but they consoled themselves by saying, *we may one day become consuls.* Now, observe, sir, that in your present form of government, you have not attached either sufficient grandeur, or dignity to any place, to render its possessor illustrious, still less the whole class from which he may be chosen. You have thrown far from you all hereditary honours, but have you bestowed sufficient personal distinctions? Have you reflected that these distinctions, far from being less considerable than those which took place among the Greeks and Romans, ought rather to surpass them? The reason of this is very obvious: the effect of honours and distinctions is by so much the more marked, as it operates on the greater number of men assembled together. When Cneius Duillius was conducted home on his return from supper to the sound of instruments, the whole city of Rome was witness to his triumph : grant the same honours to Governor Trumbull ;* three houses at most in Lebanon will hear the symphony. Men must be moved by some fixed principle ; is it not better that this should be by vanity than interest? I have no doubt that love of country will always prove a powerful motive, but do not flatter yourself that this will long exist with the same spirit. The greatest efforts of the mind, like those of the body, are in resistance ; and the same may happen with respect to the state, as in matters of opinion, to which we cease to be attached, when they cease to be contested.

Behold many objects, Sir, which have passed in review before us. We have only glanced at them, but to distinguish them more clearly, requires more penetrating eyes than mine ; you hold the telescope ; do you apply your optics and you will make good use of them. My task will be accomplished if I can only prove to you that these inquiries are not foreign to my subject. I shall observe then that to know to what precise point, and on what principle you should admit the arts and sciences in your nation, it is necessary first to understand its natural tendency ; for we may direct the course of rivers, but not to repel them to their source. Now, to discover the natural tendency of a nation, not only must we examine its actual legislation, but the oppositions which may exist between the government and prejudices, between the laws and habits ; the reaction, in short, which these different moving powers may produce, one upon the other. In the present instance, for example, it is important to foresee to what degree the democracy is likely to prevail in America, and whether the spirit of that democracy tends to the equality of fortunes, or is confined to the equality of ranks. It is melancholy to confess, that it is to a very great inequality in the distribution of wealth, that the fine arts are indebted for their most brilliant eras. In the time of Pericles, immense treasures were concentred in Athens, unappropriated to any particular purpose ; under the reign of Augustus, Rome owed her acquisition of the fine arts to the spoils of the world, if the fine arts were ever really naturalized at Rome ; and under that of the Julii and Leo the tenth. Ecclesiastic pomp and riches, pushed to the highest point, gave birth to the prodigies of that famous age. But these epochas,

---

* Mr. Trumbull, Governor of Connecticut, inhabits the town of Lebanon, which occupies a league of country, and where there are not six houses less distant than a quarter of a mile from each other.

so celebrated in the history of the arts, are either those of their birth, or of their revival ; and similar circumstances are not necessary to maintain them in the flourishing and prosperous state they have attained.   There is one circumstance, however, which we have not yet touched upon, and which seems indispensable, as well for their preservation, as for their establishment.   The arts, let us not doubt it, can never flourish, but where there is a great number of men.   They must have large cities, they must have capitals.   America possesses already five, which seem ready for their reception, which you will yourself name ; Boston, New-York, Philadelphia, Baltimore, and Charleston.   But they are seaports, and commerce, it cannot be dissembled, has more magnificence than taste ; it pays, rather than encourages artists.—There are two great questions to resolve, whether large towns are useful or prejudicial to America, and whether commercial towns should be the capitals.   Perhaps it will be imagined, that the first question is answered by the sole reflection, that rural life is best suited to mankind, contributing the most to their happiness, and the maintenance of virtue, without which there can be no happiness.   But it must be remembered, that this same virtue, those happy dispositions, those peaceable amusements, we enjoy in the country, are not unfrequently acquisitions made in towns.   If nature be nothing for him who has not learnt to observe her, retirement is sterile for the man without information.   Now this information is to be acquired best in towns.   Let us not confound the man retired into the country, with the man educated in the country.   The former is the most perfect of his species, and the latter frequently does not merit to belong to it.   In a word, one must have education ; I will say farther, one must have lived with a certain number of mankind to know how to live well in one's own family.   To abridge the question, shall I content myself with expressing to you my wishes ?   I should desire that each state of America, as far as it is practicable, had a capital to be the seat of government, but not a commercial city.   I should desire that their capital were situated in the centre of the republic, so that every citizen, rich enough to look after the education of his children, and to taste the pleasures of society, might inhabit it for some months of the year, without making it his only residence, without renouncing his invaluable country-seat.   I should desire that at a small distance, but more considerable than that which separates Cambridge from Boston, an university might be established, where civil and public law, and all the higher sciences, should be taught, in a course of study, not to be commenced before the age of fourteen, and to be of only three years' duration.   I should desire, in short, that in this capital and its appendage, the true national spirit might be preserved, like the sacred fire; that is to say, that spirit which perfectly assimilates with liberty and public happiness. For we must never flatter ourselves with the hopes of modifying, after our pleasure, commercial towns. Commerce is more friendly to individual than to public liberty,* it discriminates not between citizens and strangers. A trading town is a common receptacle, where every man transports his manners, his opinions, and his habits; and the best are not always the most prevalent. English, French, Italian, all mix together, all lose a little of their distinctive character, and in turn communicate a portion of it; so that neither defects nor vices appear in their genuine light; as, in the paintings of great artists, the different tints of light are so blended, as to leave no particular colour in its primitive and natural state.

Though it seems impossible to conclude this article without speaking of luxury, I have, notwithstanding, some reluctance to employ a term, the sense of which is not well ascertained. To avoid here all ambiguity, I shall consider it only *as an expense, abusive in its relations, whether with the fortune of individuals, or with their situation.* In the former case, the idea of luxury approaches that of dissipation, and in the latter, that of ostenta-

---

* I cannot here omit an anecdote which places, in a strong point of view, the distinction between *individual* and *public* liberty, made by the mere merchant. In the early part of life I spent some years in the compting-house of one of the most considerable merchants of the city of London, a native of Switzerland, for the moderate premium of *one thousand guineas.* This happening to be the period of the violent unconstitutional proceedings against Mr. Wilkes, the foreign merchant differing from the English apprentice, entered with zeal into all the measures of the then administration, which, though a republican by birth, he maintained with all the virulence of the tools of despotism. The American war followed, and this gentleman was no less active with offers of his life and fortune, from his compting-house in the city, in support of the arbitrary views of the same set of men, accompanied on all occasions with positions destructive of every idea of *public charity.* But mark the difference, when *individual liberty* was in question. Happening to dine with Mr. John Pringle, of Philadelphia, in 1782, the conversation fell on this merchant, who is at present one of the first in the world, and some questions were asked me respecting his politics; my answers corresponded with what I have above said of him; but judge of my astonishment, when Mr. Pringle assured me, smiling, and gave me *ocular* demonstration of the fact, that America had not a better friend; producing, at the same time, an invoice of a cargo of *gunpowder* shipped by his order on *joint account,* for the *Rebels* of America, at L'Orient, by which this Mr. ——, of London, cleared near £10,000 sterling ! !—*Trans.*

tion. Let us illustrate this thought by an example : If a Dutch merchant spends his property in flowers and shells, the sort of luxury into which he has fallen is only relative to his means, since his taste has led him farther than his faculties would admit. But if, in a republic, a very wealthy citizen expends only a part of his fortune in building a noble palace, the luxury with which he is reproached, is in that case proportionable to his situation ; it shocks the public, in the same manner as proud and arrogant behaviour inspires estrangement and hatred.

We must do justice to commerce, it loves enjoyments more than luxury ; and if we see the merchant sometimes pass the limits, it is rather from imitation than natural propensity. In France and England, we see some ostentatious merchants, but the example is given them by the nobles. There is another more ridiculous, but less culpable abuse, from which commerce is not free ; which is, fashion. This must doubtless prevail wherever there are many foreigners ; for what is *usage* among them becomes *fashion*, when they establish themselves elsewhere. On the other hand, the numerous correspondences, the interest even of the merchants, which consists in provoking, in exciting the taste of the consumers, tends to establish the empire of fashion. What obstacle must be opposed to this ? I propose this question to myself with pleasure, as it leads me back to the fine arts by an indirect road. I shall ask, what has been heretofore the remedy for those caprices of opinion which have begot so many errors, so many revolutions ? Is it not reason and philosophy ? Well, then ! the remedy against the caprices of the fashion is the study of the arts, the knowledge of abstract beauty, the perfection of taste. But, what ! do you hope to fix the standard of that taste, hitherto so variable ? How often has it changed ? How often will it not again vary ? I shall continue to answer in the manner of Socrates, by interrogating myself, and I shall say, what ridiculous opinions have not prevailed in the world, from the time of the Grecian sophists to the theologians of our days ? Has not reason, however, begun to resume her rights, and do you think, that when once recovered, she will ever lose them ? Why are you so unreasonable as to expect that objects so frivolous as furniture and dress should attain perfection before religion and legislation ? Let us never cease repeating, that ignorance is the source of evil, and science that of good. Alas ! do you not see that the Greeks, who had some how acquired very early, such just notions of the arts and taste ; do you not see, I say, that they never varied in their modes ? Witness the statues modelled at Rome by Grecian artists ; witness the noble and elegant mode of dress still retained by that people, though living among the Turks. Erect altars, then, to the fine arts, if you would destroy those of fashion and caprice. Taste, and learn to relish nectar and ambrosia, if you are afraid of becoming intoxicated with common liquors.

Perhaps, Sir, what I am about to say should only be whispered in your ear. I am going to handle a delicate subject; I am venturing to touch the ark. But be assured, that during a three years' residence in America, the progress of the women's dress has not escaped me. If I have enjoyed this as a feeling man, if the results of this progress have not been viewed by me with an indifferent eye, my time of life and character are a pledge to you that I have observed them as a philosopher. Well, Sir, it is in this capacity I undertake their defence, but so long only as things are not carried to an excess. The virtue of the women, which is more productive of happiness, even for the men, than all the enjoyments of vice, if there be only real pleasures arising from that source; the virtue of the women, I say, has two bucklers of defence; one is retirement, and distance from all danger: this is the hidden treasure mentioned by Rochefoucault, which is untouched, because it is undiscovered. The other is loftiness, a sentiment always noble in its relation to ourselves. Let them learn to appreciate themselves; let them rise in their own estimation, and rely on that estimable pride for the preservation of their virtue as well as of their fame. They who love only pleasure, corrupt the sex, whom they convert only into an instrument of their voluptuousness; they who love women, render them better by rendering them more amiable. But, you will say, is it by dress, and by exterior charms, that they must establish their empire? Yes, Sir, every woman ought to seek to please; this is the weapon conferred on her by nature to compensate the weakness of her sex. Without this she is a slave, and can a slave have virtues? Remember the word *decus,* of which we have formed *decency;* its original import is *ornament.* A filthy and negligent woman is not. decent, she cannot inspire respect. I have already allowed myself to express my opinion by my wishes: I desire, then, that all the American women may be well dressed; but I have no objection to seeing that dress simple. They are not formed to represent the severity of the legislation; neither ought they to contrast with it, and convey a tacit insult on that severity. Gold, silver, and diamonds, then, shall be banished from American dress; what excuse can there be for a luxury which is not becoming? But this indulgence, Sir, which I have expressed for the toilet of the women, I am far from allowing to the men. I am not afraid to say, that I should have a very bad opinion of them, if in a country where there are neither etiquette nor titles, nor particular distinctions, they should ever give into the luxury of dress; a luxury, which even the French have laid aside, except on marriages and entertainments, and which no longer exists any where but in Germany and Italy, where certainly you will not go in search of models.

Observe, Sir, that we have imperceptibly prepared the way for the fine arts, by removing the principal obstacles which might be opposed to them ; for if, far from rendering nations vain and frivolous, they rather tend to preserve them from the excesses of luxury, and the caprices of fashion, they can certainly be considered neither as dangerous nor prejudicial. Still, perhaps, you will retain some scruple on the article of luxury ; but recollect, sir, if you please, the definition I have given of it, and if you reflect that every fortune which exceeds the necessary demands, insensibly produces some sort of personal riches, such as valuable furniture, gold and silver trinkets, sumptuous services of plate, &c. you must perceive that this constant surplus of annual income would be infinitely better bestowed on painting, sculpture, and other productions of the arts. Luxury, we have said, is often an abusive employ of riches, relatively to the condition of him who possesses them. Now, what ostentation is there in possessing a fine painting, or a handsome statue ? Surely the parade of a magnificent side-board will be more offensive to the sight of an unwealthy neighbour, than an elegant cabinet adorned with paintings. I doubt, even, whether the man who keeps a musician in his pay, be so much an object of envy as him who maintains race-horses and a pack of hounds.

But let us go farther ; it is not only the productions of the fine arts of which I wish to procure the possession to America ; the fine arts themselves must be placed within her bosom. If I am desirous of her purchasing pictures, it is that she may have painters ;* if I encourage her to send for musicians, it is that

---

* America, in her infant state, has already burst forth into the full splendour of maturity in the immortal paintings of a *Copley* and a *West*. Further glory still attends her early progress even in the present day, in a *Stewart*, a *Trumbull*, and a *Brown* ; nor is *Peale* unworthy of ranking with many modern painters of no inconsiderable fame ; ages may possibly not elapse before posterity may apply to *America*, what Mr. *Tickell* has said, so happily heretofore of the mother country,

> See on her Titian's and her Guido's urns,
> Her fallen arts forlorn Hesperia mourns :
> While Britain wins each garland from her brow,
> Her *wit* and *freedom* first, her *painting* now.

For *wit*, let me refer the reader of taste to the poem of Mac Fingal. written by another Trumbull of Connecticut, who is justly styled the American Hudibras. *Qualis ab incepto processerit, ac sibi constet.* — *Trans.*

she may become musical in her turn. Let her not apprehend the fate of the Romans, to whom she has the apparent pride, but the real humility to compare herself. The Romans, ferocious, unjust, grasping from character, and ostentatious from vanity, were able to purchase the master-pieces, but not the taste of the arts. The Americans proceeding in general from the most polished countries of Europe, have not to strip themselves of any barbarous prejudices. They ought rather to compare themselves with the Greek colonies ; and certainly, Syracuse, Marseilles, Crotona, and Agrigentum had no reason to envy the mother country. There is one base on which, all they who like you are equally attached to good taste and to your country, may safely rest their hopes. Your fellow-citizens live, and will long continue to live, in the vicinity of nature ; she is continually under their hands ; she is always great and beautiful. Let them study ; let them consult her, and they can never go astray. Caution them only, not to build too much on the pedantic legislations of Cambridge, of Oxford, and Edinburgh, which have long assumed a sort of tyranny in the empire of opinion, and seem only to have composed a vast *classic* code for no other purpose than to keep all mankind in class, as if they were still children.

Thus, Sir, you will have the complete enjoyment of the fine arts ; since you will yourselves be artists : but is it not to be feared, that the powerful attraction with which they operate on sensible minds, may divert a rising people from several more useful, though less agreeable occupations ? I am far from being of that opinion ; I think, on the contrary, that the most distinctive, and most peculiar advantage of America is that the rapid advances she is making are not laborious, that they are not due to the excess of labour. Every American has twice as much leisure in the day as an European. Necessity alone compels our painful efforts and you are strangers to necessity. Besides that, your winters are long and rigorous, and many hours may be well spared to domestic society ; this reflection too, is applicable only to the lower classes of the people. You, who live in Virginia, know what time is sacrificed to play, to hunting, and the table ; much more than is necessary to form a Phidias or a Polycletes.

You will insist, perhaps, and you will ask, whether a taste for the arts and letters will not tend to render your fellow-citizens effeminate ? Whether it will not render them frivolous and vain ? Whether the national character and manners will not necessarily be impaired, and admitting even their utility, you will desire to have their early progress, at least, conducted with a certain measure ? I think, that you will find an answer to our present inquiry in many of the preceding observations. But it is time for me to establish a general principle.

the extensive consequences of which you will develope better than I can ; *as long as a taste for the arts can assimilate itself with rural and domestic life, it will always be advantageous to your country, and vice versa.*—Public spectacles, gaudy assemblies, horse-races, &c., drag both men and women from the country, and inspire them with a disgust for it. Music, drawing, painting, architecture, attach all persons to their homes. A harpsichord is a neighbour always at command, who answers all your questions, and never calumniates. Three or four persons in the neighbourhood join to pass the evening together ; here is a concert ready formed. A young lady, in her irksome moments, amuses herself in drawing ; when she becomes a wife and mother, she still draws, that she may instruct her children ; and here is another important article, of which I had hitherto taken no notice. Do you wish your children to remain long attached to you ? Be yourselves their teachers. Education augments and prolongs the relation that subsists between you : it adds to the consideration, the respect they entertain for you. They must long be persuaded, that we know more than them, and that he who teaches always knows more than the person to be taught. In America, as in England, parents spoil their children when they are young, and they abandon them to themselves when they grow up ; for, in these two nations, education is neither enough attended to, nor sufficiently prolonged. Indulgent to children in their tender age, the people there form them into petty domestic tyrants ; negligent of them when they attain to adolescency, they convert them into strangers.

At present, Sir, it seems to me, that there remains no good reason to hinder us from attracting the fine arts to America. Unfortunately it is not the same with artists. I do not think I can better express my good opinion of the Americans, than by declaring that they will always incur some risk in receiving a foreigner among them. The Europeans, it must be confessed have vices from which you are exempt, and they are not in general, the best among them who quit their country, especially who pass the seas. Let us, however, do this justice to painters, and sculptors, that the assiduity of their labours, and above all that the sentiment of the beautiful, that delicacy of taste which they have acquired, render them, generally speaking, better than other men.—It is different with respect to music and dancing. Custom has thought proper to place the latter among the fine arts, nor do I oppose it, since it seems to improve our exterior, and to give us that decorum, the source of which is the respect of others, and of ourselves. But this apology for the art, does not constitute that of its professors. Distrust in general the masters who come to you from Europe ; be diffident even of those you may yourselves send for. It will al-

ways be much safer not to trust to chance, but to make sub-
scriptions in each state, in each town, to engage artists to fix
themselves among you; but in this case apply only to correspondents in Europe on whom you may rely. The commission
with which you entrust them, ought to be sacred in their eyes,
and the smallest negligence on their parts, would be highly
criminal; yet even they are liable to be deceived; and as it
is much better to defer even for a long time, the progress of
the arts, than to make the slightest step towards the corruption
of your manners, it is my principal recommendation to the
Americans to naturalize as much as possible, all foreign artists;
to assimilate and identify them with the inhabitants of the
country; to effect which, I see no better method than by making them husbands and proprietors; act so as to induce them
to marry, enable them to acquire lands, and to become citizens.
It is thus that by securing the empire of morals, you will still
farther guard against the effect of those national prejudices, of
that disdain which render foreigners so ridiculous and odious,
and which reflect upon the art itself, the disgust inspired by
the artist.

Henceforward, Sir, let us enlarge our views; the fine arts are
adapted to America: they have already made some progress
there, they will eventually make much greater; no obstacle, no
reasonable objection can stop them in their career; these are
points at least on which we are agreed. Let us now see to
what purposes they may be converted by the public, the state,
and the government. Here, a vast field opens to our speculation, but as it is exposed to every eye, I shall fix mine on the
object with which it has most forcibly been struck. Recollect,
Sir, what I have said above, relative to offices and public dig-
nities; I have remarked that a jealousy, possibly well founded
in itself, but pushed to the extreme, had made honours too rare,
and rewards too moderate among you. Call in the fine arts to
the aid of a timid legislation; the latter confers neither rank,
nor permanent distinction; let her bestow statues, monuments
and medals. Astonished Europe, in admiring a Washington,
a Warren, a Green, and a Montgomery, demands what recompense can repay their services; behold that recompense, worthy of them and of you. Let all the great towns in America
present statues of .Washington, with this inscription: *pater, liberator, defensor patriæ;* let us see also those of Hancock and
of Adams, with only two words, *primi proscripti;* that of Franklin, with the Latin verse inscribed in France below his portrait,
(*eripuit cælo fulmen, sceptrumque tyranni, &c. &c.**) what glory

* This verse is of that virtuous politician and good man, Mr. Tur-
got. The translator has inserted it, as it seems by the author's omitting it, to be of too high a flavour for the French censure.—*Trans.*

would not this reflect upon America! It would be found that she has already more heroes, than she could procure marble and artists;* and your public halls, your *curiæ*, why should not

---

* Although it be highly proper to insist upon this sort of recompense it may not be amiss that the world should know that congress, as far as opportunity would admit, *have not been remiss* in bestowing such honourable rewards, which they have decreed in different forms on every suitable occasion to the Baron de Kalb, &c. &c. and a marble monument was voted by that body to the memory of my inestimable friend, Montgomery, soon after his glorious fall, in the following words :

Extract from the Journals of Congress.

Thursday, January 25, 1776.

" The committee appointed to consider of a proper method of paying a just tribute of gratitude to the memory of General Montgomery, brought in their report, which was as follows :

" It being not only a tribute of gratitude justly due to the memory of those who have peculiarly distinguished themselves in the glorious cause of liberty, to perpetuate their names by the most durable monuments erected to their honour, but also greatly conducive to inspire posterity with emulation of their illustrious actions :

" *Resolved*, That to express the veneration of the United Colonies for their late general, Richard Montgomery, and the deep sense they entertain of the many signal and important services of that gallant officer, who, after a series of successes, amidst the most discouraging difficulties, fell at length in a gallant attack upon Quebec the capital of Canada ; and to transmit to future ages, as examples truly worthy of imitation, his patriotism, conduct, boldness of enterprise, insuperable perseverance, and contempt of danger and death ; a monument be procured from Paris, or other part of France, with an inscription sacred to his memory, and expressive of his amiable character, and heroic achievements, and that the continental treasurers be directed to advance a sum not exceeding £300 sterling to Dr. Benjamin Franklin, who is desired to see this resolution properly executed, for defraying the expense thereof."

This resolve was carried into execution at Paris, by that ingenious artist, Mr. Caffiers, sculptor to the king of France, under the direction of Dr. Franklin. The monument is of white marble, of the most beautiful simplicity, and inexpressible elegance, with emblematical devices, and the following truly classical inscription, worthy of the modest, but great mind of a Franklin :—To the glory of Richard Montgomery, Major-General of the Armies of the United States of America, slain at the siege of Quebec, the 31st of December, 1775, aged 38 years.

The academy of inscriptions and Belles Lettres, have composed medals for the Generals Washington, Green, Gates, Morgan, &c. The state of Virginia also sent for Monsieur Houdon, the statuary, from Paris to America since the war expressly to take a model, in order to form the statue of General Washington ; an example, however, which

they offer in *relief*, and paintings, the battles of Bunker's Hill.
of Saratoga, of Trenton, of Princeton, of Monmouth, of Cowpens, of Eutaw Springs? Thus would you perpetuate the

---

congress do not think proper to follow, *during the lifetime* of the general, for reasons which may possibly not be disapproved of, by the
Marquis de Chastellux, even in so unexceptionable an instance.

Over this monument, the translator who was the intimate friend of
this excellent young man, shed an affectionate, tributary tear, when at
Paris in the year 1777. He had long known and looked up to him with
admiration, for he was deep in the secrets of his head and heart. His
attachment to liberty was innate, and matured by a fine education, and
a glorious understanding. The translator, whilst he indulged his private sorrow at the sight of this sad, though noble testimonial of his
friend's transcendent virtues, felt his mind awed and overwhelmed with
the magnitude of the event which led to this catastrophe, and with reflections on the wonderful revolutions, and extraordinary dispensations
of human affairs. But a few months, and he had seen the deceased
hero, an officer in the service of England; an officer, too, of the most
distinguished merit, who had fought her battles successfully with the
immortal Wolfe at Quebec, the very spot on which fighting under the
standard of freedom, he was doomed to fall in arms against her; but
a few months, and he sees his dead friend the subject of a monument,
consecrated to his memory by the united voice of a free people, and
his monument, and his fame, as a victim to tyranny, and a champion
of freedom, consigned to be celebrated by an enslaved people, against
whom he had often fought in defence of the same cause, in which he
sacrificed his life. There is a remarkable circumstance connected
with his fall, which merits to be recorded. One of General Montgomery's aids-de-camp, was Mr. Macpherson, a most promising young
man, whose father resided at Philadelphia, and was greatly distinguished
in privateering in the war of 1756. This gentleman had a brother in
the 16th regiment in the British service, at the time of Montgomery's
expedition into Canada, and who was as violent in favour of the English government, as this general's aid-de-camp was enthusiastic in the
cause of America; the latter had accompanied his general a day or
two previous to the attack in which they both lost their lives, to view
and meditate on the spot where Wolfe had fallen; on his return, he
found a letter from his brother, the English officer, full of the bitterest
reproaches against him for having entered into the American service,
and containing a pretty direct wish, that if he would not abandon it, he
might meet with the deserved fate of a rebel. The aid-de-camp immediately returned him an answer full of strong reasoning in defence
of his conduct, but by no means attempting to shake the opposite principles of his brother, and not only free from acrimony, but full of expressions of tenderness and affection; this letter he dated " from the
spot where Wolfe lost his life, in fighting the cause of England, *in
friendship with America.*" This letter had scarcely reached the officer
at New-York, before it was followed by the news of his brother's death.

memory of these glorious deeds; thus would you maintain, even through a long peace, that national pride, so necessary to the preservation of liberty; and you might, without alarming even that liberty, lavish rewards equal to the sacrifices she has received.*

It would be injurious, Sir, to you and to your country, to insist longer on these reflections: my attention is excited by a fresh object, but I should regard it also as an offence, to entertain an idea that it is necessary to call the attention of America to this object, you are desirous that the progress of the sciences also should enter into your deliberations. Is it possible not to foresee their progress in a country already so celebrated for its academies, and universities, which rival those of the old world; for its learned men, I will go farther, for its men of distinguished genius, whose names alone will mark famous epochas in the history of the human mind.† Doubt not, Sir,

---

The effect was instantaneous: nature, and perhaps reason prevailed; a thousand not unworthy sentiments rushed upon his distressed mind; he quitted the English service, entered into that of America, and sought every occasion of distinguishing himself in her service.—*Trans.*

* Mr. Trumbull, son to Governor Trumbull of Connecticut, who was imprisoned in England as a traitor, whilst he was studying painting under Mr. West, is now at Paris residing with Mr. Jefferson, and has finished two capital pictures of the death of Warren and Montgomery. They are esteemed *chef d'œuvres* by all the connoisseurs in this sublime art.—*Trans.*

† Mr. Jefferson in answer to a prejudiced remark of the Abbe Raynal, who says, " on doit être etone que l'Amerique noit pas encore produit un bon poëte, un habile mathematicien, un homme de genie dans un seul art, ou une seule science." Mr. Jefferson, amidst abundance of good reasoning, says in answer, "In war, we have a *Washington*, whose memory will be adored while liberty shall have votaries, whose name will triumph over time and will in future ages assume its just station among the most celebrated worthies of the world, when that wretched philosophy shall be forgotton, which would have arranged him among the *degeneracies* of mankind, (see Buffon's system respecting animals in America.) In physics we have produced a *Franklin*, than whom no one of the present age has made more important discoveries, nor has enriched philosophy with more ingenious solutions of the phenomena of nature. We have supposed Mr. *Rittenhouse* second to no astronomer living: that in *genius* he must be the first, because he is self-taught. As an artist he has exhibited as great a proof of mechanical genius as the world has ever produced. He has not indeed, made a world; but he has by imitation approached nearer its Maker than any man who has lived from the creation to this day, &c. &c." There are various ways, Mr. Jefferson adds, of keeping

that America will render herself illustrious by the sciences, as well as by her arms, and government ; and if the attention of the philosopher be still necessary to watch over them, it is less to accelerate than to remove the obstacles which might possibly retard their progress. Let the universities, always too dogmatical, always too exclusive, be charged only to form good scholars, and leave to an unrestrained philosophy the care of forming good men. In England, the universities have laboured to destroy skepticism, and from that period philosophy has been visibly on the decline, it seems as if the English, in every thing, wish only for a *half liberty*. Leave owls and bats to flutter in the doubtful perspicuity of a feeble twilight ; the American eagle should fix her eyes upon the sun. Nothing proves to me that it is not good to know the truth, and what has error hitherto produced ?—the misery of the world.

As for academies, they will always be useful, whilst they are very numerous. An academician is a senator of the republic of letters ; he takes an oath to advance nothing he cannot prove; he consecrates his life to truth, with a promise to sacrifice to it, even his self-love. Such men cannot be numerous ; such men ought not to be thrown into discredit, by associates unworthy of them. But if academical principles tend to make science austere and scrupulous, the encouragements proposed to the public ought to excite every mind, and furnish a free channel for opinion. Of this nature are prizes proposed by the academies ; it is by their means that the activity of men's minds is directed towards the most useful objects; it is to them that first efforts are indebted for celebrity ; it is by them also the young man thirsting for glory is dispensed with sighing long after her first favours. The more the sciences approach perfection, the more rare do discoveries become ; but America has the same advantage in the learned world, as in that which constitutes our residence. The extent of her empire submits to her observation a large portion of heaven and earth. What observations may not be made between Penobscot and Savannah ? between the lakes and the ocean ? Natural history and astronomy are her peculiar appendages, and the first of these sciences at least, is susceptible of great improvement.

---

truth out of sight. Mr. Rittenhouse's model of the planetary system has the plagiary appellation of an *orrery* ; and the *quadrant*, invented by *Godfrey*, an *American* also, and with the aid of which the European nations traverse the globe, is called *Hadley's* quadrant.—Thus too, the Translator adds, is the great *Columbus* robbed of the honour of giving his name to *America !—Trans.*

Recognise at least, Sir, in this feeble essay, my devotion to your will, and the sincere attachment with which I have the honour to be, &c. &c.

On board the frigate L'Emeraude, in the Bay of Chesapeake, the 12th of January, 1783.

LETTER II.

FROM GENERAL WASHINGTON TO THE MARQUIS DE CHASTELLUX.

New-Windsor, January 28, 1781.

DEAR SIR,—Accept my congratulations on your safe arrival at Newport in good health, after traversing so much of the American theatre of war ; and my thanks for your obliging favour of the 12th, making mention thereof, and introductory of the Count de Chartres, whose agreeable countenance alone is a sufficient index to the amiable qualities of his mind, and does not fail at first view to make favourable impressions on all who see him.

He spent a few days with us at head quarters, and is gone to Philadelphia, accompanied by Count de Dillon. I parted with him yesterday at Ringwood—to which place I had repaired, to be convenient to the suppression of a partial meeting of the Jersey troops at Pompton, who in imitation of those of Pennsylvania, had revolted, and were in a state of disobedience to their officers. This business was happily effected without bloodshed. Two of the principal actors were immediately executed on the spot, and due subordination restored before I returned.

I wish I had expressions equal to my feelings, that I might disclose to you the high sense I have of, and the value I set upon, your approbation and friendship. It will be the wish and happiness of my life, to merit a continuation of them ; and to assure you upon all occasions of my admiration of your character and virtues, and of the sentiments of esteem and regard with which I have the honour to be, dear sir,

Your most obedient and humble servant,

GEORGE WASHINGTON.

LETTER III.

New-Windsor, June 13, 1781.

My dear Chevalier—I hear from the purport of the letter you did me the honour to write from Newport on the 9th, that my sentiments respecting the council of war held on board the Duke de Burgogne, (the 31st May,) have been misconceived, and I shall be very unhappy if they receive an interpretation different from the true intent and meaning of them. If this is the case, it can only be attributed to my not understanding the business of the Duke de Lauzun perfectly. I will rely, therefore, on your goodness and candour to explain and rectify the mistake, if any has happened.

My wishes perfectly coincided with the determination of the board of war, to continue the fleet at Rhode-Island, provided it could remain there in safety with the force required, and did not impede the march of the army toward the North river; but when the Duke de Lauzun informed me that my opinion of the propriety and safety of this measure was required by the board, and that he came hither at the particular request of the Counts Rochambeau and de B—— to obtain it, I was reduced to the painful necessity of delivering a sentiment different from that of a most respectable board, or of forfeiting all pretensions to candour, by the concealment of it. Upon this ground it was, I wrote to the generals to the effect I did, and not because I was dissatisfied at the alteration of the plan agreed to at Weathersfield. My fears for the safety of the fleet, which I am now persuaded were carried too far, were productive of a belief, that the generals, when separated, might feel uneasy at every mysterious preparation of the enemy, and occasion a fresh call for militia. This had some weight in my determination to give Boston (where I was sure no danger could be encountered but that of a blockade,) a preference to Newport, where, under some circumstances, though not such as were likely to happen, something might be enterprised.

The fleet being at Rhode-Island, is attended certainly with many advantages in the operation proposed, and I entreat that you and the gentlemen who were of opinion that it ought to be risked there for these purposes, will be assured, that I have a high sense of the obligations you meant to confer on America by that resolve, and that your zeal to promote the common cause, and my anxiety for the safety of so valuable a fleet, were the only motives that gave birth to the apparent difference in our opinion.

I set that value upon your friendship and candour, and that

implicit belief in your attachment to America, that they are only to be equalled by the sincerity with which, I have the honour to be, my dear sir,

> Your most obedient and obliged servant,
> *The Marquis de Chastellux.*   GEORGE WASHINGTON.

LETTER IV.

Philadelphia, January 4, 1782.

MY DEAR CHEVALIER—I cannot suffer your old acquaintance. Mrs. Curtis, to proceed to Williamsburgh, without taking with her a remembrancer of my friendship for you.

I have been detained here by Congress, to assist in making the necessary arrangements for next campaign, and am happy to find so favourable a disposition in that body, to prepare vigorously for it. They have resolved to keep up the same number of corps as constituted the army of last year, and have called upon the states in a pressing manner, to complete them.

Requisitions of money are also made, but how far the abilities and inclinations of the states, individually, will coincide with the demands, is more than I am able, at this early period, to inform you. A farther pecuniary aid from your generous nation, and a decisive naval force upon this coast, in the latter end of May, or beginning of June, unlimited in its stay and operations, would (unless the resources of Great Britain are inexhaustible, or she can form powerful alliances) bid fair to finish the war, in the course of next campaign, (if she means to prosecute it,) with the ruin of that people.

The first, that is, an aid of money, would enable our financiers to support the expenses of the war with ease and credit, without anticipating or deranging those funds which Congress are endeavouring to establish, and which will be productive, though they are slow in the operation. The second, a naval superiority, would compel the enemy to draw their whole force to a point, which would not only be a disgrace to their arms, by the relinquishment of posts and states which they affect to have conquered, but might, eventually, be fatal to their army. Or, by attempting to hold these, to be cut off in detail. So that, in either case, the most important good consequences would result from the measure.

As you will have received, in a more direct channel than from me, the news of the surprise and recapture of St. Eustatia, by the arms of France, I shall only congratulate you on the event, and add, that it marks, in a striking point of view, the genius of the Marquis de Boulli, for enterprise, and for intrepidity in resources in difficult circumstances. His conduct, upon this occasion, does him infinite honour.

Amid the numerous friends who would rejoice to see you at this place, none (while I stay here) could give you a more sincere and cordial welcome than I should.

Shall I entreat you to present me to the circle of your friends in the army around you. With all that warmth and attachment of the purest friendship and regard, I have the honour to be, dear sir,

> Your affectionate humble servant,

The Marquis de Chastellux.   GEORGE WASHINGTON.

LETTER V.

Princeton, October 12, 1783.

MY DEAR CHEVALIER—I have not had the honour of a letter from you since the 4th of March last ; but I will ascribe my disappointment to any cause sooner than to a decay of your friendship.

Having the appearances, and, indeed the enjoyment of peace, without the final declaration of it, I, who am only waiting for the ceremonials, or till the British forces shall have taken their leave of New-York, am held in an awkward and disagreeable situation, being anxiously desirous to quit the walks of public life, and under my own vine and my own fig-tree, to seek those enjoyments, and that relaxation, which a mind that has been constantly upon the stretch for more than eight years, stands so much in want of.

I have fixed this epoch to the arrival of the definitive treaty, or to the evacuation of my country, by our newly-acquired friends ; in the meanwhile, at the request of Congress, I spend my time with them at this place, where they came in consequence of the riots at Philadelphia, of which, doubtless you have been informed, for it is not a very recent transaction.

They have lately determined to fix the permanent residence of Congress, near the falls of Delaware ; but where they will hold their sessions, till they can be properly established at that place, is yet undecided.

I have lately made a tour through the Lakes George and Champlain as far as Crown Point—then returning to Schenectady, I proceeded up the Mohawk river to Fort Schuyler, (formerly Fort Stanwix,) crossed over Wood creek, which empties into the Oneida Lake, and affords the water communication with Lake Ontario ; I then traversed the country to the head of the eastern branch of the Susquehannah, and viewed the Lake Otsego, and the portage between that lake, and the Mohawk river at Canajoharie.

Prompted by these actual observations, I could not help taking a more contemplative and extensive view of the vast inland navigation of these United States, from maps, and the information of others, and could not but be struck with the immense diffusion and importance of it, and with the goodness of that Providence which has dealt her favours to us with so profuse a hand. Would to God we may have wisdom enough to make a good use of them. I shall not rest contented till I have explored the western part of this country, and traversed those lines (or a great part of them,) which have given bounds to a new empire ; but when it may, if it ever should happen, I dare not say, as my first attention must be given to the deranged situation of my private concerns, which are not a little injured by almost nine years absence, and total disregard of them.

With every wish for your health and happiness, and with the most sincere and affectionate regard,

I am, my dear Chevalier, your most obedient servant,

The Marquis de Chastellux.   GEORGE WASHINGTON.

LETTER VI.

Mount Vernon, February 1, 1784.

MY DEAR CHEVALIER—I have had the honour to receive your favour of the 23d of August from L'Orient, and hope this letter will find you in the circle of your friends at Paris, well recovered from the fatigues of your long inspection of the frontiers of the kingdom. I am at length become a private citizen, on the banks of the Potomac, where, under my own vine and my own fig-tree, free from the bustle of a camp and the intrigues of a court, I shall view the busy world with calm indifference, and with serenity of mind, which the soldier in pursuit of glory, and the statesman of a name, have not leisure to enjoy. I am not only retired from all public employments, but am retiring within myself, and shall tread the private walks of life with heartfelt satisfaction.

After seeing New-York evacuated by the British forces on the 25th of November, and civil government established in the city, I repaired to Congress, and surrendered all my powers, with my commission, into their hands on the 23d of December.

and arrived at this cottage the day before Christmas, where I have been close locked in frost and snow ever since. Mrs. Washington thanks you for your kind remembrance of her, and prays you to accept her best wishes in return.

With sentiments of pure and unabated friendship, I am, my dear Chevalier,

Your most affectionate and obedient servant,

The Marquis de Chastellux.   GEORGE WASHINGTON.

LETTER VII.

Mount Vernon, June 2, 1784.

DEAR SIR—I had the honour to receive a letter from you by Major L'Enfort. My official letters to the Counts de Estaing and Rochambeau (which I expect will be submitted to the members of the society of the Cincinnati in France) will inform you of the proceedings of the general meeting, held at Philadelphia on the 3d ult., and the reasons which induced a departure from some of the original principles and rules of the society. As these have been detailed, I will not repeat them, and as we have had no occurrences out of the common course, except the establishment of ten new states in the Western Territory, and the appointment of Mr. Jefferson (whose talents and worth are well known to you) as one of the commissioners for forming commercial treaties in Europe, I only repeat to you the assurances of my friendship, and express to you a wish that I might see you in the shade of those trees which my hands have planted, and which by their rapid growth at once indicate a knowledge of my declination, and their willingness to spread their mantles over me before I go hence to return no more. For this, their gratitude, I will nurture them while I stay.

Before I conclude, permit me to recommend Colonel Humphreys (who is appointed secretary to the commission) to your countenance and civilities whilst he remains in France. He possesses an excellent heart and a good understanding.

With every sentiment of esteem and regard, I am, my dear Chevalier,

Your most affectionate servant,

The Marquis de Chastellux.   GEORGE WASHINGTON.

LETTER VIII.

Mount Vernon, September 5, 1785.

DEAR SIR—I am your debtor for two letters : one of the 12th of December, the other of the 8th of April. Since the receipt of the first, I have paid my respects to you, in a line or two by Major Swan, but as it was introductory only of him, it requires apology, rather than entitles me to credit, in our epistolary correspondence.

If I had as good a nack, my dear Marquis, as you have, at saying handsome things, I would endeavour to pay you in kind for the many flattering expressions of your letters. I have an ample field to work in ; but as I am a clumsy labourer in the manufactory of compliments, I must first profess my unworthiness of those which you have bestowed on me, and then, conscious of my inability of meeting you upon that ground, confess that it is better not to enter the list, than to retreat from it in disgrace.

It gives me great pleasure to find, by my last letters from France, that the dark clouds which overspread your hemisphere, are yielding to the sunshine of peace. My first wish is to see the blessings of it diffused through all countries, and among all ranks in every country, and that we should consider ourselves as the children of a common parent, and be disposed to acts of brotherly kindness toward one another ; in that case, restriction of trade would vanish. We should take your wines, your fruit, and surplusage of such articles as our necessities or convenience might require, and in return give you our fish, our oil, our tobacco, our naval stores, &c. ; and in like manner should exchange produce with other countries, to the reciprocal advantage of each : and as the globe is large, why need we wrangle for a small spot of it ? If one country cannot contain us, another should open its arms to us. But these halcyon days (if they ever did exist) are now no more. A wise Providence, I presume, has decreed it otherwise ; and we shall be obliged to go on in the old way, disputing, and now and then fighting, until the great globe itself dissolves.

I rarely go from home, but my friends in and out of Congress inform me of what is on the carpet. To hand it to you afterwards would be circuitous and idle ; as I am persuaded, that you have correspondents at New-York, who give them to you at first hand, and can relate them with more clearness and precision. I give the chief of my time to rural amusements ; but I have lately been active in instituting a plan, which, if success attend it, (and of which I have no doubt,) may be productive

of great political, as well as commercial advantages, to the
states on the Atlantic, especially the middle ones.   It is the
improving and extending the inland navigations of the rivers
Potomac and James, and communicating them with the western
waters, by the shortest and easiest portages, and good roads.
Acts have passed the assemblies of Virginia and Maryland, authorising private adventurers to undertake the work.   Companies in consequence are incorporated, and that on this river is
begun ; but when we come to the difficult parts of it, we shall
require an engineer of skill and practical knowledge in this
branch of business, and from that country where those kind of
improvements have been conducted with the greatest success.

With very great esteem and regard, I am, my dear sir,
                          Your most obedient servant,
The Marquis de Chastellux.   GEORGE WASHINGTON.

LETTER IX.

Mount Vernon, August 8, 1786.

MY DEAR MARQUIS,—I cannot omit to seize the earliest occasion to acknowledge the receipt of the very affectionate letter
you did me the honour to write me on the 22d May, as well as
to thank you for the present of your travels in America, and the
translation of Colonel Humphrey's poem ; all of which came
safe to hand, by the same conveyance.

Knowing, as I did, the candour, liberality, and philanthropy
of the Marquis de Chastellux, I was prepared to disbelieve any
imputations that might militate against those amiable qualities ;
for character and habits are not easily taken up, or suddenly
laid aside.   Nor does that mild species of philosophy, which
aims at promoting human happiness, ever belie itself, by devi-
ating from the generous and God-like pursuit. Having notwithstanding, understood, that some misrepresentation of the
work in question had been circulated, I was happy to learn
that you had taken the most effectual method to put a stop to
their circulation, by publishing a more ample and correct edition.   Colonel Humphreys (who spent some weeks at Mount
Vernon) confirmed me in the sentiment, by giving me a most
flattering account of the whole performance.   He has also put
into my hands the translation of that part in which you say
such, and so many handsome things of me, that (although no
skeptic on ordinary occasions) I may perhaps be allowed to
doubt whether your friendship and partially have not, in this

one instance, acquired an ascendancy over your cooler judgment.

Having been thus unwarily, and I may be permitted to add, almost unavoidably betrayed into a kind of necessity to speak of myself, and not wishing to resume that subject, I choose to close it forever, by observing, that, as on the one hand, I consider it as an indubitable mark of mean spiritedness and pitiful vanity to court applause from the pen or tongue of man ; so on the other, I believe it to be a proof of false modesty, or an unworthy affectation of humility, to appear altogether insensible to the commendations of the virtuous and enlightened part of our species.*

Perhaps nothing can excite more perfect harmony in the soul, than to have this spring vibrate in unison with the internal consciousness of rectitude in our intentions, and an humble hope of approbation from the supreme disposer of all things.

I have communicated to Colonel Humphreys, that paragraph in your letter which announces the favourable reception his poem has met with in France. Upon the principles I have just laid down, he cannot be indifferent to the applauses of so enlightened a nation, nor to the suffrages of the King and Queen, who have been pleased to honour it with their royal approbation.

We have no news on this side the Atlantic worth the pains of sending across it. The country is recovering rapidly from the ravages of war. The seeds of population are scattered far in the wilderness ; agriculture is prosecuted with industry ; the works of peace, such as opening rivers, building bridges, &c., are carried on with spirit. Trade is not so successful as

---

* In a letter from General Washington to Mr. Arthur Young, dated Mount Vernon, Dec. 4th, 1788, the General, after replying to a request to obtain his permission to publish his letters on agricultural subjects, concludes with the following remarks :

" I can only say for myself, that I have endeavoured, in a state of tranquil retirement, to keep myself as much from the eye of the world as I possibly could. I have studiously avoided, as much as was in my power, to give any cause for ill-natured, or impertinent comments on my conduct ; and I should be very unhappy to have any thing done on my behalf (however distant in itself from impropriety) which should give occasion for one officious tongue to use my name with indelicacy. For I wish most devoutly, to glide silently and unnoticed through the remainder of life. This is my heart-felt wish, and these are my undisguised feelings. After having submitted them confidentially to you, I have such a reliance upon your prudence, as to leave it with you to do what you think, upon a full consideration of the matter, shall be wisest and best."

we could wish. Our state governments are well administered. Some objections in our Federal government might perhaps be altered for the better. I rely much on the goodness of my countrymen ; and trust that a superintending Providence will disappoint the hopes of our enemies.

With sentiments of the sincerest friendship, I am, my dear Marquis,

Your obedient and affectionate servant,

The Marquis de Chastellux.　　GEORGE WASHINGTON.

LETTER X.

Mount Vernon, April 25, 1788.

MY DEAR MARQUIS—In reading your very friendly and acceptable letter, of the 21st of December, 1787, which came to hand by the last mail, I was, as you may well suppose, not less delighted than surprised to come across that plain American word, " My wife."—A Wife !—well my dear Marquis, I can hardly refrain from smiling to find that you are caught at last. I saw, by the eulogium you often made on the happiness of domestic life in America, that you had swallowed the bait, and that you would, as surely as you are a philosopher and a soldier, be taken one day or other. So, your day has at length come.—I am glad of it, with all my heart and soul. It is quite good enough for you :—Now, you are well served for coming to fight in favour of the American rebels, all the way across the Atlantic Ocean, by catching that terrible contagion, which, like the small pox, or the plague, a man can have only once in his life, because it commonly lasts him (at least with us in America—I dont know how you manage these matters in France) for his life time.—And yet, after all the maledictions you so richly merit on the subject, the worst wish I can find it in my heart to make against Madame de Chastellux, and yourself, is, that you may neither of you get the better of this domestic felicity during the course of your mortal existence.

If so wonderful an event should have occasioned me, my dear Marquis, to have written in a strange style, you will understand me as clearly as if I had said, (what in plain English is the simple truth,) do me the justice to believe that I take a heart felt interest in whatever concerns your happiness ; and in this view, I sincerely congratulate you on your auspicious matrimonial connection.

I am happy to find that Madame de Chastellux is so intimately connected with the Dutchess of Orleans, as I have always understood that this noble lady was an illustrious pattern of connubial love, as well as an excellent model of virtue in general.

While you have been making love under the banner of Hymen, the great personages of the north have been making war under the inspiration, or, rather the infatuation of Mars. Now, for my part, I humbly conceive you had much the best and wisest of the bargain ; for certainly, it is more consonant to all the principles of reason and religion, (natural and revealed,) to replenish the earth with inhabitants, rather than depopulate it by killing those already in existence ; besides, it is time for the age of knight-errantry and mad heroism to be at an end.

Your young military men, who want to reap the harvest of laurels, don't care, I suppose, how many seeds of war are sown ; but, for the sake of humanity, it is devoutly to be wished, that the manly employment of agriculture, and the humanizing benefits of commerce, should supersede the waste of war, and the rage of conquest ; that the swords might be turned into plough shares—the spears into pruning hooks—and, as the Scripture expresses it, " the nations learn war no more."

I will now give you a little news from this side the Atlantic, and then finish. As for us, we are plodding on in the dark road of peace and politics. We, who live in these ends of the earth only hear of the rumours of war, like the roar of distant thunder. It is to be hoped our remote local situation will prevent us from being swept into its vortex.

The constitution which was proposed by the Federal Convention, has been adopted by the states of Massachusetts, Connecticut, Jersey, Pennsylvania, Delaware, and Georgia. No state has rejected it. The Convention of Maryland is now sitting, and will probably adopt it, as that of South-Carolina will do in May. The other Conventions will assemble early in the summer. Hitherto there has been much greater unanimity in favour of the proposed government than could have reasonably been expected. Should it be adopted, (and I think it will be,) America will lift up her head again, and, in a few years, become respectable among the nations. It is a flattering and consolatory reflection, that our rising republic has the good wishes of all philosophers, patriots and virtuous men, in all nations and that they look upon it as a kind of asylum for mankind. God grant that we may not be disappointed in our honest expectations by our folly or perverseness !

With sentiments of the purest attachment and esteem, I have the honour to be, my dear Marquis,

Your most obedient and humble servant,

The Marquis de Chastellux.   GEORGE WASHINGTON.

P. S. If the Duke de Lauzun is still with you, I beg you will thank him, in my name, for his kind remembrance of me, and make my compliments to him.

May 1st.—Since writing the above, I have been favoured with a duplicate of your letter, in the hand writing of a lady, and cannot close this, without acknowledging my obligations to the flattering postscript of the fair transcriber. In effect, my dear Marquis, the characters of this interpreter of your sentiments, are so much fairer than those through which I have been accustomed to decipher them, that I already consider myself as no small gainer by your matrimonial connection ; especially, as I hope that your amiable amanuensis will not forget, at sometimes, to add a few annotations of her own to your original text.

I have just received information that the Convention of Maryland has ratified the proposed constitution, by a majority of 63 to 11. G. W.

ADDITIONAL

NOTES AND CORRECTIONS,

BY THE

AMERICAN EDITOR.

ADDITIONAL

NOTES AND CORRECTIONS.

AMERICAN EDITOR.

PAGE 18.—For Massachusetts, read *Rhode-Island*, the state in which Warren is situate.

PAGE 19.—For Connecticut, read *Conanicut*, an island opposite Newport, at the mouth of Providence river, 30 miles below Providence.

Idem.—Providence has greatly changed and doubled itself twice since the author saw it. The "Guinea trade" is no longer carried on from thence, the importation of slaves into the country having been prohibited by Congress in 1808, pursuant to the federal constitution, by which (in favour to the southern states) they were restricted from abolishing the trade before ; and traffic in human flesh in any part of the world is forbidden by the laws of England as well as the United States, and the practice declared piratical and treated as such by the two governments. France has also prohibited the slave trade. No longer dependant on this commerce for any portion of its prosperity, the citizens of Providence and its neighbourhood have turned their attention to domestic manufactures, in addition to their East and West India and other foreign trade and fisheries, and now present an example of growth and prosperity seldom equalled in this or any other country. From the number of 2,500 inhabitants, the large estimate of the Marquis, in 40 years the town has increased its population, in 1820, to 11,757 ; and 4 miles from Providence, on the Boston road, on each side of the boundary river between Rhode-Island and Massachusetts, is situate Pawtucket, a flourishing village, containing, in 1810, no less than 24 manufactories of different kinds, principally cotton, which furnish materials for the export trade of Providence.

Besides the university, the town contains 9 banks, with insurance offices, and other public buildings and institutions. There are 4 banks also in Pawtucket. The banks in Rhode-Island have small capitals, with the directors personally responsible for their paper.—When Chastellux speaks of the commerce of Rhode-Island and Boston, he means the towns of *Newport* and *Boston*.

PAGE 23, *note.*—The translator would have found, in 1827, wine of all kinds, less than 30 days from France, Madeira, or Oporto, with which to fill his cantines [canteens.]

PAGE 24.—The author is not sufficiently accurate in his description of a "town or township," in this and other places. It is always a tract or territory of land, from 4 or 5 to 10 miles square, or other convenient dimensions, bounded and described by law, within the limits of which may be an incorporated borough, a village, or two or three parishes, and several school districts, each subject to its own local regulations, although under the common government of the town for general purposes—the " space" is more properly the town, and not any " certain number of houses." All the northern and middle, and most of the other states, are surveyed and laid out in townships, without regard to the number of houses now or hereafter to be erected on them.

PAGES 25, 26.—Quenebaugh for *Quinnebaug,* and Seunganick for *Shetucket* rivers, are awkwardly spelt, neither the author nor translator being conversant with Indian names.

PAGE 28.—Vermont was admitted as a state into the federal Union, about the year 1793, and in 1820 contained 235,764 inhabitants.

Idem.—Ferries :—If the author or translator had witnessed the modern improvements in our ferry-boats, whether moved by horse power or steam, and in one of which we have seen a body of 848 men, besides other passengers, transported safely across a river at a single draught, the remarks on our ferries would have been omitted.

Idem.—The facts of Colonel Wadsworth's residence and employment on Long-Island before the revolution, and " the American expression of *contestation*" given to the struggle, will be quite new to the reader.

PAGE 30.—Line 2, for two years, read *one* year, the elections in Connecticut having always been annual, with two sessions a year for their legislature.

PAGE 31.—Hartford is mentioned, and townships again, and both in exceptionable terms. Hartford is now a city, containing a statehouse, college, deaf and dumb institution, churches, banks, &c. with a population, in 1820, of 4,726 within the city, and 2,175 in the town without, or 6,901 in the whole ; and is situate on the Connecticut, which was never called the Hartford river.

PAGE 33.—The Americans have a bird they call the blue-jay, familiar to the youth of New-England, very different from the common blue-bird. The whimsical blunder of the wall-nut tree is corrected by the translator—the walnut, or hickory, is so valuable for other purposes, that it is used less than any other kind of wood in constructing the walls of houses.

PAGE 35.—For Harrington, read *Harwinton.*

PAGE 36.—Every state in the Union, excepting South-Carolina, is organized and divided into counties, each of which has a court, embracing common pleas and criminal jurisprudence.

PAGE 37.—Washington county :—There is none thus designated in Connecticut, although one may be found in almost every other state of the twenty-four. The *town* or *township* of Washington is here meant. " The woods of Connecticut," to any considerable extent, at the present time, would be very difficult to discover. The state is more populous, in proportion to its size, than any other in the Union.

PAGE 39.—Kent is a town, not a county. Both this and Washington are in Litchfield county. Milford is also a town, not a county.

PAGE 42.—"Hopel township" is not yet " built," and may be searched for in vain among our records, as well as the account that " the greatest part of the state of New-York was exchanged for Surinam, instead of being surrendered to the English by Gov. Stuyvesant, in 1664." In the last paragraph for next, read *kept,* and recollect that half a dozen glass-houses in the country, with our weekly packets to Europe and increased population, render it less difficult now to repair broken windows than when the Marquis wrote.

PAGE 42, *note.*—Glass :—In 1810 there were ten manufactories of window-glass, (six of them in the state of New-York) besides a number for making double flint glass, and black bottles. At present, in the vicinity of the city of New-York, there are three large glass-houses, in successful operation, where the finest glass is blown, and in two of which the business of cutting the glass is carried on extensively, besides the numerous glass-cutting establishments in the city.

PAGE 46.—For Apalachian Mountains, read *Alleghany,* their more common name.

PAGES 51, 52.—Spell *Bauman* and *Lyman* right. Col. Bauman was afterwards post-master in New-York, and Maj. Lyman naval officer at Newport. For siege of New-York, read *Yorktown* in Virginia.

PAGE 57.—Read *Ramapaugh* for Romopog ; and at Totobaw road and Second river, read near the Passaic. At 60, read *Passaic* falls.

We should not forget that the English publishers had no Gazetteers of our country to assist their translation.

PAGE 75.—The name of Troy is not to be found in this neighbourhood, not even the classical memento " Here Troy was." In the state of New-York, six miles above Albany, stands a flourishing city of that name, containing, in 1825, 7,859 inhabitants, and which was not in existence at the period of the Marquis' travels, having sprung up within the last thirty years.

PAGE 79.—The remarks of the author on the " liberty" of conduct in unmarried people in this country, is not only singular in itself, but more so in coming from a Frenchman, and one whose liberal views of our manners and character are frequently so enthusiastic. But the confirmation of our loose customs, in the translator's note, especially in quoting " a grave Quaker" for his example, is too absurd and unfounded to be thought serious. The note is as false as it is indecent, and worthy only of a modern Weld, Fearon, or other national libeller. Impartiality requires a publisher to copy his author faithfully ; but so ridiculous a *slip*, in a pen however respectable otherwise, should not pass without a corrective. The translator either was a man of depraved taste, frequenting low and licentious company, or accidentally drew his picture from the worst class of American society. We cannot but smile to see customs and fashions imputed to Philadelphia, that would not be tolerated in London !

PAGE 80.—The author was at Saourland, a German settlement. Many of the local designations of our country at that day, are now lost and forgotten in our more improved and regularly established distinctions of political and natural geography.

PAGE 82.—Princeton college, though " fallen into decay since the war," has revived again and again, like the Phenix, more flourishing and brilliant from its ashes. Besides this college, another, exclusively devoted to the study of theology, is established at Princeton. The name of the town of Maidenhead has been changed to Lawrence, in honour of the late Capt. Lawrence, of the U. S. navy, who was killed in the war of 1812, and was a native of that neighbourhood.

PAGE 87.—Governor Livingston, of New-Jersey, "*passes* for a sensible man" to this day, and will pass for as much, and a little more, to posterity. The author did not fully appreciate his talents and worth. His remarks on American politeness, it should be recollected, are from a French nobleman, unaccustomed to plain republican manners.

PAGE 89.—The company and friends of the Marquis must have been select and special indeed, to have made 5 or 6 o'clock a dining hour in Philadelphia. He would have been more correct to have said the general custom was from 12 to 2. Even in New-York the most fashionable hour is now 3, or in the extreme, 4 in the afternoon : and fashionable, in this case does not mean common, but uncommon. The Marquis moved in the highest rank of official and diplomatic circles.

PAGE 91.—Mr. now Bishop, White is still living, one of the last of the revolutionary chaplains, in Philadelphia.

PAGE 98.—Robert Morris, after all his wealth, and the important services he rendered his country, suffered great pecuniary hardships, lost all his magnificent possessions, and died a bankrupt. His brother Gouverneur, who was afterwards our minister at Paris in the French revolution, was more fortunate, or prudent, in his worldly concerns.

PAGE 100.—" Mrs. Powell had read a great deal." The Marquis having formed a hasty opinion that the American women read nothing, seems to think a lady of extensive reading and literary taste quite a phenomenon. But as he frequently met with very intelligent and accomplished females in his subsequent travels, although there were no " blue stockings" in those days, it is presumed he found reason to change his opinion. The learned ladies of America were noted by an English traveller, soon after, as quite remarkable, on finding some in Connecticut familiar with the sciences and languages. See pages 144, 159, &c.

PAGE 107.—The translator's speculations on the division of the Union, so far from being supported by events, are contradicted by the history of every succeeding year. In peace or war, our confederation has proved the most popular, and therefore the most efficient and probably durable of all the known systems of government.

PAGE 112.—If " the Almanac was almost the only book of astronomy studied at Philadelphia" in 1782, the remark would not apply to the eastern states. Indeed, the present state of literature in Pennsylvania makes one smile at the author's thoughtless remark. He appears too amiable to have intended it as a sneer. Franklin, from Philadelphia, was a member of the English Royal Society, and other learned and scientific institutions, an LL. D. &c. &c. twenty years before. In 1750, Latin, Greek, and mathematical schools, were opened in the Philadelphia Academy, incorporated the preceding year. Mr. Thompson, afterwards secretary of Congress, and who was an assistant in the academy, a particular friend of the Marquis, (and who has since translated the New Testament,) as well as Mr. Peters, and others mentioned by the author, could have given him better information.

Page 122.—The objections to forts lying in one state rather than another, are all removed, by the federal constitution, which, by making it the duty of Congress to provide for the common defence of the country, has given them all the powers of location and (with the consent of the state legislatures) jurisdiction necessary to carry the proper measures into effect.

Page 134.—The character of the Quakers, or Friends, given them by Chastellux, is as inapplicable to the general habits and principles of the society or sect, as the deepest shades of night are to the brilliant gleams of noonday. The scandalous picture must have been drawn from some outcast individuals of the denomination, unworthy of trust or regard by any intelligent person. Notwithstanding the dissimilarity of their manners to the gaiety of the French court, a countryman of the Marquis, but a few years after, could find every thing to admire, and nothing to condemn, in the Friends' character.—See [Brissot de] Warville's Travels, and his Examination of Chastellux.

Page 135.—The author's account of the Quaker's praying on his knees, is a marvellous thing indeed, not known at the present day, any more than the sect of Jemima Wilkinson, in Rhode-Island, mentioned by the translator, with a circumstance equally distant from delicacy and truth. Jemima herself, who blasphemously called herself 1 AM! and marked her clothing I. A. had a child while rambling about at the head of her followers. They scarcely merited the name of a sect ; and, making but few proselytes to their extravagances, on the death of their Elect Lady, who had declared herself immortal, dispersed and soon became extinct. They should not be confounded with the Shakers, who are sedentary, numerous, and comparatively, respectable, notwithstanding they are opposed to marriage and its natural consequences.

Page 144.—For Flowy and Maddison, read *Floyd* (from New-York) and *Madison*.

Page 153.—Philadelphia did not long continue to be " the great sink" of all American speculations. The reign of the " quakers and tories" soon passed away ; the seat of government was removed, and the vices, intrigues, and corruption of its retainers and attendants, whether of the court or camp, (if such there were, in the imagination of the Marquis) left " the city of brotherly love" with their patrons. The focus of monied speculations was long since settled in New-York, to which Philadelphia has at length become second in wealth, commerce, and population. It is, however, a considerable manufacturing district, and from 40,000 souls, the estimation of the Marquis in 1782. contained, in 1820, in the city and county, 136,597.

PAGE 160.—For Romopog, read *Ramapaugh*, or Ramapo .

PAGE 164, *note.*—Londonderry is in New-Hampshire, and not Massachusetts.

PAGES 165, 166.—For Strasbourgh, or Strattsborough, read *Staats burgh* or *Staatsberg.*

PAGE 169.—The great chain of rocks, near Claverack, is not only calcareous, but full of marine shells, although 130 miles from the ocean. Where the traveller then had to turn off to Claverack, for lodging, is now the city of Hudson, containing upwards of 5,000 inhabitants.

PAGE 170, *note.*—Read Buffonic. It looks too much now as if it were derived from *buffoon*, instead of the great naturalist.

PAGE 172, &c.—Every reader will recollect that the Americans designate by the name of *sleigh*, the vehicle called by the author in the Russian phrase, *sledge.*

PAGE 174.—For Cokes, read Cohoes or Cahoos. The height of the Cahoos Falls is 70 feet, and the width of the river, at the bridge three-quarters of a mile below, 997 feet.

PAGE 179.—Line 13, for highly read *lightly ;* and at note, for Soree read *Sorel.*

PAGE 181.—For Lake Meida read *Oneida.*

PAGE 186.—For Rill and rill, read *Kill* and *kill*, signifying creek with the Dutch.

PAGE 191.—The murder of Miss Mac Rea has been differently related. The account most commonly received is, that Mr. Jones, her English lover, having offered a barrel of rum to whomsoever should conduct her to him, she was brought on her way by two Indians, who differing about the reward, one of them settled the dispute by sinking his tomahawk into the head of their helpless charge.

PAGE 192.—For Fort Stanwise read *Stanwix.*

Idem.—The *cataract* of the Hudson, it is believed, never found a place in history, before it was designated as such by the Marquis. It was called a ford, or carrying place, in the old wars, until 1755, when Fort Edward was built there. The river being frozen, and its banks and icy surface covered with snow 15 inches deep, the rushing of the waters in broken sluices down the rapids, formed a spectacle, so novel to the Marquis, that with a little of the romantic turn of the French, he easily magnified it into a frightful cataract. At this place is now the Great Dam of the Hudson, erected to provide a feeder to the Champlain Canal. This dam is of somewhat stupendous magnitude, being 27 feet high for 900 feet across the river. Two miles above Fort Edward is Baker's Falls, and 3 miles higher, at Glen's

Falls, must be the cataract meant by the author. We here find the author talking about the Totohaw [Passaic] Falls.

PAGE 199.—For Quakerbush read Quakenbos.

PAGE 201.—We are glad to perceive the Marquis here at last found a beautiful girl, with some other books than an Almanac. As our author could find so few or no handsome or elegant women in America, we must conclude he had a *different taste* from common people. He could not expect to witness the luxurious belles, the artificial charms, the practised graces, and the voluptuous manners, of the court of Marie Antoinette. Yet when he accidentally meets with such a *rare* being as an elegant and accomplished female in his travels, he takes care to inform us that she is frail as she is fair, and his translator comes in with his *delicate* explanations to support him !

PAGE 206.—The Marquis, in his rage for philosophical reflections, has made another slip. Who would think, for the worth of a squirrel, with which our country is overrun, of taking the trouble of cutting down a tree—if the tree was larger than a hoop-pole !

Idem.—For Governor Turnbull, read *Trumbull*, a character not very *great* in the estimation of the author, however solid were his merits in the eyes of his countrymen.

PAGE 218.—At line 16, read "will not be," &c.

PAGE 219.—What confusion we have about names and *sur*names ! The dictionaries tell us that *surname* is at the same time the original or family name, and also the name *added* to the name of the family : so that of the two names by which a man is known, both the first and last are surnames. The custom in New-England, and most parts of the United States, is simple, distinct, and intelligible. The first is the *given* or *Christian* name, given at baptism, as George, John, or Thomas, and the second is the *surname*, the patronymick or family name, as Washington, Adams, or Jefferson. Surname is not applied, as by lexicographers, to both names. Convenience, the origin of all grammatical rules, is necessarily preferred to theory.

PAGE 221.—In Virginia, in 1820, were 603,597 whites, and 461,769 blacks, total 1,065,366—a number that would now astonish the author and his translator, were they living to witness the fact.

PAGE 236.—Last line, for unexamined read *unexampled.*

PAGE 242.—The *lofty* banks of the Potomac (in the translator's note) excites a smile in persons accustomed to the view of northern rivers. The translator had not been with the author, at the Highlands, &c. of the Hudson, or he would have spared the ironical epithet. The town is 290 miles from the sea, but is not yet "become one of the first cities of the new world." its growth being prevented by Georgetown and Washington City, erected within a distance of 8 miles. Washington had a population, in 1820, of 13,247, and has rapidly increased ; Georgetown had 7,360 ; and Alexandria 8,218.

PAGE 244.—How a mill-stream was the only *cellar* of its owner, does not readily appear. It could not be a store-house. The author doubtless alluded to the *cellarist* or butler of a convent or religious house, who furnishes the drink to its inmates ; the stream, in this case, was the only *liquor-vault*, as well as bath, of the landlord, as we may gather from the Italian quotation.

The delicate choice of subjects in some of the notes of the translator, forbids our attracting more notice to them by any remarks.

PAGE 249.—The appellation of the " country of the curious," given by the translator, appertains to New-England exclusively. It is improper to apply Franklin's remarks on the road to Boston, to a journey through Virginia.

PAGE 251.—The translator is mistaken in designating the best kind of oak for ship-building. For firmness, strength, and durability, the Live-Oak of the southern sea-coast is long established as decidedly and materially superior to every other species.

PAGE 252.—Kentucky was admitted as a state in the Union, as the translator expected, and in 1820 contained 564,317 inhabitants.

PAGE 256.—We congratulate the author, after the pleasure he derived from the discovery of the singular and beautiful mocking-bird, the thrush, the wild turkey, the roebuck, the marmoset, and other interesting animals, on his at last meeting with a beautiful woman ; and hope his acquaintance and opinion of our countrywomen improved.

PAGE 259.—The translator says *mighty* little, &c. are favourite expressions in *America.* No such thing is known, but in *Virginia*, and some of the western states.

PAGE 260.—The women have become." far from handsome" again. But in 263, another beautiful woman was found, but with as many general reflections, by way of drawback, as Dr. Johnson would have made. At 267, in Petersburg, the author met another beauty, and indeed a second and quite accomplished lady, the descendant of an Indian princess. But Mrs. Bowling was more distinguished, it seems, by her amiable disposition, (a quality the Marquis found so rare in the American ladies) than by " her exterior beauty."

PAGE 273.—The translator as well as the author, frequently display an unkind feeling towards Philadelphia and its quaker features. Yet Major Butler ultimately settled there, and passed his last years there in prosperity and the first respectability, as a Senator in Congress from Georgia, U. S. Bank director &c.

PAGE 274.—Read *Appomattox;* the spelling not so material when it sufficiently designates the place, as in the case of many other names we have passed with incorrect orthography.

PAGE 282.—The translator's note helps the text to a pretty good *fish story;* but it is rather odd to style a fish so common in both hemispheres a *monster,* and so common a monster, too, that thousands of them may be seen at once! The sturgeon is not considered a monster at Albany, where the people are neither too indolent to catch them, nor too ignorant to make very palatable food of their flesh. Indeed, it is really singular that a fish so well known, and breeding in such " amazing numbers" in the lakes and rivers of Europe, and furnishing such valuable materials for commerce as their flesh, caviar, and isinglass, should have been so great a stranger to writers so intelligent and well informed in general. Buffon and Goldsmith could have taught them better.

PAGE 290, *note.*—Read, the river Cape Fear' *or* Clarendon. The population of North-Carolina, in 1820, was 419,200 whites, and 219,629 blacks, total 638,829. The state has in reality, " become not one of the least on the continent."

PAGE 292.—For wane read *wan,* and for land read *lands.*

PAGE 293, *note.*—Goudging [gouging] has been a savage practice in the wilds of Virginia, but long since vanished before the influence of law and refinements of civilization. In a residence in that state of some years, scarcely an instance can be recollected of seeing the want of an eye by gouging, or any more countenance given to the custom than to shooting, stabbing, cutting, or any unlawful maiming, which are prohibited as all other felonies. Enough, however, of that brutality has existed in the southern and western states, (when colonies) to give foundation to the charge, and from its singular atrocity to secure its recital by unfriendly or careless writers.

PAGE 295.—" The negroes in Virginia amount," in 1820, to 401,264, and the whites to 603,597. The remark on the difference of colour between the slaves of ancient and modern times, is highly important, and not sufficiently attended to in our discussions of the subject in free states. Some of our most wealthy and respectable citizens, being white, have been sold as slaves (for a term) for their passage to this country, and afterwards found their way into the state legislatures and congress. But of free blacks, there seems to be an everlasting and insurmountable barrier in the colour alone, to their full enjoyment of all the rights and advantages of white society. It will perhaps be as difficult to establish their claim to physical or moral equality with our species, as to convince us that their ideas of beauty in the human figure and countenance are founded on as just principles of taste as ours. If our Creator has furnished us with a skin, features, hair, &c. different from theirs, and which we shall probably always consider superior, it will ever be difficult to reconcile their moral or political elevation to our habits, our feelings, or our convictions, either of their capacity, their merits, or their natural rank in the scale of creation. Entitled originally to inherent rights, mixed with whites they can never enjoy them. With all the political equality established by our constitutions, and the eligibility (in some states) of all to office, we do not choose the ignorant, the depraved, the weak, the unfortunate, the female, nor the black, to legislate for us, or to rule over us. It is not until " the Ethiopian change his skin," that he will be able to participate in all the social enjoyments secured to him by any human laws, in a white population. Physical difference and moral inferiority, can never be counterbalanced by the theory of political equality.

Pages 298, 299.—That judges and lawyers, as well as the clergy, are excluded from all share in the government of this country, is a most singular and important error of the Marquis, and almost unaccountable, when we recollect that most of the active and influential public characters of his acquaintance had been bred to the law or bar. One half or two thirds of the members of congress and the legislatures of the United States are lawyers, to a degree of proverbial complaint. The " separate Judicial Body" mentioned by the writer, is the Judiciary department of the government in its actual administration, which is wisely kept separate from the Legislative and Executive branches, that their different and distinct powers may not be united and consolidated into despotism, nor blended and confounded into anarchy. The judges of the superior courts, whose province it is to interpret the laws, and decide on their constitutionality, alone are excluded from enacting them as legislators. The great body of lawyers, for reasons which readily suggested themselves to the author, who mistook them for the Bench, or disqualified " judicial body," have more agency and weight in managing elections and the affairs of government, than any other class or denomination of citizens (and in many districts more than all the others together,) in the country.

Page 304.—Here we are first introduced to the famous Talleyrand, who has subsequently acted so conspicuous a part in the European world. His enthusiasm in the cause of the United States, his service as a volunteer in the ranks of the army, and his travels in the country since the war, were highly conducive to his knowledge of the American character and interests, with which his diplomatic vocations have been so much connected.

Idem.—For hog-house read *log-house.*

PAGE 306.—The text should have stated the pound only, or added that it was of fourteen (nearer 15) *French* ounces ; the English pound of 16 ounces being equal to only 14⅔ ounces French.   The translation should have given us nothing but English weights and measures.   The English pound is as 109 to 100 French ; and the fathom, or French toise, is as 6 feet English to 6.0789 French, or 6 feet 4¾ inches.

PAGE 310.—Read Mr. *Buck*minster.   311, For Bittery, read *Kittery.*

PAGE 312.—The anecdote of Col. Langdon and the negro is excellently characteristic.   A regiment of blacks (with white officers,) was raised in Rhode-Island, and served well through the war, at the end of which they found themselves very properly rewarded by their personal freedom, for their aid in defending and securing the national liberty.

PAGE 313.—The anticipations of Portsmouth becoming a great naval depot, have not been realized.   It is too far distant from the seat of government and centre of commerce and naval resources.   Although we have a number of navy-yards, the Portsmouth of England has as yet been found at New-York.

PAGE 314.—The text is unintelligible again, without recollecting that the translation of the money concerns of the writer into English, (excepting when otherwise designated,) has been into *sterling* account. And in this page, line 22, for corn we should read *wheat.*

PAGE 315.—The remarks and calculations extracted from Jefferson's Notes, prove the sagacity and judgment of that profound philosopher and practical statesman, more fully, than any political speculations which have appeared from his pen.   The events of the war of 1812—15, realized his predictions with remarkable exactness.

PAGE 323.—The author is sorry to say that the Americans do not dance minuets so well as the French—others would be sorry if they did—so tastes differ.

PAGE 328.—For Milk read *Mill*-Pond.   Our land did not literally flow with milk and honey, nor were our lakes or ponds filled with milk, in the time of the Marquis or his translator.

PAGE 332.—The author, in describing Cambridge, finds himself at what has since been denominated (by flattery,) " the literary emporium of America," among a people, the Bostonians, whom he really thinks are " friends to good wine, good cheer, and hospitality," notwithstanding they are awkward at a minuet.   This is much better than he thought of Philadelphia, where he supposed they studied nothing in astronomy but an almanac, and the women did not read.   He has found also (by good luck,) some handsome women in Boston, and a variety of elegant and refined enjoyments. But alas, he makes a discovery, and the translator confirms it, that the inhabitants are fond of high play, and much addicted to gambling ! This from a resident of Paris, where gaming-houses are recognized and licensed by law, might lead one to think the practice might have been introduced by the French officers, at their nightly parties and clubs, rather than originating in native dissipation and propensities. The English translator, also, there is no reason to doubt, had seen too much of the evils of gambling in his own country, not to deprecate its prevalence or appearance in this. Its effects are horrible, every where ; but we have reason to congratulate ourselves that we are still at a great distance behind the licentiousness, the profligacy, and the vices of European courts, whatever of their fashionable follies we have adopted, and of their vices we have partly imitated. When the French and English charge us with a spirit of gambling, we may well suspect something is wrong. In this case, we may conscientiously suggest the old proverb, " When the fox preaches," &c.

Page 341.—Line 22, For Ckeat, read *Kakiat*.

Page 343.—For toises, line 13, read *fathoms*, and for their length see the preceding note on page 306.

Pages 344, 345.—The Moravians are a sect of christians, so distinguished by the purity of their manners, the scrupulous morality of their principles, and the virtuous and benevolent effects of their doctrines and example, that children of the most rigid of other denominations are sent to them for education. If sectarians are driven by the violence of despotic governments into extreme fanaticism, it is not so in a country, where " error of opinion may be safely tolerated, when reason is left free to combat it." In the United States, where no separate church or denomination is established by law, many of the singularities and asperities of the most heterodox persuasions or sects, have vanished before the liberty of discussion, the friendly interchange of sentiment, and the harmony of social intercourse. Many of the rites and practices formerly imputed to the strange schismatics which sprung up in every country where they are permitted to exist, are now matters of recollection only, and no part of present faith or practice.

Page 346, *note.*—For National read *Natural* Bridge.

Page 349.—Mr. Pinckney, in his subsequent history, as a public writer, member of congress, minister in foreign courts, &c. has fully justified the translator's expectations.

Page 353, *note.*—For Lecha, read *Lehigh*, at present one of the most abundant and profitable regions of mineral coal, found in Pennsylvania.

PAGES 355, 356.—In the description of the Natural Bridge, the points called Amont and Aval, we presume have reference to the plans or maps furnished to the author, but which do not appear in his book.

PAGE 358.—For Potama, read *Potomac.*

PAGE 359, *note.*—Line 6, read disrupture *and* convulsion.

PAGE 362.—Line 13, for Cordelliers, read *Cordilleras.*

PAGE 365.—Line 5 from bottom, for satient read *salient.*

PAGE 370.—Mr. Madison, since President, still lives in the possession of all the " eloquence, wisdom, and genius," he has so usefully displayed in the service of his country.

PAGE 373.—The author was incorrect in his anticipation of the *direction* in which the stream of population would extend. It is literally a fact in the United States, in their general and their relative situation, that

" *Westward* the tide of empire rolls."

Natives of Connecticut, and New-England generally, peopling the western part of New-York, the States of Ohio, and districts still farther west and south, not only decide the elections, but form, in many cases, nine tenths of the adult population.

PAGE 383.—Bottom line, French censure, is *Censor,* or licenser of the press in France.

PAGE 384.—The statue of Montgomery, with an additional inscription, on bringing the remains of the deceased from the place of their interment, is viewed with interest, by strangers and citizens, in the front of St. Paul's Church, in New-York.

PAGE 388.—Line 16 from bottom, for meeting read *mutiny.*

PAGE 393.—Line 11, for L'Enfort, read *L'Enfant.*

THE END.